BRAHMA-SUTRAS

BRAHMA-SUTRAS

With text, Word-for-Word Translation,
English Rendering, Comments according to
the Commentary of Śrī Śaṅkara and Index

Swami Vireswarananda

Advaita Ashrama
(Publication House of Ramakrishna Math)
5 Dehi Entally Road • Kolkata 700 014

Published by
Swami Muktidananda
Adhyaksha, Advaita Ashrama
Mayavati, Champawat, Uttarakhand, Himalayas
from its Publication House, Kolkata
Email: mail@advaitaashrama.org
Website: www.advaitaashrama.org

Fourteenth Reprint, May 2019
1M1C

ISBN 978-81-85301-95-2

Printed in India at
Gipidi Box Co.
Kolkata 700 014

CONTENTS

CONTENTS

LIST OF ABBREVIATIONS

Ai.	..	Aitareya Upaniṣad
Ai. Ā.	..	Aitareya Āraṇyaka
Bṛ.	..	Bṛhadâraṇyaka Upaniṣad
Ch.	..	Chândogya Upaniṣad
Jâ.	..	Jâbâla Upaniṣad
Ka.	..	Kaṭha Upaniṣad
Kau.	..	Kauṣîtakî Upaniṣad
Ke.	..	Kena Upaniṣad
Mâ.	..	Mâṇḍûkya Upaniṣad
Mbh.	..	Mahâbhârata
Mai.	..	Maitrâyaṇi Upaniṣad
Mu.	..	Muṇḍaka Upaniṣad
Pr.	..	Praśna Upaniṣad
Śat. Br.	..	Śatapatha Brâhmaṇa
Śv.	..	Śvetâśvatara Upaniṣad
Tai.	..	Taittirîya Upaniṣad

PREFACE

Some centres of the Ramakrishna Order have for some years past been bringing out important scriptures of the Hindus with text, word-for-word rendering, running translation and notes based on authoritative commentaries, in order to make them accessible to the English-knowing public whose knowledge of Sanskrit is limited. The Bhagavad-Gītâ by Swami Swarupananda published by the Advaita Ashrama, Mayavati, and eight major Upaniṣads by Swami Sharvananda published by the Ramakrishna Math, Madras, have already become popular. An edition of the Brahma-Sûtras on similar lines was overdue. The present work is intended to fulfil this want and to complete in this series the Prasthânatraya according to the interpretations of Śaṅkara. The word-for-word translation is very literal, but the running translation is made as literal as possible consistent with easy reading. In some places the translation of quotations from the Upaniṣads are taken from Max Müller's edition of the Upaniṣads and the quotations of the Śrī Bhâṣya from Dr. Thibaut's edition of the book (Sacred Books of the East Series), both with slight adaptations.

It is hoped the volume will be a fitting companion to the other Sanskrit works published by the Ramakrishna Order.

S.V.

ADVAITA ASHRAMA
MAYAVATI, HIMALAYAS
November 25, 1936

INTRODUCTION

THE SIX SYSTEMS OF PHILOSOPHY

The Vedas are the scriptures of the Hindus, to whatever sect or denomination they may belong. They are the earliest extant religious literature today and form the corner-stone of the Indo-Aryan cultural edifice. The Hindus believe that the Vedas are not the utterances of any person but are eternal and owe their authority to no individual. They are not inspired but expired by God. These Vedas are divided into two sections, the Karmakâṇḍa and the Jñânakâṇḍa, the former dealing with the ritualistic and the latter with the knowledge portion of the Vedas. The latter section is also known as the Vedânta, the end of the Vedas or the goal or gist of the Vedas. These are not mere speculations but the record of the spiritual experiences of the race for centuries, actual realizations or superconscious perceptions.

Though we find Vedântic thought even in some of the earliest hymns of the Rg-Veda, *e.g.* the Nâsadîya Sûkta, which forms, as it were, the basis of later Upaniṣads, yet there is no denying the fact that the Indo-Aryans in their earlier days in India were given more to rituals and sacrifices. These were elaborated to such an extent by the Brâhmaṇas, the priestly class, that persons of rationalistic bent of mind revolted and questioned the very efficacy of the sacrificial religion. They engaged themselves in metaphysical problems and arrived at different solutions of the world. The Vedântic thought that was in germ form was now developed more and more, and we have the Upaniṣads. This spirit of revolt against ritualism was carried on mainly by the Kṣatriyas. The Indo-Aryans were very bold thinkers and nothing was sacrilegious to them in their search after truth. Traces of opposition against the religion of the Vedas are found in the Vedas themselves. This tidal wave of rationalism in its extreme form gave rise to such schools of thought as the Cârvâkas, which were extremely materialistic and anti-religious.

In the age immediately preceding Buddha and during his lifetime there was a great religious and philosophical upheaval in India. From the Brahmajâla-Sûtras we learn that in his time there were as many as sixty-two different schools of philosophy in India. We also learn from Buddhistic literature the names of good number of teachers who were venerated in Āryâvarta at the time—like Purâṇa Kaśyapa, Kâtyâyana, Makkâli Gosâla, Niganṭha Nâthaputra the founder of Jainism and others. While these great souls represented Indian culture from an anti-Vedic standpoint there were many great names that represented the culture from the traditional standpoint—names that are still venerated by Hindu religion and culture.

The destructive criticism of everything in the old system by the Cârvâkas and others set the orthodox section to organize their belief on a more rationalistic basis and render it immune against all such criticism. This led to the foundation of the six systems of orthodox Hindu philosophy—orthodox[1] in the sense that they accepted the authority of the Vedas in things transcendental—while there were others who did not accept this authority and therefore were dubbed heterodox, though otherwise they too were the outcome of Upaniṣadic thought. The acceptance of the authority of the Vedas by these orthodox schools, however, does not mean that they accepted them *in toto*. Their allegiance to the Vedas varied widely and often it was too loose. Of the six orthodox schools. *viz* Nyâya, Vaiśeṣika, Sâṁkhya, Yoga, Pûrva Mîmâṁsâ and Uttara Mîmâṁsâ or Vedânta, the last two are intimately connected with the Vedas, which is one of the reasons why they are not mentioned in the Jaina and Buddhistic literature, while the others are mentioned.

These six orthodox system of thought developed side by side at different intellectual centres, of which there were a good number all over the country even during the Upaniṣadic period. Again in each system there were shades of difference. Thus for centuries philosophic thought developed in India till at last it became so unwieldy that a regular systematization of each school of thought was found a great necessity This led to the Sûtra literature.

THE SUTRAS

These systematic treatises were written in short aphorisms called Sûtras, meaning clues, and were intended as memory-aids to long discussions on any topic

1 Āstika (orthodox) and Nâstika (heterodox) had nothing to go with belief or non-belief in the existence of a God. Sâṁkhya and Mîmâṁsâ which did not accept an Īśwara were yet regarded Āstika (orthodox).

which the student had gone through with his teacher or Guru. The thought was very much condensed, for much was taken for granted. Consequently the maximum of thought was compressed into these Sûtras in as few words as possible. Madhvâcârya quotes from *Padma Purâṇa* a definition of the Sûtra in his commentary on the Brahman-Sûtras which runs as follows:

अल्पाक्षरमसंदिग्धं सारवद्विश्वतोमुखम् ।
अस्तोभमनवद्यं च सूत्रं सूत्रविदो विदुः ॥

"People, learned in Sûtra literature, say that a Sûtra should be concise and unambiguous, give the essence of the arguments on a topic but at the same time deal with all aspects of the question, be free from repetition and faultless." Though this definition states what a Sûtra ought to be, in practice, however, the desire for brevity was carried to such extremes that most part of the Sûtra literature is now unintelligible, and this is particularly so with respect to the Vedânta-Sûtras which has consequently given rise to divergent systems.

There was Sûtra literature in every branch of Indo-Aryan knowledge which had become cumbrous through centuries and required systematization. The authors of these Sûtras, as we see, are not the founders of the thought or systems they propounded, but are mere systematizers of the thought developed on the subject by successive generations of thinkers for centuries. The thought of these Sûtras was much developed by later thinkers and even modified by them, though all of them disclaimed any originality in it, declaring that they were merely interpreting the Sûtras. This was specially the case with respect to the philosophical Sûtras. All these subsequent thinkers belonged to one or other of the six systems and developed its traditionary thought from generation to generation, rendering it more and more perfect, and more and more secure against the ever new criticisms of rival schools. Such interpretations of the Sûtras gave rise to various kinds of literary writings like Vâkyas, Vṛttis, Kârikâs and Bhâṣyas, each of them being more and more elaborate than the previous ones.

THE BRAHMA-SŪTRAS

The Upaniṣads do not contain any ready-made consistent system of thought. At first sight they seem to be full of contradictions. Hence arose the necessity of systematizing the thought of the Upaniṣads. Bâdarâyaṇa, to whom the authorship of the Brahma-Sûtras or Vedânta-Sûtras is ascribed, is not the only one who had tried to systematize the philosophy of the Upaniṣads. From the Brahma-Sûtras itself we find that there were other schools of Vedânta which had their own following. We find the names of Auḍulomi, Kâśakṛtsna, Bâdari, Jaimini, Kârṣṇâjini, Āṣmarathya and others mentioned. All this shows that Bâdarâyaṇa's Sûtras do not constitute the only systematic work in the Vedânta school, though probably the last and best. All the sects of India now hold this work to be the great authority and every new sect starts with a fresh commentary on it—without which no sect can be founded in this country.

THE AUTHOR AND DATE OF THE SŪTRAS

About Bâdarâyaṇa, the author of the Sûtras, very little is known today. Tradition, however, identifies him with Vyâsa, the author of the Gîtâ and the Mahâbhârata. Śaṅkara, however, in his commentaries refers to Vyâsa as the author of the Mahâbhârata, and the author of the Sûtras he refers to as Bâdarâyana. Perhaps to him these two personalities were different. His followers, Vâcaspati, Ānandagiri and others identify Vyâsa and Bâdarâyana, while Râmânuja and other commentators on the Sûtras attribute it to Vyâsa.

Deussen infers from the cross references in the works of Jaimini and Bâdarâyaṇa that they may have been combined by a later editor into one work, and provided with the cross references. This combined work, he says, was commented upon by Upavarṣa on whose work the commentaries of Śabara on the Pûrva Mîmâṁsâ and Śaṅkara on the Uttara Mîmâṁsâ rest. Śaṅkara's commentary on 3.3.53 gives support to this last view and it also explains the popular idea that the two Mîmâṁsâs form one Śâstra. This combined work might well have been arranged by Vyâsa, the author of the Mahâbhârata. Or it may be that he had written them himself according to the views that were traditionally handed down as Bâdarâyaṇa's. This latter view easily accounts for the reference to Bâdarâyaṇa by name in the Sûtras. That such a thing was not uncommon in ancient India is established by Colebrook on the authority of Indian commentators of Manu and Yâjñavalkya. Max Müller also says that Bâdarâyaṇa and other similar names are simply eponymous heroes of different philosophies.[1]

In support of the view that the two persons are one it can be pointed out that there existed in the time of

[1] *The Six Systems of Indian Philosophy* (1912 *Impression*), p. 120.

Pâṇini Sûtras known as Bhikṣu-Sûtras which are identified by Vâcaspati with the Vedânta-Sûtras. The subject-matter of the Vedânta-Sûtras being Brahman, the knowledge of which is pre-eminently meant for Sannyâsins, it might well be called Bhikṣu-Sûtras. Pâṇini in his Sûtras ascribes these Bhikṣu-Sûtras to Pârâśarya, the son of Parâśara, *i.e.* Veda-Vyâsa, who was also called Bâdarâyaṇa as he had his Āshrama at Badari in the Himâlayas. That the Vedânta-Sûtras and Pûrva Mîmâṁsâ-Sûtras must have existed before Pâṇini can also be inferred from the commentary on both of them by Upavarṣa who is said to be the Guru of Pâṇini in the Kathâ-saritsâgara, though we must admit it cannot be conclusively proved that the two Upavarṣas are one and the same person.

The identity of the Vedânta-Sûtras and the Bhikṣu-Sûtras would no doubt fix the date of the Sûtras very early before Buddha, and a question may arise how such an early work could have referred to various other schools of philosophy of a much later date and refuted them. In this connection we must not forget that the author of the Sûtras does not refer to any founder of the different schools by name. He even does not use the technical terms of the different schools as they are known to us today. During that great philosophical ferment which followed at the close of the Upanisadic period various metaphysical views were held which later developed in definite channels. Therefore the fact that Bâdarâyaṇa is acquainted with certain systems of thought which later came to be associated with certain names does not show that Bâdarâyaṇa was later than these persons. These later names were by no means the original founders of the systems of thought.

but only gave definite shape to some particular thought that was found in that mass of philosophical speculations which existed in that period. Bâdarâyaṇa could anticipate even the Buddhistic and Jaina schools, for Buddha and Mahâvîra also were not the founders of any altogether new schools of philosophy but imbibed much of the thought current in the country at the time. There was no revolutionary departure in their philosophy, but it was their great personality that shaped the history of India for centuries. As regards Jaina thought we know definitely that it existed from even before the time of Pârśwanâtha (8th or 9th century B.C.). In fact all these systems must have belonged to the same period of philosophical ferment which preceded the rise of Buddhism. Thus a writer of the Vedânta-Sûtras before Buddha may well be acquainted with the different schools of philosophy refuted in the Tarkapâda of that book though they might not have existed in the form in which we know them today or in the form in which they have been refuted by Śaṅkara.

Moreover, that the Vedânta-Sûtras were known to exist before Buddha can also be made out from the Gîtâ. The date of the Gîtâ and the original Mahâbhârata, of which the Gîtâ is a part, can be fixed before the time of Buddha. Both of them are pre-Buddhistic, for they contain no reference to Buddha and Buddhism. Quotations from both are found in Bodhâyana who belongs to 400 B.C. The language of the Gîtâ also seems to belong to a period before Pâṇini. He is also conversant with the epic characters. So we can well say that the Gîtâ and the Mahâbhârata were known before Buddha. Now we find a clear reference to the Brahma-Sûtras, in Gîtâ 13.4, where the word 'Brahma-Sûtra-padaiḥ' occurs. This is a definite reference to the Vedânta-Sûtras. The full text runs as follows: "This has been sung by the Ṛṣis in various ways and in different metres and definitely and logically by the words of the Brahma-Sûtras." Tilak argues in his Gîtâ-Rahasya that the first half refers to teachings which are disconnected and unsystematic and therefore refers to the Upaniṣads, while the later half to something definite and logical—a difference that is clearly brought out by this stanza and therefore refers to the systematized thought in the Vedânta-Sûtras. Max Müller too is of opinion that the Vedânta-Sûtras belong to an earlier period than the Gîtâ[1] and in the text just quoted he finds a clear reference to the recognized title of the Vedânta or Brahma-Sûtras.[2] Indian commentators on the Gîtâ like Râmânuja, Madhva and others identify the Vedânta-Sûtras in this passage of the Gîtâ.

But if the Vedânta-Sûtras be of an earlier date than the Gîtâ, how could it contain references to the Gîtâ? In Sûtras 2. 3. 45 and 4. 2. 21 all the commentators quote the same text of the Gîtâ, and there seems to be no doubt that they are right. These cross references show that the author of the Gîtâ had a hand in the present recension of the Sûtras. This is also made clear by the rejection of the four-fold Vyûha of the Bhâgavatas both by the Gîtâ and the Sûtras and the great predominance given to the Sâṁkhya school in both. The Gîtâ accepts the Sâṁkhya view of creation but modifies it to some extent and makes the Pradhâna subservient to the supreme Brahman which is non-dual. In the Vedânta-Sûtras also the author refutes the dualism of the

[1] *The Six Systems of Indian Philosophy,* p. 113.
[2] *Ibid.* p. 118.

Sâṁkhyas. Otherwise he has no objection to accepting the Pradhâna or Prakṛti as a principle dependent on the supreme Lord (*vide* 1. 4. 2-3). Śaṅkara in his Bhâṣya on these Sûtras makes this quite clear.

From what has been said above we find that there are strong grounds for believing that the Vedânta-Sûtras must have existed before Buddha and that if Bâdarâyaṇa and Veda-Vyâsa are not one and the same person as tradition holds, the latter must have had a hand in the present recension of the Sûtras, though it is very difficult to say to what extent—whether it was by way of merely revising the original Sûtras of Bâdarâyaṇa or writing them down *in toto* after the teachings of Bâdarâyaṇa.

COMMENTATORS ON THE BRAHMA-SŪTRAS

It has already been shown that the Brahma-Sûtras of Bâdarâyaṇa somehow gained prominence and popularity and as a result all the great Ācâryas have written commentaries on it. The oldest of extant commentaries is by Śaṅkara, the exponent of Monism. A Vṛtti by Upavarṣa is mentioned by Śaṅkara and Bhâskara and a Vṛtti by Bodhâyana is referred to and often quoted by Râmânuja in his Śrî Bhâṣya. Śaṅkara does not refer to Bodhâyana. According to Vedânta Deśika the two are one person. Unfortunately this work of Bodhâyana is not available now. Râmânuja quotes also from the Drâmiḍa Bhâṣya which evidently belongs to the Bhakti cult of Southern India. Śaṅkara was followed by a host of commentators on these Sûtras—Yâdava Prakâśa, Bhâskara. Vijñâna Bhikṣu. Râmânuja, Nîlakaṇṭha, Srîpati. Nimbârka. Madhva,

Vallabha and Baladeva. There are even some recent commentaries, though of not much value. All these try to maintain that their system is the one that Bâdarâyaṇa propounded through his Sûtras.

At present, however, only five of these great commentators have a large following—Śaṅkara, the exponent of Monism; Râmânuja, the exponent of Viśiṣṭâdvaita or qualified Monism; Nimbârka, the exponent of Bhedâbhedavâda or the theory of difference and non-difference; Madhva, the exponent of Dualism; and Vallabha, the exponent of Śuddhâdvaitavâda. All of these systems seem to be based on the views of one or other of the ancient Vedânta schools which we find Bâdarâyaṇa referring in his Sûtras.

A question may be raised how the same work could have given rise to so many conflicting schools of thought. The reasons are many. In the first place the brevity of the Sûtras leaves much to be supplied by the commentators, and in the absence of a universally accepted unbroken tradition each is free to do this according to his own preconceived ideas. Sometimes even without supplying anything the same Sûtra is capable of being interpreted differently and even conveying quite the opposite meaning (*e.g.* Śaṅkara and Râmânuja on 3. 2. 11) by the mere shifting of the stops. Again, while there is a tradition which is accepted more or less by all as regards the arrangement into chapters and sections there is no such accepted tradition as regards the division into Adhikaraṇas (topics), nor is there anything authoritative to guide us as to which Sûtras form the Pûrvapaksa or the *prima facie* view and which give the Siddhânta or the author's view. So every one is free to divide the Sûtras into topics according to his own choice and regard any Sûtras as giving the author's view. Then again, the Sûtras do not give any reference as to which texts of the scriptures are being discussed and as a result the commentator is free to select any texts from that vast repertory, so much so that it often happens that different commentators see different topics discussed in the same set of Sûtras. Added to all this is the difficulty that Bâdarâyaṇa is often silent as regards his own decision and that on fundamental questions. He merely gives the views of different Vedântins and ends the topic (*vide* 1.4.20-22).

The five great commentators more or less agree on certain points, especially where the author attacks the principles of the non-Vedântic schools. All of them agree that Brahman is the cause of this world and that knowledge of It leads to final emancipation which is the goal to be attained; also that Brahman can be known only through the scriptures and not through mere reasoning But they differ amongst themselves as to the nature of this Brahman, Its causality with respect to this world, the relation of the individual soul to It and the condition of the soul in the state of release.

Brahman, according to Śaṅkara, is attributeless, immutable, pure Intelligence. Īśvara, according to him, is a product of Mâyâ—the highest reading of the nirguṇa Brahman by the individualized soul. The world is a Vivarta or apparent transformation through Mâyâ of the nirguṇa Brahman but not in reality. The Jîva in reality is all-pervading and identical with Brahman, though as individualized by its Upâdhi (adjunct), the internal organ, it regards itself as atomic, as an agent, and as a part of the Lord. The knowers of the nirguṇa

Brahman attain It directly and have not to go by "the path of the gods". It is the knowers of the saguṇa Bṛahman that go by that path to Brahmaloka from where they do not return but attain Brahman at the end of the cycle. Knowledge is the only means to Liberation.

To Râmânuja and the other commentators Brahman is not attributeless but an essentially personal God possessing infinite benign attributes. They hold that though personality as we experience it in man is limited, it need not be invariably connected with personality as Śaṅkara thinks, so as to contradict infinity. They do not accept the Mâyâ doctrine, for to them the world is real, and so they accept that the world is produced from Brahman. Madhva, however, accepts It only as the efficient cause and not as the material cause also. The Jîva, according to them, is really atomic, an agent, and a part of the Lord. The knower of Brahman goes by the path of the gods to Brahmaloka where he attains Brahman and does not return to this mortal world. They do not make any distinction of higher and lower knowledge like Śaṅkara. According to them Bhakti is the chief means to Liberation, and not Jñâna.

Thus to all of them Brahman, the world, and the souls are all realities. Râmânuja integrates the three into one organic whole and says that Brahman has for Its body the other two. Nimbârka integrates the three by his Bhedâbhedavâda *i.e.* the relation of the sentient and insentient world with Brahman is one of difference and non-difference. Madhva, a thoroughgoing dualist, regards these three as quite independent, eternal entities, though Brahman is the ruler of the other two. To Vallabha the world and the souls are Brahman Itself.

They are real and their relation to Brahman is one of identity, as that of parts to a whole.[1]

ŚAṄKARA'S INTERPRETATION OF THE SŪTRAS

There is a strong opinion current amongst scholars today that whatever be the merit of Śaṅkara's metaphysical doctrines considered by themselves or even as doctrines elucidating the teachings of the Upaniṣads, he is not faithful to Bâdarâyaṇa in his interpretation of the Sûtras. They hold that Bâdarâyaṇa was ignorant of a two-fold Brahman and consequently of a two-fold knowledge; that he was not aware of the doctrine of Mâyâ and so did not hold that the world was unreal, but that Brahman underwent a real change into this world-order; and that the Sûtras do not hold the view of absolute identity of the individual soul and Brahman. In short their view is that the system of Bâdarâyaṇa is a theistic system which has more affinities with the systems of Râmânuja and Nimbârka than with Śaṅkara's pure Non-dualism. This view is nothing new. Bhâskara at the beginning of his commentary on the Sûtras accuses Śaṅkara of this very thing. But at the same time we can also cite Śâṇḍilya, the author of the Bhakti-Sûtras, who in Sûtra 30 of his work refers to Bâdarâyaṇa as a Monist, which shows that the view that Bâdarâyaṇa was an Abhedavâdin was prevalent in ancient days, even as early as the Sûtra period.

It is not possible to deal with such a controversial subject in a short Introduction like this. All the same we shall take some salient points connected with this

[1] For details, see the various Bhāṣyas on Sûtras 1.1.2. 1.4.23. 26, 2. 1. 26-28, 2. 3. 18-53, 3. 2. 11-30, 4. 2. 12-14 and 4. 4. 1-7.

discussion and try to see how far such a criticism against Śaṅkara is justified. At the outset, however, it is fair to admit that at places Śaṅkara's interpretations seem to be far-fetched; but this is by no means a defect of his Bhâṣya alone but of all the other extant Bhâṣyas as well. Moreover, in such a critical study we shall not gain much if we follow the letter of the Sûtras, missing the general spirit of the work as a whole. It is possible to give a consistent interpretation of the Sûtras by following the letter of the Sûtras and at the same time miss the general spirit of the work as a whole.

पौर्वापर्यापरामृष्टः शब्दोऽन्यां कुरुते मतिम् ।

"The Śruti texts give rise to a wrong view if they are not studied as one connected whole"—in other words the letter often kills the spirit.

Sûtra 2 aims at a nirguṇa Brahman:

To start with, let us take the definition of Brahman given by Bâdarâyaṇa in Sûtra 2. Sûtra 1 says that Brahman is to be inquired into, for the knowledge of It leads to Mokṣa (Liberation). The next Sûtra defines Brahman and so naturally we have to understand that the Brahman the knowledge of which gives Mokṣa is defined here. As such we get a saguṇa Brahman as the subject-matter of the Śâstra and not the nirguṇa Brahman of Śaṅkara which is Existence, Knowledge, Bliss Absolute. So it appears that the author at the very beginning of the work precludes any chance of Śaṅkara's doctrine being read in his Sûtras. But let us investigate into the matter a little and see whether it is actually so.

After the statement in Sûtra 1 that Brahman is to be known, naturally the question about the nature of Brahman arises. The Sûtrakâra (aphorist) here anticipates an objection that Brahman cannot be defined at all. For whatever we cognize in this world is limited and as such cannot be a characteristic of Brahman which is infinite. A limited thing cannot define an unlimited thing. Nor can any characteristic which is absolutely beyond our experience, like Reality etc., define Brahman, for it is only a well-known characteristic that defines a thing and distinguishes it from other things. Again the scriptures cannot define Brahman, for being absolutely unique It cannot be expressed in speech. Thus in the absence of any definition Brahman cannot be a thing worth inquiring into and cannot serve any human purpose. To refute all such objections the Sûtrakâra defines Brahman in Sûtra 2. Granted that the world we experience cannot define Brahman as being a quality of It or as being identical with It, yet the quality of being the (supposed) cause of the world may indicate It. "Birth etc." mentioned in the Sûtra define Brahman *per accidens*. Though they inhere in the world and do not pertain to Brahman, the causality connected therewith pertains to Brahman and therefore the definition holds good. This causality indicates Brahman even as the snake indicates the rope when we say that which is the snake is the rope, where the rope is indicated by the snake owing to the illusory connection between the two. This definition, therefore, actually aims at the nirguṇa Brahman and cannot be taken as a definition of the saguṇa Brahman.[1]

[1] *Bhāmati* and *Ratnaprabhā* on Śaṅkara's comments on Sûtra 2.

Again the Sûtra refers to the Taittirîya text, "That from which these beings are born....That is Brahman" etc. (3.1) and the word 'that' here refers to the Brahman defined as Existence, Knowledge, and Infinite in the immediately preceding section, the Ānanda Valli. Therefore from this text itself we get at the real nature of Brahman.

Yet it may be questioned why the author should give an indirect definition of Brahman instead of defining It in Its real nature as, "Existence, Knowledge, Bliss is Brahman." The answer is that the author has followed here the universally accepted principle of taking a student step by step from a lower to a higher truth, from a grosser to a subtler one. It is indeed by first pointing to the end of the branch of a tree that one points out the moon to the child. Similarly, first Brahman as the Cause is distinguished from this world of products, and finally by saying that from Bliss this universe is born, It is differentiated from other probable causes like atoms, the Pradhâna, etc. In this way finally Brahman's real nature as distinguished from everything else is described. The aspirant whose mind is turned away from the world of the senses first comprehends Brahman as the cause of the world. Though in Itself as the inner Self Brahman is immediate, yet we have the idea that It is remote. Hence the Śruti first teaches that Brahman is the cause of the world, and then to remove this false notion of remoteness it teaches that It is one with the inner Self. So long as this identity is not realized, It appears to be the cause of the world.

That Bliss which admits of no difference is Brahman we learn from the Chândogya Upaniṣad. "The Bhuman (Infinite) only is Bliss. This Infinite we must desire to understand" (7. 23. 1). What is this Infinite which is called Bliss? The Upaniṣad explains: "Where one sees nothing else, hears nothing else, understands nothing else, that is the Infinite. Where one sees something else, hears something else, understands something else, that is the finite. The Infinite is immortal, the finite is mortal" (*Ibid.* 7. 24. 1). This non-dual Bliss is the Infinite, the Brahman defined in Ânanda Valli as Existence, Knowledge, Infinite is Brahman, and from this all creation springs—so understood Bhṛgu, the son of Varuṇa.

Again the Taittirîya text, "That from which all beings are born. . . .Try to know that. That is Brahman," aims at defining a non-dual Brahman as the only reality and does not define a saguṇa Brahman. It defines Brahman as the efficient and also as the material cause of the universe, since It is the place of dissolution of the world. Being the material cause of everything, It is the basic reality behind everything and this gives rise to the intuition that Brahman is non-dual and that everything else is unreal. Its being the efficient cause also establishes the fact that It is non-dual, as it precludes anything else being such an efficient cause. Thus this definition, which is but one, qualifies *per accidens* the non-dual Brahman as both the efficient and material cause of the universe. This material causality of Brahman which is non-dual, immutable Intelligence cannot be one of origination, as by primeval atoms by whose combination something new is created; nor can it be one of modification, as of the Pradhâna of the Sâṁkhyas. It is through Vivarta or apparent modification through Mâyâ or Nescience that Brahman is transformed into this universe. This universe is therefore illusory.[1] That this is in accordance with Bâdarâyaṇa's view is made clear by the fact that he uses the word 'Sat' as a characteristic epithet to denote Brahman which he would not have done if he had considered the Jîvas and the world also real like Brahman (*vide* Sûtra 2. 3. 9). The word 'Sat' here is interpreted by all commoentators to denote Brahman.

Thus we find that this definition is given by Bâdarâyaṇa to indicate a nirguṇa (attributeless) and nirviśeṣa (absolute) Brahman and not a saguṇa Brahman and he has selected a significant text from the wide range of scriptural texts for defining his Brahman.

Is Brahman the real or apparent cause of the world?

Now let us take up the Sûtras about the causality of Brahman, *viz* Sûtras 1. 4. 23-27 and Sûtra 2. 1. 14. Before that let us have a brief summary of the work up to 2. 1. 14. After defining Brahman in Sûtra 2 the Sûtrakâra from 1. 1. 5 to 1. 4. 13 and in 1. 4. 23-27 shows that all the scriptural texts teach that Brahman is both the efficient and the material cause of the universe, refuting the Sâṁkhyas in 1.1. 5-11 and in 1.4.1-13. Sûtras 1.4. 14-22 refute the Sâṁkhyan objection that there are contradictions in the Śruti texts with respect to the first Cause. Finally Sûtra 28 says that by what has been said against the Sâṁkhyas the others also are refuted. Sûtras 2.1. 1-2 reject the authority of the Sâṁkhya and Yoga Smṛtis as against the scriptures. Sûtras 4-11 answer through reasoning without the aid of texts the Sâṁkhyan objection based on reasoning that Brahman cannot be the material cause of the world, for It and the world are of different nature and

[1] *Siddhāntaleśa*, Brahmalakṣaṇavicāra.

as such the relation of cause and effect cannot exist between them. Sûtra 12 refutes the validity of reasoning in matters transcendental and thus refutes all schools which arrive at their doctrines through reasoning Sûtra 13 answers another objection of the Sâṁkhyas that if Brahman be the material cause, then there would result non-distinction between enjoyer and things enjoyed, a fact established by experience. The Sûtra refutes it saying that such a difference can exist in non-different things even as we have waves, foam, etc. in the sea and so the Vedântic doctrine cannot be set aside on the ground of contradiction to our experience. Now, duality and non-duality cannot exist in one and the same thing, for they are mutually contradictory. The example of the sea and the waves would be apt if Brahman had aspects, but non-dual reality does not admit of such aspects. Moreover, Sûtra 13 has not established the truth of the scriptural statement, "By the knowledge of the one everything else is known" which was referred to in Sûtra 1. 4. 23. To establish these two things Sûtras 14-20 declare that the effects are in reality non-different from the cause, *i.e.* they have no existence apart from the cause.[1]
Non-difference here does not mean identity but that there is no difference.[2] In other words the two Brahman and the world, have not the same grade of reality.[3] That is what is meant. If the world is something different from Brahman, it would contradict such Śruti texts as, "All this was but the Self" (Bṛ. 1.4.1., 1.4.17). Again if the world is real, it would contradict texts

[1] Śaṅkara on Sûtra 14.
[2] *Bhāmati* on Sūtra 14.
[3] *Siddhāntaleśa*, Brahmakāraṇatvavicāra.

like, "There is nothing whatsoever here" (Bṛ. 4.4.19). Therefore the world is non-different from Brahman. But identity is not what is meant by non-difference, for this is impossible between the world and Brahman, they being mutually different in nature. Hence non-difference means that it has no existence apart from Brahman, it precludes difference. The denial of identity, however, does not establish the difference of the world and Brahman, but establishes the apparent identity or the illusory nature of the world, even as the illusory snake is seen in he rope. This is what the Chândogya text 6.1.4 tries to teach. Thus only by the knowledge of one thing can everything be known, on any other assumption it would be impossible to establish it. The non-difference of the world from Brahman being established, the question naturally arises that Brahman would then be responsible for creating evil for the Jîva which is one with It. This is answered in Sûtras 2. 1. 21-23. Sûtras 24-25 show how Brahman, though destitute of materials and instruments, yet is the cause of the world even as milk turns into curbs without any extraneous help. The example cited raises a fresh objection in Sûtra 26 that Brahman cannot at the same time be both immutable and be transformed into the world. Against this Sûtra 27 says that the Śruti states both these views and so they have to be accepted, as the Śruti is the only authority with respect to Brahman As to how these two views are to be reconciled, Sûtra 28 says that even as in the individual soul diverse creation exists in the dream state without marring its indivisibility, so also this world springs from Brahman. This example which is cited is very significant as it shows that Bâdarâyaṇa was quite familiar with

Mâyâvâda—that he considered this world unreal in a higher sense even as the dream world is Mâyâ (3.2.3). These two Sûtras together with Sûtras 2. 3. 50 and 3. 2. 18 show that he viewed the world as unreal. The subsequent Sûtras establish that Brahman through Mâyâ possesses all powers necessary for creation and so on.

In the above summary we find how logically and consistently Śaṅkara has interpreted the Sûtras which leaves no room for dispute as to what Bâdarâyaṇa meant in these Sûtras.

Thus in the whole of Chapter I and Section 1 of Chapter II Bâdarâyaṇa establishes the efficient and material causality of Brahman and in this his opponents are primarily the Sâṁkhyas who deny Its material causality. As they also quote the scriptures often in their support, they are the foremost opponents in Bâdarâyaṇa's view. He disposes of others by saying that they too are refuted by these arguments. Śaṅkara also, as shown above, has in Ch. I, Sec. 4 and Ch. II, Sec. 1 consistently interpreted the Sûtras as directed against the Sâṁkhyas or as answering their objections.

Some critics of Śaṅkara, however, think that the reasoning employed by the aphorist against the Sâṁkhyas in Sûtras 4--11 of Ch. II, Sec. 1, especially Sûtra 6, would be hardly appropriate from Śaṅkara's point of view, for according to him the world springs not from Brahman as Intelligence, but in so far as It is associated with Mâyâ. Similarly, Sûtra 24 which says that Brahman transforms Itself into the world like milk would be inappropriate if the world were unreal; Sûtra 1.4.23 where Brahman is said to be the material and efficient cause of the world does not say that Brahman is the material cause through Mâyâ; on the other hand Sûtra 1.4.26 uses the word 'Pariṇâmât' to show how Brahman is changed into the world.

This criticism does not seem to be relevant. In Sûtras 2.1.4-11 the Sâṁkhyas' objection against the Vedântic doctrine of the material causality of Brahman in answered. Here the author is concerned only with establishing Brahman as the material cause and thus refuting the dualism of the Sâṁkhyas who posit an independent principle, the Pradhâna, as the first Cause, and not with the true nature of this causality. Up to Sûtra 13 he refutes the objection from the Sâṁkhyas' own realistic standpoint. His own view as to the true significance of the causality is established in Sûtra 14. It is not true that Śaṅkara holds that Brahman as pure Intelligence is not the material cause, but only as endowed with Mâyâ. Brahman or pure Intelligence as such is the material cause of the world as Sûtra 1. 4. 23. says. But because of this, we cannot expect the effect, the world, to be similar to the cause in all respectes. This is made clear by Śaṅkara in his commentary on Sûtra 2.1.6 where he says that they cannot be similar in all respects, for if they were, then there would be nothing like cause and effect, for would they be called by different names. What is essential for establishing the relation of cause and effect is that some qualities of the cause must be found in the effect also, and this is satisfied in the case of Brahman and the world. Everything in this world exists and this quality is obtained from Brahman which is Existence; everything is also illumined by Intelligence which is Brahman. So Sûtra 1.4.23 which says that Brahman as Intelligence is the cause is not contradicted according to Śaṅkara's view. This Sûtra further says, "This view not contradicting the proposition and illustration cited in Ch. 6. 1. 14." In what sense the material causality of Brahman as Intelligence does not contradict this enunciation, is shown by the aphorist in 2.1.14. From these Sûtras Śaṅkara says that both Brahman and Mâyâ are the cause of the world. Brahman through Vivarta, and Mâyâ through Pariṇâma; and the qualities of both are found in the effect, the world, as we gather from our cognition of a pot, 'The pot exists,' 'The pot is inert' where as existence the pot is identical with Brahman which is existence itself, and as inert it is identical with Mâyâ which is inert. Everything in this world has five elements in its make-up, *viz* Asti, Bhâti, Priya, Nâma, and Rûpa, the former three have Brahman for its material cause corresponding to the three factors, Existence Intelligence and Bliss, and the last two consist of Mâyâ, and are unreal. No doubt the aphorist takes the Pariṇâma view as a workable basis in refuting the Sâṁkhyas. But we have aldeady said that it is a well established principle of Indian teachers to take the aspirant step by step to the final truth. So Bâdarâyaṇa, by taking the Pariṇâma view-point in his earlier Sûtras where Brahman is referred to as the Cause and establishing Vivarta in 2.1.14, has only followed this universaly accepted methods. That the author is not for Pariṇâmavâda is made clear by him in Sûtras 26-28. Sûtra 28 clearly establishes the unreality of the world, it being illusory like the dream world.

Coming to Râmânuja's commentary, we find that he is not so logical or consistent as Śaṅkara. According to him Brahman has for Its body the entire universe with all its sentient and insentient beings in all Its states. When the souls and matter are in the subtle state,

Brahman is in the causal condition and when they are in the gross state It is in the effect state. The effect, *i.e.* the world, is thus seen to be non-different from the cause, *i.e.* the supreme Brahman (*vide* Śrî Bhâṣya, Sûtras 1.4.27 and 2.1.15). Bâdarâyaṇa does not seem to hold this view, for nowhere does he say that Brahman has for Its body the souls and matter. Even if 2.3.43 should mean that the souls are the body of Brahman, there is no similar Sûtra to show that matter too is Its body. Moreover, if Brahman is the material cause of the world through Its insentient part only, as the above view leads to, then Sûtra 1.4.23 which says that Brahman as Intelligence is the material cause would be contradicted and Sûtras 2. 1. 26-28 also would be useless, for the question of the whole of Brahman passing over into the world does not arise at all. Nor can the relation of cause and effect exist between Brahman in the causal and the effect state for it is the same Brahman in either case. Even if such a relationship be granted, it would make Sûtras 2.1.4-6 meaningless, for there can be no difference of nature in Brahman in the two states as between Brahman and the world—the sentient and the insentient. Râmânuja directs Sûtra 14 against the Vaiśeṣikas, but we do not find the author making anybody else but the Sâṁkhyas the opponents. The rest he disposes of by saying that the arguments against the Sâṁkhyas refute others also (*vide* 1.4.28 and 2.1.12). The interpretation of Sûtra 2.1.28 by Râmânuja is very far-fetched. His explanation that because things possess different qualities owing to the difference in their essential nature, Brahman which is unique can possess qualities beyond our experience, is not to the point, while Śaṅkara's interpretation is very happy as it gives us an idea as to how it is possible for Brahman to create the world and yet remain immutable. Moreover, Râmânuja has not explained in Sûtras 26-28 the contradiction in the Śruti texts, while Śaṅkara's interpretation reconciles the contradiction through reasoning, and such reasoning as is not against the Śruti texts is quite acceptable to all Vedântins; in fact that is what the author proposes to do in this Uttara Mîmâṁsâ work of his.

Coming to Nimbârka, his line of argument on these Sûtras relating to the causality of Brahman is to establish the Bhedâbheda doctrine. Sûtra 2. 1. 13 he interprets first like Śaṅkara. But in Sûtra 14 the word 'अनन्यत्वम्' he interprets as ,न तु अत्यन्तभिन्नत्वम्' 'not absolutely different'. That is, the effect is not absolutely different from the cause: it has no separate existence from Brahman. Thus from Sûtra 13 which says that Brahman and the Jîva are different, Sûtras 4-6 which says that the insentient world is different from It and Sûtra 14 which says that they have no separate existence apart from Brahman, Nimbârka concludes that between Brahman and the sentient and insentient world there is difference as well as non-difference. But such a thing in one and the same entity is impossible. The Chândogya text says that the clay alone is real and not the things made of clay, for they are mere names, unreal. Take for example a clay pot: when we cognize it as a pot we are not conscious of its being clay and when we cognize it as clay we miss the pot, though both these aspects are inherent in it. So we have to conclude that its nature is illusory, for it is not cognized as what it is. That which is non-different from a thing and yet appears to be different and which depends upon the non-difference for its existence cannot but be illusory. So between the pot and the clay, the latter alone is real and not the pot. Similar is the case with Brahman and the world. Brahman alone is real and world is unreal. "When all this is but the Self, how could one see another?" (Bṛ. 2.4.14). Chândogya 6.16 calls one who sees variety as false-minded and the one who sees unity as true-minded. But to people who are in ignorance both difference and non-difference seem to be real, the unity being understood through the scriptures and variety through direct perception. This is only a relative or Vyâvahârika state. The truth is unity. Therefore Nimbârka's view cannot be correct.

Does Bâdarâyaṇa accept the Pâñcarâtra view?

In Section 2 of Chapter II the author takes the offensive. So long he was on the defensive. In the whole of this section he refutes through reasoning alone, without recourse to the Śruti texts, the various schools of philosophy of the time. In this Section he refutes those schools of thought that were regarded by the orthodox section as outside the sphere of the Vedas. We have enough references in ancient works like the Mahâbhârata and some of the Purânas that all these schools refuted in Section 2 by the author were so regarded. The Śiva Mahimnaḥ Stotra contains the verse 'त्रयी सांख्य योग: पशुपतिमतं वैष्णवमिति', which shows that Sâṁkhya, Yoga, Pâśupata and Vaiṣṇava (which includes Pâñcarâtra) schools of thought were regarded as different from त्रयी or the Vedic religion with its two branches, Karmakâṇḍa and Jñânakâṇḍa. Moreover, we find that in many works of the Pâñcarâtra school the Vedas are held in contempt. Śaṅkara himself quotes such a text. The scholiasts Govindânanda and Ānandagiri also quote similar texts. Therefore they must have been definitely regarded by the ancients as outside the pale of the Vedas and we cannot reasonably expect Bâdarâyaṇa to have accepted their view as his final conclusion in a work meant to systematize the orthodox thought of the Upaniṣads. Of course, to that portion which does not contradict the Vedas he has no objection; nor has Śaṅkara, as he has made it clear in his Bhâṣya on Sûtras 42 and 43. Râmânuja, however, sees in Sûtras 44 and 45 the acceptance of the Pâñcarâtra doctrine by a refutation of the objections raised against it in Sûtras 42-43. But his interpretations are stretched. Sûtra 45 he twists to mean, "And because the creation of the soul is contradicted by this Śâstra," saying thereby that the question raised in Sûtra 42 as to the creation of the soul does not arise at all, as this school does not hold the view. The way in which this Sûtra is stretched by Râmânuja can easily be seen by comparing it with Sûtra 10 where Bâdarâyaṇa uses the same wording, "And on account of contradiction," etc. to mean that contradiction in the Sâṁkhya system makes it unacceptable to the wise. This seems to be the Sûtrakâra's view here also Dr. Thibaut thinks "It would not be unnatural proceeding to close the polemical section with a defence of that doctrine which in spite of objections has to be viewed as the true one." But that being the purpose of the whole work itself, we cannot reasonably think that the author establishes his doctrine in these two Sûtras. Moreover, no other commentator sees the acceptance of the Pâñcarâtra doctrine in this topic. Vallabha follows Śaṅkara. Nimbârka sees the refutation of Śaktivâda in the topic

He is therefore consistent in that. He regards the whole of Section 2 as being devoted to a refutation of views not acceptable to the author. He accepts the Pâñcarâtra system and so he finds some other subject in this topic, though on this account his interpretation is not happy. But if Vyâsa had any hand in this work as already shown, then we cannot but see the refutation of the Pâñcarâtra system in these Sûtras, for we find that he does not accept this doctrine even in his Gîtâ.

The Jîva's real nature:

Now we come to Sûtras 2.3.16-53 which deal with the nature of the soul and its relation to Brahman. All except Śaṅkara interpret these Sûtras to mean that the soul is atomic, an agent, and a part of the Lord. Śaṅkara alone says that the atomicity, agency, and being a part are not the Jîva's real nature, but its nature as a Saṁsârin (transmigrating entity) and that in reality it is all-pervasive and identical with Brahman.

The author defines Brahman as the cause etc. of this world of sentient and insentient things in Sûtra 2, referring to the Taittirîya text, "That out of which all these creatures are born" etc. (3.1). It is clear, therefore, that the world of sentient and insentient things has sprung from Brahman. Hence the Jîvas too have sprung from the Lord. But in Sûtra 17 the author says that the individual soul is not produced. Thus he contradicts his definition and also the enunciation of the scriptures that "by the knowledge of one thing everything else is known" (Ch. 6.1). The Sûtrakâra at every place makes this enunciation the corner-stone of his argument. So we have to reconcile it and the author's definition of Brahman with his statement in Sûtra 17 which drives us to the conclusion that the Jîva as such, as a Saṁsârin, is an effect, but in its real nature it is eternal and identical with Brahman. That the nature of Jîva as we experience it is unreal is made clear by him in Sûtra 16. What originates is its connection with its adjuncts, gross and subtle, which is unreal. From this standpoint it is also clear why the author treats the question of the Jîva's nature and its relation to Brahman in this section which reconciles contradictions in the Śruti texts with respect to creation. There are different statements about the nature of the Jîva also and these he reconciles in this section, showing thereby that in its real nature it is not created and is identical with Brahman, but as a Saṁsârin it is an effect, atomic, an agent, and a part of Brahman. Even as Īśvara or Brahman limited by Nescience is not eternal, so is the Jîva limited by the body, mind, etc. not eternal, but in its true nature it is eternal. Bereft of their Upâdhis both are pure Intelligence and identical. That is why the Taittirîya Upaniṣad after saying, "Existence, Knowledge, Infinite is Brahman" (2. 1) says, "From That verily—from this Self—is the ether born" etc. (2.1), thus identifying the self as bereft of all its Upâdhis with Brahman. Taittirîya 2. 1, and 3. 1 cited by the Sûtrakâra in his definition of Brahman all refer to the same pure Intelligence. Thus the one 'Existence, Knowledge, Infinite' which is pure Intelligence, reflected in Nescience is Īśvara, and reflected in the Antaḥkarana (internal organ) is the Jîva, which is borne out by the scriptural statement, "This Jîva has the effect for the adjunct and Īśvara has the cause for the adjunct" (Śukarahasya Up. 2. 12). This seems to be the true viewpoint which has guided the aphorist in framing the

Sûtras of Section 3, Chapter II and in which sense Śaṅkara also has interpreted them. The enunciation also is not contradicted according to this interpretation.

According to Râmânuja, the souls are realy effects of Brahman but have existed in It from all eternity as a mode or Prakâra of Brahman. So also have the elements. Yet the latter are said to originate, as at the time of creation they undergo an essential change of nature. But the souls do not undergo such a change, they are always cognizing agents, but at the time of creation there is an expansion of their intelligence and in this sense alone, *i.e.* in the sense that there is no essential change in their nature at creation, are the souls said to be not created (*vide* Śri Bhâṣya 2. 3. 18) while the elements which undergo change in their essential nature are said to be created. Bâdarâyaṇa nowhere says that the souls and Prakṛti which form the body of Brahman are Its effects; nor does he anywhere declare such a difference between the souls and the elements. Again, according to Râmânuja, Brahman means not pure Being but as qualified by the souls and matter for Its body. This very conception of Brahman establishes that the relation between the souls and Brahman is as between a quality and the thing qualified and consequently 2. 3. 43 is redundant if the word 'part' there should be interpreted to convey this idea.

Râmânuja sees a refutation of Advaita in Sûtras 50-53. This does not seem to be intelligible at all, for the Advaitins do not say that the Jîva is all-pervading in its relative state. It is so in the state of release. Śaṅkara makes it clear that the Jîva as such is limited and subject to injunctions and prohibitions, through its connection with a gross body (2.3.38), and that even after the gross body falls, on account of its finer Upâdhis, the Antaḥkaraṇa etc. which accompany it even after death (4. 2. 1-6), it still continues to be individualized (2. 3. 30), and so there is no confusion in fruits of actions done in the gross body (2.3.49 and 50). It is only when this Upâdhi also, which being something created and not eternal (*vide* 2. 4) and therefore liable to destruction, is rent asunder, that the Jîva attains its real nature and is all-pervading. As such, Râmânuja's refutation of Advaita falls flat. Śaṅkara's interpretation of these Sûtras on the other hand is happy. The Sûtrakâra, having established that the Jîva in its relative state is atomic and an agent but in reality all-pervading, refutes the view of those who hold that the Jîvas are many and all-pervading in their relative state itself. Nimbârka and Vallabha also see the same subject in this topic which shows that Râmânuja's attempt to refute Advaita is far-fetched and not at all what the Sûtrakâra (aphorist) means.

Nimbârka too regards the Jîvas and Prakṛti as effects of Brahman; but while matter undergoes further modification after creation, the souls do not and in this sense the soul is said to be eternal by him also. Such a view stands refuted by the same arguments as are applied against Râmânuja's view. Coming to Sûtra 43 which says the Jîva is different as well as non-different from Brahman, it has already been shown by Śaṅkara in 2. 1. 14 that such a thing is not possible in the same entity and that non-difference alone is real.

Let us now conclude this topic by considering the reasonableness or otherwise of taking Sûtras 19-28 as the decisive view of the author. According to this view the soul is atomic, for the Śruti declares it to be so

(Mu. 3. 1. 9) and other texts mention its passing out of the body, going to heaven, etc. But then the Śruti also describes the supreme Self as atomic in texts like, "Smaller than a grain of rice, smaller than a grain of barley" etc. (Ch. 3. 14. 3). So how can we say that the Jîva alone is atomic and not the Lord? It may be said that texts say that Brahman is all-pervading. "All-pervading like the ether and eternal" etc.; "Greater than the sky, greater than heaven" etc. But then the Śruti texts describe the soul also as all-pervading: "He is indeed the great unborn Self" (Bṛ. 4. 4. 22); "Just as when a pot is carried, the pot alone is carried, not the ether inside it, even so is the Jîva compared to the ether," which expressly says it is all-pervading. Nor will it serve any purpose to say that Brahman, being the material cause of the world, must be all-pervasive for even the atomic Jîva creates several bodies (Kâyavyûha) and rules them and so Brahman though the material cause can yet be atomic. So neither by the Śruti texts nor by reasoning can the differentiation of Brahman and the Jîva as all-pervasive and atomic be justified. But, according to Advaita, there is no disparity in its reasoning in the two cases. Brahman due to Upâdhi (adjunct) appears atomic but in reality It is all-pervasive. So also is the Jîva in its real nature all-pervading and therefore identical with Brahman, though it appears to be atomic, an agent and so on owing to its limiting adjunct, the Antaḥkaraṇa. The primary texts say that Brahman and the Jîva in its real nature are all-pervading. The texts which speak of atomicity etc. are of a secondary import and so have to be explained otherwise.[1]

[1] *Siddhāntaleśa,* Jīvāṇutvavicāra.

Is Brahman with or without attributes?

Now let us take up the Sûtras in Chapter III, Section 2, where Bâdarâyaṇa describes the nature of Brahman. Sûtras 11-12, according to Śaṅkara, deal with the reconciliation of texts which describe Brahman both as attributeless and as possessing attributes and mean that even from difference of place a two-fold characteristic cannot be predicated of Brahman, because the scriptures teach throughout that Brahman is without attributes (11). If it be said that such difference is taught by the scriptures, we deny it because with respect to each form the Śruti declares just the opposite of that. The Śruti explains at every instance that the form is not true and that behind all Upâdhis there is one formless principle (*vide* Bṛ. 2. 5. 1.) (12). Moreover, some teach thus (*vide* Ka. 4. 11) (13). Verily Brahman is formless, for that is the purport of the texts (14). And as formless light takes form, so does Brahman take form in connection with Upâdhis which serve the purpose of Upâsanâ (meditation) (15). It is pure Intelligence (16). The Śruti and Smṛti teach that It is attributeless (17). Therefore we have with respect to Brahman comparisons like the images of the sun. The forms are mere reflections, they are not real (18).

Râmânuja and Nimbârka on the other hand see quite a different subject discussed in these Sûtras. The topic is not whether Brahman is attributeless or possesses attributes, but whether It is polluted by imperfections owing to Its being inside everything as the inner Ruler, even as the soul being embodied is subject to imperfections due to its states of waking, dream, and dreamless sleep described in Sûtras 1-10 Therefore according to Râmânuja the Sûtras mean that even on account of place such as matter and soul there is not the possibility of the supreme Lord being contaminated by imperfections, since everywhere in the scriptures Brahman is described as having a two-fold characteristic, *viz* freedom from imperfections and possessing all blessed qualities (11). If it be said that since the soul also by nature possesses according to Ch. 8.7 the two-fold characteristic of Brahman and yet is subject to imperfections due to its connection with a body, the inner Ruler will likewise be subject to such conditions owing to its connection with bodies, we deny it, for the Śruti at every place denies it by saying the Brahman is immortal and therefore free from imperfections (*vide* Br. 3. 7. 3-22). The imperfections in the soul are due to Karma and the Lord who is not subject to it is therefore free from such imperfections (12). Brahman can be said to have no form, as It is the originator of name and form and therefore is not subject to Karma like the souls which being embodied are subject to it (14). To an objection that the differentiated form of Brahman is false, Sûtra 15 answers thus: Even as on account of texts like "Brahman is Existence, Knowledge, Infinite" we have to accept that intelligence constitutes the essential nature of Brahman, so also we have to admit that It possesses a two-fold characteristic, as otherwise such texts become meaningless (15). And the texts say that much only, *i.e.* that Brahman has intelligence for its essential nature, and does not negative the other attributes of Brahman (16). The Śruti and Smṛti state thus (17) For this very reason are comparisons such as reflected images of the sun. Brahman, although abiding in manifold places, ever possesses the two-fold characteristic and is not contaminated even as the sun refllected in dirty water is not polluted (18).

Nimbârka also more or less follows Râmânuja's interpretation as regards Sûtras 11-14. Sûtras 15 and 16 he interprets in a different way, and sees in them an argument for establishing the authority of the Śruti as absolute in the matter discussed in 11-14. Sûtras 17-21 he interprets like Râmânuja, though he reads 21 as a separate Sûtra and not as a part of 20 as Râmânuja does.

A glance through these three commentaries on these Sûtras convinces one of the superiority and reasonableness and also of the logical consistency of Śaṅkara's interpretation. Moreover, it has the merit of dealing with the solution of an important doubt that arises in the mind of even a casual reader of the Upaniṣads, *viz* as to the nature of Brahman—whether it is qualified or non-qualified; for the Śruti texts seem to support both views though they are contradictory. Râmânuja and Nimbârka ignore such an important subject and see a less important subject discussed in these Sûtras. Secondly, they fail to bring out the force of the words of the Sûtras in bold relief as Śaṅkara does, *e.g.* 'two-fold characteristic' of Sûtra 11 which refers to contradictory qualities in Śaṅkara, but not so in the other two. They therefore seem to overlook what is actually taught in the Sûtras and bring in a subject-matter not meant by the aphorist. We shall be doing an injustice to Bâdarâyaṇa to think with Râmânuja and Nimbârka that he had omitted to discuss such an important subject in his work meant to systematize the teachings of the Upanisads. No doubt Râmânuja broaches this subject in Sûtras 15 and 16 and says that both these views are to be accepted; but his interpretation of Sûtra 16 is indeed stretched and cannot be accepted, while Nimbârka does not discuss the subject at all. We cannot think with Râmânuja that Bâdarâyaṇa disposed of such an important subject in one or two Sûtras in a topic which deals with quite a different subject-matter and of less importance. Râmânuja's introducing this subject in Sûtras 15 and 16 is against the spirit of the Adhikaraṇa (topic) even according to his own interpretation. It is something which he forcibly introduces out of all relation to the context, as anybody can easily see.

In fact, according to their interpretation of this Adhikaraṇa the whole of it looks redundant after what has been stated by them in 2.1.13. Finally the simile of the reflections of the sun is happier according to Śaṅkara's interpretation than according to that of the other two and the text cited by Râmânuja in Sûtra 18 holds good according to Śaṅkara's view also and more aptly.

Sûtras 22-30 Śankara takes as a separate topic and interprets 22 to 24 as follows: What has been mentioned up to this (*i.e.* the two forms of Brahman mentioned in Bṛ. 2.3.1) is denied by the words "Not this, not this" (Bṛ. 2. 3. 6) and the Śruti says something more than that afterwards. It does not deny Brahman but Its forms mentioned earlier, their transcendental reality (22). The objection that Brahman is denied because It is not experienced is not reasonable, for the Śruti says that Brahman exists, though It is not manifest on account of ignorance (23). And moreover It is realized in perfect meditation, so say the Śruti and Smṛti (24). Therefore the Jîva becomes one with the Infinite when Knowledge dawns, for thus the scripture indicates (26). In the next two Sûtras an objection is raised against Sûtras 25 and 26. But on account of both difference and non-difference being taught by the Śruti, the relation between them is as between the serpent and its coil (27), or like that between light and its orb (28). Sûtra 29 refutes this view and says: Or the relation is as given before in Sûtras 25-26. And on account of the denial of everything else besides Brahman by the Śruti texts (30).

Râmânuja continues the previous topic up to 26. Sûtras 22-26 according to him mean: The text (Bṛ. 2.3.6) denies the previously mentioned thatmuchness and says more than that. The two forms of Brahman (Bṛ. 2.3.1) do not exhaust Its attributes, for the text states further qualities after that. "For there is nothing higher than this 'not this'. Then comes the name, 'the Truth of truth'; for the Prâṇas are true and It is the truth of them." 'Prâṇas' here mean the souls, because they accompany the latter at death. The souls are true, because they do not undergo any change in their essential nature. The Lord is the Truth of these true souls, for these contract and expand with respect to intelligence while He is unaffected. Thus the subsequent part of the text connects Brahman with some qualities. The clause "Not this, not this" does not deny the attributes of Brahman, but denies that Its nature is confined to these two forms only (22). The Śruti instruction is not unnecessary here, for though the world is seen, yet it is not known as a Prakâra or mode of Brahman and that is what can be gathered only from the Śruti texts. So declares the Śruti (23). And Brahman's being differentiated by these two forms is realized even as Its being of the nature of intelligence is realized by repeated meditation (25). For all these reasons Brahman is regarded as Infinite, *i.e.* as possessing infinite attributes; for thus the attributes hold good, *i.e.* the two-fold characteristic of Sûtra 22 (26). Sûtras 27-30 are treated by Râmânuja as a separate topic. Sûtras 27 and 28 give the Pûrvapakṣa, as Śaṅkara also says, and 29 gives the Siddhânta; but the words 'as before' in the Sûtra refer not to Sûtras 25 and 26, but to 2.3.43.

Nimbârka follows Râmânuja in Sûtras 22-24. The next two Sûtras he interprets somewhat differently. Just as fire is manifested through the rubbing of wooden sticks, so is Brahman manifested in meditation (25). On realizing Brahman the soul becomes one with It (26). Sûtras 27 and 28 he takes as the author's and not as the opponent's view. Sûtra 27 describes that the relation between Brahman and the insentient world is as between the serpent and its coils (27) and the relation between the soul and Brahman is as between the orb and the light (28). But to an objection of the kind raised in Sûtra 2.1.25 the answer is as before, *i.e.* 2. 1. 26 (29). Moreover, the supreme Self is not affected by the imperfection of the soul (30).

Śaṅkara thus interprets "Not this, not this" as a denial of the two forms of Brahman mentioned in Bṛ. 2.3.1. Brahman can be described only as "Not this, not this," *i.e.* It is not what we see. Whatever we see is not Brahman as It is. Brahman is something different from all this manifested world. This interpretation is in keeping with scriptural teaching. Râmânuja and Nimbârka interpret that "Not this, not this" denies only the limitation of Brahman's nature to only these two forms, in other words It has many more attributes than these two. The two forms are real and are only two of the infinite attributes of the Lord. This seems to be a total denial of the Upaniṣadic teaching. "Not this, not this" occurs in four different places in the Bṛ. Even if Râmânuja's explanation be allowed in Bṛ. 2.3.6—however strange and twisted it might seem, Bṛ. 4.2.4, 4.4.22 and 4.5.15 do not by any means yield to such an interpretation. These texts after saying, "This Self is that which has been described as 'Not this, not this,' " says, "It is imperceptible" etc. Other texts also describe the Self or Brahman as beyond comprehension. "There goes neither the eye, nor speech nor the mind; we know It not nor do we see how to teach about It. Different It is from all that is known, and is beyond the unknown as well" (Ke. 1. 3-4); "Whence speech returns along with the mind without realizing It" (Tai. 2.4); also *Ibid.* 2.9 and Ka. 1.3.15. From these texts we find that nothing can be predicated of Brahman. From the Kena Upaniṣad texts we find that we cannot say that Brahman is this and this in a positive way. It is not what we see and therefore It can only be described as "Not this, not this" by denying everything we see in It. It is true that we do find the scriptures dealing with both difference and non-difference; but with what object, is the question. It is not to establish that both are true, for they are mutually contradictory. A careful study of the scriptures convinces one that duality is taught in order to take the aspirant step by step through it to non-duality. Râmânuja in his Bhâṣya on these Sûtras criticizes Śaṅkara saying that the Śruti could not have described these two forms only to deny them later on. But that this is process the Śruti adopts is clear from Prajâpati's instruction to Indra in the Châandogya or Varuna's teaching to Bhṛgu in the

Taittirîya Upaniṣad. The aspirant is gradually taken to higher and higher truths. Through duality he is led up to non-duality, the goal or final truth. Duality has not been praised anywhere in the scriptures, and no fruit is ascribed to it. On the other hand it is censured (*vide* Ka. 2.4.10-11; Bṛ. 4.4.9; Mai. 4.2. and 6.3), which shows that the scriptures do not intend to posit duality. But non-duality is praised and immortality is said to be achieved by the knowledge of unity. According to the Pûrva Mîmâṁsâ principle, that which has no result of its own but is mentioned in connection with something else which has a result, is subordinate to the later. Therefore duality which has no fruit of its own is subsidiary to non-duality which is the main purport of the Śruti texts. Again we have texts like "The Ātman is smaller than the smallest, greater than the greatest" (Ka. 1.2.20); "Neither gross nor fine" etc.—which negate all duality and establish the Infinity of Brahman beyond all doubts.

A question, however, may arise: If everything is negated, what will be left? We shall by such a process arrive at a nonentity. Not so. We cannot go on negating *ad infinitum,* but have to come finally to some basic reality, and this basic reality behind everything is the Ātman or Brahman. When we remove an object, space is left behind. Similarly, when everything we see is removed or negated, Brahman is left behind, which cannot be negated and which is the witness of everything. We cannot say that by negation we come to nonentity, for the very fact that we comprehend this nonentity shows that it is being illumined by the witnessing consciousness, the basic reality even behind this idea of nonentity. In this Sûtra the Sûtrakâra solves this doubt, showing that the negation concerns not Brahman, but only the two forms of It. To turn the drift of this discussion topsy turvy and establish the reality of the two forms is to ignore the spirit of scriptural teaching.

Mâyâvâda in the Upaniṣads:

There is a common belief that Mâyâvâda is not found in the scriptures and that it is Śaṅkara's own doctrine borrowed from the Buddhists. But such a statement is scarcely justified. In the Bṛhadâraṇyaka text under discussion we have, "Now its name: "The Truth of truth.' The vital force is truth, and It is the Truth of that" (Bṛ. 2.3.6). If the vital force, *i.e.* Prâjña (the soul in a state of deep-sleep) of which the vital force is an Upâdhi is true or real, Brahman is the Truth or Reality of this real. In other words, Brahman's reality is of a different grade from that of the universe. If this world is real and not Mâyâ, as Śaṅkara would call it, then Brahman is the Reality of this real, which shows that the world's reality is of an inferior kind from that of Brahman and when It is realized this world is no more. A similar idea is conveyed by Ch. 7. 24. 1 where Brahman, the Infinite, is said to be immortal and the world, the finite, is said to be mortal. But this is exactly what Śaṅkara too says—that the two, Brahman and the world, have two grades of reality, even as the dream world and the world we experience while we are awake have two grades of reality, and as a result we are justified in saying that the dream world is Mâyâ, as the Sûtrakâra says in 3.2.3, or unreal as compared with the waking state. Similarly, this world we experience is Mâyâ or unreal as compared with the reality of

Brahman. The dream world has a reality for the time being; so has this world so long as we are in ignorance; and Śaṅkara nowhere denies the Vyâvahârika (phenomenal) reality of this world. The scriptures explain this difference between the reality of the two, Brahman and the world, by using symbology, as for example in Ch. 6.1.4, which we had occasion to explain in Sûtra 2.1.14 where the Śruti tries to explain that the one, the clay, is more real than the many, which is identified with name and form only. We find the same idea again in Bṛ. 1.6.3: "This immortal entity is covered by truth (the five elements): The vital force is the immortal entity, and name and form are truth; (so) this vital force is covered by them." Name and form, *i.e.* the world we experience, are called truth, but Brahman is distinguished from them by saying that It is immortal —Its reality is of a different grade from the reality of that which is called truth. And as the reality of this world is of a lesser grade or illusory as compared with that of Brahman, It can be the cause of such an illusory world of manifoldness without undergoing any change in Itself; for an illusory manifoldness can exist in It without in any way affecting Its immutability, like a snake in a rope or the manifold dream world in the dreaming self, as the Sûtrakâra exemplifies in 2.1.28, which brings us to the conclusion that this world is a Vivarta of the non-dual Brahman, as Śaṅkara says.

Coming to the interpretation of Sûtras 27-30, Śaṅkara connects "or as before" in Sûtra 29 with what immediately precedes in Sûtras 25-26 and so it is happy. Râmânuja connects it with Sûtra 2. 3. 43 and so it is not so apt. Nimbârka's explanation is still farfetched; for while Râmânuja refers for the Siddhânta only to a previous Sûtra, Nimbârka refers for an objection as well as a decision to Sûtras in 2.1. His interpretation of the whole topic thus appears to be much stretched.

That Śaṅkara has followed the Sûtrakâra faithfully in his interpretation of Sûtras 11-30 will be clearer if we just try to see the reason why the latter treats of dream and deep-sleep in this section which deals with the nature of Brahman. Śaṅkara at the beginning of Chapter III, Section 1, says that the transmigration of the soul is taught in order to generate a spirit of Vairâgya (dispassion).

Sûtra 1-10 of Section 2 treat of the soul's states of dream and dreamless-sleep. According to Śaṅkara the very fact that the dream world does not fulfil the conditions of the time and space factors as in the waking state, shows that the dream world is illusory and therefore a creation of the soul and not of the Lord. From this he shows that the real nature of the Jîva is self-luminous and beyond all these states. Thus Sûtras 1-10 elucidate the real nature of the 'Thou' in "Thou art That". Sûtras 11-21 give the nature of 'That' and Sûtras 22-30 identify the two. Thus the place of Sûtras 1-10 in this section is very significant. Râmânuja and Nimbârka say that the creation of the dream world belongs to the Lord and not to the soul. If it were so, it should be as real as this world. Granting that it is the Lord's creation, of what significance is this subject in a section that deals with the nature of Brahman? It would have been apt in 2.3 where creation is the Lord's creation, of what significance is this Râmânuja says at the beginning of Chapter III, then it ought to have been included in Section 1 which treats of the soul's transmigration with the same object and thus be separated from Section 2 where it is out of place.

The above analysis of Sûtras 3. 2. 1-30 shows that Śaṅkara has rightly grasped the spirit of Bâdarâyaṇa, while Râmânuja and Nimbârka have sadly missed it.

A two-fold knowledge of Brahman established:

Finally, let us consider Sûtras 4.2.12-14 and Sûtras 4.4.1-7. The former set of Sûtras as they stand are interpreted better by Râmânuja and Nimbârka than by Śaṅkara. According to Śaṅkara they run as follows: If it be said (that the Prâṇas of a knower of Brahman do not depart), on account of the Śruti denying it (we say) not so, for the Śruti (Mâdhyandina recension of the text) denies the departure of the Prâṇas from the soul and not from the body (12). For the denial is clear in the texts of some schools (13). So in Sûtra 12 the Siddhânta view is first expressed on the basis of Bṛ. 4.4.6, Kâṇva recension, and the objection against this is raised by the opponent in the second half of the Sûtra, basing his argument on the Mâdhyandina recension of the text, which is answered again in Sûtra 13 by Bṛ. 3.2.11, Kâṇva recension. By such an interpretation the significance of 'some schools' is lost, for it ought to have referred to some text of the Mâdhyandina school and not of the same Kâṇva school on which the Siddhânta is based in Sûtra 12.

Râmânuja and Nimbârka on the other hand read these Sûtras as one, which runs as follows: "If it be said that the Prâṇas of a knower of Brahman do not depart on account of the denial by the Śruti text (Bṛ 4.4.6. Kâṇva), we deny it; for the Śruti says that they do not depart from the soul (*i.e.* they accompany the soul) and this is clear according to some, *viz* the Mâdhyandina recension of Bṛ. 4.4.6." We cannot but say that this is more happy, as the force of 'some school' and the word 'hi' (because) in the Sûtra are well brought out.

Though the interpretation according to the letter of the Sûtrá forces us to side with Râmânuja and Nimbârka, yet if we consider the Śruti text, *viz* Bṛ. 4.4.6, on which the discussion is based and also the arrangement of the Sûtras in this Section 2 up to Sûtra 16, we find that Śaṅkara is more reasonable than the other two and it looks as though the Sûtrakâra himself had made a slip, though he meant otherwise. Bṛ. 4.4.6 says in the first half of the text how one who is attached transmigrates, and concludes the first half by saying, "Thus does the man who desires transmigrate." The second half speaks of the man without desires and says, "Of him who is without desires...and to whom all objects of desire are but the Self—the organs do not depart. Being but Brahman, he is merged in Brahman." Here it is quite clear that the Śruti contrasts the two cases of one who is attached and one who is not attached and so does not transmigrate but is merged in Brahman. Now it is well known both from the scriptures and the *Vedânta-Sûtras* itself that a transmigrating soul at the time of death goes out with the organs and so when in contrast to this it is said, "His organs do not depart," it is quite clear that the denial of departure of the Prâṇas is from the body as in the case of one who is attached, and consequently the expression 'from him' in the Mâdhyandina recension even ought to mean the body and not the soul.

From what has been stated above we find Śaṅkara

more reasonable and consistent and therefore we can safely say that his interpretation of Sûtras 12-14 as establishing a two-fold knowledge is after Bâdarâyaṇa's view, though according to the wording of the Sûtras it is not so happy. This sort of interpretation of the Sûtrakâras is not without its precedent, as we find Upavarṣa and Śabara doin the same in their commentaries on the *Pûrva Mîmâṁsâ-Sûtras*.

We now come to the last section of the work where the state of the released soul is described. Sûtras 1-3 describe that on the attainment of Knowledge the soul manifests itself in its own nature. Sûtra 4 says that it attains non-distinction with Brahman. The question as to what the nature of that state is naturally arises after this and Sûtras 5-7 attempt a description. The views of Jaimini and Auḍulomi are given and finally in Sûtra 7 Bâdarâyaṇa says that both these views are true, for they are not contradictory. The question is, whether the views of Jaimini and Auḍulomi are true of the released soul in succession or simultaneously. Bâdarâyaṇa's decision is that they are true at one and the same time according as the subject is viewed from the relative or transcendental standpoint. Śaṅkara makes this clear in his Bhâṣya. His critics find fault with him here. They say that he is obliged in this Sûtra to ascribe to the truly released soul qualities which clearly cannot belong to it, since for such a soul no Vyavahâra exists. They say thereby that his interpretation is not faithful. Such a criticism shows that they have failed to understand what Śaṅkara means here. He does not say that the released soul is conscious of itself as possessing all the qualities described by Jaimini, but that we who are in bondage are obliged in describing the state of such a soul to have recourse to such a description. In reality the soul when released exists as pure Intelligence, but as pure Intelligence is beyond our conception, we in our ignoronce view it as identified with Īśvara, for that is the highest reading of pure Intelligence or the nirguṇa Brahman that we can possibly conceive. Certainly there exists no Vyavahâra at all for the released soul, which is free from ignorance; but it exists for us who are in ignorance; and Jaimini's description of the state of a released soul is our description of it. Īśvara's possession of powers is not like that of an ordinary Jîva which being subject to Nescience thinks of itself as an experiencer, an agent, and so on. He is beyond all taint and therefore not subject to Nescience, and consequently does not think of Himself as possessing all these lordly powers; but these powers exist in Him, because we in our ignorance ascribe them to Him. Even so are these lordly powers ascirbed to the released soul by us and it is regarded as identical or having attained non-distinction with Īśvara. This is the full import of Sûtra 7 both according to Bâdarâyaṇa and Śaṅkara. So till all souls are released, the state of the released partakes of a two-fold characteristic according to the view-point from which it is described—transcendental or relative, even as Brahman has a two-fold characteristic of which one is illusory or real from the relative standpoint (*vide* 3.2.11-21). This attainment of lordly powers by souls on identification with Īśvara is not the same as the attainment of such powers by the knowers of the saguṇa Brahman who go to Brahmaloka, for it is made clear in 4. 4. 17 that their lordly powers do not include the power of creation etc., but only power to create objects of enjoyments at will (4. 4. 8), while this power is not negated in the case of souls which get identified with Īśvara according to Sûtra 4. 4. 5 and 7.

That the Sûtrakâra makes a distinction between the attainment of Liberation by the knowledge of the nirguṇa Brahman and that by the knowledge of the saguṇa Brahman, is clear from Sûtra 4.1.19, where he makes no reference to any going forth in the case of a Jîvanmukta, but simply says that on the exhaustion of the Prârabdha Karma he attains Brahman and this is also in keeping with texts like Bṛ. 4.4.6 and especially Ch. 6.14.2 where it is clearly stated that his merging in Brahman is delayed just as long as the body lasts. But going to Brahmaloka by "the path of the gods" is also a kind of Liberation, for from there the soul does not return to this mortal world, but gets merged in Brahman at the end of the cycle together with Brahmâ, as stated in Sûtra 4.3.10. As the author is concerned in this section with the result of Upâsanâs, *viz* Liberation, he describes the result of the knowledge of the nirguṇa Brahman in Sûtras 1-7 and from 8-22 the result of the knowledge of the saguṇa Brahman. If, as according to Râmânuja and Nimbârka, there is no such distinction at all, but the description is of one kind of Liberation only, then when it is said in Sûtra 4.4.5 that the released soul attains a nature like that of Brahman, there is no further necessity of saying that it can create at will all objects of enjoyment. Moreover, if being free from sin, old age etc. (Ch. 8.1.5) are qualities of the soul as well as of the Lord, then they will cease to be the defining characteristic of the Lord. In this case the objection raised in the first part of Sûtra 1.3-19 will not be answered by the second half of the Sûtra. The Sûtra runs as follows: "If it be said that from the subsequent texts which refer to the Jîva 'small Ākâśa,' means the Jîva, we say that the reference to the soul is in so far as its real nature is made manifest (*i.e.* as non-different from Brahman)." In the previous Sûtra it was established that the 'small Ākâśa' in Ch. 8.1.1 is Brahman and not the Jîva, in spite of the reference to the Jîva in Ch. 8.3.4, for 'free from evil' etc. which are said to be qualities of the 'small Ākâśa' are not true of the soul. At the end of his commentary on Sûtra 18, Śaṅkara says that Sûtra 20 will make it clear why the individual soul is referred to in Ch. 8.3.4. In Sûtra 19 cited above a fresh objection is raised that subsequent texts also refer to the Jîva (*vide* Ch. 8.7-11 in which the waking, dream, and deep-sleep state of the soul are described) and therefore 'small Ākâśa' means Jîva. The second half answers it by saying that the reference to the Jîva is in so far as its real nature is made manifest (*vide* Ch. 8.12.3). The reference to the individual soul in Ch. 8.3.4 is to show that in reality it is beyond the three states of waking, dream, and deep-sleep and non-different from Brahman. If under the circumstances 'free from sin' etc. are its qualities even as different from Brahman, as Râmânuja says, then 'small Ākâśa' cannot be established to be Brahman against the objection raised in Sûtra 1.3.19. Moreover, in Sûtra 1.3.20 (according to him 19) the explanation given by him for the reference to the Jîva in Ch. 8.3.4 is not at all satisfactory. He says, "This reference to the Jîva serves the purpose of giving instruction not about the Jîva, but about the nature of that which is the cause of the qualities of the individual soul, *i.e.* qualities specially belonging to the Lord. The reason is that such information about the released soul helps the doctrine with respect to 'small Ākâśa'. The individual soul which wants to attain Brahman must also know its true nature, so that it as being endowed with auspicious qualities will finally arrive at the intuition of the Lord who is a mass of auspicious qualities raised to the highest excellence." But according to Śaṅkara we have seen that its reference is to identify the two—the released soul and the Lord. It is quite apparent that between the two explanations Râmânuja's falls to the ground. Such an argument does not at all fit in as an explanation for the reference to the released soul in Ch. 8. 3. 4 and is against the spirit of the teaching of the whole of chapter 8 of the Chāndogya. Śaṅkara's critics find fault with him taking into consideration only Sûtra 1. 3. 19; but if they only try to understand the Sûtrakâra taking into consideration Sûtras 18-20 and the Śruti texts to which they refer, they will find that Śaṅkara's interpretation is by far the best.

The defects that are shown in Râmânuja's interpretation of Section 4 hold good in the case of Nimbârka also.

Śaṅkara's interpretation justified by the Gîtâ:

Thus a comparative study of these three commentaries on the most important topics treated by Bâdarâyaṇa in his work establishes a strong case for Śaṅkara's interpretation of the Sûtras. We find similar views also expressed in the Gîtâ. And if, as has been shown at the beginning, the author of the Gîtâ had a hand in the Sûtras—and this fact is not questioned by Râmânuja and Nimbârka, for according to them it is the same person Veda-Vyâsa—then it goes all the more to show that Śaṅkara's interpretation is correct.

for we cannot expect that the same author has expressed different views in the two works. We shall cite a few texts from the Gîtã which tally with Śaṅkara's interpretation of the Sûtras.

"I shall describe that which has to be known,...the beginningless supreme Brahman. It is called neither being nor non-being...Without and within all beings... Impartible, yet It exists *as if divided* in beings" (13.12-16)—these texts describe the attributelessness of Brahman. The text says that the one Immutable appears *as if divided* into many and not in reality. It Itself, therefore, is "the sustainer, generator, and devourer of all beings" (13.16); also 7.6 and 7. That Brahman has a two-fold nature, the Nirguṇa which is Its real nature and the Saguṇa which is the creation of Mâyâ, is made clear by Arjuna's question in 12.1 and the Lord's answer in 12.2-5, where He recognizes the Nirguṇa aspect, but says at the same time that those devoted to the Saguṇa aspect are better versed in Yoga, as devotion to it is easier and, therefore, best suited to Arjuna and the generality of mankind, even as He says in 5.6 for the same reason that Karma Yoga is better than Jñâna Yoga.

The individual soul in its real nature is described in 2.11-25. Specially verses 16-18 say that it is real all-pervading, changeless, immutable, indestructible and illimitable, while verse 24 again says it is all-pervading. Again 6.31 establishes the identity of the self and Brahman contained in the Vedic dictum, "That thou art," verses 29 and 30 having described the real nature of 'thou' and 'That'; while 13.29-34 describe the real nature of the soul as identical with Brahman. But the soul in its state of bondage being deluded considers itself an agent and experiencer, atomic and a part of the Lord. "The Guṇas of Prakṛti perform all action. With the understanding *deluded* by egoism, man thinks, 'I am the doer' " (3.27). See also 14.23 and 15.7.

The doctrine of Mâyâ is clearly referred to in the following texts: "Knowledge is enveloped in ignorance, hence do beings get deluded" (5.15); "This world knows Me not, being deluded by the modifications of the Guṇas. Verily this divine Mâyâ of Mine is difficult to cross over...deprived of discrimination by Mâyâ they follow the Āsuric ways" (7.13-16); "I am not manifest to all, being veiled by My Yogamâyâ" (7.25); "The Lord dwells in the heart of all beings causing them to revolve by His Mâyâ" (18.61). Finally, though stress is laid on Bhakti in the Gîtâ, nowhere does it say that Bhakti is superior to Knowledge. On the other hand we find Knowledge highly praised. "The fire of Knowledge burns all Karma to ashes. There exists nothing so purifying like Knowledge" (4.37-38); "Supremely dear is the wise man to Me. I regard him as My very Self" (7.17-18).

Conclusion:

In conclusion, we would like to state that from what all has been said above we do not mean to suggest that Śaṅkara's interpretation of the Sûtras is the only true one. Rather our object has been to show that Śaṅkara too, like the other great commentators, is justified in interpreting the Sûtras in the way he has done. The fact is, Bâdarâyaṇa has systematized the philosophy of the Upaniṣads in his work, and like them his Sûtras also are all-comprehensive. The Upanisads, we must remember, do not teach throughout any particular doctrine. They contain various doctrines which are meant for people at different stages of spiritual evolution. They are not contradictory, but rather they are based on the principle of Adhikâribheda, as all are not capable of apprehending the same truth. The old idea of Arundhatî-darśananyâya[1] applies. Nearly every chapter in the Upaniṣad begins with dualistic teaching or Upâsanâ and ends with a grand flourish of Advaita. God is first taught as a Being who is the creator of this universe, its preserver, and the destruction to which everything goes at last. He is the one to be worshipped, the Ruler, and appears to be outside of nature. Next we find the same teacher teaching that God is not outside of nature, but immanent in nature. And at last both ideas are discarded and it is taught that whatever is real is He; there is no difference. "Śvetaketu, thou art That." The Immanent One is at last declared to be the same that is in the human soul.[2] This fact is recognized by Bâdarâyaṇa too and so commentators make a mistake when they think that the Sûtras propound only their doctrine and nothing else.

This grand principle of Adhikâribheda is the foundation on which the teachings of the Upaniṣads, the *Brahma-Sûtras,* and the Gîtâ are based and that is the reason why they have been universally accepted by the Hindus of all classes and denominations. From this point of view we are inclined to think that of all the commentators Śaṅkara has done the greatest justice to the Sûtrakâra by his two-fold doctrine of the absolute and phenomenal reality.

1 The method of spotting the tiny star Arundhatî with the help of bigger near it, calling them Arundhatî.

2 *Complete Works of Swami Vivekananda,* Vol. III. pp. 281 397, and 398.

ADHYĀSA OR SUPERIMPOSITION

The whole of Śaṅkara's philosophy may be summed up as follows: ब्रह्म सत्यं जगन्मिथ्या जीवो ब्रह्मैव नापरः ।—The Brahman of the Upaniṣads is the only Reality, and everything else—this world of manifoldness—is unreal, is a mere appearance; the individual soul (Jîva) is identical with Brahman, the One without a second, which the scriptures define as Existence-Knowledge-Bliss Absolute. "Brahman is Existence, Knowledge, Infinity" (Tai. 2.1); "Brahman is Knowledge, Bliss" (Bṛ. 3.9.28). This identity of the Jîva and Brahman is clearly stated by the scriptures in texts like: "Thou art That, O Śvetaketu" (Ch. 6.8.7), "I am Brahman" (Bṛ. 1.4.10), and "The Self alone is to be meditated upon" (Bṛ. 1.4.7).

The question then naturally arises: If Truth is one, whence arises this many which we experience through the senses? Truth cannot contradict experience. So Śaṅkara had to explain this apparent contradiction between Truth and our everyday experience. He says that this plurality is an illusion (Mâyâ). It has no reality, for it disappears when the knowledge of the true nature of Brahman is realized. It is just like seeing a snake in a rope in the dark. This wrong perception is brought about by ignorance (Avidyâ), which is beginningless. It is this ignorance which is the cause of all this duality, Brahman being mistaken for the world. On account of this ignorance the individual soul identifies itself with its adjuncts (Upâdhis) *viz* the body, senses, etc., which are only superimposed on it. This identification makes the soul think that it is the doer, enjoyer, etc.—though the truth is that it is none of these—and thereby it comes under the sway of birth, death, happiness, misery, etc., in short, becomes bound down to this world (Saṁsâra).

When Śaṅkara says that the world is false, he does not mean that it is absolutely nothing, but that our experience is liable to be stultified by means of knowledge of things as they are. The world has a relative existence; it is true for the time being, but disappears when true knowledge dawns. It is not real for all times, in other words, it is not real from the absolute standpoint. Mâyâ or ignorance is not a real entity. We can neither say that it exists nor that it does not exist. It is a mystery which is beyond our understanding; it is unspeakable (Anirvacanîya). As Mâyâ is not real, it cannot be related to Brahman, the Reality, in any way whatsoever; for any relation between truth and falsehood is impossible. The relation is only apparent, and therefore Brahman is in no way affected by this illusion which is superimposed upon It, even as the rope is not affected by the snake that is assumed to exist in it.

Therefore the only way to liberation from this worldly existence (Saṁsâra) is to get rid of this wrong notion through the real knowledge of Brahman. Just as in the case of the rope and the snake, it is the knowledge of the rope *alone* that removes the illusion of the snake and nothing else, so also it is the knowledge of Brahman alone that brings about the cessation of this relative existence (Saṁsâra). "A man who knows It alone truly, passes beyond death; there is no other path to go by" Śv. 3.8); "He comes not to death who sees that one". Pilgrimages, austerities, worship and charity—these by themselves, without Knowledge, cannot help us to attain Liberation. Their utility lies only in purifying our mind (Cittaśuddhi), cleansing it of all worldliness, and thus making it fit to comprehend the Truth. When Brahman is realized this phenomental world disappears automatically, without any further effort on the part of the individual. Knowledge of Brahman being thus the only way to Liberation, an inquiry into Brahman through the study of the *Brahma-Sûtras* is absolutely necessary.

Śaṅkara's explanation of the world as an illusion has given his philosophy the name of Mâyâvâda or Anirvacanîya Khyâtivâda. It is also known as Vivartavâda, the doctrine of the apparent modification of Brahman into this phenomenal world, as opposed to Pariṇâmavâda or the doctrine of the actual modification of Brahman into this phenomenal world, as held by some other schools of Vedânta like the Viśiṣṭâdvaitavâda of Râmânuja.

Śaṅkara anticipated that this method of explaining the phenomenal world would raise a protest from the various other schools of his time. So at the beginning of his commentary on the *Brahma-Sûtras,* he writes a masterly introduction, which is well known as the Adhyâsa Bhâṣya or the section dealing with superimposition, wherein he establishes superimposition as a statement of fact and not a mere hypothesis. He starts with the objections that can possibly be raised against his theory of superimposition and then refutes them. He says: It is well known that the subject and the object, which have for their spheres or contents the notions of 'I' and 'Thou' respectively, and which are opposed to each other as darkness and light cannot be indentified. Hence their attributes also cannot be identified. Consequently the superimposition of the object and its attributes on the subject, whose essence is pure intelligence, and *vice versa, ought to be* a logical impossibility.

If the world phenomena are a case of superimposition, like the snake in the rope, then which is superimposed on which? Is the world superimposed on Brahman, or is it the reverse? In the latter case, the world, which is the substratum, like the rope in the example, would be a reality. If it is the other way—the world on Brahman—it is not possible, for Brahman is not an object which can be perceived by the senses like the rope. A thing becomes an object when it is limited by time, space, and causation. Since Brahman is unlimited, It is beyond these, and so cannot be an object of perception: as such It cannot be the substratum of a superimposition. Brahman is also the inner Self of everyone and therefore can never be separate and in front of a person like a rope, when alone the world can be superimposed on It.

Neither can Brahman be both subject and object of the thinking process, for one and the same being cannot both be the agent and the object of its activity at the same time. An object is that on which is concentrated the activity of the agent and hence it must be different from the agent. If, again, Brahman is manifested by some other knowledge and thus becomes an object, It ceases to be self-luminous and becomes limited, and this the scriptures do not accept. Further, in all cases of superimposition there is an antecedent real knowledge of the object which is superimposed, as of the snake in the example. So to superimpose the world on Brahman a *real knowledge* of the world is necessary, and this would make the world a reality, with the result that the cessation of the world phenomena would be an impossibility and Liberation would be impossible. Thus in whatever way we may try to establish the theory of superimposition, we are not able to do so.

Yet, says Śaṅkara, it is natural (a self-evident fact) on the part of man, because of ignorance, not to distinguish between the two entities (the subject and the object), which are quite contradictory, and to superimpose the one on the other, and their attributes as well, and thus mixing up the real and the unreal to use such phrases as "That is I", or "This is mine". The Self again is not altogether a non-object, for it is the object of the notion of the Ego. The Self does not entirely elude our grasp. Though the inner Self is not an object and is also without parts, yet owing to ignorance, which is unspeakable and without a beginning, attributes like mind, body, senses, etc., which are products of ignorance, are superimposed on the Self, and it behaves as if it were an agent, enjoyer, possessed of parts, and many—although in truth it is none of these—and thus becomes an object. The real Self can never be an object of knowledge. Self-consciousness is possible only with respect to a Self already qualified by these adjuncts (Upâdhis). This sounds like an argument in a circle; for to establish superimposition we have to accept the Self to be an object and the Self can be an object only through the superimposition of adjuncts (Upâdhis); it is actually not so. It is a case like the seed and the tree. The seed gives rise to the tree, which again produces the seed, the cause of the future tree, and so on. So in this series of illusions without a beginning, the Self, which is the substratum of the present superimposition, is an object on account of a past superimposition and that one had for its substratum the Self, which had become an object of a still earlier superimposition, and so on *ad infinitum*. The pure Self without the limiting adjuncts is never the substratum of a superimposition. It is the difference in the limiting adjuncts, as shown above, that makes it possible for the Self to be at the same time an agent and the object of action.

Superimposition, again, is due to ignorance and hence it is not necessary that the knowledge of the object superimposed must be a real knowledge. It is enough if we have a knowledge; it need not necessarily be real; it can itself be another illusory knowledge. That the Self exists is proved by the intuitive knowledge we have of it. This is well known and but for it nothing would have been cognized in this world. "He shining, everything else shines" (Ka. 2. 2. 15). We know things in and through it; no consciousness or experience is possible independently of it. Everyone is conscious of his own Self, for no one thinks, "I am not". Nor, again, is it necessary that the object to be a substratum of a superimposition should be before us, for we see that Ākâśa (sky), which is not visible to the senses, becomes a substratum for superimpositions by the ignorant, who impute blueness, spherical shape, etc., to it in such expressions as, "The sky is blue", and "It is spherical". Thus superimposition is an established fact.

But then direct perception, which is the best of all proofs—since it is the basis of all other means of knowledge like inference etc.—affirms this world of manifoldness. How can the scriptures that deny it carry conviction as against direct experience? They cannot. Hence scriptural texts that deny the many and uphold unity will have to be interpreted in a manner so as not to contradict our experience. This view cannot stand, for the scriptures (Śrutis) are impersonal, eternal, self-luminous, and so on. Their validity is direct and self-evident and therefore infallible. They constitute by themselves an independent source of knowledge. Hence they too are to be accepted as authoritative. The fact is that each evidence of knowledge has its own sphere wherein it is absolutely authoritative. Perception has its supreme validity in knowledge through the senses. There a hundred texts cannot prevail against it. The scriptures (Śrutis) on the other hand have their absolute authority in a province where perception cannot be of any avail. Their province is transcendental knowledge, which cannot be attained in any other way. Here revelation, which does not depend on other sources of knowledge, is the final authority, and not perception or even reason. The scriptures do not deny the empirical validity of perception; they deny only its absolute or transcendental validity.

SUPERIMPOSITION DEFINED

Superimposition, says Śaṅkara, is the apparent presentation to consciousness, by way of remembrance, of something previously observed in some other thing.

It is an *apparent presentation,* that is knowledge which is subsequently falsified; in other words, it is illusory knowledge. According to Vâcaspati Miśra this is the fundamental characteristic of superimposition, and the rest of the definition only differentiates it from those given by other schools of philosophy. But the author of the commentary *Ratnaprabhâ* takes *apparent presentation in some other thing* as the characteristic mark of superimposition, and this seems to be more in keeping with Śaṅkara, who says in his commentary: "But all these definitions agree in so far as they represent superimposition as the apparent presentation of the attributes of one thing in another thing."

As it is impossible to have illusory knowledge without the mixing up of two things, we find the words *something previously observed* in the definition. These words, together with the words *apparent presentation,* make it clear that the thing superimposed is not the real object seen some time before, but something like it. A mere experience, and not the reality, is what is necessary; hence the word *observed.* The experience should not be a present one, but a past one, and that is the significance of the word *previously.* So the thing superimposed is a false or unreal thing. But the thing on which it is superimposed is a real thing. The words *by way of remembrance* excludes all cases of recognition where the object previously observed again presents itself to our senses, as when a person seen at a particular place is again seen at another place. In remembrance the object previously observed is not in renewed contact with the senses. It is mere remembrance that operates in the case of superimposition.

This definition of superimposition meets an objection of the Mîmâṁsakas, who say that an unreal thing cannot be an object of experience. According to them all knowledge is real; there can be nothing like false knowledge. They uphold the intrinsic validity of all knowledge, for every knowledge produces a sense of certainty in us and we have no doubt about it at the time. If it were otherwise, then we should always be in doubt and never arrive at any certainty. So every knowledge is true for the time being, though subsequent experience may prove that it was wrong, as in the case of an illusion. But from the definition of superimposition given by Śaṅkara we find that because a particular thing is experienced it does not for that very reason become real. A thing may be unreal and at the same time may be experienced. Otherwise the water in a mirage would be a reality, which in fact we know it is not.

The Prâbhâkara school of Mîmâṁsakas raise a fresh objection. How can the world be unreal or non-existent? Non-existence is not a category by itself; it can be conceived only in relation to a real object. We speak of non-existence when one *real* object is predicated in terms of another real object. When we think of a pot in terms of a cloth, we say *the negation of the cloth* is the pot. That is all that is meant by non-existence; apart from this, it has no reality. An unreal object can never be the object of our experience. So this world, if it were unreal, could never be the object of our experience.

Applying this argument in the case of a mirage, we find that the reality, the sun's rays refracted by layers of air, is, according to the Mîmâṁsakas, nothing but *the negation of water,* and it is therefore self-evident that the phenomenon we experience cannot be water. Neither can they say that the water in the mirage is not real, since it is experienced. So the water in the mirage is neither real nor unreal, nor can it be both at the same time. Therefore we have to accept the phenomenon as something beyond our comprehension (Anirvacanîya), which is exactly the view of Śaṅkara.

Śaṅkara says that the nature of objects is two-fold, real and unreal. The first manifests by its very nature, depending on the object itself; the second, the unreal appearance, depends on some other thing for its manifestation. In a mirage the rays of the sun are a reality, but their appearance as water is unreal and depends on something else, the impressions (Saṁskâras) produced by seeing water elsewhere before. That which is real always continues to be so, but the unreal is ever changing. Brahman, the Reality, remains unchanged; but Mâyâ and its products, which are assumed to exist in Brahman, are unreal and therefore everchanging, yet experienced by us. The world phenomena are neither real nor unreal, nor both; they are unspeakable (Anirvacanîya).

DEFINITION OF SUPERIMPOSITION ACCORDING TO OTHER SCHOOLS

The four schools of philosophy in Buddhism define superimposition as "the superimposition of the attributes of one thing on another." They maintain that in superimposition forms of cognition, or modes of the internal organ in the form of the object, are superimposed on an external object which itself may be real or illusory. The Prâbhâkaras refute this definition, for according to the Buddhists there is no separate entity called the Self apart from consciousness (Vijñâna). The Self is but a form of consciousness. If in an illusion, where a rope is taken for a snake, the snake also be a form of cognition, then our experience ought to be of the kind "I am a snake" or "My snake", and not as "This is a snake". Therefore Prâbhâkaras define superimposition as "an error arising from the non-perception of the difference of that which is superimposed from that on which it is superimposed". There is no positive wrong or illusory knowledge, but a mere non-perception of the difference between two real experiences, one of which is a past experience. Where a mother-of-pearl is taken for silver, the difference between the mother-of-pearl seen at a moment and the silver remembered is not perceived. Naiyâyikas refute this definition on the ground that mere non-perception of the difference cannot induce us to action. But as a matter of fact we are tempted to posses the silver seen in a mother-of-pearl. Where there is no positive knowledge, as, for example, in profound sleep (Suṣupti), there is no activity. It is positive knowledge that is responsible for our activity, as we find from our experience in the dream and waking states. Nor can a mere remembrance induce us to action. So in illusion we are conscious of silver as a reality present before us, and not as a mere remembrance.

The Naiyâyikas therefore define superimposition as "the fictitious assumption of attributes (like those of silver) contrary to the nature of the thing (*e.g.* the mother-of-pearl) on which something else (silver) is superimposed". An identity is established between the object present before us (the mother-of-pearl) and the silver remembered, which is not here and now, but imagined, and which *exists as a reality somewhere else.* The person is not conscious that it is only a memory of silver, and not an actuality. This identity between the silver seen elsewhere and the mother-of-pearl is what gives rise to the illusion. There is thus a positive factor in this experience, which is not the case in the Prâbhâkaras' definition. Yet it may be questioned how the silver which exists elsewhere can be in contact with the senses, which is essential if the silver is to be experienced as an actuality in front of us and not a mere memory. If it be said that there is transcendental contract (Alaukika Jñânalakṣaṇa Sannikarśa) of the senses with it, then where fire is inferred from smoke we can say it is also a case of transcendental contact, and inference as a means to knowledge becomes unnecessary. Therefore we have to accept that in illusion an indescribable (Anirvacanîya) silver is produced, which is a reality for the time being. It is this silver which is directly perceived by the senses and gives rise to the knowledge, "This is silver". The silver that is seen in the mother-of-pearl is not present somewhere else, for in that case it could not have been experienced as here and now; nor is it in the mind. Neither is it a mere nonentity, for then it could not have been an object of perception; nor can it be inherent in the mother-of-pearl, for in that case it could not have been sublated afterwards. So we are forced to say that the silver has no real existence anywhere, but has only an apparent reality for the time being which is unspeakable.

This superimposition is called ignorance (Avidyâ) metaphorically, the effect being put for the cause. Ignorance does not mean want of knowledge, but that kind of knowledge which is stultified later on by the knowledge of things as they are. Its counterpart is called knowledge (Vidyâ). When the Self is discriminated from its limiting adjuncts through Vedântic discipline and practice (Sâdhanâ), *viz* hearing of scriptural texts, reflection, and meditation on them, then knowledge dawns, which destroys this superimposition. A mere intellectual knowledge is however not meant here, but actual realization. Since through this superimposition the two objects are not in the least affected by the good or bad qualities of each other, once true knowledge dawns, it roots out ignorance with all its effects, leaving no chance of its cropping up again. The recrudescence would have been possible if owing to the superimposition the Self was in any way contaminated by the non-Self and its properties.

This superimposition (Adhyâsa) due to ignorance is the presumption on which are based the distinctions among the means of knowledge, objects of knowledge, and knowing persons, in our career of daily activity, and so are also based all scriptural texts, whether they refer to rituals (Karma) or knowledge (Jñâna). All our experience starts in this error which identifies the Self with the body, senses, etc. All cognitive acts presuppose this kind of false identification, for without it the pure Self can never be a knower, and without a knowing personality, the means of right knowledge cannot operate. Therefore the means of right knowledge and the scriptural texts belong to the sphere of ignorance (Avidyâ). They are meant only for one who is still under ignorance and has not realized the Self. They are valid only so long as the ultimate Truth is not realized; they have just a relative value. But from the standpoint of the ultimate Truth, our so-called knowledge is all Avidyâ or no knowledge at all. In the phenomenal world, however, they are quite valid and are capable of producing empirical knowledge.

That our knowledge (empirical) is no knowledge at all is further proved by the fact that we do not differ from animals in the mater of cognition. Just as a cow runs away when she sees a man with a raised stick in his hand, while she approaches one with a handful of green grass, so also do men, who possess higher intelligence, walk away from wicked persons shouting with drawn swords, while they approach those of an opposite nature. The behaviour of animals in cognition, etc. is well known to be based on ignorance. Therefore it can be inferred that man's conduct in the matter of cognition, etc., so long as they are under delusion, is also similarly based.

It may seem rather strange to say that even the scriptures belong to the field of ignorance (Avidyâ); for though in ordinary matters of cognition, etc., we may resemble animals and act through ignorance, yet in matters religious, such as the performance of sacrifices, the person who engages himself in them has the knowledge that the Self is separate from the body, since otherwise he cannot expect to enjoy the fruits of his ritualistic acts in heaven, the body being destroyed at death. But we forget that though a person who engages himself in ritualistic acts may have a knowledge of the Self as distinct from the body, yet it is not necessary that he should have a knowledge of the real nature of the Self as given by the Vedânta texts; rather such knowledge is destructive to him. For how can a person who knows the Self to be not an enjoyer, agent, and so forth undertake any sacrifice enjoined by the scriptures? Scriptural texts like, "A Brâhmaṇa should perform a sacrifice", are operative only on the supposition that attributes such as caste, stage of life, age, and circumstances are superimposed on the Self, which is none of these. Not only is ritualism (Karmakâṇḍa) meant for persons under ignorance (Avidyâ), but even so is the Vedânta; for without the distinction of the means of knowledge, objects of knowledge, and knower it is not possible to comprehend the meaning of the Vedânta texts. A person who is conscious of these distinctions is under the sway of ignorance (Avidyâ), being in the world of duality. But there is a difference between Vedânta and ritualism. While the latter has for its goal that which is within the sphere of ignorance, like enjoyment in heaven etc., the former helps one to realize his true nature, which destroys all ignorance.

How can ignorance lead to knowledge? Empirical knowledge can produce transcendental knowledge through its empirical validity. To put it in Sri Ramakrishna's beautiful language, "When we run a thorn in our hand we take it out by means of another thron and throw out both. So relative knowledge alone can remove that relative ignorance which blinds the eye of the Self. But such knowledge and such ignorance are both alike included in Avidyâ; hence the man who attains to the highest Knowledge (Jñâna), the knowledge of the Absolute, does away in the end with both knowledge and ignorance, being free himself from all duality." But before the dawning of real knowledge the authority of the Vedas stands unquestioned, for a knowledge that has not been realized cannot prevent a person from entering on ritualistic activities. It is only after realization that scriptural texts cease to be operative. But before that, "Let the scriptures be thy authority in ascertaining what ought to be done and what ought not to be done. Having known what is said in the ordinance of the scriptures thou shouldst act here" (Gîtâ 16.24). But when realization dawns, then, "To the sage who has known the Self, all the Vedas are of so much use as a reservoir is when there is flood everywhere" (Gîtâ 2.46). It is only for the knower of Brahman that they have no value, and not for others.

CHAPTER I

SECTION I

Topic 1: The inquiry into Brahman and its prerequisites.

अथातो ब्रह्मजिज्ञासा ॥ १ ॥

अथ Now अत: therefore ब्रह्मजिज्ञासा the inquiry (into the real nature) of Brahman.

1. Now (after the attainment of the requisite spiritual qualities) therefore (as the results obtained by sacrifices etc., are ephemeral, whereas the result of the knowledge of Brahman is eternal), the inquiry (into the real nature) of Brahman (which is beset with doubts owing to the conflicting views of various schools of philosophy, should be taken up).

At the very beginning the utility of such an inquiry is questioned.

Objection: Such an inquiry is not worth the trouble. An intelligent man generally does not enter into an inquiry about an object which is already known, or the knowledge of which does not serve any useful purpose. He is always guided by utility. Now Brahman is such an object. As Brahman pure and unconditioned, there is no doubt or indefiniteness about it, for we have such definitions as, "Brahman is Truth, Knowledge, Infinity" (Tai. 2.1). As identical with the Self (Ātman)—which the Vedânta holds—also, there is no doubt about Brahman; for the Self is nothing but the object of the notion of 'I', the empirical self which is well known to exist as something different from the body, senses, etc. Moreover, no one doubts his own existence. There is therefore no indefiniteness about Brahman, which would induce one to make an inquiry into It. The objection that this empirical self is a result of superimposition (Adhyâsa) of the non-Self on the Self and *vice versa,* and is therefore not the true Self, cannot be accepted, for such a superimposition between two absolutely contradictory objects is not possible.

Again, the knowledge of this Self or Brahman which, as shown above, everyone possesses, cannot destory the world phenomena and help one to attain Liberation, for they have been existing together side by side all along from time immemorial. And as there is no other knowledge of the Self besides 'Egoconsciousness', which can be called the true knowledge of Self, there is no chance of the world phenomena ever ceasing to exist. In other words, the world is a reality, and not something illusory. So the knowledge of Brahman serves no useful purpose such as the attainment of Liberation from relative existence (Saṁsâra). For these reasons an inquiry into Brahman is not desirable.

Answer: An inquiry into Brahman is desirable, because there is some indefiniteness with respect to It, for we find various conflicting views concerning Its nature. Different schools of philosophy hold different views. Superimposition would have been an impossibility, and there would have been no indefiniteness about Brahman, if the empirical self had been the real Self. But it is not. The scriptures (Śrutis) say that the Self is free from all limiting adjuncts and is infinite, all-blissful, all-knowing, One without a second, and so on. This the scriptures repeatedly inculcate, and as such it cannot be interpreted in any secondary or figurative sense. But the empirical self is felt as occupying definite space, as when we say, 'I am in the room', as involved in manifold miseries, as ignorant, etc. How can this kind of notion be regarded as the true knowledge of the Self? To regard the Self, which is beyond limitation etc., as being limited etc., is itself an illusion, and hence superimposition is a self-evident fact. The result of the true knowledge of the Self leads to Liberation and so serves a very, very fruitful purpose. Therefore an inquiry about Brahman through an examination of the Vedânta texts dealing with It is worth while and should be undertaken.

The word *now* in the Sûtra is not used to introduce a new subject that is going to be taken up, in which sense it is generally used in other places, as for example, in the beginning of the Yoga--Sûtras or the Pûrva Mîmâṁsâ-Sûtras. Neither is it used in any other sense, except that of immediate consecution, that is, it implies an antecedent, which existing, the inquiry about Brahman would be possible, and without which it would be impossible. This antecedent is neither the study of the Vedas, for it is a common requisite for Pûrva Mîmâṁsâ as well as Vedânta, nor the knowledge and performance of rituals prescribed by the Karmakâṇḍa, for these in no way help one who aspires after knowledge, but certain spiritual requisites. The spiritual requisites referred to are: (1) discrimination between things permanent and transient, (2) renunciation of the enjoyment of fruits of action in this world and in the next, (3) the six treasures, as they are called, *viz* not allowing the mind to externalize and checking the external instruments of the sense organs (Śama and Dama), not thinking of things of the senses (Uparati), ideal forbearance (Titikṣâ), constant practice to fix the mind in God (Samâdhâna), and faith (Śraddhâ); and (4) the intense desire to be free (Mumukṣutvam).

Topic 2: Definition of Brahman.

जन्माद्यस्य यतः ॥ २ ॥

जन्मादि Origin etc. (*i.e.* sustenance and dissolution) अस्य of this (world) यतः from which.

2. (Brahman is that omniscient, omnipotent cause) from which proceed the origin etc., (*i.e.* sustenance and dissolution) of this (world).

In the previous Sûtra it has been established that an inquiry into Brahman should be made as it helps Liberation. Knowledge of Brahman leads to Liberation. Now in order that we may attain this knowledge of Brahman, It must have some characteristics by which It can be known; otherwise it is not possible to have such knowledge. The opponent holds that Brahman has no such characteristics by which It can be defined, and in the absence of definition there can be no knowledge of Brahman, and consequently no Freedom.

This Sûtra refutes that objection and gives a definition of Brahman: "That which is the cause of the world is

Brahman"—where the imagined "cause of the world" is indicative of Brahman. This is called the Taṭastha Lakṣaṇa, or that characteristic of a thing which is distinct from its nature and yet serves to make it known. In the definition given by this Sûtra, the origin, sustenance, and dissolution are characteristics of the world and as such are in no way related to Brahman, which is eternal and changeless; yet these indicate Brahman, which is imagined to be the cause of the world, just as an imagined snake indicates the rope when we say, "that which is the snake is the rope".

The scriptures give another definition of Brahman which describes Its true nature: "Truth, Knowledge, Infinity is Brahman." This is called the Svarûpa Lakṣaṇa, that which defines Brahman in Its true essence. These words, though they have different meanings in ordinary parlance, yet refer to the one indivisible Brahman, even as the words, father, son, brother, husband, etc. refer to one and the same person according to his relation with different individuals.

It must not however be thought that the first Cause of the universe is arrived at by this Sûtra through mere reasoning, inference, and other means of right knowledge usually valid in this sense world. Brahman cannot be so established independently of the scriptures (Śruti) Though from the effect, the world, we can infer that it must have a cause, we cannot establish with certainty what exactly is the nature of that cause. We cannot say that Brahman alone is the cause and nothing else, as Brahman is not an object of the senses. The relation of cause and effect can be established where both the objects are perceived. Inference etc. may give only strong suggestions of Brahman's being the first Cause of the world. A thing established by mere inference, however well thought out, is explained otherwise by greater intellects. Reasoning also is endless according to the intellectual capacity of people and therefore cannot go far in the ascertainment of Truth. So the scriptures ought to be the basis of all reasoning. It is experience that carries weight, and the scriptures are authoritative because they are the records of the experience of master minds that have come face to face with Reality (Āptavâkya). That is why the scriptures are infallible. Hence in ascertaining the first Cause the scriptures alone are authority.

The prime object of this Sûtra, therefore, is not to establish Brahman through inference but to discuss scriptural passages which declare that Brahman is the first Cause—texts like: "That from which these beings are born, by which they live after birth and into which they enter at death—try to know That. That is Brahman" (Tai. 3.1). The Sûtra collects the Vedânta texts for the full comprehension of Brahman. Once the scriptures have declared Brahman to be the first Cause, reasoning etc. may be taken advantage of in so far as they do not contradict the scriptures, but rather supplement them, in ascertaining the sense of the Vedânta texts. Such reasoning must be corroborative of the truth inculcated. This kind of reasoning include the hearing of the texts (Śravaṇa), thinking about their meaning (Manana), and meditation on them (Nididhyâsana). This leads to intuition. By intuition is meant that mental modification (Vṛtti) of the mind (Citta) which destroys our ignorance about Brahman. When the ignorance is destroyed by this mental modification in the form of Brahman (Brahmâkârâ Vṛtti).

Brahman, which is self-luminous, reveals Itself. In ordinary perception when we cognize an object the mind (Citta) takes the form of the external object, which destroys the ignorance about it, and consciousness reflected in this modification of the mind manifests the object. In the case of Brahman, however, the mental modification destroys the ignorance, but Brahman, which is consciousness pure and simple, manifests Itself, being self-luminous. That is why the scriptures describe Brahman as 'Not this', 'Not this', thus removing the ignorance about it. Nowhere is Brahman described positively, as 'It is this', 'It is this'.

There is thus a difference between an inquiry into Brahman and an inquiry into religious duty (Dharma Jijñâsâ). In the latter case, the scriptures alone are authority. Pûrva Mîmâṁsâ says that if you do such and such a thing, you will get such and such results. It is something yet to come and does not exist at the time. So no other proof is available regarding the truth of these statements except faith in them. But Vedânta speaks about Brahman, which is an already existing entity, and not dependent on human endeavour. Therefore, besides faith in the scriptural texts there are other means available to corroborate its statements. That is why there is room for reasoning etc. in Vedânta.

Topic 3: Brahman cognizable only through the scriptures.

शास्त्रयोनित्वात् ॥ ३ ॥

शास्त्र-योनित्वात् The scripture being the means of right knowledge.

*3. The scriptures (alone) being the means of right knowledge (with regard to Brahman, the proposition laid in Sûtra 2 becomes corroborated).

This Sûtra makes the idea expressed in Sûtra 2 clearer. If any doubt has been left regarding the fact that Brahman as the origin etc. of the world is established by scriptural authority and not by inference etc. independently of it, this Sûtra makes it clear that Śrutis alone are proof about Brahman.

Objection: Brahman is an already existing thing like a pot, and so It can be known by other means of right knowledge independently of the scriptures.

Answer: Brahman has no form etc. and so cannot be cognized by direct perception. Again in the absence of inseparable characteristics, as smoke is of fire. It cannot be established by inference or analogy (Upamâna). Therefore, It can be known only through the scriptures. The scriptures themselves say, "One who is ignorant of the scriptures cannot know that Brahman." No doubt, as already referred to in the previous Sûtra, these means of right knowledge also have a scope, but it is only after Brahman is established by the scriptures—as supplementary to them and not independent of them.

---

*This Sûtra can also be interpreted in another way. It has been said in Sûtra 2 that Brahman, which is the cause of this manifold universe, must naturally be omniscient. This Sûtra corroborates it. In that case it would read: "(The omniscient and omnipotence of Brahman follow from Its) being the source of the scriptures." The scriptures declare that the Lord Himself breathed forth the Vedas. So He who has produced these scriptures containing such stupendous knowledge cannot but be omniscient and omnipotent.

Topic 4: Brahman the main purport of all Vedânta texts.

तत्तु समन्वयात् ॥ ४ ॥

तत् That तु but समन्वयात् because It is the main purport.

4. But that (Brahman is to be known only from the scriptures and not independently by any other means is established) because It is the main purport (of all Vedânta texts).

Objection by Pûrva Mîmâṁsakas: The Vedânta texts do not refer to Brahman. The Vedas cannot possibly aim at giving information regarding such self-established, already existing objects like Brahman, which can be known through other sources. They generally give information only about objects that cannot be known through other means of right knowledge, and about the means to attain such objects. Again Brahman, which is our own Self, can neither be desired nor shunned and as such cannot be an object of human effort. So a mere statement of fact about an existing object like Brahman, incapable of being desired or shunned and therefore useless, would make the scriptures purposeless.

Vedic passages hae a meaning only in so far as they are related to some action. So the Vedânta texts, to have a meaning, must be so construed as to be connected with action (rituals), as supplementing them with some necessary information. The texts dealing with the individual soul in the Vedânta, therefore, refer to the agent; those dealing with Brahman refer to the Deities; and those dealing with creation refer to spiritual practices (Sâdhanâs). In that case, being supplementary to action, the Vedânta texts will have a purpose. But if they are taken to refer to Brahman only, they will be meaningless, inasmuch as they will not be helpful to any action.

Answer: The word *but* in the Sûtra refutes all these objections. The Vedânta texts refer to Brahman only, for all of them have Brahman for their main topic. The main purport of a treatise is gathered from the following characteristics: (1) Beginning and conclusion, (2) repetition, (3) uniqueness of subject-matter, (4) fruit or result, (5) praise, and (6) reasoning. These six help to arrive at the real aim or purport of any work. In chapter six of the Chândogya Upaniṣad, for example, Brahman is the main purport of all the paragraphs; for all these six characteristics point to Brahman. It begins, "This universe, my boy, was but the Real (Sat), in the beginning" (Ch. 6.2.1), and concludes by saying, "In it all that exists has its self. It is true. It is the Self" (*Ibid.* 6.15.2)—which also refers to the Sat or Brahman. In the frequent repetition, "Thou art That, O Śvetaketu", the same Brahman is referred to. The uniqueness of Brahman is quiet apparent, as It cannot be realized either by direct perception or inference in the absence of form etc. and characteristics respectively. Reasoning also has been adopted by the scriptures here by citing the example of clay to elucidate their point. As different objects are made out of clay, so are all things created from this Brahman. The description of the origin of the universe from Brahman, and of its sustenance by and reabsorption in It is by way of praise

(Arthavâda). The result or fruit (Phala) is also mentioned, *viz* that through the knowledge of Brahman everything else is known. When we realize Brahman the universal Reality, we know all the particulars involved in It. So all these six characteristics go to show that the main topic of the Vedânta texts, as cited above, is Brahman.

Again, these texts cannot be made to refer to the agent etc., for they are treated in quite a different section from the Karmakâṇḍa. Neither are the texts useless, for from the comprehension of these texts results Liberation, without any reference to action on the part of the person, even as a mere statement that it is a rope and not a snake helps to destroy one's illusion. A mere intellectual grasp of the texts, however, will not help the person to attain Liberation; actual realization is what is meant here.

Objection: The scriptures have a purpose in so far as they lay down injunctions for man. They either induce him to or prohibit him from some action. The very meaning of the word 'Śâstra' is this. Even the Vedânta texts are related to injunctions and thus have a purpose. For though they have Brahman for their main purport, yet they do not end there, but after describing the nature of Brahman they enjoin on man to realize Brahman through intuition. "The Self is to be realized — to be heard of, thought about, and meditated upon"—in passages like this the scriptures, after enjoining on man to be conversant first with the nature of Brahman, further enjoin thinking and meditation on the meaning of those passages for the attainment of direct experience. Thus they formulate injunctions with regard to the knowledge of Brahman.

Answer: "He who knows the supreme Brahman becomes Brahman indeed" (Mu. 3.2.9)—texts like this show that to know Brahman is to become Brahman But since Brahman is an already existing entity, we cannot say that to know Brahman involves an act, like a ritualistic act, having for its result Brahman. When ignorance is removed Brahman manifests Itself, even as when the illusion of the snake is removed the rope manifests itself. Here the rope is not the creation of any act. The identity of the individual soul and Brahman set forth in texts like, "I am Brahman" (Bṛ. 1.4.10), is not a fancy or imagination, but an actuality, and therefore differs from meditation and devout worship as prescribed by the scriptures in texts like, "One should meditate on the mind as Brahman", and "The Sun is Brahman" (Ch. 3.18.1; 3.19.1). The knowledge of Brahman, therefore, does not depend on human endeavour, and hence it is impossible to connect Brahman or the knowledge of It with any action. Neither can Brahman be said to be the object of the act of knowing; for there are texts like, "It is different from the known, again It is beyond the unknown" (Ke. 1.4), and "Through what, O Maitreyî, can the knower be known?" (Bṛ. 2. 4. 14) In the same way Brahman is denied as an object of devout worship (Upâsanâ)—"Know that alone to be Brahman, not that which people adore here" (Ke. 1.5). The scriptures, therefore, never describe Brahman as this or that, but only negate manifoldness which is false, in texts like, "There is no manifoldness in It" (Ka. 2.4.11), and "He who sees manifoldness in It goes from death to death" (*Ibid.* 2.4.10).

Moreover, the result of action is either creation, modification, purification or attainment. None of these is applicable to the knowledge of Brahman, which is the same thing as Liberation. If Liberation were created or modified, it would not be permanent, and no school of philosophers is prepared to accept such a contingency. Since Brahman is our inner Self, we cannot attain It by any action, as a village is reached by our act of going. Nor is there any room for a purificatory ceremony in the eternally pure Self.

Knowledge itself, again, cannot be said to be an activity of the mind. An action depends upon human endeavour and is not bound up with the nature of things. It can either be done, or not done or modified by the agent. Knowledge, on the other hand, does not depend upon human notions, but on the thing itself. It is the result of the right means, having for its objects existing things Knowledge can therefore neither be made, nor not made, nor modified. Although mental, it differs from such meditations as "Man is fire, O Gautama", "Woman is fire", etc. (Ch. 5.7.1; 5.8.1).

Thus Brahman or the knowledge of Brahman being in no way connected with action, injunctions have no place with regard to It. Therefore texts like, "The Ātman is to be realized" etc., though imperative in character, do not lay down any injunction, but are intended to turn the mind of the aspirant from things external, which keep one bound to this relative existence, and direct it inwards. Further it is not true that the scriptures can have a purpose if only they enjoin or prohibit some action, for even by describing existing things they serve a useful purpose, if thereby they conduce to the well-being of man, and what can do this better than the knowledge of Brahman, which results in Liberation? The comprehension of Braman includes hearing, reasoning, and meditation. Mere hearing does not result in full comprehension or realization of Brahman. Reasoning and meditation are also subservient to that full comprehension. Hence it cannot be said that they are enjoined. If after full comprehension Brahman was found to be related to some injunction, then only it could be said to be supplementary to action.

So Brahman is in no way connected with action. All the Vedânta texts deal with an independent topic, which is Brahman, and these texts are the only proof of this Brahman, as it is not possible to know It through any other source.

So far it has been shown in the previous Sûtras that all the Vedânta texts refer exclusively to Brahman without any connection whatsoever with action, and that Brahman is the omniscient, omnipotent cause of the origin etc. of this universe. Here the Sâmkhyas raise an objection: The Vedânta texts about creation do not refer to Brahman but to the unintelligent Pradhâna made up of the three Gunas (constituents)—Sattva, Rajas, and Tamas, as the first Cause. The Pradhâna is omnipotent with respect to its effects. Again the Pradhâna has Sattva for one of its components, of which, according to Smrti (Gîtâ 14.17), knowledge is an attribute. Therefore the Pradhâna can figuratively be said to be omniscient, because of its capacity for all knowledge. To Brahman, on the other hand, which is isolated and pure intelligence itself, you cannot ascribe all-knowingness or partial-knowledge. Moreover, as the Pradhâna has three components, it seems reasonable that it alone is capable of undergoing modifications, like clay, into various objects of name and form, and not Brahman, which is uncompounded, homogeneous and unchangeable. Moreover, the first Cause is already existing entity and so can be established by inference from its effects and even the scriptures recommend inference of the cause from the effect. So what the Vedânta texts about creation say with respect to the first Cause holds good, and more aptly so, in the case of the Pradhâna, and therefore it is the first Cause referred to by the scriptures.

Topic 5: The first Cause an intelligent principle.

Sûtras 5-11 refute these arguments of the Sâṁkhyas and establish Brahman as the first Cause. The discussion mainly, refers to the sixth chapter of the Chândogya Upaniṣad.

ईक्षतेर्न, अशब्दम् ॥ ५ ॥

ईक्षतेः On account of thinking (seeing) न is not अशब्दम् not based on the scriptures.

5. On account of thinking (being attributed to the first Cause by the scriptures, the Pradhâna) is not (the first Cause referred to by them); it (Pradhâna) is not based on the scriptures.

The first Cause is said, in the scriptures, to have willed or thought before creation. "This universe, my dear, was but the Real (Sat) in the beginning—One only without a second. It thought, 'may I be many, (the Ātman) willed, 'Let me project world!'. So It projected these worlds" (Ai. 1.1.1-2). Such thinking or willing is not possible to the insentient Pradhâna. It is possible only if the first Cause is an intelligent principle like Brahman.

The all-knowingness attributed to the Pradhâna because of its Sattva component is inadmissible, as Sattva is not predominant in the Pradhâna, since all the three Guṇas are in a state of equilibrium. If in spite of this it is said to be capable of producing knowledge, then the other two Guṇas must be equally capable of retarding knowledge. So while Sattva will make it all-knowing, Rajas and Tamas will make it partly knowing, which is a contradiction.

That all-knowingness and creation are not possible to Brahman, which is pure intelligence itself and unchangeable, is also not true. For Brahman can be all-knowing and creative through Mâyâ. So Brahman, the Sat of the text quoted, which thought, is the first Cause.

The Sâṁkhyas again try to avoid the difficulty created by thinking being attributed to the first Cause thus: In the same text quoted above it is said further on, "That fire thought, 'may I be many, may I grow!' and it projected water....Water thought,... it projected earth" (Ch. 6.2.3-4). Here fire and water are material things, and yet thinking is attributed to them. Similarly the thinking by the Sat (Real), in the text originally quoted, can also be taken figuratively, in which case the Pradhâna, though insentient, can yet be the first Cause.

This argument the following sûtra refutes.

गौणश्चेत्, न, आत्मशब्दात् ॥ ६ ॥

गौणः Secondary (figurative) चेत् if (it be said) न not आत्मशब्दात् because of the word 'Self' (Ātman).

6. If it be said (that 'thinking') is used in a secondary sense (with regard to Sat); (we say) not so, because of the word 'Self' (by which the first Cause is referred to in the scriptures).

The Sat (Real) of the text cited in the previous Sûtra after creating fire, water, etc. thought, "Let me now enter into these three as this living self (Jîva) and evolve names and forms" (Ch. 6.3.2). The Sat, the first Cause, refers to the intelligent principle, the Jîva, as its self. The insentient Pradhâna cannot refer to an intelligent principle like the Jîva as its self or as its own nature.

The Sâṁkhyas again try to word off this objection by saying that the word 'Self' (Ātman) is equally used to refer to intelligent and non-intelligent things, as, for example, in expressions like Bhûtâtmâ (the self of the elements), Indriyâtmâ (the self of the senses), etc., and so can be used in connection with the Pradhâna also. The next Sûtra refutes this argument.

तन्निष्ठस्य मोक्षोपदेशात् ॥ ७ ॥

तन्निष्ठस्य To one who is devoted to that (Sat) मोक्षोपदेशात् because Liberation is declared.

7. (That Pradhâna cannot be designated by the word 'Self' is established) because Liberation

is declared to one who is devoted to that Sat (the first Cause).

The sixth chapter of the Chândogya Upaniṣad ends by instructing Śvetaketu thus: "Thou art that." An intelligent being such as Śvetaketu cannot be identified with the insentient Pradhâna. Moreover, in section 14, paragraphs 2-3 of this chapter, Liberation is said to result to one who is devoted to this Sat, and it cannot result from meditation on the insentient Pradhâna. For these reasons, given in the previous Sûtra and in this, the 'Sat', the first Cause, does not refer to the Pradhâna but to an intelligent principle.

हेयत्वावचनाच्च ॥ ८ ॥

हेयत्वावचनात् Fitness to be abandoned not being stated (by the scriptures) च and.

8. And because it is not stated (by the scriptures) that It (Sat) has to be abandoned, (Pradhâna cannot be denoted by the word 'Sat').

If the intention of the scriptures had been to take the aspirant step by step from grosser to subtler truths till finally the real nature of the Ātman was presented to him, and for this purpose they had referred to the Pradhâna—denoted by the word 'Sat' according to the Sâṁkhyas—as the Self, then there would have been later on a statement to the effect that this Pradhâna must be dropped, for it was not the real Self. But there is no such statement in the texts in question. On the contrary, the whole chapter of the Chândogya Upaniṣad, in which the texts occur, deals with the Self as nothing but that Sat. Moreover, this chapter begins with the question, "What is that which being known everything is known?" Now if the Pradhâna were the first Cause, then by knowing it everything would be known, which is not a fact. The enjoyer (Puruṣa), which is different from it, not being a product of the Pradhâna like the objects of enjoyment, cannot be known by knowing the Pradhâna. Therefore the Pradhâna is not the first Cause, knowing which everything is known, according to the scriptures. Such a view will contradict the premiss.

स्वाप्ययात् ॥ ९ ॥

स्वाप्ययात् On account of resolving or merging in one's own Self.

9. On account of (the individual soul) merging in its own Self (or the universal Self referred to as the Sat, in deep sleep, the Pradhâna cannot be denoted by the word 'Self').

"When a man is said to be thus asleep, he is united with the Sat, my child—he merges in his own Self" (Ch. 6.8.1). Here it is taught that the individual soul merges in the Sat, and as it is impossible for the intelligent soul to merge in the insentient Pradhâna, the latter cannot be the first Cause denoted by the word 'Sat' in the text.

गतिसामान्यात् ॥ १० ॥

गतिसामान्यात् On account of the uniformity of views.

10. Because (all the Vedânta texts) uniformly refer to (an intelligent principle as the first Cause, Brahman is to be taken as that Cause).

See Ch. 7.26.1, Pr. 3. 3, Tai. 2.1, etc. The scriptures themselves say, "Whom all the Vedas proclaim" (Ka. 1. 2. 15).

श्रुतत्वाच्च ॥ ११ ॥

श्रुतत्वात् Being declared by the Vedas च also.

11. (That all-knowing Brahman alone is the first Cause of this world) because (it is so known directly) from the Vedas also.

"He is the Cause, the Lord of the ruler of the sense organs (Jîvâtman) and has neither parent nor Lord" (Śv. 6. 9)—where 'He' refers to the all-knowing Lord described in that chapter.

Therefore it is established that the omniscient, omnipotent Brahman is the first Cause and not the insentient Pradhâna or anything else.

From Sûtra 12 onwards till practically the end of the first chapter a new topic is taken up for discussion, *viz* whether certain terms found in the Upanisads are used in their ordinary senses or as referring to Brahman. Again the Upaniṣads speak of two types of Brahman, the Nirguṇa or Brahman without attributes and the Saguṇa or Brahman with attributes. It is the latter which is within the domain of Nescience and is the object of meditation (Upâsanâ), which is of different kinds yielding different results; while the nirguṇa Brahman, which is free from all imaginary limiting adjuncts of the other type is the object of knowledge. Meditation on the saguṇa Brahman cannot lead to immediate Liberation. It can at best lead to gradual Liberation (Krama-Mukti). The knowledge of the nirguṇa Brahman alone leads to immediate Liberation. Now in many places in the Upaniṣads Brahman is described apparently with qualifying adjuncts; yet the scriptures say that the knowledge of that Brahman leads to immediate Liberation. If Brahman is worshipped as limited by those adjuncts, it cannot lead to such Liberation. But if these qualifying adjuncts are regarded as not being ultimately aimed at by the Śruti, but used merely as indicative of Brahman, then these very texts would refer to the nirguṇa Brahman and Liberation would be the immediate result of knowing that Brahman. So by reasoning we have to arrive at a conclusion as to the true significance of these texts, which obviously have a doubtful import.

The issue of the saguṇa and nirguṇa Brahman as shown above is not, however, kept up all through, for in many places it is not between them but between the saguna Brahman and the individual soul or something else.

Topic 6: Concerning "the Self consisting of bliss".

आनन्दमयोऽभ्यासात् ॥ १२ ॥

आनन्दमयः "The Self consisting of bliss" अभ्यासात् because of the repetition.

12. (In the passage) "The Self consisting of bliss" etc. (Brahman, which is spoken of as the

tail, is put forward as an independent entity and not as something subordinate to Ānandamaya, the Self consisting of bliss) on account of the repetition (of Brahman as the main topic in many passages of that chapter).

In topic 5 the word 'thinking' attributed to the first Cause is interpreted in its direct sense, thus establishing the intelligent principle Brahman as the first Cause, and the figurative meaning, which would have established the Pradhâna, is thrown out as being doubtful. But here such a thing, that is the establishing of Brahman, is impossible, for the terms denoting parts allow no room for doubt, thus making it impossible to interpret the texts as referring to Brahman. This connects the present topic with the last one by way of objection.

The passage in question is: "Different from this self, which consists of understanding (Vijñânamaya), is the inner self which consists of bliss. . . . Joy is the head, satisfaction is its right wing, rapture is its left wing, bliss is its trunk, Brahman is the tail, the support" (Tai. 2.5). The Sûtra says that here Brahman, which is spoken of as the tail, is treated as an independent entity and is not to be taken as a part of "the self consisting of bliss", for 'tail' here does not mean the limb, in which sense it is generally used, but the support of the individual soul made up of "the self consisting of bliss", as Brahman is the substratum of the imaginary individual soul. This conclusion is arrived at, because Brahman without any limiting adjuncts whatsoever is again and again reiterated in these Taittirîya texts.

[Sûtras 12-19 are interpreted by the Vṛttikâra (who is probably Upavarṣa) as follows: The Taittirîya Upaniṣad (2. 1-4) after enumerating the selves consisting of food, vital force, mind, and understanding, speaks of "the self consisting of bliss" in the passage quoted above (Tai. 2. 5). The question is whether this refers to the individual soul or Brahman. The opponent holds that it refers to the individual soul, because the word 'Ānandamaya' denotes a modification and therefore cannot refer to Brahman, which is unchangeable, Moreover, five different parts are enumerated of this Ānandamaya, the self consisting of bliss; this is not possible in the case of Brahman, which is without parts. Sûtras 12-19, according to this interpretation, maintain that 'Ānandamaya', the self consisting of bliss, refers to Brahman on account of the repetition of the word 'Ānandamaya' in these Taittirîya texts. Repetition has already been said to be one of the characteristics by which the subject-matter of a passage is ascertained. Brahman, again, has been proved to be the main topic of the Vedânta texts (Ch. 1, Sec. 1, Sûtra 4). Therefore 'Ānandamaya' refers to Brahman. Moreover, the opening words of the second chapter of the Taittirîya Upaniṣad, "Truth, Knowledge, Infinity is Brahman" (Tai. 2.1), and texts like, "He projected all this" (*Ibid.* 2.6), make it clear that Brahman is the topic. The termination 'mayaṭ' is also not out of place in Brahman, for it is used here to denote an abundance of bliss. The possession of a body having parts is also ascribed to It, only because of the immediately preceding limiting condition, *viz* the self consisting of understanding and does not really belong to It. Hence "the self consisting of bliss" is the highest Brahman.

Śaṅkara objects to this interpretation of the Sûtras and says that Ānandamaya cannot be the highest Brahman. First of all, there is no justification for suddenly changing the interpretation of the affix 'mayaṭ' from *modification* in the case of Vijñânamaya, Prâṇmaya, etc. in the preceding passages to *abundance* in the case of Again the very idea of preponderance or abundance of bliss suggests that there is also misery in it, however slight. Such an idea with respect to Brahman is absurd. So Śaṅkara replaces this interpretation of the Sûtras, which Ānandagiri attributes to the Vṛttikâra, by another, which we have reproduced above.]

विकारशब्दान्नेति चेत्, न, प्राचुर्यात् ॥ १३ ॥

विकारशब्दात्, On account of a word ('tail') denoting part न is not इति चेत् if it be said न not so प्राचुर्यात् on account of abundance (of terms denoting parts).

13. If it be said (that Brahman) is not (spoken of as an independent entity in the passage) on account of a word ('tail') denoting part, (we reply) not so, on account of abundance (of terms denoting parts).

Owing to the abundance of phraseology denoting parts or limbs in the Taittirîya texts 2.1-5, Brahman is designated as the tail just to keep up the foregoing imagery; but it is not intended to convey the idea that Brahman is actually a part or member of "the self consisting of bliss" The object of the seriptures is to teach the knowledge of the real Self. If the "self consisting of bliss" were the real Self the scriptures would refer to this in the concluding texts, but as a matter of fact they do not; on the other hand they refer to the nirguṇa Brahman, which is therefore the real subject-matter. Brahman's being the tail means, not that It is a part, but that It is the main support or abode of everything.

तद्धेतुव्यपदेशाच्च ॥ १४ ॥

तद्धेतुव्यपदेशात् Because (It) is declared to be the cause of it च and.

14. And because (Brahman) is declared to be the cause of it (the self consisting of bliss, Brahman cannot be taken as part of it).

Brahman is the cause of everything, even of "the self consisting of bliss", as also of the four earlier named ones, *viz* the self consisting of food, vital force, mind, and understanding. "He projected all this whatever there is" (Tai. 2.6). The cause cannot be a part of the effect.

मान्त्रवर्णिकमेव च गीयते ॥ १५ ॥

मान्त्रवर्णिकम् That which has been referred to in the Mantra portion एव the very same च moreover गीयते is sung.

15. Moreover that very Brahman which has been referred to in the Mantra portion is sung (in this Brâhmaṇa passage as the tail).

The second chapter of the Taittiriya Upaniṣad begins, "He who knows Brahman attains the the Highest.... Brahman is Truth, Knowledge and Infinity." This very Brahman is finally declared to be the tail. Otherwise there would be a contradiction between the Mantra and Brâhmaṇa portions, which cannot be, for the Brâhmaṇas only explain what the Mantras declare. Therefore Brahman is the primary subject-matter and is not treated as a part of "the self consisting of bliss".

नेतरोऽनुपपत्तेः ॥ १६ ॥

न Not इतर: the other (Jîva) अनुपपत्ते on account of impossibility.

16. (Brahman and) not the other (the individual soul, is meant here) on account of the impossibility (of that assumption).

He who is referred to in the passage, "The self consisting of bliss" etc. is said to be the creator of everything "He projected all this whatever there is" (Tai. 2.6). This the individual soul cannot possibly do and so is not referred to in the passage, "The self consisting of bliss" etc.

भेदव्यपदेशाच्च ॥ १७ ॥

भेदव्यपदेशात् On account of the declaration of difference च and.

17. And on account of the declaration of difference (between the two, *i.e.* the one referred

to in the passage, "The self consisting of bliss" etc. and the individual soul, the latter cannot be the one referred to in passage).

That which is referred to in the passage, "The self consisting of bliss" etc. is said to be of the essence of flavour, attaining which the individual soul is blissful. "It (That which is referred to in the passage, 'The self consisting of bliss' etc.) is flavour; only after attaining (this essence of) flavour is this (soul) blissful" (Tai. 2.7). Now that which is attained and the attainer cannot be the same. So the individual soul is not referred to in that passage under discussion.

कामाच्च नानुमानापेक्षा ॥ १८ ॥

कामात् On account of the word 'bliss', literally 'desire', (denoting Brahman) च and नानुमानापेक्षा (Ānandamaya also) cannot be inferred as Brahman.

18. And on account of the word 'bliss', literally 'desire', (referring to Brahman), (you) cannot infer (Ānandamaya is also Brahman, since the suffix 'mayaṭ' is used to denote modification).

In the scriptures the word 'bliss' is often used for Brahman; from this we cannot infer that Ānandamaya, the self consisting of bliss, is also Brahman, for the suffix 'mayaṭ' shows that it is a modification. This sets aside the whole of the interpretation of the Vṛttikâra mentioned under Sûtra 12.

अस्मिन्नस्य च तद्योगं शास्ति ॥ १६ ॥

अस्मिन् In this अस्य its (the Jîva's) च also तद्योगं mergence as that शास्ति teaches.

19. (The Vedas) also teach of its (the Jîva's) becoming (on the dawning of Knowledge) one with this (referred to in the passage under discussion).

Since the individual soul, on the dawning of Knowledge, becomes one with that which is referred to in the passage under discussion, the latter must be Brahman.

Hence "the self consisting of bliss" is in no way the principal topic of these texts. It is Brahman which is the support of everything that is dealt with as an independent entity in these texts.

Topic 7: The person in the sun and the eye is Brahman.

अन्तस्तद्धर्मोपदेशात् ॥ २० ॥

अन्त: Within तद्धर्मोपदेशात् because Its characteristics are mentioned.

20. (The one) within (the sun and the eye is Brahman), because Its characteristics are mentioned (therein).

"Now that golden person who is seen within the sun, with a golden beard and golden hair...is named

Ut, for he has risen (udita) *above all evils*...Ṛk and Sâman are his joints...He is the lord of the worlds beyond the sun and of all objects desired by the gods" (Ch. 1. 6. 6-8). "Now the person who is seen in the eye *is Ṛk; he is Sâman, Uktha, Yajus, Brahman.* The form of that person in the eye is the same as that of the other (the person in the sun), the joints of the one are the joints of the other, the name of the one is the name of the other...He is the lord of the world beneath the body and of all objects desired by men" (Ch. 1.7.5-8). In the last topic, in spite of things to the contrary, the very fact of the repetition of Brahman in the texts helped us to arrive at the conclusion that Brahman was the topic of those texts. Following the same argument, the repetition of abode, form, limitations, etc., in the texts cited ought to make some individual soul which has attained to that eminence of being the presiding deity of the solar orb, and not Brahman, the topic of these texts—this is the objection.

The Sûtra refutes this and says that the person spoken of is the highest Brahman, as its characteristics —such as being above all evils, being the self of everything like Ṛk, Yajus, Sâman (these few being mentioned only by way of example), and his being the lord of the worlds beyond the sun and also of the worlds beneath the body—are mentioned. The mention of a particular abode, *viz* the sun, and the eye, of form, as having a beard, and being golden in colour, and of a limitation of powers is only for the purpose of meditation (Upâsanâ). The highest Lord may, in order to gratify His devout worshippers, assume through Mâyâ any form He likes. It is for the convenience of meditation that these limitations are imagined in Brahman, which otherwise, in Its true nature, is beyond them.

भेदव्यपदेशाच्चान्यः ॥ २१ ॥

भेदव्यपदेशात् On account of a distinction being made च also अन्यः different.

21. Also on account of a distinction being made (in another text between the two, *i.e.* the person in the sun and the individual soul animating the sun) (the Lord) is different (from) the latter).

"He who dwells in the sun and is within the sun, *whom the sun does not know,* whose body the sun is and who rules the sun from within, is thy Self, the ruler within, the immortal" (Br. 3. 7. 9)—this text clearly shows that the highest Lord is within the sun and yet different from the individual soul identifying itself with the sun. This confirms the view expressed in the last Sûtra.

Topic 8: The word Ākāśa' (ether) to be understood as Brahman.

In the last topic the characteristics like "being above all evil" etc. being of doubtful import were made to refer to Brahman and not to the deity of the solar orb and accordingly the mention of form, etc. were interpreted to be imagined in Brahman for the sake of meditation. But now the characteristics mentioned in the text that are taken up for discussion are not of

doubtful import but refer clearly to elemental ether, so
how will you interpret these texts—seems to be the
view of the objector.

आकाशस्तल्लिङ्गात् ॥ २२ ॥

आकाश: (The word) Ākâśa तल्लिङ्गात् on account of
the characteristic marks of that (Brahman).

22.   (The word) Ākâśa (ether) (is Brahman) on
account of the characteristic marks of That
(*i.e.* Brahman) (being mentioned).

" 'What is the goal of this world?' 'Ākâśa', he replied.
For all these beings take their rise from Ākâśa', only
and dissolve in it. Ākâśa is greater than these. It
is their ultimate goal. It indeed is the supreme Udgîtha
...He who knowing this as such meditates on the
supreme Udgîtha..." (Ch. 1. 9. 1-2). Here 'Ākâśa'
refers to Brahman and not to the elemental 'Ākâśa'
(ether), as the characteristics of Brahman, namely, the
rise of the entire creation from it and its return to it at
dissolution are mentioned. No doubt these marks may
also refer to the ether, as the scriptures say that from
the ether is produced air, from air fire, etc., and they
return o the ether at the end of a cycle. But then the
force of the words 'all these' and 'only' in the text
quoted would be lost. To preserve it the text should
be taken to refer to the fundamental cause of all,
including the ether, which can be Brahman alone. The
word Ākâśa' is also used for Brahman in other texts;
"That which is called Ākâśa is the revealed of all forms

and names" (Ch. 8. 14. 1). Again Brahman alone can be 'greater than all' and 'their ultimate goal' as mentioned in the text. In other scriptural passages like, "He is greater than the earth. He is greater than the heavens" (Ch. 3. 14. 3), "Brahman is Knowledge and Bliss. It is the ultimate goal of him who makes gifts" (Bṛ. 3. 9. 28)—these qualities of being greater and the ultimate goal of everything are mentioned, and therefore this interpretation is justified. Hence the Udgîtha in the text cited is to be meditated upon not as a symbol of the ether but of Brahman.

Topic 9: The word 'Prâṇa' to be understood as Brahman

अत एव प्राणः ॥ २३ ॥

अत एव For the same reason प्राणः (the word) Prâṇa (refers to Brahman).

23. For the same reason (the word) 'Prâṇa' (also refers to Brahman).

" 'Which is that deity?' 'Prâṇa', he said. For all these beings merge in Prâṇa alone and from Prâṇa they arise" (Ch. 1. 11. 4-5). The question is whether Prastâva (a division of Sâman) is a symbol of the vital force or Brahman. Here Prâṇa does not mean the vital force but Brahman, in which sense it is used in texts like, "The Prâṇa of Prâṇa" (Bṛ. 4. 4. 18). Why? Because the characteristic of Brahman, "All these beings merge in Prâṇa," etc. is mentioned. All the Jîvas merge in Prâna and that is possible only if 'Prâṇa' is Brahman and not the vital force (the ordinary sense of the word), in which only the senses get merged in deep-sleep.

Topic 10: The word 'light' to be understood as Brahman.

In the two previous topics, on account of the characteristics of Brahman being present in the texts quoted, it was possible to conclude that Brahman was referred to in them. The next Sûtra takes up for discussion a text which itself does not mention the characteristics of Brahman, but the text prior to it does.

ज्योतिश्चरणाभिधानात् ॥ २४ ॥

ज्योतिः Light चरणाभिधानात् on account of the mention of feet.

24. (The word) 'light' (is Brahman) on account of the mention of feet (in a complementary passage).

"Now that light which shines above this heaven, beyond all, ... Let a man meditate on this" etc. (Ch. 3. 13. 7). Here the question is whether the meditation is to be on the light as such or on Brahman. The Sûtra says that 'light' here does not mean physical light which helps vision, such as the sun, but Brahman, because feet (quarters) are mentioned in a preceding text: "This much is Its glory, greater than this is the Puruṣa. One foot of It is all beings while Its (remaining) there feet are immortal in heaven" (Ch. 3. 12. 6). The Brahman that has been so described in this passage is recognized in the one first quoted, where 'light' occurs, because there also it is said to be connected with 'heaven'. Brahman is the subject-matter of not only the previous texts, but also of the subsequent texts; for in the section immediately following that which contains the passage under discussion (*i.e.* in Ch. 3. 14) Brahman is also the main topic. It is therefore but reasonable to say that the intervening section (Ch. 3. 13) also deals with Brahman. Hence 'light' here means Brahman. The word 'light' can be used for Brahman, which manifests the world even as light manifests objects. The mention of limiting adjuncts with respect to Brahman, denoted by the word 'light' is only for the sake of meditation.

छन्दोऽभिधानान्नेति चेत्, न तथा चेतोऽर्पणनिगदात्,
तथा हि दर्शनम् ॥ २५ ॥

छन्दोऽभिधानात् The metre (Gâyatrî) being mentioned न is not इति चेत if it be said न no तथा in that way चेतोऽर्पणनिगदात the application of the mind has been inculcated तथा हि for so दर्शनम् it is seen (in other texts).

25. If it be said (that Brahman is) not referred to) on account of the metre (Gâyatrî) being mentioned; (we reply) no, because in that way (*i.e.* by means of the metre), the application of the mind (on Brahman) has been inculcated; for so (*i.e.* through the help of the modifications of Brahman) it is seen (in other texts).

An objection is raised that in the text "One foot of It is all beings", Brahman is not referred to, but the metre Gâyatrî, for the first paragraph of the preceding section of the same Upaniṣad begins with, "Gâyatrî is everything, whatever here exists," etc. Therefore the feet referred to in the text cited in the last Sûtra refer to this metre and not to Brahman. In reply it is said: Not so; for the next, "Gâyatrî is all this" etc., teaches that one should meditate upon the Brahman which is connected with this metre, because Brahman, being the cause of everything, is connected with that Gâyatrî also, and it is that Brahman which is to be meditated upon. This interpretation would be in keeping with the other texts in the same section, *e.g.* "That which is that Brahman" (Ch. 3. 12. 7) and also with "All this indeed is Brahman" (*Ibid.* 3. 14. 1), where Brahman is the chief topic. Meditation on Brahman through Its modifications or effects is seen in other texts also. "Him the Bahvṛcas meditate upon in the great hymn" etc. (Ai. Ā. 3. 2. 3. 12). Therefore Brahman is meant here, and not the metre Gâyatrî.

भूतादिपादव्यपदेशोपपत्तेश्चैवम् ॥ २६ ॥

भूतादिपादव्यपदेश: The representation of beings etc. as feet उपपत्ते: is possible च also एवम् thus.

26. Thus also (we have to conclude, *viz* that Brahman is the topic of the previous passage, where Gâyatrî occurs) because (thus only) the representation of the beings etc. as the feet (of Gâyatrî) is possible.

The beings, earth, body, and heart can be feet only of Brahman and not of Gâyatrî, the metre—a mere collection of syllables. (See Ch. 3. 12. 2-4). So by Gâyatrî is here meant Brahman as connected with the metre Gâyatrî. It is this Brahman so particularized by Gâyatrî that is said to be the self of all in the text, "Gâyatrî is everything" etc. This same Brahman is again recognized as 'light' in Ch. 3. 13. 7.

उपदेशभेदान्नेति चेत्, न, उभयस्मिन्नप्यविरोधात् ॥ २७ ॥

उपदेशभेदात् On account of the difference in specification न not इति चेत् if it be said न no उभयस्मिन् अपि in either (description) अविरोधात् because there is no contradiction.

27. If it be said (that Brahman of the Gâyatrî passage cannot be recognized in the passage dealing with 'light'), on account of difference in specification, (we reply) no, there being no contradiction in either (description to such a recognition).

In the Gâyatrî passage heaven is specified as the abode of Brahman, while in the other, Brahman is described as existing above heaven. How then can it be said that one and the same Brahman is referred to in both the passages? It can; there is no contradiction here, even as when we say, with reference to a bird perching on the top of a tree, that it is perching on the tree, or that it is above the tree. The difference in the case-ending of the word दिव् is no contradiction, since the locative case is often used in scriptural passage to express, secondarily, the meaning of the ablative.

Therefore the word 'light' has to be understood as Brahman.

Topic 11 : Indra's instruction to Pratardana.

प्राणस्तथानुगमात् ॥ २८ ॥

प्राण: Prâṇa तथा (like) that अनुगमात् being so comprehended (from the texts).

28. Prâṇa is Brahman, it being so comprehended (from the purport of the texts).

In the previous topic the fact that Brahman's three feet (quarters) were spoken of in an earlier text as being in heaven helped us to recognize that the same Brahman is spoken of as the light above heaven. The connection with heaven helped us to this recognition. Now another text is taken up for discussion, in which there is no such decisive factor.

In the Kauṣîtaki Upaniṣad there occurs the following conversation between Indra and Pratardana, in which the latter says to Indra: "You yourself choose for me that boon which you deem most beneficial to man." Indra said, "Know me only, that is what I deem most beneficial to man. ... I am Prâṇa, the intelligent self (Prajñâtman), meditate on me as life, as immortality.... And that Prâṇa is indeed the intelligent self, blessed, undecaying, immortal" (Kau. 3. 1-8). The question is raised whether these passages refer to the god Indra, or the individual self, or the vital force, or Brahman. The decision is that as the characteristics of Brahman are more in evidence in these passages than those of the god India, individual soul, or the vital force (Prâṇa), therefore Brahman is referred to in these passages; hence Prâṇa here means Brahman. The characteristics of Brahman referred to are: (1) Indra says in reply to Pratardana's request for that which is most beneficial to man, "Know me, I am Prâṇa" etc., and since Brahman alone is most beneficial to man, Indra's answer refers to Brahman. (2) Prâṇa is spoken of as blessed, undecaying, immortal, which can be true only of Brahman. (3) The knowledge of this Prâṇa is also said to absolve one from all sing; "He who knows me thus, by no deed of his is his achievement harmed, neither by matricide nor by patricide..." (Kau. 3. 1).

न वक्तुरात्मोपदेशादिति चेत्, अध्यात्मसम्बन्धभूमा ह्यस्मिन् ॥ २९ ॥

न Not वक्तु: the speaker's आत्मोपदेशात् on account of the instruction about himself इति चेत् if it be said अध्यात्म-सम्बन्ध-भूमा abundance of reference to the inner Self हि because अस्मिन् in this.

29. If it be said that (Brahman is) not (referred to in these passages) on account of the speaker's instruction about himself; (we reply not so), because there is abundance of reference to the inner Self in this (chapter).

An objection is raised that the word 'Prâṇa', cannot as stated in the last Sûtra, refer to Brahman, since the speaker Indra describes himself by the word 'Prâṇa' in, "I am Prâṇa" etc. But as in this conversation there are profuse references, as already pointed out in Śûtra 28, to the inner Self or Brahman, 'Prâṇa' here must be taken as Brahman. And Indra's describing himself as Prâṇa is apt, since he identifies himself with Brahman in that instruction, as did the sage Vâmadeva.

शास्त्रदृष्ट्या तूपदेशो वामदेववत् ॥ ३० ॥

शास्त्रदृष्ट्या Through realization of the Truth confirmed by the scriptures तु but उपदेशः instruction वामदेववत् like Vâmadeva.

30. But (Indra's) instruction (to Pratardana is justified) by his realization of the Truth confirmed by the scriptures (*viz* that he is Brahman), as did (the sage) Vâmadeva.

Ṛṣi Vâmadeva having realized Brahman said "I was Manu, and the sun," etc., which is justified by the passage: "Whichsoever of the gods knew It (Brahman) became That" (Bṛ. 1. 4. 10). Indra's instruction also is like that. Having realized the truth, "Thou art That", declared by the scriptures, he identifies himself in the instruction with the supreme Brahman.

जीवमुख्यप्राणलिङ्गान्नेति चेत्, न, उपासात्रैविध्यात्, आश्रितत्वात् इह तद्योगात् ॥ ३१ ॥

जीवमुख्यप्राणलिङ्गात् On account of the characteristics of the individual soul and the vital energy न not इति चेत् if it be said न not so उपासा-त्रैविध्यात because it would enjoin three-fold meditation आश्रितत्वात् on account of Prâṇa being accepted (elsewhere in the sense of Brahman) इह here तद्योगात् because words denoting Brahman as mentioned with reference to Prâṇa.

31. If it be said that (Brahman) is not referred to on account of the characteristics of the individual soul and the vital force (being mentioned), (we say) not so, because (such an interpretation) would enjoin three -fold meditation (Upâsanâ); because Prâṇa has been accepted (elsewhere in the sense of Brahman); and because here also (words denoting Brahman) are mentioned with reference to Prana. (Hence it is to be understood to mean Brahman).

The passages under discussion might as well refer to the individual soul and the vital force, for their characteristics also are found: "One should know the speaker and not inquire into speech" (Kau. 3. 8), "Prâṇa, leaving hold of this body, makes it rise up" (*Ibid.* 3. 3). The Sûtra refutes such a view and says that Brahman alone is referred to by 'Prâṇa'; for the above interpretation would involve a three-fold Upâsanâ, *viz* of the individual soul, of the chief vital force, and of Brahman, which is against the accepted rules of scriptural interpretation. No single passage can be made to yield three different meditations in this way by splitting it up. Moreover in the beginning we have, "Know me only", followed by, "I am Prâṇa", and in the end again we have, "And that Prâṇa indeed is the intelligent self, blessed, undecaying, immortal", which shows that the same topic is kept up throughout. Therefore 'Prâna' must be taken in the sense of Brahman and that on the ground that Its characteristics are found in this passage which have already been referred to in Sûtra 1. 1. 28. This meaning of 'Prâṇa' is found in other scriptural passages, and we are justified in taking it in that sense here, since words denoting Brahman are mentioned with reference to 'Prâṇa'.

CHAPTER I

SECTION II

In the latter part of section 1, certain scriptural terms generally used in a different sense have been shown through reasoning to refer to Brahman, and consequently certain passages of the scriptures of doubtful sense, but containing clear characteristics of Brahman, have been shown to refer to Brahman. Now in this and the next section some more passages of doubtful import, especially with no clear mention of the characteristics of Brahman in them, are taken up for discussion.

Topic 1: The Being consisting of the mind is Brahman.

सर्वत्र प्रसिद्धोपदेशात् ॥ १ ॥

सर्वत्र Throughout (the scriptures) प्रसिद्धोपदेशात् because there is taught (the Brahman which is) well known.

1. (That which consists of the mind [Manomaya] is Brahman) because there is taught (in this text) (that Brahman which is) well known (as the cause of the universe) throughout (the scriptures).

Sûtras 1-8 show that the Being who consists of the mind (Manomaya) and is prescribed as the object of Upâsanâ or meditation in the text, "All this indeed is Brahman, for it has its beginning, end, and subsistence in It; so let a man meditate with a calm mind. ...*He who consists of the mind,* whose body is Prâṇa (the subtle body)" etc. (Ch. 3. 14. 1-2) is Brahman and not the individual soul. Why? Because the text begins with, "All this is Brahman", wherein that Brahman which is treated as the cause of the universe in all scriptural texts is described. Since the Beginning refers to Brahman, it is but proper that the latter sentence where "He who consists of the mind" occurs, should also refer to Brahman as distinguished by certain qualities; otherwise there would arise the inconsistency of suddenly introducing a new subject and dropping the previous one. Moreover the text here speaks of Upâsanâ, meditation, and as such it is but apt that Brahman which is described in all other texts as an object of meditation is also taught here and not the individual soul which is nowhere prescribed as such. Moreover, one can become calm as the text asks only by meditating on Brahman which is bereft of all anger, hatred, etc.

विवक्षितगुणोपपत्तेश्च ॥ २ ॥

विवक्षित-गुणोपपत्ते: Because qualities desired to be expressed are befitting च moreover.

2. Moreover, the qualities desired to be expressed are befitting (only in the case of Brahman; and so the passage refers to Brahman).

"He who consists of the mind, whose body is Prâṇa (the subtle body), whose form is light, resolve is true, whose nature is like that of ether omnipresent and invisible", etc. (Ch. 3. 14. 2)—the qualities mentioned in this text as topics of meditation are possible in the case of Brahman alone. Therefore the conclusion is that such a qualified Brahman alone is to be meditated upon.

अनुपपत्तेस्तु न शारीरः ॥ ३ ॥

अनुपपत्तः Because (they) are not appropriate तु on the other hand न is not शारीरः the individual soul.

3. On the other hand the individual soul is not (referred to by the text) because these qualities are not appropriate (to it).

कर्मकर्तृव्यपदेशाच्च ॥ ४ ॥

कर्म Object कर्तृ agent व्यपदेशात् on account of the mention च and.

4. And on account of the mention of the attainer and the object attained ("He who consists of the mind" refers to Brahman and not to the individual soul).

In the same chapter of the Chândogya Upaniṣad there occurs the passage, "When I shall have departed from hence, I shall attain Him" (3. 14. 4), where 'Him' refers to "Who consists of the mind", the object of meditation spoken of in the earlier passage. Therefore He is necessarily different from the person who meditates, the individual soul referred to in the above text by the pronoun 'I'.

शब्दविशेषात् ॥ ५ ॥

5. Because of the difference (indicated by the case-endings) of the words.

In the Śatapatha Brâhmaṇa, where the same idea is expressed in similar words, we have, "As is a grain of rice, or a grain of barley...so is that golden Being in the self" (10. 6. 3. 2), where the individual soul and 'the self consisting of the mind' are clearly described as two different entities, for 'the self consisting of the mind'—which is denoted by a word in the nominative case—is described as being in the individual self, the word denoting it being in the locative case. Therefore it is clear that the individual self is not referred to in the text under discussion.

स्मृतेश्च ॥ ६ ॥

स्मृते: From the Smṛti च also.

6. From the Smṛti also (we learn that the individual soul is different from the one referred to in the text under discussion).

The Smṛti referred to is, "The Lord, O Arjuna, is seated in the hearts of all beings" etc. (Gîtâ 18. 61). We must not forget, however, that according to Advaita Vedânta this difference is only imaginary and not real. The difference exists only so long as ignorance lasts, and the full import of the text "Thou art That" has not been realized.

अर्भकौकस्त्वात् तद्व्यपदेशाच्च नेति चेत्, न, निचाय्य-त्वादेवं व्योमवच्च ॥ ७ ॥

अर्भकौकस्त्वात् Because of the smallness of the abode तद्व्यपदेशात् on account of its being designated as such (i.e. small) च also न not इति चेत् if it be said न not so निचाय्यत्वात् for the sake of contemplation एवं so व्योमवत् like the ether च and.

7. If it be said that (the passage does) not (refer to Brahman) because of the smallness of the abode (referred to, *viz* the heart) and also on account of its being designated as such (*i.e.* as minute); (we say,) not so, (because Brahman has been so characterized) for the sake of contemplation and because the case is similar to that of the ether.

"He is myself within the heart, smaller than a grain of rice, smaller than a grain of barely" etc. (Ch. 3.14.3). This text occurs in the same section in which we also find "the self consisting of the mind". The objection is raised that since these limitations are apt not in the case of Brahman but of the individual soul, it is the latter that is referred to by "the self consisting of the mind". The Sûtra refutes it and says that Brahman here is thus characterized for the convenience of contemplation, as otherwise it is difficult to mediate on the all-pervading Brahman. This does not mar Its omnipresence, as these limitations are merely imagined in Brahman and are not real. The case is analogous to that of the ether in the eye of the needle, which is spoken of as limited and small, whereas in fact it is all-pervading.

संभोगप्राप्तिरिति चेत्, न, वशेष्यात् ॥ ८ ॥

सभोगप्राप्ति: That it has experience (of pleasure and pain) इति चेत् if it be said न not so वैशेष्यात् because of the difference in nature.

8. If it be said that (being connected with the hearts of all individual souls on account of Its omnipresence, It would also) have experience (of pleasure and pain), (we say,) not so, because of the difference in the nature (of the two).

The mere fact that Brahman is all-pervading and connected with the hearts of all individual souls, and is also intelligent like them, does not make It subject to pleasure and pain. For the individual soul is an agent, the doer of good and bad deeds, and therefore experiences pleasure and pain, while Brahman is not an agent, and therefore does not experience pleasure and pain. A fallacious argument is often put forward that because Brahman and the individual soul are in reality identical, therefore the former is also subject to the pleasure and pain experienced by the latter. But then this identity only refutes the experience of pleasure and pain even by the individual soul as being due to ignorance; for in reality there is neither the individual soul nor pleasure and pain. Therefore the argument of identity cannot be turned the other way to make even the ever pure Brahman subject to evil.

Topic 2: The eater is Brahman.

In the last topic the experience of pleasure and pain in Brahman is denied. Here, in this topic, the fact that Brahman is not an agent is established—which is its connection with the previous topic.

अत्ता चराचरग्रहणात् ॥ ६ ॥

अत्ता The eater चराचरग्रहणात् because the movable and immovable (*i.e.* the whole universe) is taken (as his food).

9. The eater (is Brahman), because both the movable and immovable (*i.e.* the entire universe) is taken (as his food).

"Who thus knows where He is, to whom the Brâhmaṇas and Kṣatriyas are (as it were) but food and death itself a condiment" (Ka. 1. 2. 25)? This passage says that there is some eater. Who is this eater referred to by 'He'? Is it the fire referred to in another text as eater: "Soma indeed is food, and fire the eater" (Bṛ 1.4.6); or is it the individual soul referred to as eater in, "One of them eats the sweet fruit" (Mu. 3.1.1). This Sûtra says it is neither, but the supreme Lord, for the text says that in Him the whole of creation, movable and immovable, is reabsorbed. The fact that death, which destroys everything else, is swallowed up as a condiment, shows that the entire creation is referred to as His food. The Brâhmanas and Kṣatriyas are mentioned as mere examples, since they are the foremost of created beings. The eater of such a stupendous thing can be Brahman alone and none else.

प्रकरणाच्च ॥ १० ॥

प्रकरणात् From the context च and.

10. And because (Brahman) is the subject of the discussion.

In an earlier text Naciketas asks Yama: "Tell me of that which you see as neither good nor bad action, as neither effect nor cause, as neither past nor future" (Ka. 1.2. 14). In this text Brahman is inquired into and Yama answers: "I will tell you in brief—it is Aum" (*Ibid.* 1.2.15). Further on he says, "The Self is neither born nor does it die" (*Ibid.* 1.2.18), and finally concludes with the passage in which the eater is mentioned. All this clearly shows that Brahman is the topic, and therefore the 'eater' is Brahman. It also follows from the peculiar characteristic, *viz* the difficulty to cognize It, which is referred to in the text under discussion.

An objection may be raised on the ground that the scripture itself in another place denies that Brahman is the 'eater': "The other (Brahman) looks on without eating" (Mu. 3.1.1). But 'eating' in this text refers to the experience of pleasure and pain, while in the text under discussion it means the reabsorption of the universe at the time of dissolution, which the scriptures attribute to Brahman alone.

Topic 3: The two that have entered the cavity of the heart are the individual soul and Brahman.

गुहां प्रविष्टावात्मानौ हि, तद्दर्शनात् ॥ ११ ॥

गुहां cavity (of the heart) **प्रविष्टौ** the two that have entered **आत्मानौ** are the two selves (individual and Supreme) **हि** indeed **तद्दर्शनात्** because it is so seen.

11. The two that have entered into the cavity (of the heart) are indeed the individual self and the supreme Self, because it is so seen.

In the Katha Upanisad there occurs the passage, "Having entered the cavity of the heart, the two enjoy the reward of their works, in the body" (1.3.1). The question is whether the couple referred to are the individual soul and Brahman, or the individual soul and intellect (Buddhi). The opponent, following the argument of the previous topic, says it is the latter. In the last topic the nearness of the word 'death' helped us to interpret 'Brâhmaṇa' and 'Kṣatriya' as typical of the whole phenomenal world, similarly the nearness of the word 'enjoy' would make the two in the text refer to limited things like the individual soul and intellect. The Sûtra refutes this and says that the couple referred to are the individual soul and Brahman, for numerals denote things of the same class. When a cow is brought to us and we say, "Bring another", it means another cow. So if with an intelligent self, the individual soul, another is said to enter the cavity of the heart, it must refer to another of the same class, *i.e.* to another sentient being, and not to the intellect (Buddhi), which is insentient. The fact that both are said to enjoy the fruits of actions, which cannot apply to the highest Brahman, is thus explained: Sometimes the characteristics of one in a group are indirectly applied to the whole group, as when we say, "The men with an umbrella", where only one has an umbrella and not the whole group. So here also, though it is only one that is enjoying the fruits of actions, both are so spoken of.

विशेषणाच्च ॥ १२ ॥

विशेषणात् From the specification च and.

12. And from the (distinctive) qualities (of the two mentioned in subsequent texts).

The texts subsequent to the one under discussion mention the characteristics of the two that have entered the cavity of the heart, which show that these are the individual soul and Brahman. 'Know that the soul is the charioteer" etc. (Ka. 1.3.3). and "He attains the end of the journey, that supreme state of Viṣṇu" (*Ibid.* 1. 3. 9), where the two are mentioned as the attainer and the goal attained, *i.e.* as the Jîva and Brahman. In a previous passage also the two are spoken of as the meditator and the object of meditation. "The sage relinquishes joy and sorrow, having realized by meditation...that effulgent One...seated in the heart" (*Ibid.* 1. 2. 12).

Topic 4: The person within the eye is Brahman.

In the last topic the reference to 'two' occurring at the beginning of the text discussed, was interpreted to denote two of the same class, *i.e.* two sentient beings, and the entrance into the cavity of the heart, mentioned later on, was interpreted accordingly. The same line of argument should be used, says the opponent, to interpret the text of this topic. That is, the person in the eye ought to be taken as a reflection in the eye, as it occurs at the beginning of the text, and the subsequent mention of immortality, fearlessness, etc. ought to be explained away, as praise or otherwise. The inverse method, *i.e.* taking these words to refer to Brahman and thus fixing the person in the eye to be Brahman, should not be followed. In this way the opponent wants to show that the argument of the previous one is defective, for it will launch us into difficulties with respect to other texts of the Śruti.

अन्तर उपपत्तेः ॥ १३ ॥

अन्तरः Inside (the eye) उपपत्तेः on account of the appropriateness of (attributes).

13. (The person) inside (the eye is Brahman) on account of (the attributes mentioned therein) being appropriate (only to Brahman).

"This person that is seen in the eye is the self. This is immortal and fearless; this is Brahman" (Ch. 4.15.1) The question is whether the person referred to here is the reflection of a person in the eye, or the individual soul, or the sun, which helps sight, or Brahman. The Sûtra says that this person in the eye is Brahman because the qualities 'immortal', 'fearless', etc. mentioned here with respect to that person can be true only of Brahman, and they cannot be otherwise explained away.

स्थानादिव्यपदेशाच्च ॥ १४ ॥

स्थानादिव्यपदेशात् Because abode etc. (*i.e.* name and form) are attributed to it च and.

14. And because abode etc. (*i.e.* name and form) are attributed to It (Brahman) (by other scriptural texts also, for the sake of contemplation).

But, how can the all-pervading Brahman be in a limited space like the eye? The assignation of a definite locality to the all-pervading Brahman only serves the purpose of meditation (Upâsanâ). In other scriptural texts, the disc of the sun, the cavity of the heart, even the eye itself (Bṛ. 3.7.18) and similar pure spots have been prescribed as places for the contemplation of Brahman. So here it is prescribed that Brahman should be contemplated in the eye. Not only abode, but even name and form are attributed to Brahman for the purpose of meditation, as Brahman without attributes cannot be an object of contemplation. (*Vide* Ch. 1.6. 6-7).

सुखविशिष्टाभिधानादेव च ॥ १५ ॥

सुखविशिष्ट-अभिधानात् On account of the reference (to Brahman) distinguished by bliss एव verily च and.

15. And verily on account of the reference

(in the passage to Brahman) distinguished by bliss (mentioned at the beginning of the Prakaraṇa).

"The vital energy is Brahman, bliss is Brahman, the ether is Brahman" (Ch. 4.10.5)—so taught the fires to Upakosala Kâmalâyana about Brahman, and this same Brahman is further elucidated by his teacher as "the person in the eye".

श्रुतोपनिषत्कगत्यभिधानाच्च ॥ १६ ॥

श्रुत-उपनिषत्क-गति The way of those who have realized the Truth of the Upaniṣads अभिधानात् on account of the statement च also.

16. Also on account of the statement of the way (after death) of those who have known the Truth of the Upaniṣads (*i.e.* knowers of Brahman) (with reference to the knower of the person in the eye).

The Devayâna path or the path of the gods, by which a knower of Brahman travels after death and which is described in the Praśṇa Upaniṣad 1.10 and other scriptural texts, is referred to here. Since the knower of "the person in the eye" also goes by this path after death, and since it is known from scriptures that none other except the knower of Brahman goes by this path after death, "the person in the eye" must be Brahman.

अनवस्थितेरसंभवाच्च नेतरः ॥ १७ ॥

अनवस्थितेः Not existing always असंभवात् on account of the impossibility च and न not इतरः any other.

17. (The person in the eye is the supreme Self) and not any other (*i.e.* individual soul etc). as these do not exist always; and on account of the impossibility (of the qualities of the person in the eye being attributed to any of these).

The reflection in the eye, for example, does not exist always, nor can the qualities like immortality, fearlessness, etc. be appropriately ascribed to this reflection. So no other self except the supreme Self is here spoken of as the person in the eye.

Topic 5: The ruler within is Brahman.

In the last topic, while interpreting the person in the eye as Brahman it has been taken for granted that the eye is prescribed in Bṛ. 3.7.18 as an abode of Brahman for contemplation, and that therefore here also the eye is prescribed as an abode. The present topic takes up for discussion this text of Bṛhadâraṇyaka and establishes the conclusion that was taken for granted in the last topic.

अन्तर्यामी, अधिदैवादिषु तद्धर्मव्यपदेशात् ॥ १८ ॥

अन्तर्यामी The Ruler within अधिदैवादिषु in the gods etc. तद्धर्म-व्यपदेशात् on account of Its qualities being mentioned.

18. The Ruler within of the gods and so on (is Brahman) on account of the qualities of that (Brahman) being mentioned.

"Dost thou know the internal Ruler" etc. (Bṛ. 3. 7. 1); and again, "He who inhabits the earth, but is within it, whom the earth does not know,...is the internal Ruler, your own immortal self" (*Ibid.* 3.7.3). The "internal Ruler" spoken of here is Brahman and not the individual soul endowed with Siddhis (powers) or the presiding deity, or anything else, for the characteristics of Brahman are mentioned in the concluding part of the text cited, wherein the Ruler is spoken of as identical with the individual soul and immortal, which can be true only of Brahman. He is also described in this section as being all-prevading, since he is inside and the Ruler within of everything, *viz* the earth, the sun, water, fire, sky, the ether, the senses, etc., and this also can be true only of Brahman.

न च स्मार्तम्, अतद्धर्माभिलापात् ॥ १९ ॥

न Neither च and स्मार्तम् that which is mentioned in the (Sâṁkhya) Smṛti अतत्-धर्म-अभिलापात् because attributes contrary to its nature are mentioned.

19. And neither is (the Ruler within) that which is talked of in (Sâṁkhya) Smṛti (*i.e.* Pradhâna), because attributes contrary to its nature are mentioned (here).

The Pradhâna is not this "internal Ruler", as the attributes: "He is the immortal"; "unseen but seeing, unheard but hearing," etc. (Bṛ. 3.7.23), do not hold true of the non-intelligent Pradhâna.

शारीरश्च, उभयेऽपि हि भेदेनैनमधीयते ॥ २० ॥

शारीर: The individual soul च also (न not) उभये अपि (the followers of) both (the recensions—Kâṇva and Mâdhyandina) हि for भेदेन as different एनम् this (the Jîva) अधीयते read.

20. Also the individual soul (is not the Ruler within), for this is read as different (from the internal Ruler) by the followers of both (the recensions, *viz* the Kâṇva and Mâdhyandina Śâkhâs of the Bṛhadāraṇyaka Upaniṣad).

The negative 'not' is to be supplied from the last Sûtra.

"He who dwells in knowledge" etc.—says Bṛ. 3. 7. 22, Kâṇva reading, where 'knowledge' stands for the individual soul, for it consists of knowledge. "He who dwells in self"—is the Mâdhyandina reading of the same passage, where 'self' stands for the individual soul These quotations make it clear that in either reading the individual soul is spoken of as different from the "internal Ruler", for it is the ruler of the individual soul also.

Here again we should not forget that the difference of the internal Ruler, the supreme Lord, and the individual soul is merely the product of Nescience. There is only one Self within, for two selves are not possible. But owing to limiting adjuncts the one Self is treated as if It were two.

Topic 6: That which cannot be seen is Brahman.

In the last topic the ruler within was interpreted as

the supreme Lord and not the Pradhâna, for qualities like, 'seeing', 'hearing', etc., which are contrary to the nature of the Pradhâna, were present. Now certain texts which do not mention such qualities so as to exclude the Pradhâna are taken up for discussion.

अदृश्यत्वादिगुणको धर्मोक्तेः ॥ २१ ॥

अदृश्यत्वादि-गुणकः: Possessor of qualities like invisibility etc. धर्मोक्तेः: on account of the qualities being mentioned.

21. The possessor of qualities like invisibility etc. (is Brahman) on account of (Its) characteristics being mentioned.

"That which cannot be seen nor seized, which is without origin...eternal, all-pervading, omnipresent, extremely subtle..., the source of all beings, which the wise behold" (Mu. 1. 1. 6). The Being which is the source of all beings is not the Pradhâna but Brahman, for qualities like "He is all-knowing, all-perceiving" (*Ibid*. 1. 1. 9) are true only of Brahman and not of the Pradhâna, which is non-intelligent. Obviously it cannot refer to the individual soul as it is limited.

विशेषणभेदव्यपदेशाभ्यां नेतरौ ॥ २२ ॥

विशेषण-भेद-व्यपदेशाभ्यां On account of the mention of characteristic qualities and differences न not इतरौ the other two.

22. The other two (*viz* the individual soul and the Pradhâna) are not (referred to in the

passage), because the characteristics of Brahman and the difference (of the Being which is the source of all beings from the individual soul and the Pradhâna) are mentioned.

"That heavenly person is without body, comprises the external and the internal, is birthless, without the vital force and without mind, pure, higher than the high, Imperishable" (Mu. 2.1.2). Epithets like 'heavenly', 'birthless', 'pure', etc. apply to Brahman and not to the individual soul, which considers itself limited, impure, corporeal, etc. "Higher than the high Imperishable (Pradhâna)" shows that the source of all beings spoken of in the last Sûtra is not the Pradhâna but something different from it.

रूपोपन्यासाच्च ॥ २३ ॥

रूप-उपन्यासात् Form being mentioned च also.

23. Also because (its) form is mentioned (the passage under discussion refers to Brahman).

Subsequent to the text quoted in the previous Sûtra we have the following text, "The Person indeed is all this sacrifice, knowledge, etc." (Mu. 2.1.10) which shows that "the source of all beings" referred to in the text under discussion, is none other than the supreme Lord or Brahman, because it is the self of all beings.

Topic 7: Vaiśvânara is Brahman.

In the last topic a general quality like invisibility equally applicable to Brahman and the Pradhâna was interpreted to refer to Brahman taking into consideration qualities like all-knowingness etc. mentioned later on in the section. Following this argument the objector takes some texts for discussion and insists that the Vaiśvânara referred to in them must be the ordinary fire in view of specifications like "the support of sacrifice" mentioned later on.

वैश्वानरः साधारणशब्दविशेषात् ॥ २४ ॥

वैश्वानर Vaiśvânara साधारण-शब्द-विशेषात् because of the qualifying adjuncts to the common words (Vaiśvânara and self).

24. Vaiśvânara (is Brahman), because of the qualifying adjuncts to the common words ('Vaiśvânara' and 'Self').

"But he who worships this Vaiśvânara Self extending from heaven to the earth as identical with his own self eats food in all beings, in all selves; of that Vaiśvânara self Sutejas (heaven) is the head, the sun the eye", etc. (Ch. 5.18.1-2). Now what is this Vaiśvânara Self? 'Vaiśvânara' generally means fire, the presiding deity of fire and the gastric fire. 'Self' refers to both the individual soul and the supreme Self. Which of these is referred to in the passage? Whatever be the ordinary meaning of these two words, the Sûtra says that here the supreme Self is referred to, on account of the qualifying adjuncts to those words. The adjuncts are: Heaven is the head of this Vaiśvânara Self, the sun its eyes, etc. and this is possible only in the case of the supreme Self. Again the result of meditation on this

Vaiśvânara Self having the parts stated is the attainment of all desires, and freedom from all sin (*vide* Ch. 5. 24. 3). This also can be true if the highest Self is meant. Moreover the chapter begins with the inquiry, "What is our Self? What is Brahman?"—where the word 'Brahman' is used in its primary sense, and so it is proper to think that the whole chapter delineates Brahman.

स्मर्यमाणमनुमानं स्यादिति ॥ २५ ॥

स्मर्यमाणम् Described in the Smṛti अनुमानम् indicatory mark स्यात् must be इति because.

25. Because that (cosmic form of the supreme Lord) which is described in the Smṛti must be an indicatory mark (from which we arrive at the meaning of this śruti text under discussion).

The Smṛtis are interpretations of Śruti texts. So where a doubt arises as to the meaning of a Śruti the former may be consulted to throw light on the subject. The Smṛti describes the cosmic form of the supreme Lord as "He whose mouth is fire, whose head is heaven, ...whose ears are the regions—salutation to Him, whose body is the universe", which agrees with the description in the text under discussion. Hence we have to conclude that the highest Lord is referred to in the text.

शब्दादिभ्योऽन्तः प्रतिष्ठानाच्च नेति चेत्, न, तथा दृष्ट्युपदेशात्, असंभवात्, पुरुषमपि चैनमधीयते ॥ २६ ॥

शब्दादिभ्यः Because of the word and other reasons अन्तः inside प्रतिष्ठानात् on account of (its) existing च and न

not इति चेत् if it be said न not so तथा as such दृष्टयुपदेशात् on account of the instruction to conceive it असम्भवात् being impossible पुरुषम् as person अपि also एनम् him च also अधीयते (they) describe.

26. If it be said that (Vaiśvânara) is not (Brahman) because of the word ('Vaiśvânara', which has a definite meaning *viz* gastric fire) and other reasons, and on account of its existing inside (which is true of gastric fire), (we say) not so, because there is the instruction to conceive (Brahman) as such (as the gastric fire), because it is impossible (for the gastric fire to have the heaven etc. for its head and other limbs) and also because (the Vâjasaneyins) describe him (Vaiśvânara) as a person (which the gastric fire is not).

Objection: The ordinary meaning of 'Vaiśvânara' is fire and the Śruti also says that it is seated inside: "He who knows this Vaiśvânara abiding within man" (Śat. Br. 10.6.1.11), which applies to the gastric fire only. Hence it alone, and no Brahman is referred to in the text under discussion.

The Sûtra refutes this objection firstly because the scripture here teaches the worship of Brahman in the gastric fire by way of meditation (Upâsanâ), even as in the passage, "Let a man meditate on the mind as Brahman" (Ch. 3.18.1). Secondly because the gastric fire cannot have heaven for its head, and so on. Thirdly because Vaiśvânara is conceived as a person by the Vâjasaneyins: "This Agni Vaiśvânara is a person" etc. (Śat. Br. 10.6.1.11). Hence 'Vaiśvânara' here refers to

Brahman, which is all-pervading and can also be conceived of as a person.

अत एव न देवता भूतं च ॥ २७ ॥

अत एव For the same reason न (is) not देवता deity भूतं element च and.

27. For the same reason (Vaiśvânara) is not the deity (fire) or the element (fire).

For the same reason—as stated in the previous Sûtra.

साक्षादप्यविरोधं जैमिनिः ॥ २८ ॥

साक्षात् Directly अपि even अविरोधं no contradiction जैमिनि (so says) Jaimini.

28. Even (if by 'Vaiśvânara' Brahman is) directly (taken as the object of worship), there is no contradiction; (so says) Jaimini.

In the last Sûtra it was explained that meditation on Brahman in the gastric fire, taking it as a symbol, was taught. This Sûtra says that 'Vaiśvânara' can be taken directly to mean Brahman as an object of contemplation, for 'Vaiśvânara' is the same as Vaiśvânara, which means the universal man, *i.e.* the all-pervading Brahman Itself.

अभिव्यक्तेरित्याश्मरथ्यः ॥ २९ ॥

अभिव्यक्तेः On account of manifestation इति so आश्मरथ्यः (so says) Āśmarathya.

29. On account of manifestation—so says Āśmarathya.

The reference to Vaiśvânara in the text under discussion as extending from heavens to the earth is explained here. Even though the Lord is all-pervading, yet He specially manifests Himself as extending from heaven to the earth for the sake of the devotees.

अनुस्मृतेर्बादरिः ॥ ३० ॥

अनुस्मृतेः For the purpose of constant remembrance बादरिः (so says) Bâdari.

30. For the purpose of constant remembrance —so says Bâdari.

The highest Lord may be called "measured by a span" (to render the term 'Prâdeśamâtra' differently), because He is remembered through the mind, which is seated in the heart, and the heart is of the size of a span.

संपत्तेरिति जैमिनिः, तथा हि दर्शयति ॥ ३१ ॥

संपत्तेः Because of imaginary identity इति so जैमिनिः (says) Jaimini तथा हि for so दर्शयति declares (the Śruti).

31. Because of imaginary identity (the supreme Lord may be called span long), so says Jaimini; for so (the Śruti) declares.

Sampat Upâsanâ is a kind of meditation in which Something is imagined as identical with something else on account of some kind of similarity or likeness. As, for example, when the cosmic being (Puruṣa) is worshipped through the identification of His different limbs with the different parts of the worshipper's body from the top of the head to the chin. The head of the worshipper is heaven, the eyes the sun and the moon, and so on. In this meditation of the cosmic Person He is limited to the size of a span, the distance from the top of the head to the chin. Therefore, says Jaimini, in the text under discussion, the supreme Lord is regarded as of the size of a span.

आमनन्ति चैनमस्मिन् ॥ ३२ ॥

आमनन्ति Teach च moreover एनम् this अस्मिन् in this.

32. Moreover (the Jâbâlas) teach that this (supreme Lord is to be meditated upon) in this (space between the head and the chin).

See Jâbâla Upaniṣad 1.

Sûtras 27—32 justify the reference to the supreme Lord by the term 'Prâdeśamâtra' "as extending from heaven to the earth", or "as measured by a span".

CHAPTER I

SECTION III

In the last section texts of doubtful import wer interpreted to refer to Brahman, and in so doing th fact that Brahman is the one object of all devou meditations helped us much. In this section some mor texts of doubtful import are taken up for discussio and are interpreted to refer to Brahman, and in thi interpretation the fact that Brahman is the one objec of knowledge is taken advantage of.

Topic 1: The resting-place of heaven, earth, etc. is Brahman.

In the last topic of the last section the word 'Vaiś vânara', which usually means the gastric fire, wa interpreted as Brahman, in view of the words, "It head is heaven", occuring at the end of the text Following this argument the opponent takes up fo discussion a text where the word 'immortal' shoul refer to the Pradhâna and not to Brahman, on accoun of the word 'bridge' which occurs at the end of th text. A bridge connects with something beyond, an as there can be nothing beyond Brahman, the wor 'bridge' excludes Brahman, and so 'immortal' refer not to Brahman but to the Pradhâna.

द्युभ्वाद्यायतनं स्व-शब्दात् ॥ १ ॥

द्यु-भू-आदि-आयतनं The resting-place of heaven, earth etc. स्व-शब्दात् on account of the word 'Self'.

1. The resting-place of heaven, earth, etc. (is Brahman) on account of the word 'Self' (or on account of the actual words of the Śruti) (designating this resting-place).

"In Him heaven, the earth, and the sky are woven, as also the mind with all the senses. Know that Self alone and leave off other talk! He is the bridge of Immortality" (Mu. 2. 2. 5). He who is spoken of as the abode, in whom the earth, heaven, etc. are woven is Brahman, on account of the term 'Self', which is appropriate only if Brahman is referred to in the text and not Pradhâna or Sûtrâtman. Or there are actual texts in which Brahman is spoken of as the abode by terms properly designating Brahman. For example: "All these creatures, my dear, have their root, their abode, and their rest in the being" (Ch. 6. 8. 4). It may also mean Brahman because in the texts preceding and following this one, *i.e.* in Mu. 2.1.10 and 2.2.11, Brahman is spoken of, and so it is but proper to infer that It is also referred to in the intervening text, which is under discussion.

From the text cited above, where mention is made of an abode and that which abides, and also from "Brahman indeed is all this" (Mu. 2. 2. 11) we are not to take that Brahman is of manifold, variegated nature like a tree consisting of leaves, branches, etc. This would lead us to Pantheism, and Advaita does not uphold it. So in order to remove the possibility of such a doubt the passage under discussion, says, "Know Him alone, the Self" *i.e.* know the Self alone and not that which abides in it, which is merely a product of Nescience and has to be set aside as false.

मुक्तोपसृप्यव्यपदेशात् ॥ २ ॥

मुक्त-उपसृप्य to be attained by the liberated व्यपदेशात् because of the statement.

2. Because of the statement (in the scriptures) that is to be attained by the liberated.

A further reason is given to show that Brahman is meant in the passage under discussion. It is the goal of the liberated (*vide* Mu. 2.2.9; 3.2.8). Therefore it can be Brahman alone.

नानुमानम्, अतच्छब्दात् ॥ ३ ॥

न Not अनुमानम् what is inferred (Pradhâna) अतत्-शब्दात् owing to want of any term indicating it.

3. (The abode of heaven etc.) is not what is inferred (*i.e.* Pradhâna), owing to want of any term indicating it.

The abode of heaven etc. cannot be the Pradhâna, for there is no term indicative of it in the text, as we have 'Self' indicative of Brahman. There are no terms whatsoever referring to inert matter, but on the other hand there are terms indicating intelligence: "Who knows all, understands all" etc. (Mu. 1. 1. 9).

प्राणभृच्च ॥ ४ ॥

प्राणभृत् The living or individual soul च also (न not).

4. (Nor) also the individual soul.

The word 'not' has to be inferred from the previous Sûtra.

Nor is it the individual soul, though it is an intelligent principle and can therefore be denoted by the word 'Self'; for it is impossible to conceive the individual soul as omniscient and as the resting-place of the whole universe.

भेदव्यपदेशात् ॥ ५ ॥

भेद-व्यपदेशात् On account of difference being mentioned.

5. (Also) on account of difference being mentioned (between the individual soul and the abode of heaven etc.).

"Know Him alone as the Self," says the text under discussion, thereby differentiating the individual soul desirous of release and the abode of heaven etc. as the knower and the thing to be known.

प्रकरणात् ॥ ६ ॥

6. On account of the subject-matter.

The Upaniṣad begins with, "What is that by knowing which everything else becomes known" (Mu. 1. 1. 3), and concludes by saying, "The knower of Brahman becomes Brahman" (Mu. 3. 2. 9), which shows that the subject-matter of the whole Upanisad from beginning to end is Brahman, and therefore it is the same Brahman which is spoken of as the abode of heaven etc.

स्थित्यदनाभ्याम् च ॥ ७ ॥

स्थिति-अदनाभ्याम् On account of remaining unattached and eating च also.

7. Also on account of (the mention of two conditions:) remaining unattached and eating (which are the characteristics of the supreme Self and the individual self respectively).

"Two birds, inseparable friends, cling to the same tree. One of them eats the sweet fruit, the other looks on without eating" (Mu. 3. 1. 1). Here Brahman is described as the witness and the individual soul as experiencing the fruits of good and evil actions and hence different from the other. This description, which distinguishes the two, can be apt only if the abode of heaven etc. is Brahman. Otherwise there will be no continuity of topic. Nor can we take this text as merely describing the nature of the individual soul, for the scriptures nowhere aim at describing the individual soul, which is known to everyone as the agent, enjoyer, etc. Their aim is always to describe and establish Brahman which is not so known.

Topic 2: The Bhûman is Brahman

In the last section the abode of heaven etc. was interpreted as referring to Brahman on account of the word 'Self' in the text. The opponent now takes up for discussion another text, where the word 'Self' according to his view is used to denote Prâna, the vital force, and not Brahman. See Ch. 7. 23 and 24.

The following Sûtra however says that here also it is Brahman and not Prâna.

भूमा संप्रसादादध्युपदेशात् ॥ ८ ॥

भूमा The Bhûman संप्रसादात्-अधि after or beyond the state of deep-sleep, (here, the vital force) उपदेशात् because of the teaching.

8. The Bhûman (is Brahman) because it is taught after the state of deep-sleep (*i.e.* afer Prâṇa or the vital force, which alone functions even in that state).

In the seventh chapter of the Chândogya Upanisad, Sanatkumâra teaches Nârada several truths. He begins with 'name' and goes higher and higher, till he teaches the highest truth, which is Bhûman. "The Bhûman (infinite) is bliss....The Bhûman you should seek to understand...Where one sees nothing else, hears nothing else, understands nothing else, that is the Bhûman" (Ch. 7. 23 and 7. 24. 1). The question is, what does this Bhûman refer to. The opponent holds that it is the vital force. He argues as follows: After Sanatkumâra finished teaching every truth from name up to the vital force, Nârada asks him, "Is there anything higher than this?"—to which Sanatkumâra answers, "Yes, there is," and takes up the next higher truth. But after being taught about the vital force Nârada does not ask whether there is any higher truth, and yet Sanatkumâra gives this dissertation on the Bhûman—which shows that this Bhûman is not different from the vital force taught already.

Not only that, he calls the knower of the vital force an Ativâdin (one who makes a statement surpassing previous statements), thereby showing that the vital force is the highest truth, and in accordance with this he further elucidates the truth as Bhûman.

This Sûtra refutes this argument and says that Bhûman is Brahman, for though the Sûtra calls the knower of vital force an Ativâdin, yet it says, "But he indeed is an Ativâdin who is such through the realization of the Truth" (Ch. 7. 16. 1), which clearly shows that it refers to something higher than the vital force, knowing which one becomes truly an Ativâdin. Thus it is clear that a new topic about Brahman which is the highest Truth is begun, though Nârada does not ask whether there is any truth higher than the vital force. Sanatkumâra, in accordance with Nârada's desire to be an Ativâdin through Truth, now leads him by a series of steps to the knowledge of the Bhûman, showing that this Bhûman in Brahman. Moreover, if the vital force, says the Sûtra, were the Bhûman, then the Śruti would not give any information about it—as it does in Ch. 7. 24. 1. cited above—beyond what it has already given in section 15.

धर्मोपपत्तेश्च ॥ ९ ॥

धर्म-उपपत्तेः Because the qualities are appropriate; च and.

9. And because the qualities (mentioned in the texts) are appropriate (only in the case of Brahman).

The qualities referred to are: Truth, resting on its own greatness, non-duality, bliss, all-pervadingness. immortality, etc. mentioned in the text under discussion, which hold good only in the case of Brahman and not of the vital force, which is but an effect and as such cannot possess any of these qualities. Moreover the chapter begins thus: "The knower of the Self goes beyond misery", which shows that the Self or Brahman is the subject to be known. It is therefore delineated in the subsequent texts.

Topic 3: Akṣara is Brahman.

In the previous section because the epithet 'Truth' is generally applied to Brahman, the Bhûman was interpreted as Brahman. Following the same argument the opponent holds that the word 'Akṣara' should mean the syllable 'Om' in the texts to be taken up for discussion in this section, for 'Akṣara' generally means word or syllable.

अक्षरमम्बरान्तधृते ॥ १० ॥

अक्षरम् The Akṣara अम्बर-अन्त-धृते: (because) it supports all up to Ākâśa (ether).

10. The Akṣara (the Imperishable) (is Brahman) because it supports (everything) up to Ākâśa (ether).

"O Gârgî, the Brâhmaṇas call this Akṣara" etc. (Bṛ. 3.8.8). Here the question is whether 'Akṣara' means the syllable 'Om' or Brahman. The doubt arises because 'Akṣara' etymologically means a syllable and therefore commonly represents the syllable 'Om', which is also an object of meditation. The Sûtra however says 'Akṣara' here stands for Brahman. Why? For the text says, "In that Akṣara, O Gârgî, is the ether woven like warp and woof" (Bṛ. 3. 8. 11). This attribute of supporting everything, even the Ākâśa, the first entity in the order of creation, can be true only of Brahman. Then again "it is neither gross nor minute, neither short nor long" etc. (Bṛ. 3.8.8) shows that all relative qualities are absent in it. Therefore the 'Aksara' is Brahman.

सा च प्रशासनात् ॥ ११ ॥

सा This (supporting) च also प्रशासनात् because of the command.

11. Because of the command (attributed to Akṣara) this (supporting) (can be the work of the highest Self only and not of the Pradhâna).

"Under the mighty rule of that Immutable (Akṣara), O Gârgî, the sun and the moon are held in their positions" (Br. 3.8.9) This command or rulership cannot be the work of the non-intelligent Pradhâna. So the Pradhâna cannot be the 'Akṣara' which supports everything up to Ākâśa.

अन्यभावव्यावृत्तेश्च ॥ १२ ॥

अन्य-भाव-व्यावृत्तेः Because the qualities of any other than Brahman have been negated च also.

12. And because the qualities of any other than Brahman have been negated (by the Śruti).

All other qualities referred to in the text, as, for example, seeing, hearing, thinking, knowing, etc. (Bṛ. 3.8.11) point to a conscious principle and therefore negate the Pradhâna etc. Nor can it be the individual soul, which is not free from limiting adjuncts as the Aksara is described.

Topic 4: The highest Person to be meditated upon is the highest Brahman.

In the last section the word 'Akṣara', though it generally means syllable, was interpreted to refer to Brahman on account of the characteristic quality of supporting everything and we had to go to the etymological meaning of the word 'Akṣara', *viz* that which does not perish or undergo change, *i.e.* Brahman. Similarly in the text to be taken up for discussion the opponent holds that on account of the attainment of Brahmaloka as the result of the meditation we have to take by the highest Person the lower Brahman or Hiraṇyagarbha which is relatively speaking higher, and not the higher Brahman.

ईक्षतिकर्मव्यपदेशात् सः ॥ १३ ॥

ईक्षति-कर्म Object of seeing व्यपदेशात because of his being mentioned स: he.

13. Because of his being mentioned as an object of (the act of) seeing, he (who is to be meditated upon is Brahman).

"Again he who meditates with the syllable 'Om' of three Mâtrâs (A-u-m), on the highest Person" etc.

(Pr, 5.5). A doubt arises whether the highest Brahman or the lower Brahman is meant, because, in 5.2 both are mentioned, and also because Brahmaloka is described as the fruit by the worship of this highest Person. The Sûtra says that this highest Person is the highest Brahman and not Hiraṇyagarbha (the lower Brahman). Why? Because the paragraph ends thus: "He sees the highest Person," which shows that he realizes or actually gets identified with the highest Person. It is not a mere imagination but an actuality, for the object of an act of seeing is an actuality, as we find from experience. But Hiraṇyagarbha is an imaginary being, since it is a product of ignorance. Hence the highest Person means the highest Brahman, which is a reality, and this very Brahman is taught at the beginning of the paragraph as the object of meditation, for it is not possible to realize one entity by meditating on another.

The attainment of Brahmaloka by the worshipper should not be regarded as an insignificant fruit of the worship of the highest Person, for it is a step in gradual emancipation (Krama Mukti). First he attains this Loka and then final beatitude.

Topic 5: The 'small Ākâśa' is Brahman

In the previous section the epithet 'highest Person', being generally used with reference to the highest Brahman, was taken to mean that. The opponent now follows this argument and wants to interpret the word Ākâśa occuring in the texts to be taken up for discussion in this section, as ether, that being the ordinary meaning of the word.

दहर उत्तरेभ्यः ॥ १४ ॥

दहर: Small उत्तरेभ्य: because of subsequent texts.

14. The small (Ākâśa) (is Brahman) because of subsequent texts (which give ample indication to that effect).

"Now there is in this city of Brahman (the body) a small lotus-like place (the heart), and in it a small Ākâśa. What exists within that small Ākâśa is to be sought, that is to be understood" (Ch. 8.1.1). Here the 'small Ākâśa' is Brahman and does not mean ether, though it is the ordinary meaning of the word; nor does it mean the Jîva or individual soul, though there is the qualification 'small', which may show that it is a limited something. Why? Because the characteristics of Brahman occur later on in the text, "As large as this (external) ether is, so large is that Ākâśa within the heart" (Ch. 8.1.3), which clearly shows it is not actually small. Again Ākâśa cannot be compared with itself, nor can the limited individual soul be compared with the all-pervading ether. Therefore the two are precluded. Then we have the characteristics of Brahman. 'Both the earth and heaven are contained in it" (*Ibid.* 8.1.3), which shows that this Ākâśa is the support of the whole world. "It is the Self, free from sin, free from old age" (*Ibid.* 8. 1. 5), all of which are distinctly qualities of the highest Brahman.

गतिशब्दाभ्यां, तथा हि दृष्टं लिङ्गं च ॥ १५ ॥

गतिशब्दाभ्याम् From going and the word तथा हि likewise दृष्ट it is seen लिंगम् indicatory sign च and.

15. The small Ākâśa (is Brahman) on account of going (into Brahman) and of the word (Brahmaloka); it (*i.e.* the individual soul's going into Brahman) is likewise seen (from other Śruti texts); and (the daily going) is an indicatory sign (by which we can interpret the word Brahmaloka).

This Sûtra gives further reasons that the 'small Ākâśa' is Brahman.

"All these creatures day after day go into this Brahmaloka (*i.e.* they are merged in Brahman while fast asleep) and yet do not discover it" etc. (Ch. 8.3.2). This text shows that in deep sleep all Jîvas go daily into the 'small Ākâśa,' called here Brahmaloka (the world of Brahman), thus showing that the 'small Ākâśa' is Brahman. In other Śruti texts also we find that this going of the individual soul into Brahman in deep-sleep is mentioned: "He becomes united with the Real (Sat), he is merged in his own self" (*Ibid.* 6.8.1). The word 'Brahmaloka' is to be interpreted as Brahman Itself, and not as the world of Brahmâ, because of the indicatory sign in the text where it is said that the soul goes to his world every day, for it is not possible to go to the world of Brahmâ every day.

धृतेश्च, महिम्नोऽस्यास्मिन्नुपलब्धेः ॥ १६ ॥

धृतेः On account of the supporting (of the world by the Ākâśa) च moreover अस्य महिम्नः this greatness अस्मिन् in Brahman उपलब्धेः being seen.

16. Moreover on account of the supporting

(of the world by the small Ākâśa it is Brahman) for this greatness is seen in this (Brahman only from other scriptural texts).

"That Self is a bank, a limiting support, so that these worlds may not get confounded", (Ch. 8.4.1)—in which text is seen the glory of the 'small Ākâśa' by way of holding the worlds asunder. It is learnt beyond doubt from other texts that this greatness of supporting belongs to Brahman alone: "Under the mighty rule of that Immutable (Akṣara), O Gârgî, the sun and moon are held in their positions" (Bṛ. 3.8.9). See also *Ibid.* 4.4.22.

प्रसिद्धेश्च ॥ १७ ॥

प्रसिद्धेः Because of the well-knowing (meaning) च also.

17. Also because of the well-known meaning (of Ākâśa as Brahman the 'small Ākâśa' is Brahman).

"Âkâśa is the revealer of all names and forms" (Ch. 8.14.1); "All these beings take their rise from Ākâśa alone" (*Ibid.* 1.9.1). In all these passages 'Ākâśa' stands for Brahman.

इतरपरामर्शात् स इति चेत्, न, असम्भवात् ॥ १८ ॥

इतर-परामर्शात् Because of the reference to the other (*i.e.* the individual soul) सः he (the individual soul) इति चेत् if it be said न no असम्भवात् on account of impossibility.

18. Because of the reference to the other (*i.e.* the individual soul in a complementary passage) if it be said that he (the individual soul) (and not Brahman is meant by the 'small Ākâśa'), (we say) no, on account of the impossibility (of such an assumption).

"Now that being, the individual soul (Jîva) in deep sleep, which having risen above this earthly body" etc. (Ch. 8.3.4). Since in this complementary passage the individual soul is referred to, one may say that the 'small Ākâśa' of Ch. 8. 1. 1 is also the individual soul. It cannot be; for a comparison is made in Ch. 8. 1. 3 between the 'small Ākâśa' and the ether, which would be absurd if by 'small Ākâśa' Jîva were meant, because there can be no comparison between a thing that is limited like the individual soul and the all-pervading ether. The attributes like 'free from evil' of this Ākâśa, referred to in the passage under discussion, cannot be true of the individual soul. So Brahman is meant in that passage.

उत्तराच्चेत्, आविर्भूतस्वरूपस्तु ॥ १९ ॥

उत्तरात् From subsequent texts (in the chapter) चेत् if आविर्भूत-स्वरूप: with its real nature made manifest तु but.

19. If (it be said) that from subsequent texts (which contain references to the Jîva, 'small Ākâśa' means the Jîva) (we say) but (that reference to the Jîva is in so far as its) real nature (as non-different from Brahman) is made manifest.

An objection is again raised to justify that the 'small Ākâśa' refers to the individual soul. In Ch. in the later sections, *viz* sections 7-11 of chapter 8, the different states of the individual soul are mentioned. Section 7 begins thus: "That self which is free from sin...is what is to be searched" etc. Then we have, "That person who is seen in the eye (the individual soul) is the self" (Ch. 8. 7. 4); "He who moves glorified in dreams is the self" (*Ibid.* 8. 10. 1), "When a being is thus asleep, drawn in, perfectly serene, and sees no dreams, that is the self" (*Ibid.* 8. 11. 1). And in each of these descriptions of the self we have for it the qualifying terms, "immortal and fearless', which show that it is free from evil. It is clear that here the individual soul is meant, and not the supreme Lord, for the latter is free from these three states, *viz* waking, dream, and deep-sleep; and it is also said to be free from evil. Therefore 'small Ākâśa' in the preceding section refers to the soul and not to the supreme Lord.

This Sûtra refutes this and says that the reference is to the individual soul in its real nature as indentical with Brahman and not to the individual soul as such "As soon as it has approached the highest light it appears in its own form. It (then) is the highest Puruṣa" (*Ibid* 8. 12. 3). It is only as non-different from Brahman that the Jîva is free from evil etc. and not as the individual soul.

अन्यार्थश्च परामर्शः ॥ २० ॥

अन्यार्थः For a different purpose च and परामर्शः reference.

20. And the reference (to the individual soul) is for a different purpose.

The detailed reference to the three states of the individual soul (Jîva) is meant not to establish the nature of the individual soul as such, but to show finally its real nature, which is non-different from Brahman.

अल्पश्रुतेरिति चेत्, तदुक्तम् ॥ २१ ॥

अल्पश्रुतेः Because of the Śruti declaring its smallness इति चेत if it be said तत् that उक्तम् has already been explained.

21. If it be said that because the Śruti declares the limitedness (of this Ākâśa, therefore it cannot refer to the all-pervading Brahman); (we say) that has already been explained (as having reference to devout meditation only. *vide* 1. 2. 7).

Topic 6: That which shining, everything shines is Brahman.

In the last section, in the text quoted (Ch. 8. 12. 3) there is mention of 'the highest light'. This section is introduced to prove that what was referred to as 'light' is Brahman, and for this other texts are taken up for discussion in which this 'light' is mentioned.

अनुकृतेस्तस्य च ॥ २२ ॥

अनुकृतेः Because of the acting after तस्य Its च and.

22. Because of the acting after (*i.e.* shining after) (That which shining, everything else

shines) and (because by) Its (light everything else is lighted).

"There the sun does not shine, nor the moon...It shining, everything else shines after It, by Its light all this is lighted" (Mu. 2. 2. 11). Here 'It' refers to the supreme Brahman, the pure Consciousness, and not to any material light besides the sun and the moon. It is absurd to say that one light is lighted by another. Nor do we know of any material light besides the sun that can light it. 'It shining, everything else shines' shows that it is the principle of Intelligence which shines first of all. 'By its light all this is lighted' shows that it is the light of Intelligence, Consciousness or Brahman which illumines the whole world, luminous and non-luminous. That Brahman is self-luminous we learn from texts like, "It is the light of lights".

अपि च स्मर्यते ॥ २३ ॥

अपि च Moreover स्मर्यते the Smṛti states.

23. Moreover the Smṛti states (It to be the universal light).

"That the sun illumines not" etc. (Gîtâ 15. 6) and also "The light which residing in the sun illumines the whole world, that which is in the moon and in the fire—know that light to be Mine" (Gîtâ 15. 12).

Topic 7: The person of the size of a thumb is Brahman.

शब्दादेव प्रमितः ॥ २४ ॥

शब्दात् From the word एवं itself प्रमितः measured.

24. From the very word ('Lord' by which it is referred to in the text) (the being) measured (by the size of the thumb is Brahman).

"The being of the size of a thumb, resides in the centre of the body. (Knowing that) Lord of the past and future, one does not seek to hide oneself any more. This is That" (Ka. 2. 4. 12). The being referred to is Brahman, because he is spoken of as the Lord or ruler of the past and future. It cannot be the individual soul, though the limitation in size and residence in the centre of the body by themselves might be more applicable in its case. Moreover in reply to the request of Naciketa who wanted to know Brahman, Yama refers to this being of the size of a thumb thus: "That which you wanted to know is this."

हृद्यपेक्षया तु मनुष्याधिकारत्वात् ॥ २५ ॥

हृदि-अपेक्षया With reference to the heart तु but मनुष्य-अधिकारत्वात् man (alone) being entitled.

25. But with reference to (the space in) the heart (the highest Brahman is said to be of the size of a thumb); (and because) man alone is entitled (to the study of the Vedas).

How could the all-prevading Brahman be of the size of a thumb, as stated by the previous Sûtra? Because the space in the heart is of the size of a thumb, therefore Brahman, with reference to Its abiding within that space, is described as being of the size of a thumb. Since Brahman abides within the heart of all living creatures, why is the 'thumb' used as a standard?

Because man alone is entitled to the study of the Vedas and to the different Upâsanâs of Brahman prescribed in them, therefore it is with reference to him that thumb is used as the standard of measurement.

Topic 8: The right of the gods to the study of the Vedas

तदुपर्यपि बादरायणः संभवात् ॥ २६ ॥

तदुपरि Above them अपि also बादरायण: Bâdarâyaṇa सभवात् because (it is) possible.

26. (Beings) above them (men) also (are entitled to the study of the Vedas) because (it is) possible (for them also to attain Knowledge according to) Bâdarâyaṇa.

In Sûtras 26-38 there is a digression from the main topic in the Section. A doubt may arise from the previous Sûtra that as it is said that men alone are entitled to the study of the Vedas, the gods are thereby debarred. To remove this doubt that Sûtra is given. The gods are also entitled to it, according to Bâdarâyaṇa. How? Because it is possible for them also—since they too are corporeal beings—to have a desire for Brahmaloka or for final illumination and also to possess the necessary requisites (the four-fold qualification) for such illumination. In the Śruti also we find Indra and other gods living the life of Brahmacarya for attaining this knowledge of Brahman. For instance, Ch. 8. 11. 3; also Tai. 3. 1, where the god Varuṇa is said to have possessed that Knowledge which he teaches to his son Bhṛgu.

विरोधः कर्मणीति चेत्, अनेकप्रतिपत्तेर्दर्शनात् ॥ २७ ॥

विरोध: Contradiction कर्मणि to sacrifices इति चेत् if it be said न not अनेक-प्रतिपत्ते: the assumption of many (forms) दर्शनात् because it is found (in the scriptures).

27. If it be said (that the corporeality of the gods would involve) a contradiction to sacrifices; (we say) no, because we find (in the scriptures) the assumption (by the gods) of many (forms at one and the same time).

If gods possess bodies, then it would not be possible for one and the same god to be present in sacrifices performed simultaneously at different places. This is the objection, which is refuted by the latter part of the Sûtra on the ground that the gods, like the Yogîs, owing to their Yoga powers are capable of assuming several forms (Kâyavyûha) simultaneously. See Ch. 7. 26. 2. Again as a sacrifice consists in making offerings by the sacrificer to some divinity, many persons at the same time may make such offerings to a single divinity, even as many persons can at the same time salute a single person.

शब्द इति चेत्, न, अतः प्रभवात् प्रत्यक्षानुमानाभ्याम् ॥ २८ ॥

शब्दे With regard to (Vedic) words इति चेत् if it be said न no अत: from these (words) प्रभवात् because of the creation प्रत्यक्ष-अनुमानाभ्याम् from direct perception and inference.

28. If it be said (that the corporeality of the gods would involve a contradiction) with regard

to (Vedic) words, (we say) no, because of the creation (of the world together with the gods) from these (words), (as is known) from direct perception (Śruti) and inference (Smṛti).

A further objection is raised with respect to the corporeality of the gods. If they have a body, they too like men would be subject to births and deaths. Now all the words in the Vedas according to Pûrva Mîmâṁsâ are eternal. So also every word has for its counterpart a form, an object which it denotes. The relation between a name or word and form (the object) is eternal. The word or name, its object, and their relation are eternal verities. Now in the Vedas we find words like Indra, Varuṇa, etc.—the names of the gods. If these gods are eternal, since they possess bodies, then these words cannot have their eternal counterpart, the object. So the eternity and authoritativeness of the Vedas, which are based on the eternal relation between the word and its object, would be a myth. This is the main objection. It is answered thus. Each word of the Vedas has an objective counterpart, which is not an individual but a type. The word 'cow', for instance, has for its counterpart the object, which is a type and as such is eternal and does not depend on the birth or death of individuals belonging to that type. Similar is the case with words like Indra, Varuṇa, etc. Words representing the gods etc. have for their counterpart objects that are types and not individuals. Again Indra is the name of any one who would occupy that exalted position, like the word 'king' in ordinary parlance. So there is no contradiction to Vedic words. As a matter of fact, the world including the gods etc. have originated from Vedic words. This does not mean that the Vedic words constitute the material cause of these things, which Brahman alone is, as stated in Sûtra 1. 1. 2. What then is meant? According to Indian philosophy the universe and its objects have both name and form as the conditions of their manifestation. There can be no mental state (Citta-vṛtti) unconditioned by name and form. The thought wave first manifests as a word and then as the more concrete form. The idea is the essence, and the form is, as it were, the outer crust. What is true of the individual mind is also true of the cosmic mind. In this sense only is the world said to be created, rather manifested, from the Vedic words. This is endorsed by the Śruti and Smṛti. In the Vedas it is said that the Lord uttered different words before creating different types of beings (*vide* Bṛ. 1. 2. 4). "The several names, actions, and conditions of all things He shaped in the beginning from the words of the Vedas" (Manu 1.21).

अत एव च नित्यत्वम् ॥ २९ ॥

अत एव From this very reason च also नित्यत्वम् the eternity.

29. From this very reason also (results) the eternity (of the Vedas).

Since the objects are eternal, that is, gods etc. as types are eternal, the Vedic words are eternal. This establishes the eternal nature of the Vedas. The Vedas were not written by anybody. They are impersonal and eternal. The Ṛṣis only discovered them but were not authors of the Vedic texts. "By means of their past good deeds (the priests) attained the capacity to understand the Vedas; (then) they found them dwelling in the Ṛṣis" (Ṛg-Veda 10.71.3), which shows that the Vedas are eternal.

समाननामरूपत्वाच्चावृत्तावप्यविरोधो दर्शनात्
स्मृतेश्च ॥ ३० ॥

समान-नामरूपत्वात् Because of similar names and forms च and आवृत्तौ in the revolving of the world cycles अपि even अविरोधः no contradiction दर्शनात् from the Śruti स्मृतेः from the Smṛti च and.

30. And because of the sameness of names and forms (in every fresh cycle) there is no contradiction (to the eternity of the Vedic words) even in the revolving of the world cycles, as is seen from the Śruti and the Smṛti.

An objection is raised. Since at the end of a cycle everything is completely destroyed and creation begins afresh at the beginning of the next cycle, there is a break in the continuity of existence; so even as types the gods are not eternal. This upsets the eternal relation of Vedic words and the objects they represent, and consequently the eternity of the Vedas and their authority fall to the ground. This Sûtra refutes it. Just as a person after waking from deep-sleep finds no break in the continuity of existence, so also in the state of Pralaya (end of a cycle) the world is in a potential state—in seed form—in ignorance, and not completely destroyed; at the beginning of the next cycle it is again manifested into a gross form with all the previous variety of names and forms. As the world does not become absolutely non-existent, the eternity of the relation between Vedic words and their objects is not contradicted, and consequently the authoritativeness of the Vedas remains. This eternal existence of the world in gross and fine forms alternatively and the similarity of the names and forms are brought out by the Śruti and Smṛti texts. "As formerly the Lord ordered the sun and the moon, heaven, earth, the sky" etc. Ṛg-Veda 10.190. 3).

मध्वादिष्वसंभवादनधिकारं जैमिनिः ॥ ३१ ॥

मध्वादिषु In Madhu Vidyâ etc. असंभवात् on account of the impossibility अनधिकारं disqualification जैमिनिः Jaimini (is of opinion).

31. On account of the impossibility (of the gods) being qualified for Madhu Vidyâ etc. Jaimini (is of opinion that the gods) are not qualified (either for Upâsanâs or for the knowledge of Brahman).

In many of the Upâsanâs (devout meditations) a person is asked to meditate on the self of some god or other. For example, in Madhu Vidyâ one is to meditate on the sun as honey (something helpful). Such a meditation will be impossible for the sun-god. Hence in Upâsanâs where one has to meditate on the self of certain gods, these divinities themselves would naturally be disqualified; for the same person cannot be both the object of meditation and the worshipper. So Jaimini thinks that the gods are not qualified for these devout meditations or for the knowledge of the supreme Brahman.

ज्योतिषि भावाच्च ॥ ३२ ॥

ज्योतिषि As mere spheres of light भावात् because (used) in the sense च and.

32. And (the gods are not qualified for Vidyâs) because (the words 'sun', 'moon', etc. spoken of as gods) are used in the sense of mere spheres of light.

A further objection is given. There is no proof as to the existence of gods with hands, feet, etc., and with desires—which would qualify them for meditations and Knowledge. These are mere names of planets and luminary objects and as such are material inert things. Consequently they are not qualified for any kind of Vidyâ (meditation) prescribed in the scriptures.

भावं तु बादरायणः, अस्ति हि ॥ ३३ ॥

भावं The existence (of qualification) तु but बादरायणः (sage) Bâdarâyaṇa(maintains) अस्ति does exist हि because.

33. But Bâdarâyaṇa (maintains) the existence (of qualification on the part of the gods for the knowledge of Brahman), because (all those causes like body, desires, etc., which qualify one for such knowledge) do exist (in the case of the gods).

Bâdarâyaṇa thinks that besides the luminary orbs like the sun, moon, etc., each of them has a presiding deity of that name with body, intelligence, desires, etc., and as such there being all the causes which can qualify them for the Upâsanâs and supreme Knowledge, the gods also are entitled to them. The fact that the sun-god cannot be entitled to Madhu Vidyâ because he cannot meditate on the sun, *i.e.* himself, does not disqualify him for other devout meditations or for the knowledge of Brahman. Similar is the case with other gods.

Topic 9: The right of the Śūdras to the Study of the Vedas discussed.

शुगस्य तदनादरश्रवणात्, तदाद्रवणात्, सूच्यते हि ॥ ३४ ॥

शुक् Grief अस्य his तत्-अनादरश्रवणात् from hearing his (the Ṛṣi's) contemptuous words तत् that (grief) आद्रवणात् owing to his approaching सूच्यते is referred to हि because.

34. His (king Jânaṣruti's) grief (arose) from hearing the contemptuous words (of the Ṛṣi in the form of a swan); owing to his approaching (Raikva overwhelmed with) that (grief) (Raikva called him Śûdra); because it (the grief) is referred to (by Raikva, who could read his mind).

In the previous Sûtra it has been shown that the gods are entitled to the Vedas and Knowledge. This Sûtra discusses whether the Śûdras are entitled to them or not. Since, like the gods, the Śûdras also are possessed of a body, strength, and desires, it naturally follows that they too are entitled. In Chândogya 4.2.5 Raikva at first calls Jânaśruti, a Śûdra, when he comes for instruction with presents, which are refused. But when he appears a second time, Raikva again calls him a Śûdra, but this time accepts his presents and teaches him. So it is maintained that the Śûdras also are qualified for Knowledge.

This Sûtra refutes the view and denies the right to the study of the Vedas for a Śûdra by caste, since the word 'Śûdra' occurring in the text referred to does not denote a Śûdra by birth, which is its conventional meaning, for Jânaśruti was a Kṣatriya king (Ch. 4.1.3). Here we must take the etymological meaning of the word, which is "He rushed into grief" or "He in his grief immediately approached Raikva". The following Sûtra also shows that he was a Kṣatriya.

क्षत्रियत्वगतेश्चोत्तरत्र चैत्ररथेन लिङ्गात् ॥ ३५ ॥

क्षत्रियत्वगतेः (His) Kṣatriyahood being known च and उत्तरत्र later on चैत्ररथेन लिङ्गात् by the indicatory sign (of his being mentioned) along with a descendant of Chitraratha (a Kṣatriya).

35. And because the Kṣatriyahood (of Jânaśruti) is known later on by the indicatory sign (of his being mentoined) along with a descendant of Chitraratha (a Kṣatriya).

Jânaśruti is mentioned with the Kṣatriya Chaitraratha Abhipratârin in connection with the same Vidyâ, and so we can infer that Jânaśruti also was a Kṣatriya, for as a rule equals alone are mentioned together.

संस्कारपरामर्शात् तदभावाभिलापाच्च ॥ ३६ ॥

संस्कार-परामर्शात् Purificatory ceremonies being mentioned तत्-अभाव-अभिलापात् its absence being declared च and.

36. Because purificatory ceremonies are mentioned (in the case of the twice-born) and their absence are declared (in the case of the Śûdras).

Purificatory ceremonies like Upanayana etc. are declared by the scriptures to be a necessary condition of the study of all kinds of knowledge or Vidyâ; but these are meant only for the higher castes. Their absence in the case of the Śûdras is repeatedly declared in the scriptures. "Śûdras do not incur sin (by eating prohibited food), nor have they any purificatory rights" etc. (Manu 10.12.6). Consequently they are not entitled to the study of the Vedas.

तदभावनिर्धारणे च प्रवृत्तेः ॥ ३७ ॥

तदभाव-निर्धारणे On the ascertainment of the absence of that (Śûdrahood) च and प्रवृत्तेः from inclination.

37. And because the inclination (on the part of Gautama to impart Knowledge is seen only) on the ascertainment of the absence of Śûdrahood (in Jâbâla Satyakāma).

That Śûdras are not qualified is known also from the fact that great teachers like Gautama made sure before imparting Knowledge that disciples like Jâbâla Satyakâma were not Śûdras. See Ch. 4.4.5.

श्रवणाध्ययनार्थप्रतिषेधात् स्मृतेश्च ॥ ३८ ॥

श्रवण-अध्ययन-अर्थ-प्रतिषेधात् Because of the prohibition of hearing, studying, and understanding स्मृतेः in the Smṛti च and.

38. And because of the prohibition in the Smṛti of hearing and studying (the Vedas) and knowing their meaning and performing Vedic rites (to Śûdras, they are not entitled to the knowledge of Brahman).

Sûtras 34-38 disqualify the Śûdra for the knowledge of Brahman through the study of the Vedas. But it is possible for them to attain that knowledge through the Purâṇas and the epics (*Râmâyana* and *Mahābhārata*).

The digression begun from Sûtra 26 ends here and he general topic is again taken up.

Topic 10: The Prâṇa in which everything trembles is Brahman.

In topic 7 it was proved that the reference to the îva was to inculcate the knowledge of Brahman, as the ɔrmer is really identical with Brahman. But in the text ɔ be discussed 'Prâna' cannot refer to Brahman as ıch identity is not possible—this seems to be the line f thinking of the opponent, who therefore takes up his topic for discussion.

कम्पनात् ॥ ३९ ॥

कम्पनात् On account of vibration.

39. (Prâṇa is Brahman) on account of the vibration (spoken of the whole world).

"Whatever there is in the whole world has come out of and trembles in the Prâṇa" etc. (Ka. 2.6.2). Here 'Prâṇa' is Brahman and not the vital force. Why? First because of the context, since Brahman is the topic in the previous and subsequent texts. Again "The whole world trembles in Prâṇa"—in this we have reference to an attribute of Brahman, It being the abode of the whole world. It is the cause of the life of the whole world including the Prâṇa. Lastly, immortality is declared to him who knows this Prâṇa, and 'Prâṇa' is also often used to denote Brahman in the Śruti.

Topic 11: The 'light' is Brahman.

In the last topic 'Prâṇa' was taken to mean Brahman from the context. But in the text taken up for discussion in this topic, there is no such context by which 'light' can be taken to be Brahman—so says the opponent.

ज्योतिर्दर्शनात् ॥ ४० ॥

ज्योतिः Light दर्शनात् on account of (Brahman) being seen.

40. Light (is Brahman) on account of (Brahman) being seen (as the subject of the texts).

"Thus does that serene being, arising from the body, appear in its own form as soon as it has approached the highest light." (Ch. 8.12.3). Here 'highest light' stands for Brahman. Why? Because Brahman is the subject of the whole section. The 'highest light' is also called the highest Person in that text itself later on. Freedom from the body is said to belong to that being which is one with this 'light'. Disembodied state or Freedom can arise only from being identified with Brahman.

Topic 12: The Ākâśa which reveals names and forms is Brahman

आकाशोऽर्थान्तरत्वादिव्यपदेशात् ॥ ४१ ॥

आकाशः Ākâśa अर्थान्तरत्वादि-व्यपदेशात् because it is declared to be something different etc.

41 Ākāśa (is Brahman) because it is declared to be something different etc. (from names and forms and yet their revealer).

"That which is called Ākâśa is the revealer of all names and forms. That within which these names and forms are, is Brahman, the immortal, the Self" (Ch. 8.14.1).

Here 'Ākâśa' is Brahman. Why? Because names and forms are said to be within this Ākâśa, which is therefore different from these. In this phenomenal world everything is conditioned by name and form, and Brahman alone is beyond them. Ākâśa is said to be the revealer of names and forms; and as the inner Ruler of the whole world of names and forms it cannot be anything else but Brahman. Moreover, epithets like 'Infinite', 'Immortal', 'Self' also show that 'Ākâśa' here refers to Brahman.

Topic 13: The Self consisting of knowledge is not the individual soul but Brahman.

In the previous topic because Ākâśa was spoken of as different from names and forms, it was taken as Brahman. This argument is objected to by the opponent, who cites that even difference is spoken of with respect to the individual soul and Brahman, who are really identical. So this topic is taken up for discussion.

सुषुप्त्युत्क्रान्त्योर्भेदेन ॥ ४२ ॥

सुषुप्ति-उत्क्रान्त्योः In deep-sleep and death भेदेन as different.

42. Because of the supreme Self being shown as different (from the individual soul) in the states of deep-sleep and death.

In the sixth chapter of the Bṛhadâraṇyaka Upaniṣad in reply to the question, "Which is that Self" (4.3.7), a lengthy exposition of the nature of the Self is given. The question is whether the Self is the supreme Self or the individual soul. This Sûtra says it is the supreme Self. Why? Because it is shown to be different from the individual self in the state of deep-sleep and at the time of death. "This person, embraced by the supremely in telligent Self, knows nothing that is without or within" (Bṛ. 4.3.21), which shows that in deep-sleep the 'person' which represents the individual soul, is different from the supreme Self, called here the supremely intelligent Self.

The 'person' is the individual soul, because the absence of the knowledge of external things and things within in deep-sleep can be predicated only of the individual soul, which is the knower, and the supremely intelligent Self is Brahman because such intelligence can be predicated of Brahman only. Similarly at the time of death (Bṛ 4.3.35). Therefore Brahman is the chief topic in this section. The extensive discourse on the individual soul in this section is not to establish its Jîvahood, but to show that it is in reality not different from Brahman.

पत्यादिशब्देभ्यः ॥ ४३ ॥

43. On account of words like 'Lord' etc. (the Self in the text under discussion is the supreme Self).

Epithets like 'Lord', 'Ruler', etc. are applied to the 'Self' discussed in the text (*Vide* Bṛ. 4.4.22), and those are apt only in the case of Brahman, for these epithets show that the thing spoken of is beyond bondage. So the word 'Self' denotes the supreme Self and not the Jîva.

CHAPTER I

Section IV

In top c 5, section I, it has been shown that as the Sâṁkhyan Pradhâna is not based on scriptural authority and that as the Śruti texts all refer to an intelligent principle as the first Cause, Brahman is that first Cause. In all the subsequent Sûtras of the first three sections it has been shown how all the Vedânta texts refer to Brahman. Now the fact that the Pradhâna is *not* based on scriptural authority is questioned by the opponent, and his objections are being answered. The whole of section 4 practically answers all objections from the Sâṁkhyan standpoint.

Topic 1: The Mahat and Avyakta of the Kaṭha Upaniṣad do not refer to the Sâṁkhyan categories.

In the last topic of the previous section, by a reference to the well-known individual soul, Brahman, which is not so well known, was taught. So the opponent in this topic holds that the reference to Avyakta in the text to be quoted should be taken to deal with the well-known Sâṁkhyan category.

आनुमानिकमप्येकेषामिति चेत्, न, शरीररूपकविन्यस्तगृहीतेः, दर्शयति च ॥ १ ॥

आनुमानिकम् That which is inferred (*i.e.* the Pradhâna) अपि also एकेषाम् in some (recensions of the texts) इति चेत् if it be said न no शरीर-रूपक-विन्यस्त गृहीतेः because it is mentioned in a simile referring to the body दर्शयति (the Śruti) explains च too.

1. If it be said that in some (recensions of the Vedas) that which is inferred (*i.e.* the Pradhâna) (is) also (mentioned), (we say) no, because (the word 'Avyakta' occurring in the Kaṭha Upaniṣad) is mentioned in a simile referring to the body (and means the body itself and not the Pradhāna of the Sāṁkhyas); (the Śruti) too explains (it).

An objection is again raised here by the Sâṁkhyas that the Pradhâna is also based on scriptural authority, for some Śâkhâs (Vedic recensions) like the Kaṭha Śâkhâ (school) contain expressions wherein the Pradhâna seems to be referred to: "Beyond the Mahat (Great) there is the Avyakta (Undeveloped), beyond the Undeveloped is the Puruṣa (Being)" etc. (Ka. 1.3.11). The word 'Avyakta', they say, here refers to the Pradhâna. Because the words 'Mahat', 'Avyakta', and 'Puruṣa', which occur in the same order as mentioned in the Sâṁkhya philosophy, occur in the text, and so they are recognized to be the same categories of the Sâṁkhyas.

This Sûtra after raising this objection refutes it thus: The word 'Avyakta' is used in connection with a simile referring to the body, and does not refer to the Pradhâna. In that word we recognize something mentioned in an earlier text. "Know that the soul is the rider of the chariot and the body the chariot. Consider the intellect to be the charioteer and the mind the reins. The senses, they say, are the horses, and their roads are the sense-objects" etc. (Ka. 1.3.3-4). All these things that are referred to in these verses are to be found in the following: "The objects are superior to the senses, the mind is superior to the objects, the intellect is superior to the mind, the Mahat is superior again to the intellect, the Avyakta is superior to the Mahat, and the Purusa is superior to the Avyakta. Nothing is superior to the Puruṣa," etc. (Ka. 1.3.10-11).

Now compare these two quotations. The senses, mind and intellect, mentioned in the earlier texts, are to be found in these later texts. The Ātman of the earlier texts is denoted by the 'Puruṣa' of the later ones. The Mahat of the later texts mean the cosmic intellect and so is included in the intellect of the earlier texts, where it is used in a comprehensive sense to include both the individual and cosmic intellects. What remains is only the body in the earlier texts, and Avyakta in the later texts; and so Avyakta means the body here and not the Pradhâna. We shall not be justified in interpreting a Śruti according to Sâṁkhyan technicalities. For the purpose of recognition a comparison should be made not with the Smṛti, but with similar passages of the Śruti itself, like those cited above.

सूक्ष्मं तु तदर्हत्वात् ॥ २ ॥

सूक्ष्मं Subtle तु but तदर्हत्वात् because it can be properly so designated.

2. But the subtle (cause of the body is meant

by the term 'Avyakta') because it can be properly so designated.

An objection is raised. As the body is gross and developed, how can it be referred to by the term 'Avyakta' (Undeveloped)? The answer is, here, not the gross body but the causal substance, *e.* the five uncompounded elements out of which the body is built, is meant. They, being subtle and not fully manifest and also being beyond sense perception, can be properly designated by the term 'Avyakta' (Undeveloped) It is also a common thing to denote the effect by the cause and hence indirectly the gross body is referred to here. "Mix the Soma with the cow (*i.e.* milk)" (Ṛg-Veda 9.46.4).

तदधीनत्वादर्थवत् ॥ ३ ॥

तदधीनत्वात् On account of its dependence अर्थवत् is fitting.

3. On account of its dependence (on the Lord), it fits in (with our theory).

It may be said that if a subtle causal condition of the gross world is thus admitted, it is as good as accepting the Pradhâna. This Sûtra makes the difference clear. While the Pradhâna of the Sâṁkhyas is an independent entity, the subtle causal condition admitted here is dependent on the supreme Lord. Such a causal condition has necessarily to be admitted, for without that the Lord cannot create. It is the potential power, the causal potentiality inherent in Brahman. It is Nescience. That explains why, when one's ignorance is destroyed by Knowledge, there is no possibility of that liberated soul getting into bondage again. About this ignorance you can neither say that it is, nor that it is not; it is an illusion and so it is reasonably called Undeveloped (Avyakta). This ignorance or creative power cannot create of itself without the instrumentality of the Lord. The illusion of a snake in a rope is not possible merely through ignorance without the rope. So also the world cannot be created merely by ignorance without the substratum, the Lord. Hence it is dependent on the Lord. Yet the Lord is not in the least affected by this ignorance, even as the poison does not affect the snake which has it. "Know then Prakṛti is Mâyâ and the great Lord the ruler of Mâyâ" (Śv. 4.10). So the Avyakta is a helper, as it were, to Īśvara in His creation, and hence such an Avyakta dependent on the Lord is significant and has to be admitted, says the Sûtra.

ज्ञेयत्वावचनाच्च ॥ ४ ॥

ज्ञेयत्वावचनात् Because it is not mentioned (as something) to be known च and.

4. And because it is not mentioned (that the Avyakta) is to be known (it cannot be the Pradhâna of the Sāṁkhyas).

Liberation, according to the Sâṁkhyas, results when the difference between the Puruṣa and the Avyakta (Prakṛti) is known. Hence the Avyakta, with them, is to be known. But here there is no question of knowing the Avyakta, and as such it cannot be the Pradhâna of the Sâṁkhyas.

वदतीति चेत्, न, प्राज्ञो हि प्रकरणात् ॥ ५ ॥

वदति Does state इति चेत् if it be said न no प्राज्ञः intelligent Self हि for प्रकरणात् from the context.

5. If it be said (that the Śruti) does state (that the Avyakta has to be known and therefore it is the Pradhâna); (we say) no, for (it is) the intelligent (supreme) Self (which is meant), since that is the topic.

"He who has perceived that which is without sound, without touch...beyond the Mahat (Great) and unchangeable, is freed from the jaws of death" (Ka. 1.3 15). The Sâṁkhyas hold that in this text the Śruti says that the Pradhâna has to be known to attain Freedom; for the description given of the entity to be known tallies with the Pradhâna, which is also beyond the Mahat. The Sûtra refutes this saying that by Avyakta, the one beyond the Mahat (Great) etc., the intelligent (supreme) Self is meant, as that is the subject-matter of that section.

त्रयाणामेव चैवमुपन्यासः प्रश्नश्च ॥ ६ ॥

त्रयाणाम् Of three एव only च and एवम् thus उपन्यासः introduction प्रश्नः question च and.

6. And thus the question and elucidation with

reference to three only (of which the Pradhâna is not one) (is consistent).

In the Kaṭha Upaniṣad, Naciketas asks Yama three questions only, *viz.* about the fire (sacrifice), the individual soul, and the supreme Self. The Pradhâna is not mentioned. So we cannot expect Yama to go out of his way and treat of the Pradhâna, which has not been inquired into

महद्वच्च ॥ ७ ॥

महद्वत् Like Mahat च and.

7. And like Mahat (the word 'Avyakta' does not refer to any Sāṁkhyan category).

The Mahat according to the Sâṁkhyas means the first-born, the cosmic intelligence; but in the Vedic texts it is associated with the word 'Self'. Passages like "The Mahat (Great) is superior to the intellect" (Ka. 1.3.10), clearly show that it is used in a different sense from the intellect and refer to the Self in different aspects. Similarly though the Avyakta in the Sâṁkhya philosophy may mean the Pradhâna or Prakṛti, in the Śruti texts it means something different. So the Pradhâna is not based on scriptural authority but is a mere inferred thing.

Topic 2: The tri-coloured Ajâ of the Śvetâśvatara Upaniṣad is not the Sâṁkhyan Pradhâna.

In the last topic the opponent was refuted on the ground that the mere mention of the word 'Avyakta' was not sufficient reason to identify it as the Sâṁkhyan category called the Pradhâna. The opponent here gives more analogies from the Śruti texts to uphold his view.

चमसवदविशेषात् ॥ ८ ॥

चमसवत् Like the bowl अविशेषात् for want of special characteristics.

8. (The word 'Ajâ' cannot be asserted to mean the Pradhâna) for want of special characteristics, as in the case of the bowl.

"There is one Ajâ, red, white, and black producing manifold offspring of the same appearance (colour)" (Śv. 4.5). The question is whether this 'Ajâ' refers to the Sâṁkhya category Prakṛti or to the fine elements fire, water, and earth. The Sâṁkhyas hold that 'Ajā' here means the Pradhâna, the unborn; and red, white, and black refer to its three constituents, the Guṇas—Sattva, Rajas, and Tamas. This Sûtra refutes this, saying that in the absence of special characteristics there is no basis for such a special assertion. The text can be interpreted otherwise also. "There is a bowl that has its opening below and bulging at the top" (Bṛ. 2.2.3) It is impossible to decide from the text itself what kind of bowl is meant. So also it is impossible to fix the meaning of 'Ajā' from the text alone. As in the case of the bowl the complementary texts fix what kind of bowl is meant, so also here we have to refer this passage to supplementary scriptural texts to fix the meaning of 'Ajâ' and not assert that it means the Pradhâna.

ज्योतिरुपक्रमा तु, तथा ह्यधीयत एके ॥ ९ ॥

ज्योतिरुपक्रमा (Elements) beginning with light but तथा so हि because अधीयते read एके some.

9. But (the elements) beginning with light (are meant by the word Ajâ), because some read so.

The Chândogya assigns to the elements fire, water, and earth, created by the Lord, red, white, and black colours. *Vide* Ch. 6.2.2-4 and 6.4.1.

This passage fixes the meaning of the word 'Ajâ' here. It refers to the three elementary substances, *viz* fire, earth, and water, from which the rest of the creation has been produced. It is not the Prakṛti of the Sâṁkhyas consisting of the three Guṇas. In the former interpretation the three colours can be taken in their primary sense, whereas they can represent the three Guṇas in a secondary sense only. Moreover, the force of the recognition of the Śruti is stronger; that is to say, if we can beyond doubt recognize in this passage what is elsewhere mentioned in the Śruti, that will be more reasonable than to recognize categories of a Smṛti in the Śruti texts

कल्पनोपदेशाच्च मध्वादिवदविरोधः ॥ १० ॥

कल्पनोपदेशात् Instruction having been given through imagery च and मध्वादिवत् as in the case of 'honey' etc अविरोधः no incongruity.

10. And instruction having been given through

the imagery (of a goat) (there is) no incongruity, (even) as in the case of 'honey' (standing for the sun in Madhuvidyâ for the purpose of devout meditation) and such other cases.

The word 'Ajâ' refers to something unborn; so how can it refer to the three causal elements of the Chândogya, which are something created? It is incongruous, says the objector.

There is no incongruity in it, answers the Sûtra, as the elements are spoken of through the imagery of a she goat (Ajâ). Even as the sun in Madhuvidyâ is represented as honey in the text, "The sun indeed is the honey" (Ch. 3.1.1), so also are the three elementary substances of the Chândogya represented as the goat. A she-goat may be black, white, and red, and may give birth to offspring representing her in colour. Similarly out of the combination of fire, water, and earth, having red, white, and black colours respectively, are produced all the inanimate and animate beings of similar colours. The combination of the fine elements, fire, water, and earth is here spoken of by the imagery of a tri-coloured goat, and that is why it is called an Ajâ, which does not however mean unborn.

Topic 3 : The five-fold people of Bṛ. 4.4.17 are not the twenty-five Sâṁkhyan categories.

न संख्योपसंग्रहादपि, नानाभावादतिरेकाच्च ॥ ११ ॥

न Not संख्योपसंग्रहादपि even from the statement of the number नानाभावात् on account of the differences अतिरेकात् on account of the excess च and.

11. Even from the statement of the number (five-fold five, *i.e.* twenty-five categories, by the Śruti, it is) not (to be presumed that the Śruti refers to the Pradhâna) on account of the differences (in the categories) and the excess (over the number of the Sâṁkhyan categories).

"That in which the five groups of five and the (subtle) ether are placed, that very Ātman" etc. (Bṛ. 4.4.17). Now five times five makes twenty-five, which is exactly the number of the Sâṁkhyan categories. So the Sâṁkhyas say that here is the scriptural authority for their philosophy. This Sûtra refutes such an assumption. For the Sâṁkhyan categories cannot be divided into groups of five on any basis of similarity, for all the twenty-five categories differ from each other. Secondly, the mention of the ether in the text as a separate category would make the number twenty-six in all, contrary to the Sâṁkhyan theory.

प्राणादयो वाक्यशेषात् ॥ १२ ॥

प्राणादय: The vital force etc. वाक्यशेषात् because of the complementary passage.

12. (The five people referred to are) the vital force etc., because (we find it to be so) from the complementary passage.

"They who know the vital force of the vital force, the eye of the eye, the ear of the ear, the food of the food, the mind of the mind," etc. (Bṛ. Mâdhyandina recension 4.4.21). The 'five people' refer to this vital force and the other four of the text, which are cited to describe Brahman.

ज्योतिषैकेषामसत्यन्ने ॥ १३ ॥

ज्योतिषा By light एकेषाम् of some असति अन्ने food not being mentioned.

13. (In the text) of some (the Kâṇva recension) food not being mentioned (in the complementary passage referred to in the previous Sûtra), (the number is made up) by 'light' (mentioned in the previous verse).

"That immortal Light of lights the gods worship as longevity" (Bṛ. 4.4.16). Though food is not mentioned in the text cited in the last Sûtra according to the Kâṇva recension of the Śatapatha Brâhmaṇa, yet the four of that verse, together with 'light' mentioned in the text cited above, would make the 'five people'.

Topic 4: There is no contradiction in the scriptures as regards the fact that Brahman is the first Cause.

In the last three topics it has been shown that the Pradhâna of the Sâṁkhyas is not based on the scriptures, and consequently it was established that all the Śruti texts refer to Brahman as the first Cause. The opponent now tries to show that as the Vedânta texts contradict each other with respect to the order of creation, they are therefore of doubtful import, and consequently it is safer to accept the Pradhâna, which is established by reason and inference, as the first Cause.

कारणत्वेन चाकाशादिषु यथाव्यपदिष्टोक्तेः ॥ १४ ॥

कारणत्वेन As the (first) Cause च and आकाशादिषु as regards ether and so on यथा व्यपदिष्टोक्तेः being represented (in other texts) as taught (in one text).

14. (Although) as regards (things created, like ether and so on the Vedânta texts differ), (yet there is no such conflict with respect to Brahman) as the first Cause, (on account of Its) being represented (in other texts) as taught (in one text).

The Sâṁkhyas contend that though the Pradhâna cannot be the first Cause according to the Śruti, yet Brahman also cannot be taken to be the first Cause taught by the Śruti. Why? Because there is conflict as regards the order of creation; for some texts say that it is Ākâśa that was first produced from Brahman, some say that it is Prâṇa, others that it is fire. This Sûtra says that though there are conflicting views with respect to things created, that is, as regards the order of creation, yet since it is not the main object of the Śruti to teach about creation, it matters little. The main object in these descriptions is to teach that Brahman is the first Cause, and with respect to this there is no conflict; for every Vedânta text holds that Brahman is that.

समाकर्षात् ॥ १५ ॥

15. On account of the connection (with passage referring to Brahman, non-existence does not mean absolute non-existence).

A further objection is raised that even as regards

the first Cause there is a conflict, for some texts say that the Self created these worlds (Ai. Ā. 2.4.1.2-3), others say that creation originated from non-existence (Tai. 2.7). Again existence is taught as the first Cause in some texts (Ch. 6.2.1-2). Spontaneous creation also is taught by some texts (Bṛ. 1.4.7). On account of these conflicting texts it cannot be said that all the Vedânta texts refer to Brahman uniformly as the first Cause. These objections are answered as follows: "This was indeed non-existence in the beginning" (Tai. 2.7). Non-existence here does not mean absolute non-existence but undifferentiated existence. Existence was at the beginning undifferentiated into name and form. In the texts of the Taittirîya Upaniṣad Brahman is definitely described as not being non-existence. "He who knows Brahman as non-existing becomes himself non-existing. He who knows Brahman as existing is known by sages as existing" (Tai. 2.6). This Brahman is again described as having wished to be many and created this world. Again "How can that which is be created from non-existence?" (Ch. 6.2.2) clearly denies such a possibility. "Now this was then undifferentiated" (Bṛ. 1.4.7), does not speak of spontaneous creation without a ruler, for it is connected with another passage where it is said, "He has entered here to the very tips of the finger-nails" (Br. 1.4.7), where 'He' refers to this ruler, and hence we have to take that the Lord, the ruler, developed what was undeveloped. Similarly Brahman, which is described in one place as existence, is referred to in another place as being the Self of all by the word 'Ātman' So all texts uniformly point to Brahman as the first Cause, and there is no conflict as regards this.

Topic 5: He who is the maker of the sun, moon, etc. is Brahman and not Prâṇa (the vital force) or the individual soul.

In the last topic the word 'existence' occurring in one passage helped us to interpret non-existence occuring in another passage as undifferentiated existence and not absolute non-existence. But the opponent now takes up for discussion texts where the words 'Prâṇa' etc. cannot be reasonably interpreted to mean Brahman, though It is mentioned in another text.

जगद्वाचित्वात् ॥ १६ ॥

जगत्-वाचित्वात् Because (it) denotes the world.

16. (He of whom all this is the work is Brahman) because (the work) denotes the world.

"He, O Bâlâki, who is the maker of these persons (whom you mentioned), and whose work this is—is alone to be known" (Kau. 4.19). In this section Bâlâki first describes the several individual souls residing in the sun, moon, ether, etc. as Brahman. Ajâtaśatru says that these are not the true Brahman and proceeding to teach the real Brahman says, "He who is the maker of these persons is alone to be known and not these persons." Here who is the maker of the sun, moon, etc. is the question. The opponent holds he is either the chief Prâṇa or the individual soul. He is the chief Prâṇa, for the activity of motion connected with work refers to Prâṇa, and Prâṇa is also mentioned in a complementary passage: "Then he becomes one vith that Prâṇa alone" (Kau. 4.20). It may also be the ïva, for in "As the master feeds with his people...thus loes the conscious self feed with the other selfs" (Kau. .20) it is referred to. The Sûtra refutes all this and says t is Brahman that is referred to by 'maker' in the text; or Brahman is taught here. "I shall teach you Brahnan." Again 'this', which means the world, is his work—vhich clearly points out that the 'he' is none other han Brahman. Therefore the maker is neither Prâṇa ıor the individual soul, but the supreme Lord.

जीवमुख्यप्राणलिङ्गान्नेति चेत्, तद्व्याख्यातम् ॥ १७ ॥

जीव-मुख्यप्राण-लिङ्गात् On account of characteristics of he individual soul and the chief Prâṇa न not इति चेत् if t be said तत् that व्याख्यातम् has already been explained.

17. If it be said that on account of the characeristics of the individual soul and the chief 'râṇa (to be found in the text, Brahman is) not referred to by the word 'maker' in the passage ited), (we reply) that has already been explained.

See note on 1.1.31.

अन्यार्थं तु जैमिनिः प्रश्नव्याख्यानाभ्यामपि चैवमेके ॥ १८ ॥

अन्यार्थं For another purpose तु but जैमिनिः Jaimini श्नव्याख्यानाभ्याम् because of the question and elucidation पि च moreover एवम thus एके some.

18. But (the sage) Jaimini (thinks that the reference to the individual soul in the text) has another purpose because of the question and answer; moreover thus some (the Vâjasaneyins) (read in their recension).

Even the reference to the individual soul in the said chapter of the Kauṣîtakī Upaniṣad has a different purpose, and that is not to propound the individual soul but Brahman by showing that the individual soul is different from Brahman. The questions, "Where did the person thus sleep? Where was he? Whence came he thus back?" (Kau. 4.19) refer clearly to something different from the individual soul. And so does the answer (*Ibid*. 4.20) say that the individual soul is merged in Brahman in deep sleep. The Bṛhadâranyaka Upaniṣad, where also this conversation occurs, clearly points out the individual soul by the term 'Vijñânamaya', the person consisting of cognition, and distinguishes it from the supreme Self (Bṛ 2.1.16-17).

Topic 6: The Self to be seen through hearing etc. is Brahman.

In the last topic the text under discussion was interpreted to refer to Brahman, because the section begins with Brahman: "I will teach you Brahman." Following the same argument the opponent cites Bṛ. 2.4.5 and argues that since the section begins with the individual soul, the self to be seen referred to in this text is the individual soul and not Brahman.

वाक्यान्वयात् ।। १९ ।।

वाक्य-अन्वयात् On account of the connected meaning of passages.

19. (The Self to be seen, to be heard, etc. is Brahman) on account of the connected meaning of the passages.

"The Self, my dear Maitreyī, should be realized—hould be heard of, reflected on and meditated upon. By the realization of the Self, my dear, through hearing, eflection, and meditation, all this is known" (Bṛ .4.5). In this passage the supreme Self is referred to, nd not the individual soul. Why? In the whole section Brahman is treated. It begins with Maitreyî's question Will wealth get me immortality?" and Yâjñavalkya nswers that wealth, sacrifice, etc. will not obtain that mmortality. She then asks for that which will give her mmortality, and Yâjñavalkya teaches her the knowedge of the Self; finally the section concludes with, Thus far goes immortality". Now immortality cannot e gained by the knowledge of the individual soul, but nly by the knowledge of the supreme Self or Brahman herefore Brahman alone is the subject-matter and It lone is to be seen through hearing etc. Moreover, the xt quoted says that by the knowledge of the Self ooken of there, everything is known, which clearly onnects the Self referred to with Brahman; for how n the knowledge of a limited individual self give us nowledge of everything?

प्रतिज्ञासिद्धेर्लिङ्गमाश्मरथ्यः ।। २० ।।

प्रतिज्ञा-सिद्धे: Of the proof of the proposition लिङ्गम् dicatory mark आश्मरथ्य: Āśmarathya.

20. (The fact that the individual soul is

taught as the object of realization is an) indicatory mark (which is) proof of the proposition, so Āśmarathya thinks.

In this Sûtra the text quoted in the last Sûtra (Bṛ. 2.4.5.) is interpreted from the standpoint of Bhedâbhedavâda of sage Āśmarathya. According to this school the individual soul (Jîva) and Brahman, which are related as effect and cause respectively, are different, yet not different, from each other, even as sparks are different yet not different from fire. If the individual soul (Jîva) were quite different from Brahman, then by the knowledge of the one (Brahman) everything else would not be known. Hence this school interprets the text thus: The individual soul alone is to be seen. But as it is not different from Brahman, the knowledge of the individual soul gives knowledge of Brahman and consequently knowledge of everything. It is this non-difference between Brahman and the individual soul (Jîva) that establishes the proposition, "By the knowledge of one everything else is known", and in this sense alone the text speaks of the individual soul in Bṛ. 2.4.5.

It can also be interpreted as follows. If the individual soul is something different from Brahman, then the knowledge of Brahman would not give the knowledge of the individual soul. Therefore the individual soul is different, yet not different, from Brahman. It is to show this that the Śruti text begins with the individual soul.

उत्क्रमिष्यत एवंभावादित्यौडुलोमिः ॥ २१ ॥

उत्क्रमिष्यतः Of the one which rises from the bo

एवं-भावात् because of this nature **इति** thus **औडुलोमिः** (the sage) Auḍulomi.

21. (The statement at the beginning identifies the individual soul with Brahman) because of this nature (*viz.* its identity with Brahman) of the one (*i.e.* the soul) which rises from the body (at the time of release), thus (thinks) Auḍulomi.

This Ācârya, while taking that the self to be seen is the individual soul (Jîva), explains it as follows: The soul, when it rises from the body, *i.e.* is free and has no body consciousness, realizes that it is identical with Brahman. It is to show this non-difference in the state of release that the Śruti speaks of the individual soul as indentical with Brahman, even though the difference between the individual soul (Jîva) and Brahman in the state of ignorance is a reality. It is spoken of as non-different from the supreme Self or Brahman because in the state of release it is one with It. The text transfers the future state of non-difference to that time when difference actually exists. This school of Vedânṭa is known as Satya-bheda-vâda (*i.e.* the theory which holds that the difference between the individual soul and Brahman is a reality).

अवस्थितेरिति काशकृत्स्नः ॥ २२ ॥

अवस्थितेः Because of the existence **इति** so holds **काशकृत्स्नः** Kâśakṛtsna.

22. (The initial statement is made) because

of the existence (of Brahman as the individual soul), so holds (sage) Kāśakṛtsna.

As it is impossible that an individual soul (Jîva) quite different in nature from Brahman can be one with it in the state of release, this sage thinks that the supreme Self Itself exists as the individual soul. They are absolutely non-different, the apparent difference being due to Upâdhis or limiting adjuncts, which are but products of ignorance, and therefore unreal from the absolute standpoint. Hence also follows that by the knowledge of Brahman everything else is known.

Of the three schools of Vedânta depicted in the last three Sûtras, that of Kâśakṛtsna is justified by the Vedânta texts. According to Āśmarathya the individual soul is a product of the supreme Self, and hence the knowledge of the cause leads to the knowledge of everything including the individual soul. But is the effect or any portion of it different from the cause? And is the whole cause involved in each of its effects? The answer to the second question is evidently, no. If the effect or some portion of it is different from this cause, whence does it come? And is it separable from that? If separable, it is not its nature, for nature cannot be separated. If not separable, the cause cannot be known, and the proposition, "The soul being known, all else is known", falls to the ground. So Āśmarathya's view cannot stand.

According to Auḍulomi the individual soul (Jîva) is only a state of the supreme Self. If the Jîvahood is a reality, it can never be destroyed and freedom would be impossible. If on the other hand it becomes one with the supreme Soul on release, then there is nothing like Jîvahood which can be a reality. So Auḍulomi's view cannot stand. Jîvahood is an unreality, a creation of ignorance, the Jîva being identical with Brahman. Even the creation of Jîvas like sparks issuing from a fire does not speak of any real creation but only with reference to Upâdhis. In reality the Jîva is neither created nor destroyed. It is our ignorance that makes us see the individual soul (Jîva) limited by Upâdhis as something different from Brahman.

Topic 7: Brahman is also the material cause of the world.

प्रकृतिश्च प्रतिज्ञादृष्टान्तानुपरोधात् ॥ २३ ॥

प्रकृतिः Material cause च also प्रतिज्ञा-दृष्टान्त-अनुपरोधात् not being contradictory to the proposition and illustrations.

23. (Brahman is) the material cause also, (on account of this view alone) not being contradictory to the proposition and the illustration (cited in the Śruti).

Granted that Brahman is the cause of the world; but what kind of cause? Is It the efficient cause, or the material cause, or both? The *prima facie* view is that Brahman is only the efficient cause, as texts like "He thought, ... he created Prâna (Pr. 6.3-4) declare.

This view is refuted by this Sûtra. Brahman is also the material cause of the world. Here 'also' shows that it is the efficient cause as well. It is only if Brahman is the material cause of the world that it is possible to know everything through the knowledge of Brahman, as texts like "By which that which is not heard becomes heard" etc. (Ch. 6.1.3) say; for the effects are not different from the cause. The illustrations referred to are: "My dear, as by one lump of clay all that is made of clay is known" etc. (Ch. 6.1.4). These texts clearly show that Brahman is the material cause of the world; otherwise they would be meaningless. Again texts like "Brahman alone was at the beginning one without a second" show that It is also the efficient cause, for who else could be such a cause when there was nothing else?

अभिध्योपदेशाच्च ॥ २४ ॥

अभिध्योपदेशात् On account of the statement of will (to create) च also.

24. Also on account of the statement of will (to create on the part of the supreme Self, It is the material cause).

"It wished, 'May I be many, may I grow forth' " etc. (Ch. 6.2.3). In this text the desire shows that Brahman is the efficient cause, and next 'may I be many' intimates that Brahman Itself became many. Hence It is the material cause as well.

साक्षाच्चोभयाम्नानात् ॥ २५ ॥

साक्षात् Direct च and उभयाम्नानात् because the Śruti states both.

25. And because the Śruti states that both (the creation and the dissolution of the world) (have Brahman as) the direct (cause).

That from which a thing springs and into which it is re-absorbed is its material cause. "All these things spring from Ākâśa (Brahman) alone and return to Ākâśa" (Ch. 1.9.1), "That from which these things are produced, by which, when produced, they live, and into which they enter at their dissolution—try to know that. That is Brahman" (Tai. 3.1). These texts show that Brahman is the material cause also. A thing may be said to be produced from its efficient cause, but it cannot return to that at dissolution unless it is also the material cause.

आत्मकृतेः परिणामात् ॥ २६ ॥

आत्मकृतेः As It created Itself परिणामात् by undergoing modification.

26. (Brahman is the material cause of the world) because (the Śruti says that) It created Itself by undergoing modification.

"That Itself manifested Itself" (Tai. 2.7), which shows that Brahman alone created the world, out of Itself, which is possible only by undergoing modification. The word 'Itself' in the text shows that there was no other cause operating. The modification is apparent according to Śaṅkara and real according to Râmânuja.

योनिश्च हि गीयते ॥ २७ ॥

योनिः Origin च and हि because गीयते is called.

27. And because (Brahman) is called the origin.

"That which the wise regard as the origin of all beings" (Mu. 1.1.6)—this shows that Brahman is the material cause of the world. Hence Its being the material cause is established.

Topic 8: The arguments which refute the Sâṁkhyas refute also others.

एतेन सर्वे व्याख्याता व्याख्याताः ॥ २८ ॥

एतेन By this सर्वे all व्याख्याताः are explained.

28. By this all (doctrines with reference to the origin of the world contrary to the Vedânta texts) are explained.

By this identity of the material and the efficient cause of the world all doctrines that speak of two separate causes for it are refuted. That is, not only the Sâṁkhyan, but also the atomic and other theories are refuted, as they are not based on scriptural authority and contradict many scriptural texts. The repetition of the verb in the aphorism only shows that the chapter ends here.

Those who hold the atomic theory, or who say that the first Cause is non-existence, or that it is Śûnya (Void)—as the Nihilists say—cite respectively the following texts as authority: "These seeds, almost infinitesimal" (Ch. 6.12.1); "This was indeed non-existent at the beginning" (Ch. 3.19.1); "Some learned men being deluded, speak of nature, and others of time, as the cause of everything" (Śv. 6.1). But the arguments put forward against the Sâṁkhyas, *viz.* that contrary to the scriptures their first Cause is insentient, that the proposition that through the knowledge of the one everything is known, will not be true, etc. will apply here also, and so these views cannot be held to be authoritative and based on the scriptures. The Śrutis quoted are explained thus:

The word infinitesimal' or 'atomic' refers to the Ātman, which can be so-called as it is very fine. The non-existence spoken of is only a fine causal condition of the world undeveloped into name and form as yet, and not absolute non-existence; and the fact of nature being the first Cause is mentioned as a Pûrvapakṣa by the Śruti, which itself refutes it further on in the succeeding texts. So Brahman alone is the first Cause, and nothing else.

CHAPTER II

SECTION I

In the first chapter it has been proved that all the Vedânta texts deal with Brahman as the first Cause, yet the arguments based on reasoning against this doctrine remain to be refuted. With this object in view this section is begun. In section IV of Chapter I it was shown that the Pradhâna of the Sâṁkhyas, as also the atoms of the Vaiśeṣikas, are not based on scriptural authority. In this section arguments, claiming their authoritativeness from the Smṛtis, to establish the Pradhâna and the atoms etc. are refuted.

Topic 1: Refutation of Smṛtis that are not based on the Śrutis.

स्मृत्यनवकाशदोषप्रसङ्ग इति चेत्, न,
अन्यस्मृत्यनवकाशदोषप्रसङ्गात् ॥ १ ॥

स्मृति-अनवकाश-दोषप्रसङ्गः There would result the defect of leaving no scope for certain Smṛtis इति चेत् if it be said न no अन्यस्मृति-अनवकाश-दोषप्रसङ्गात् because there would result the defect of leaving no scope to some other Smṛtis.

1. If it be said that (from the doctrine of Brahman being the cause of the world) there

would result the defect of leaving no scope for certain Smṛitis, (we say) no; because (by the rejection of that doctrine) there would result the defect of leaving no scope for some other Smṛitis.

In the last chapter it has been shown that the Sâṁkhyan view is not based on scriptural authority. Now its authority even as a Smṛti is denied and refuted.

If the doctrine of the Pradhâna is rejected, then the Sâṁkhya Smṛti, propounded by a great seer like Kapila and acknowledged by other great thinkers, would cease to be authoritative; hence it is but reasonable that the Vedânta texts be so interpreted as to preserve the authoritativeness of this Smṛti and not contradict it *in toto*. So says the opponent. The Sûtra answers this by saying that if the doctrine of Brahman being the cause of the world be rejected to accommodate the Sâṁkhya Smṛti, which goes counter to the Śrutis, then by that rejection many other Smṛtis like the Manu Smṛti, which are based on the Śrutis and therefore more authoritative, and, which also propound the doctrine of Brahman, an intelligent principle, being the cause of the world, would find no scope. So between the two it is desirable that the Smṛtis which go counter to the Vedas be rejected.

इतरेषां चानुपलब्धेः ॥ २ ॥

इतरेषां Of the others च and अनुपलब्धेः : there being no mention.

2. And there being no mention (in the scriptures) of the other entities, (*i.e.* the categories

beside the Pradhâna), (the Sâṁkhya system cannot be authoritative).

Even accepting the Pradhâna of the Sâṁkhyas for argument's sake—for the Vedântins also recognize Mâyâ as the cause of the world, the difference between the two being that the Pradhâna according to the Sâṁkhyas is an independent entity, whereas Mâyâ is a dependent entity, being a power of Brahman—yet there is no mention of the other categories of the Sâṁkhyas anywhere in the Vedas. Hence the Sâṁkhya philosophy cannot be authoritative.

Topic 2: Refutation of the Yoga philosophy.

एतेन योगः प्रत्युक्तः ॥ ३ ॥

एतेन By this योगः the Yoga philosophy प्रत्युक्तः is (also) refuted.

3. By this the Yoga philosophy is (also) refuted.

After the refutation of the Sâṁkhyas, who recognize an independent entity called the Pradhâna as the cause of the world, this Sûtra refutes the Yoga Smṛti, which also recognizes a separate entity called the Pradhâna as the first Cause, though unlike the Sâṁkhyas they recognize an Īśvara who directs this inert Pradhâna in its creative evolution. The Yoga system is spoken of in Upaniṣads like the Śvetâśvatara. It helps concentration of the mind, which is necessary for the full comprehension of Brahman, and as such it is a means to Knowledge. So this Smṛti, being based on the Śruti is authoritative. But it also recognizes the Pradhâna, which therefore is the first Cause—so says the opponent. This Sûtra says that the arguments given in the last Sûtra refute also the Yoga Smṛti, for it also speaks of a Pradhâna and its products which are not to be found in the Śrutis. Though the Smṛti is partly authoritative, yet it cannot be so with respect to that part which contradicts the Śrutis. There is room only for those portions of the Smṛti as do not contradict the Śrutis.

Topic 3: Brahman, though of a different nature from the world, can yet be its cause.

न विलक्षणत्वादस्य, तथात्वं च शब्दात् ॥ ४ ॥

न Not विलक्षणत्वात् because of the contrary nature अस्य of this तथात्वं its being so च and शब्दात् from Śruti.

4. (Brahman is) not (the cause of the world) because this (world) is of a contrary nature (from Brahman); and its being so (*i.e.* different from Brahman) (is known) from the scriptures.

Brahman is intelligence, pure, etc. while the world is something material, impure, etc. and so is different from the nature of Brahman; as such, Brahman cannot be the cause of this world. The effect is nothing but the cause in another form; therefore the cause and effect cannot be altogether of a different nature. Intelligence cannot produce material effects and *vice versa*. That the world and Brahman differ entirely in their characteristics is known from texts like "Brahman became intelligence as also non-intelligent" (Tai. 2.6), where "non-intelligent" stands for the world. So Brahman cannot be the first Cause of the material world, though the scriptures may say so.

अभिमानिव्यपदेशस्तु विशेषानुगतिभ्याम् ॥ ५ ॥

अभिमानिव्यपदेशः The reference (is) to the presiding deities तु but विशेष-अनुगतिभ्याम् because of the special characterization and the fact of being so presided.

5. But the reference is to the presiding deities (of the organs) on account of the special characterization (as 'deities') and also from the fact of a deity so presiding (over the function of an organ being approved by the Śruti in other texts).

The opponent, who says that the world and Brahman being different in nature—sentient and material respectively—cannot be related to each other as cause and effect, anticipates a plausible objection and answers it in this Sûtra. There is a text, "These organs quarrelling over their respective greatness," etc. (Bṛ. 6.1.7), which shows that even the organs are not material but sentient. The opponent says that from this we are not to infer the sentiency of the world, since the reference is to the presiding deities of these organs. For the same topic occurs in the Kauṣîtakî Upaniṣad, where they are expressly mentioned. "These deities (speech etc.) quarrelling over their respective greatness" (Kau. 2.14). Also because other texts show the existence of such presiding deities. "Fire becoming speech entered the mouth" (Ai. Ā. 2.4.2.4). The same argument applies to texts of the Chândogya, (Ch. VI) where fires etc. are said to have thought and produced the next element in the series. The thought here spoken of is of the highest Deity, Brahman, which is connected with Its effects as a superintending principle. From all such texts we cannot infer the sentiency of the world, which is material and so different in nature from Brahman. Therefore Brahman cannot be the cause of the material world.

दृश्यते तु ॥ ६ ॥

दृश्यते Is seen तु but.

6. But it is seen.

'But' refutes the opponent's view expressed in the last Sûtra, *viz* that this world cannot have originated from Brahman because it is different in character. For it is seen that intelligent things like scorpions etc. are produced from non-intelligent cowdung etc. Again from a sentient spider there comes forth the thread for its web. So also do nails, hair, etc. come forth from a man, who is an intelligent being. Therefore it is quite possible that this material world could be produced by an intelligent Being, Brahman. It may be objected that a man's body is the cause of the hair and nails, and not the man; similarly the cowdung is the cause of the body of the worms. Even then it must be admitted that there is a difference between the cause and the effect since, in both the examples cited, one of them is the abode of something sentient while the other is not; they are not similar in all respects. If they were, then there would be nothing like cause and effect, nor would they be called by different names. So we have to admit that the cause and its effects are not similar in every respect, but something in the cause, or some qualities of it, must be found in the effects also, as the clay in the lump is found in the pot also, though the shape etc. of the two differ. So we say that even in the case of Brahman and the world, some qualities of the cause, Brahman, such as existence and intelligence, are to be found in its effect, the world. Everything in the world exists, and this quality it gets from Brahman, which is existence itself. Again the intelligence of Brahman lights the whole universe. So these two qualities of Brahman are found in the world, which justify our relating them as cause and effect in spite of differences in other respect between them.

असदिति चेत्, न, प्रतिषेधमात्रत्वात् ॥ ७ ॥

असत् Non-existent इति चेत् if it be said न no प्रतिषेधमात्रत्वात् for it is merely a negation.

7. If it be said (that the world, the effect, would then be) non-existent (before creation), (we say) no, for it is merely a negation (without any basis).

If Brahman, which is intelligent, pure, and without qualities, is the cause of the world of an opposite character, it follows that before creation the world was non-existent, for Brahman was then the only existence. This means that something which was non-existing is brought into existence, which is not accepted by the

Vedântins. This argument of the opponent this Sûtra refutes by saying that this negation is a mere statement without any objective validity. The effect exists in the cause before its origination as well as after it. It can never exist independent of the cause either before or after creation. Therefore the world exists in Brahman even before creation and is not absolutely non-existent.

अपीतौ तद्वत्प्रसङ्गादसमञ्जसम् ॥ ८ ॥

अपीतौ At the time of dissolution तद्वत् like that प्रसङ्गात् on account of the fact असमञ्जसम् is absurd.

8. On account of the fact that at the time of dissolution (the cause becomes) like that (*i.e.* like the effect) (the doctrine of Brahman being the cause of the world) is absurd.

Says the opponent: If Brahman is the cause of the world, then the world being dissolved in Brahman at the time of dissolution, its defects would affect Brahman, even as salt affects the water in which it is dissolved. Hence Brahman would become impure and would no more be the omniscient cause of the world, as the Upaniṣads maintain. Again at the time of dissolution all things having gone into a state of oneness with Brahman, there will be no special causes left for a new creation. If in spite of this we consider a new creation possible, then it would mean that there is a chance of even the liberated souls, who have become one with Brahman, reappearing in the world. Nor can it be said that the world remains separate from Brahman in the state of dissolution, for in that case it would be no dissolution at all. So the Vedânta doctrine of Brahman being the cause of the world is objectionable, as it leads to all sorts of absurdities.

न तु, दृष्टान्तभावात् ॥ ९ ॥

न Not तु but दृष्टान्त-भावात् on account of the existence of illustrations.

9. But not (so) on account of the existence of illustrations.

The objection is being answered: That the effect, when it gets dissolved in the cause, does not pollute the latter by its defects, is borne out by innumerable instances. A clay pot, for instance, when it is broken and reabsorbed into its original substance, *i.e.* clay, does not impart to it its special features. The very fact of absorption shows that all the qualities of the effect cannot abide, for in that case it would be no absorption at all. Moreover, we have to remember that the effect is of the nature of the cause and not *vice versa*. Hence the qualities of the effect cannot touch the cause. It may, however, be objected that since the effect is but the cause in a new condition, all the good and bad traits of the effect must have been in the cause. But we forget that the world is after all an illusion. Brahman has only apparently changed into the world and as such is never affected by it, even as a magician is not affected by the illusion produced by him.

The other incongruity shown, *viz* that since at the time of dissolution the world is resolved into Brahman and becomes one with It, there can be no furthe creation, and if it takes place there will be the possibility of even free souls coming into bondage again, cannot stand, for there are parallel instances with respect to this also. In deep-sleep we do not perceive anything, there is no diversity, but on awakening we find the world of duality. A similar phenomenon can be expected to happen at the time of dissolution. In the former case it is the existence of ignorance (Avidyâ), which is not destroyed, that is responsible for the reappearance of the world. So also at dissolution the power of distinction remains in a potential state as Avidyâ or ignorance. But in the case of the liberated no ignorance being left, there is no chance of their being brought back into bondage from their state of oneness with Brahman.

स्वपक्षदोषाच्च ॥ १० ॥

स्वपक्ष-दोषात् Because of the objections to his own view च and.

10. And because of the objections (cited) (being applicable) to his own (Sâṁkhyan) view (also).

The objections raised by the Sâṁkhyas against Vedânta are equally true of their view of the first Cause, viz the Pradhâna. Form, taste, etc. are not to be found in the Pradhâna, yet we find these things in the world produced out of it. The objection as regards reabsorption at the time of Pralaya applies also in the case of the Sâṁkhyan Pradhâna. Thus whatever objections are raised against Vedânta in this respect are also true of the Sâṁkhyas. Hence they should be dropped. Of the two, however, Vedânta being based on the Śrutis is more authoritative. Moreover, the objections have all been answered from the Vedânta standpoint, whereas from the Sâṁkhyan standpoint it is not possible to answer them.

तर्काप्रतिष्ठानादपि, अन्यथानुमेयमिति चेत्,
एवमप्यविमोक्षप्रसङ्गः ॥ ११ ॥

तर्क-अप्रतिष्ठानात् Because reasoning has no sure basis अपि also अन्यथा otherwise अनुमेयम् should be inferred or reasoned इति चेत् if it be said एवम् so अपि even अविमोक्ष-प्रसङ्गः there will result the contingency of non-release.

11. Also because reasoning has no sure basis (it cannot upset the conclusions of Vedânta). If it be said that it should be reasoned otherwise (so as to get over this defect), (we say) even so there will result the contingency of non-release (from this defect, with respect to the matter in question).

What one man establishes through reason can be refuted by another more intelligent than he. Even a sage like Kapila is refuted by other sages like Kaṇâda. Hence reasoning having no sure basis cannot upset the conclusions of Vedânta, which are based on the Śrutis. But, says the opponent, even this judgement about reasoning is arrived at through reasoning; so it is not true that reasoning has never a sure basis. Sometimes it is perfectly sound. Only we must reason properly. The latter part of the Sûtra says that even though in some cases reasoning is infallible, yet with respect to the matter in hand it cannot transcend this defect. For the cause of the world (Brahman) is beyond the senses and has no characteristic signs. It cannot therefore be an object of perception, or of inference, which is based on perception. Or again if we take 'release' in the Sûtra to mean Liberation, it comes to this: True knowledge of a real thing depends on the thing itself, and therefore it is always uniform. Hence a conflict of views with respect to it is not possible. But the conclusions of reasoning can never be uniform. The Sâṁkhyas arrive through reasoning at the Pradhâna as the first Cause, while the Naiyâyikas (logicians) mention Paramāṇus (atoms) as that. Which to accept? So no conclusion can be arrived at through reasoning independent of the scriptures, and since the truth cannot be known through this means, there will be no Liberation. Therefore reasoning which goes against the scriptures is no proof of knowledge and cannot contradict the Śruti texts.

Topic 4: The line of reasoning against the Sâṁkhyas is valid also against others like the Atomists.

एतेन शिष्टापरिग्रहा अपि व्याख्याताः ॥ १२ ॥

एतेन By this शिष्टापरिग्रहाः not accepted by the wise अपि also व्याख्याताः are explained.

12. By this (*i.e.* by the arguments against the Sâṁkhyas) (those other views) also not accepted by the wise (like Manu and others) are explained.

When the Sâṁkhya philosophy, parts of which are accepted by the wise as authoritative, has been refuted, there is no question as regards the non-authoritativeness of all doctrines based merely on reasoning like the atomic theory of Kaṇâda and non-existence as the first Cause propounded by the Buddhists, which are wholly rejected by the wise. They are also refuted by these very arguments against the Sâṁkhyas, as the reasons on which the refutation is based are the same.

Topic 5: The distinctions like enjoyer and enjoyed do not contradict the truth which is oneness.

भोक्त्रापत्तेरविभागश्चेत्, स्याल्लोकवत् ॥ १३ ॥

भोक्त्रापत्तेः On account of turning into the enjoyer अविभागः non-distinction चेत् if it be said स्यात् may exist लोकवत् as is experienced in the world.

13. If it be said (that if Brahman be the cause then) on account of (the objects of enjoyment) turning into the enjoyer, non-distinction (between enjoyer and things enjoyed would result), (we say, such distinction) may exist (all the same), as is experienced commonly in the world.

A further objection is raised against Brahman being the cause. We perceive differences in the world. Now, perception as a means of knowledge is stronger than the Śruti. Hence what the Śrutis say in contradiction to such an experience cannot stand. The idea is this: The distinction between the enjoyer (the Jîva) and the objects of enjoyment is well established by experience.

Brahman is the material cause, then the world, the effect, would be non-different from Brahman, and under the circumstances, the Jîva and Brahman being identical in Vedânta, the difference between the subject and object would be destroyed, since the old would pass over into the other. Hence Brahman cannot be held to be the material cause of the world as it contradicts perception.

The latter part of the Sûtra refutes this giving examples. It says that nevertheless there can be such differences in non-different things. For instance, waves, foam, etc. are non-different, being alike sea water; yet as waves and foam they are different from each other. As sea water, their cause, they are one, but as waves, foam, etc. they are different, and there is no contradiction here. Hence it is possible to have difference and non-difference in things simultaneously, owing to name and form. Therefore from the standpoint of Brahman the enjoyer and the enjoyed are not different, but as enjoyer and things enjoyed they are different; there is no contradiction in this.

The Sûtra can also be interpreted otherwise. If Brahman be the cause, then It would also be the enjoyer, the individual soul (Jîva), there being no difference between cause and effect. Consequently, there will be no such difference as the bondage of the individual soul and the freedom of Brahman. The Sûtra says that even as there is a distinction between the object, which is clear, and its image, which is disfigured in an unclean mirror, so also owing to the impurities of the Antaḥkaraṇa (mind) the ever-free Brahman may give rise to the image of the individual soul, which is bound.

Topic 6: The non-difference of the effect from the cause

तदनन्यत्वमारम्भणशब्दादिभ्यः ॥ १४ ॥

तदनन्यत्वम् Its non-difference आरम्भण-शब्दादिभ्यः from words like 'origin' etc.

14. Its (of the effect) non-difference (from the cause results) from words like 'origin' etc.

In the last Sûtra the objection against Brahman being the material cause, that it contradicts perception, was answered from the standpoint of Pariṇâmavâda or the theory of Brahman actually undergoing modification. Now the same objection is refuted from the standpoint of Vivartavâda or apparent modification, which is the standpoint of Advaita. The objection is: Texts like "There is no manifoldness whatever here (in Brahman)" (Ka. 2. 4. 11) contradict perception. Reason also says that among things which get transformed into each other there cannot be difference and non-difference at the same time. Hence the doubt. In a single moon we cannot see two moons. What was spoken of in the last Sûtra, *viz* that the difference between them is one of name and form, even that is unreal, for in a thing which is one without a second, which is non-duality, even the difference due to name and form is impossible. The example of the sea is not apt, for here both the sea and its modifications, waves and foam, are objects of the senses, but Brahman is not. It is realized only through the scriptures and in Samâdhi. What then is the truth? It is oneness, non-duality. As the effect is non-different from the cause, the latter alono is real. The Śruti also establishes this by the example of clay etc. in the Chândogya Upaniṣad. "Just as, by the knowledge of on lump of earth, my dear, everything made of earth is known, the modification being only a name arising from speech, but the truth being that all is earth...thus, my dear, is that instruction" (Ch. 6. 1. 4-6). Here the Śruti by using the word 'modification' tries to prove that there is no separate reality of the pots etc. which are mere modifications of the lump of earth. They are not separate things but merely different conditions, just as the boyhood, youth, etc. of Devadatta are mere conditions, and not real. So by knowing the lump of earth the real nature of the pots etc. is known. It matters little that the various forms are not known, for they are not worth knowing, being unreal. Even though these pots etc. are objects of the senses, yet discrimination tells us that besides earth nothing real is found in these. They are merely names arising out of speech and nothing more. They are cognized through ignorance, hence they are unreal. The clay, on the other hand, is realized even apart from name and form and is therefore real. Similarly Brahman alone is real and this world is unreal. The world being non-different from its cause, Brahman, the truth is oneness, non-duality, Brahman, the one without a second. To people who through want of experience have not this insight into things, there will always be difference and non-difference, even as in the case of the sea and its waves, but in reality these differences are relative and not true.

भावे चोपलब्धेः ॥ १५ ॥

भावे On the existence च and उपलब्धेः is experienced

15. And (because) on the existence (of the cause) is (the effect) experienced.

The effect is not experienced in the absence of the cause, which shows that the effect is not different from the cause. The world phenomena appear only because Brahman exists and not without It. Hence the world is non-different from Brahman.

सत्त्वाच्चावरस्य ॥ १६ ॥

सत्त्वात् On account of (its) existing च and अवरस्य of the posterior.

16. And on account of the posterior (*i.e.* the effect, which comes into being after the cause) existing (as the cause before creation).

The Śruti says that before creation the world had its being in the cause, Brahman, as one with It: "Verily in the beginning this was Self, one only" (Ai. Ā. 2. 4. 1. 1); "In the beginning, my dear, this was only existence" (Ch. 6. 2. 1). Now since before creation it was non-different from the cause, it continues to be so even after creation.

असद्व्यपदेशान्नेति चेत्, न, धर्मान्तरेण वाक्यशेषात् ॥ १७ ॥

असत्-व्यपदेशात् On account of its being described as non-existent न not इति चेत् if it be said न no धर्मान्तरेण by another characteristic वाक्यशेषात् from the latter part of the text.

17. If it be said that on account of (the effect) being described as non-existent (before creation) (the conclusion of the previous Sûtra is) not (true); (we say) not so, (it being described) by another characteristic (as is seen) from the latter part of the text.

"Non-existent indeed this was in the beginning" (Ch. 3. 19. 1). The word "non-existent" does not mean absolute non-existence, but that the world did not exist in a differentiated condition. It was undifferentiated—had not yet developed name and form—in which sense the word "non-existence" is also used in common parlance. It was in a fine condition, and after creation it became gross, developing name and form. This sense is shown by the immediately succeeding portion of the text, "It became existent, it grew." Hence the conclusion of the last Sûtra is all right.

युक्तेः शब्दान्तराच्च ॥ १८ ॥

युक्तेः From reasoning शब्दान्तरात् from another Śruti text च and.

18. From reasoning and another Śruti text (this relation between cause and effect is established).

From reasoning also we find that the effect is non-different from the cause and exists before its origination. Otherwise everything could have been produced from anything Particular causes producing particular effects only shows this relationship between cause and effect. Before creation the effect exists in the cause as unmanifest. Otherwise something new being created anything could have been created from all things. The fact is, it gets manifested on creation, that is all. That which is absolutely non-existent like the horns of a hare can never come into existence. So the cause cannot produce altogether a new thing which was not existing in it already. Moreover, that the effect exists even before creation we find from such Śruti texts as "In the beginning, my dear, this was only existence, one without a second" (Ch. 6.2.1).

पटवच्च ॥ १९ ॥

पटवत् Like cloth च and.

19. And like a piece of cloth,

Even as is cloth folded and spread out, so is the world before and after creation. In the folded state one cannot make out whether it is a cloth or anything else, which is clearly discernible when it is spread out. In the state of Pralaya (dissolution), *i.e.* before creation, the world exists in a fine potential state in Brahman and after creation takes the gross form.

यथा च प्राणादि ॥ २० ॥

यथा As च and प्राणादि in the case of Prâṇas.

20. And as in the case of the different Prâṇas.

When the five different Prâṇas (vital forces) are controlled by Prâṇâyâma, they merge and exist as the chief Prâṇa (which regulates respiration) merely maintaining life. From this we find that the effects, the various Prâṇas are not different from their cause, the chief Prâṇa. So also with all effects; they are not different from their cause. Therefore it is established that the effect, the world, is identical with its cause, Brahman. Hence by knowing It everything is known.

Topic 7: Refutation of the objection that if Brahman were the cause of the world, then It and the Jîva being really one, Brahman would be responsible for creating evil.

इतरव्यपदेशाद्धिताकरणादिदोषप्रसक्तिः ॥ २१ ॥

इतर-व्यपदेशात् On account of the other being stated (as non-different from Brahman) हित-अकरणादि-दोष-प्रसक्तिः defects of not doing what is beneficial and the like would arise.

21. On account of the other (the individual soul) being stated (as non-different from Brahman) there would arise (in Brahman) the defects of not doing what is beneficial and the like.

In the previous topic the oneness of the world with its cause, Brahman, has been established. But the Sûtra also states the identity of the individual soul and Brahman, and if Brahman at the same time were the cause of the world. It would be open to the charge of not doing what is good for Itself. Being omniscient, It would not have ordained anything which would do the individual soul harm, or abstained from doing that which would be beneficial to it; for nobody is seen to do so with respect to oneself. Rather It would have created a world where everything would have been pleasant for the individual soul, without the least trace of misery. Since that is not a fact, Brahman is not the cause of the world, as Vedânta holds.

अधिकं तु, भेदनिर्देशात् ॥ २२ ॥

अधिकं Something more तु but भेद-निर्देशात् on account of the statement of difference.

22. But on account of the statement (in the Śrutis) of difference (between the individual soul and Brahman) (Brahman the Creator is) something more (than the individual soul).

'But' refutes the objection of the last Sûtra.

The Creator of the world is omniscient and omnipotent. As such He knows the unreality of the Jîvahood and the world, and also His own non-attachment to them, being a mere witness. He has neither good nor evil. So His creating a world of good and evil is not objectionable. For the individual soul, however, there is good and evil so long as it is in ignorance. The Śrutis clearly point out the difference between the individual soul and the Creator in texts like "The Ātman is to be realized" etc. (Bṛ. 2. 4. 5). All these differences, however, are based on imaginary distinctions due to ignorance. It is only when Knowledge dawns that the individual soul realizes its identity with Brahman. Then all plurality vanishes, and there is neither the individual soul nor the Creator. Thus the individual soul not being the creator of the world, the objection raised does not hold good.

अश्मादिवच्च तदनुपपत्तिः ॥ २३ ॥

अश्मादिवत् Like stones etc. च and तदनुपपत्तिः its untenability.

23. And because the case is similar to that of stones (produced from the same earth) etc. the objection is untenable.

An objection may be raised that Brahman, which is Knowledge, Bliss, and unchangeable, cannot be the cause of a world of diversity, of good and evil. This Sûtra refutes that. The objection is untenable, for we see that from the same material, earth, stones of different values like the precious jewels as also useless stones are produced. So also from Brahman, which is Bliss, a world of good and evil can be created.

Topic 8: Brahman though destitute of material and instruments is yet the cause of the world.

उपसंहारदर्शनान्नेति चेत्, न, क्षीरवद्धि ॥ २४ ॥

उपसंहार-दर्शनात् Because collection of accessories is seen not इतिचेत् if it be said न no क्षीरवत् like milk हि since.

24. If it be said (that Brahman without extraneous aids) cannot (be the cause of the world)

because (an agent) is seen to collect materials (for any construction), (we say) no, since (it is) like milk (turning into curds).

A fresh objection is raised against Brahman being the cause of the world. There is nothing extraneous to Brahman to help in the work of creation, for there is nothing besides Brahman. Brahman is one without a second and so free from all differentiations internal or external. It is ordinarily seen that one who creates something, the potter, for example, uses extraneous aids like the wheel, clay, etc. But Brahman, being one without a second, has not these accessories and so is not the Creator. The Sûtra refutes this objection by showing that such a thing is possible even as milk turns into curds without the help of any extraneous thing. If it be urged that even in this case heat or some such thing starts curdling, we say it only accelerates the process but the curdling takes place through the inherent capacity of the milk. One cannot turn water into curds by the application of heat! But Brahman being infinite no such aid is necessary for It to produce this world. That It is of infinite power is testified by such Śrutis as the following: "There is no effect and no instrument known of Him, no one is seen like unto Him or better. His high power is revealed as manifold and inherent, acting as force and knowledge" (Śv. 6.8).

देवादिवदपि लोके ॥ २५ ॥

देवादिवत् Like gods and others अपि even लोके in the world.

25. (The case of Brahman creating the world is) even like the gods and other beings in the world.

It may be objected that the example of milk turning into curds is not in point, since it is an inanimate substance. One never sees a conscious being, a potter, for instance, turning out things without the help of external aids.

This Sûtra refutes that objection by giving an example of creation by a conscious agent without any extraneous help. Even as gods, in the sacred books, are seen to create without extraneous means simply through their inherent power, so also the Lord through His infinite power of Mâyâ is able to create this world of diversity. The examples cited above show that it is not necessary that creation be limited by the conditions observed in the creation of pots. They are not universal.

Topic 9: Brahman though without parts is yet the material cause of the world.

कृत्स्नप्रसक्तिर्निरवयवत्वशब्दकोपो वा ॥ २६ ॥

कृत्स्न प्रसक्ति: Possibility of the entire (Brahman being modified) निरवयवत्वशब्द-कोप: violation of the scriptural statement that Brahman is without parts वा or.

26. (Brahman's being the cause of the world involves) either the possibility of the entire Brahman being modified) or the violation of the scriptural statement that Brahman is without parts.

If Brahman is without parts and yet the material cause of the world, then we have to admit that the entire Brahman becomes changed into this multiform world. So there will be no Brahman left, but only the effect, the world. Moreover, it would contradict the scriptural text that Brahman is immutable. If on the other hand it is said that the whole of It does not undergo modification, but only a part, then we shall have to accept that Brahman is made up of parts, which is denied by scriptural texts. In either case it leads to dilemma, and so Brahman cannot be the cause of the world.

श्रुतेस्तु, शब्दमूलत्वात् ॥ २७ ॥

श्रुते: On account of scriptural texts तु but शब्दमूलत्वात् on account of being based on the scripture.

27. But (it cannot be like that) on account of scriptural texts (supporting both the apparently contradictory views) and on account of (Brahman) being based on the scripture only.

'But' rufutes the view of the former Sûtra.

The entire Brahman does no undergo change, though the scriptures say that the world originates from Brahman. Witness such texts as, "One foot (quarter) of Him is all beings, and three feet are what is immortal in heaven" (Ch. 3. 12. 6). And as in matters supersensuous the Śrutis alone are authority, we have to accept that both these opposite views are true though it does not stand to reason. The thing is, the change in Brahman is only apparent and not real. Hence both the views expressed by the Śruti are true. It is on this basi that the apparently contradictory texts become reconciled and not otherwise.

आत्मनि चैवं विचित्राश्च हि ॥ २८ ॥

आत्मनि In the individual soul च and एवं thus विचित्राः diverse च also हि because.

28. And because in the individual soul also (as in the case of magicians etc.) diverse (creation exists). Similarly (with Brahman).

This Sûtra establishes the view of the former by citing an example.

In the dream state there appears in the individual self, which is one and indivisible, diversity resembling the waking state (See Bṛ 4. 3. 10), and yet the indivisible character of the self is not marred by it. We see also magicians, for instance, producing a multiple creation without any change in themselves. Similarly this diverse creation springs from Brahman through Its inscrutable power of Mâyâ, though Brahman Itself remains unchanged.

स्वपक्षदोषाच्च ॥ २९ ॥

स्वपक्ष-दोषात् On account of the opponent's view being subject to these very objections च and.

29. And on account of the opponent's own view being subject to these very objections.

If the Pradhâna is taken to be the first Cause, as the opponents of the Vedântic view (the Sâṁkhyas) hold, in that case also, as the Pradhâna too is without parts, the Sâṁkhyan view will be equally subject to the objections raised against Brahman as the first Cause. The Vedânta viewpoint has, however, answered all these objections, while the Sâṁkhyas and Vaiśeṣikas cannot answer them, the change being real according to them.

Topic 10: Brahman's power of Mâyâ established.

सर्वोपेता च तद्दर्शनात् ॥ ३० ॥

सर्वोपेता Endowed with all च and तत्-दर्शनात् because it is seen.

30. And (Brahman is) endowed with all (powers), because it is seen (from the scriptures).

Generally we see that men endowed with a physical body possess such powers. But since Brahman has no body, it is not likely that It can possess such powers—so says the opponent.

This Sûtra gives proof of Brahman's being endowed with Mâyâ Śakti, the power of Nescience. Various scriptural texts declare that Brahman possesses all powers. "The great Lord is the Mâyin (the ruler of Mâyâ)" (Śv. 4. 10). See also Ch. 3. 14. 4 and 8. 7 1

विकरणत्वान्नेति चेत्, तदुक्तम् ॥ ३१ ॥

विकरणत्वात् Because devoid of organs न not इति चेत् if it be said तत् that उक्तम् has been explained

31. If it be said that because (Brahman) is devoid of organs (it is) not (able to create, though endowed with powers), (we say) this has (already) been explained.

As Brahman is devoid of organs, It cannot create. Moreover, It is described as "Not this, not this", which precludes all attributes; so how can It possess any powers? This Sûtra replies that it has already been explained in 2. 1. 4. and 2. 1. 25 that with respect to Brahman the scripture alone is authority and not reason. The scripture declares that Brahman, although devoid of organs, possesses all capacities. 'Grasping without hands, moving swiftly without feet" etc. (Śv. 3. 19). Though Brahman is without attributes, yet on account of Mâyâ or Nescience It can be taken to possess all powers.

Topic 11: Brahman's creation has no motive behind except a sportive impulse.

न प्रयोजनवत्त्वात् ॥ ३२ ॥

न Not प्रयोजनवत्त्वात् on account of having motive.

32. (Brahman is) not (the creator of the world) on account of (every activity) having a motive.

Granting that Brahman possesses all powers for creation, a further objection is raised against Its being the cause. Nobody engages himself in anything without a motive or purpose. Everything is undertaken by people to satisfy some desire. But Brahman is self-sufficient, therefore It has nothing to gain by the creation; hence we cannot expect It to engage Itself in such a useless creation. Therefore Brahman cannot be the cause of the world.

लोकवत्तु, लीलाकैवल्यम् ॥ ३३ ॥

लोकवत् As is seen in the world तु but लीलाकैवल्यम mere pastime.

33. But (Brahman's creative activity) is mere pastime, as is seen in the world.

Even as kings without any motive behind are seen to engage in acts for mere pastime, or even as men breathe without a purpose, for it is their very nature, or even as children play out of mere fun, so also Brahman without any purpose engages Itself in creating this world of diversity. This answers the objection raised in the previous Sûtra against Brahman's being the cause of the world.

Topic 12: Partiality and cruelty cannot be attributed to Brahman.

वैषम्यनैर्घृण्ये न, सापेक्षत्वात्,
तथा हि दर्शयति ॥ ३४ ॥

वैषम्यनर्घृण्ये Partiality and cruelty न not सापेक्षत्वात् on account of Its taking into consideration (other reasons) तथा so हि because दर्शयति declares.

34. Partiality and cruelty cannot (be attrib-

uted to Brahman) on account of Its taking into consideration (other reasons in that matter), because (the scripture) declares (it to be) so.

Some are created poor, some rich; hence the Lord is partial to some. He is cruel, inasmuch as He makes people suffer. To such an objection this Sûtra replies that the Lord cannot be accused of partiality and cruelty, because He dispenses according to the merit and demerit of the individual soul. The scripture declares to that effect, "A man becomes good by good work, bad by bad work" (Bṛ. 3. 2. 13). But this does not contradict the independence of the Lord, even as the king's status is not compromised by his giving presents to his servents according to their action. Just as rain helps different seeds to sprout, each according to its nature, so God is the general efficient cause in bringing the latent tendencies of each individual to fruition. Hence he is neither partial nor cruel.

न कर्माविभागादिति चेत्, न, अनादित्वात् ॥ ३५ ॥

न Not कर्माविभागात् for want of distinction in work इति चेत् if it be said न no अनादित्वात् because of (the world) being without a beginning.

35. If it be said (that is) not (possible) for want of any distinction in work (before creation), (we say) no, because of (the world) being without a beginning.

Since before the first creation the individual soul cannot possibly have had a previous existence, whence comes the difference in the condition of beings in that first creation, unless the Lord has caused it out of His partiality? This objection is answered by the Sûtra, which says that creation is without a beginning and the question of first creation cannot arise. It is like a seed and its sprout. So the individual souls have always had a previous existence and done good or bad deeds in accordance with which theïr lot in a subsequent creation is ordained by the Lord.

उपपद्यते चाप्युपलभ्यते च ॥ ३६ ॥

पउपद्यते Is reasonable च and अपि and उपलभ्यते is seen च also.

36. And (that the world is without a beginning) is reasonable and is also seen (from the scriptures).

Reason tells us that creation must be without a beginning. For if the world did not exist in a potential state in the form of Saṁskâras (impressions), then an absolutely non-existing thing would be produced at creation. In that case even liberated souls might be reborn. Moreover people would be enjoying or suffering without having done anything to deserve it—an instance of an effect without a cause, which is absurd. It cannot be attributed to primeval ignorance, which, being one, requires the diversity of individual past work to produce varied results. The scriptures also posit the existence of the world in former cycles in texts like "The Lord devised the sun and moon as before" (Ṛg-Veda, 10. 190. 3).

So partiality and cruelty cannot be imputed to the Lord.

Topic 13: Brahman endowed with all attributes necessary for creation.

सर्वधर्मोपपत्तेश्च ॥ ३७ ॥

सर्व-धर्म-उपपत्तेः From the possibility of all attributes

च and.

37. And because all attributes (required for the creation of the world) are possible (only in Brahman, It is the cause of the world).

This Sûtra answers the objection that because Brahman is attributeless It cannot be the material cause of the world.

Objection: Material cause is that which undergoes modification as the effect. Such a cause is generally seen to possess attributes in the world. Therefore an attributeless Brahman cannot be the material cause of the world, as it goes counter to our everyday experience.

Answer: Though the material cause undergoes change to produce the effect, yet this can take place in two ways. An actual modification, as when milk turns into curds, or an apparent modification due to ignorance, as when a rope is taken for a snake. Therefore though in the attributeless Brahman an actual change is impossible, yet an apparent modification is possible owing to Its power of Mâyâ. Because of this power all the attributes required in the cause for such a creation are possible only in Brahman. Therefore Brahman is the material cause of this world, not through actual modification, but through apparent modification, and It is also the efficient cause of the world. Therefore the fact that Brahman is the cause of the world is established.

CHAPTER II

SECTION II

In the last section all arguments against Brahman being the first Cause have been answered. In this section all the doctrines of the other schools are taken up for refutation through reasoning alone without reference to the authority of the Vedas.

In the last Sûtra it has been shown that Brahman possesses all the attributes, though through Mâyâ, for equipping It to be the first Cause of the universe. Now the question is taken up whether the Sâṁkhyan Pradhâna can satisfy all those conditions.

Topic 1: Refutation of the Sâṁkhyan theory of the Pradhâna as the first Cause.

रचनानुपपत्तेश्च नानुमानम् ॥ १ ॥

रचनानुपपत्तेः Because of the impossibility of design च and न not अनुमानम् that which is inferred.

1. And that which is inferred (*viz* the Pradhâna of the Sâṁkhyas can) not (be the first Cause) because (in that case it is) not possible (to account for the) design (found in the creation).

In the preceding portion the Sâṁkhyan doctrine has been refuted here and there on scriptural authority.

Sûtras 1-10 refute it through reasoning independent of the Vedânta texts.

The inert Pradhâna does not possess the intelligence that is required for creating such a diverse and well-designed world as this, and so it cannot be the first Cause.

प्रवृत्तेश्च ॥ २ ॥

प्रवृत्तेः Of a tendency च and.

2. And on account of (the impossibility of such) a tendency (to create).

Even granting that such a creation is possible for the Pradhâna, still there are other objections.

Inert Pradhâna cannot again be credited with the desire or tendency to create. Clay by itself is never seen to create a pot without the agency of an intelligent being. So the inert Pradhâna cannot be the cause, for in that case the activity necessary for the production of the world would be impossible. There must be some ruling intelligence for that purpose.

पयोऽम्बुवच्चेत् तत्रापि ॥ ३ ॥

पयोऽम्बुवत् Like milk and water चेत्, if it be said तत्र there अपि even.

3. If it be said (that the Pradhâna spontaneously undergoes modification) like (the flowing of) milk and water, (we say that) even there (it is due to intelligence).

The Sâṁkhyas try to get over the difficulty by saying that even as water flows in rivers spontaneously or milk from the udder to the calf, so also the inert Pradhâna may become active of its own accord and undergo modification into intellect, Ahaṅkâra, etc. without the agency of any intelligence. The latter part of the Sûtra refutes this and says that even the flowing of water and milk is directed by the Supreme Lord. The scriptures also say: "Under the mighty rule of this Immutable, O Gârgî, some rivers flow to the east" etc. (Bṛ. 3. 8. 9); "He who inhabits water, but is within it, ... who controls water from within" (Bṛ. 3. 7. 4). The Lord is behind everything directing the material world.

व्यतिरेकानवस्थितेश्चानपेक्षत्वात् ॥ ४ ॥

व्यतिरेकानवस्थितेः There being no extraneous agency besides it च and अनपेक्षत्वात् because it is not dependent.

4. And because (the Prâdhana) is not dependent (on anything), there being no extraneous agency besides it (its activity and nonactivity cannot be explained).

The Pradhâna of the Sâṁkhyas being inert, it cannot of itself start to be active, or when once set in motion, cease to be active of itself. So in the absence of an intelligent guiding principle it is impossible for the Sâṁkhyas to explain creation and dissolution at the beginning and end of a cycle, which they admit. The only other principle besides the Pradhâna that they admit is the Puruṣa or soul, but according to them it is not an agent, for it is indifferent. All other principles which they admit including even Karma are but products of the Pradhâna and as such cannot have any determining effect on it. Hence their position launches them into a contradiction.

अन्यत्राभावाच्च न तृणादिवत् ॥ ५ ॥

अन्यत्र Elsewhere अभावात् because of its absence च and न not तृणादिवत् even as grass etc.

5. And (it can) not (be said that the Pradhâna undergoes modification spontaneously) even as grass etc. (turn into milk); because of its absence elsewhere (than in the female mammals).

Nor is the spontaneous modification of the Pradhâna possible. If you cite grass as an instance, we say it is not changed into milk spontaneously but only when eaten by female mammals. Otherwise it would be converted into milk independently of them. Since the analogy itself does not stand, we cannot accept the Pradhâna's undergoing modification of itself.

अभ्युपगमेऽप्यर्थाभावात् ॥ ६ ॥

अभ्युपगमे Accepting अपि even अर्थाभावात् because of the absence of any purpose.

6. Even accepting (the Sâṁkhyan position with regard to the spontaneous modification of the Pradhâna, it cannot be the first Caues) because of the absence of any purpose.

Granting the spontaneity of the Pradhâna, it will lead to a contradiction in their philosophy. If the Pradhâna is active spontaneously, then this activity cannot have any purpose, which would contradict the Sâṁkhyan view that the modification of the Pradhâna is for the experience and Liberation of the soul. Moreover, the soul being perfect, it is already free and nothing can be added to or taken away from it. Hence the Pradhâna cannot be the first Cause.

पुरुषाश्मवदिति चेत्, तथापि ॥ ७ ॥

पुरुष-अश्म-वत् Even as a person or a magnet इति चेत् if it be said तथापि even then.

7. If it be said (that the Puruṣa can direct the Pradhâna) even as a (crippled) person (can direct a blind man), or a magnet (the iron filings), even then (the difficulty cannot be surmounted).

The Sâṁkhyas hold that though the Puruṣa is itself inactive yet it can direct the Pradhâna; the Sûtra refutes it. According to the Sâṁkhyas, the Pradhâna is independent, and so it is not in keeping with this to say that it depends on the nearness of the Puruṣa for its activity, even as the iron filings depend on the magnet for their motion. Moreover, the Puruṣa being always near the Pradhâna, there would be permanency of creation. Again, the case of the lame and the blind is not an apt example, for the lame man can give directions to the blind one and direct him; but since the Puruṣa is altogether indifferent according to the Sâṁkhyas, it cannot do that with respect to the

Pradhâna. In Vedânta, though Brahman is indifferent, yet through Mâyâ It is endowed with attributes and activity; so It becomes the Creator. Again the Puruṣa and the Pradhâna are altogether separate and independent; the one is intelligent and indifferent, the other inert and independent. Now if these two are to be connected, a third principle will be required, and since no such principle is recognized in the Sâṁkhya philosophy, their connection is impossible.

अङ्गित्वानुपपत्तेश्च ॥ ८ ॥

अङ्गित्व-अनुपपत्तेः Owing to the impossibility of the relation of principal (and subordinate) च and.

8. And because the relation of principal (and subordinate) is impossible (among the Guṇas, the Pradhâna cannot be active).

The Pradhâna, according to the Sâṁkhyas, consists of the three Guṇas (constituents), Sattva, Rajas, and Tamas, which are independent of each other and in a state of equilibrium before creation. Creation begins when this equilibrium is upset and one Guṇa becomes more predominant than the other two. Equilibrium cannot be upset without any external force, nor can the Guṇas, which are absolutely independent in the state of Pradhâna, take of themselves a subsidiary position to another Guṇa without losing their independence. Hence creation would be impossible.

अन्यथानुमितौ च ज्ञशक्तिवियोगात् ॥ ९ ॥

अन्यथा Otherwise अनुमितौ if it be inferred च even

ज्ञशक्ति-वियोगात् owing to the absence of the power of intelligence.

9. Even if it be inferred otherwise, owing to the absence of the power of intelligence (the other objections to the Pradhâna being the first Cause remain).

If it be inferred from the effects that the cause, the Pradhâna, consists of Guṇas which are not absolutely independent, but contain some characteristics inherent in them, like instability, owing to which they themselves enter into a state of inequality even while they are in a state of equilibrium, then also because of the want of intelligence the objections founded on design in the world and that it would lead to continuous creation, stand against accepting the Pradhâna as the first Cause. *Vide* Sûtras 1 and 4.

विप्रतिषेधाच्चासमञ्जसम् ॥ १० ॥

विप्रतिषेधात् Because of contradictions also च असमञ्जसम् inconsistent.

10. Also because of contradictions (the Sâṁkhyan theory) is inconsistent.

There are various contradictions in the Sâṁkhya philosophy, as, for example, sometimes the senses are said to be eleven and again they are said to be seven; again the Tanmâtras are said to be produced from Mahat in one place and in another place from Ahaṅkâra (Ego), and so on Its differences with Śruti and

Smṛti are well known. Hence the doctrine of the Pradhâna of the Sâṁkhyas cannot be accepted.

Topic 2: Refutation of the objection from the Vaiśeṣika standpoint against Brahman being the first Cause.

महद्दीर्घवद्वा ह्रस्वपरिमण्डलाभ्याम् ॥ ११ ॥

महत्-दीर्घ-वत् Even as the great and long वा or ह्रस्व-परिमण्डलाभ्याम् from the short and the infinitesimal.

11. (The world may originate from Brahman) even as the great and long (triad etc.) originate from the short (and the minute dyad) or (this kind of dyad) from the infinitesimal (atom).

The Sâṁkhyas having been refuted, the Vaiśeṣika philosophy is taken up in Sûtras 11-17 and refuted. First, the plausible objection against Brahman being the first Cause is answered from the standpoint of the Vaiśeṣikas in Sûtra 11. According to them the qualities of the cause produce similar qualities in the effects, even as the whiteness of the threads produce that of the cloth woven out of them. So if the world is created from Brahmaṇ, the quality of intelligence should abide in the world also; but as a matter of fact it does not. So Brahman cannot be the cause of the world. This argument is refuted on the ground that the same objection applies to the Vaiśeṣika view of creation also; hence it is no special objection against Vedânta. According to them the ultimate condition of the world is atomic, and all things in this world are but aggregates of the different kinds of atoms. The atoms are eternal and the ultimate cause of the world. In the state of dissolution the world exists in the atomic state. At the time of creation the atoms of air are set in motion by Adṛṣṭa, the unseen principle, and two atoms combine to form a dyad. Again, three dyads combine to form a triad. and four dyads form a tetrad, and in this way gross air is created. Similarly, the other elements are created from their respective atoms and dyads. An atom, according to this philosophy, is infinitesimal, a dyad is minute and short, and compounds from the triad upwards are great and long. Now, if two atoms which are spherical, produce a dyad which is minute and short, but in which the sphericity of the atom is not reproduced, or if four dyads, which are short and minute, produce a tetrad, which is great and long, but the minuteness and shortness of the dyad are not handed down, it is clear that all the qualities of the cause are not reproduced in the effect. So there can be no objection to an intelligent Brahman being the cause of the world, which is not intelligent. Brahman, which is Knowledge and Bliss, can produce a world which is inert and full of misery.

Topic 3: Refutation of the atomic theory of the Vaiśeṣikas.

Having answered the objection against the Vedântic view, the author of the Sûtras now proceeds to refute the Vaiśeṣika philosophy.

उभयथापि न कर्मातस्तदभावः ॥ १२ ॥

उभयथापि In either case न is not कर्म activity अतः therefore तत्-अभावः negation of that.

12. In either case (*viz* the Adṛṣṭa, the unseen principle, inhering either in the atoms or in the soul) the activity (of the atoms) is not (possible), therefore the negation of that (*viz* of creation through the combination of atoms).

If the world is created by the combination of atoms, the question is, what causes this combination? If it is a seen cause, it is not possible before the creation of the body. A seen cause can either be an endeavour, or an impact, or the like. Unless there is the connection of the soul with the mind, there can be no endeavour on the part of the soul, according to the Vaiśeṣika assumption. And since before creation there is no body and therefore no mind, endeavour cannot take place. Similarly with impact etc. If the cause is Adṛṣṭa (the unseen principle), does it inhere in the soul or in the atoms? In either case, it cannot be the cause of the first motion of the atoms; for this Adṛṣṭa is non-intelligent and so cannot act by itself. If it is inherent in the soul, the soul being then inert, there is no intelligence to guide this Adṛṣṭa. If it is inherent in the atoms, it being always present, a state of dissolution would be impossible, for the atoms will be always active. Again, the soul is without parts like the atoms, and so there is no possibility of any connection between the soul and the atoms. Consequently, if the Adṛṣṭa inheres in the soul, it cannot influence the motion of the atoms not connected with the soul. So in all cases original activity in the atoms is not possible, and in the absence of that there can be no combination of atoms, as the Vaiśeṣikas say. Consequently, the theory that the world is created by the combination of atoms is untenable.

समवायाभ्युपगमाच्च साम्यादनवस्थितेः ॥ १३ ॥

समवाय-अभ्युपगमात् Samavâya being admitted च also साम्यात् equality of reasoning अनवस्थितेः *regressus in infinitum* would result.

13. (The Vaiśeṣika theory is untenable) also (because it involves) a *regressus in infinitum* on similar reasoning, since it accepts Samavāya.

Samavâya or inseparable inherence is one of the seven categories of the Vaiśeṣikas. They say it is this that connects the dyad with its constituents, the two atoms, since the dyad and the atoms are of different qualities. In that case Samavâya (inherence) itself also being different from these dyads and atoms, which it connects, another Samavâya will be required to connect it with these, and that in its turn will require another Samavâya to connect it with the first Samavâya and so on without an end. Hence the argument would be defective, and consequently the atomic doctrine, which admits Samavâya for combination, is inadmissible.

नित्यमेव च भावात् ॥ १४ ॥

नित्यम् एव Permanently च and भावात because existing.

14. And because of the permanent existence (of the tendency to act or otherwise of the atoms, the atomic theory is inadmissible).

The atomic theory involves another difficulty. If the atoms are by nature active, then creation would be permanent, for dissolution would mean a change in the nature of the atoms, which is impossible. If on the other hand, they are by nature inactive, then dissolution would be permanent, and there will be no creation for the same reason. Their nature cannot be both activity and inactivity, they being contradictory. If they are neither, their activity and inactivity would depend on an efficient cause, like Adṛṣṭa, which being always connected with the atoms, they will always be active, and creation would be permanent. If on the other hand, there is no efficient cause, there will be no activity of the atoms and hence no creation. Consequently the atomic theory is again inadmissible.

रूपादिमत्वाच्च विपर्ययो, दर्शनात् ॥ १५ ॥

रूपादिमत्वात् On account of possessing colour etc. च and विपर्ययः the opposite दर्शनात् because it is seen.

15. And on account of (the atoms) possessing colour etc., the opposite (of what the Vaiśeṣikas hold would be true), because it is seen.

The atoms are said to have colour etc., for otherwise the effects will not possess these qualities, since it is the qualities of the cause that are found in the effects. In that case the atoms would cease to be atomic and permanent. For whatever possesses colour etc. is found to be gross, not minute, and impermanent as compared with its cause. So the atoms also, which have colour etc., must be gross and impermanent, and this contradicts the Vaiśeṣika tenet that they are minute and permanent. So the atoms cannot be the ultimate cause of the world.

उभयथा च दोषात् ॥ १६ ॥

उभयथा In either case **च** and **दोषात्** because of defects.

16. And because of defects in either case (the atomic theory is untenable).

The four gross elements earth, water, fire, and air are produced from atoms. Now these elements are different as regards qualities. Earth, for example, has the qualities of touch, taste, smell, and colour, while water has only three of these, fire only two, and air one. If we suppose that their respective atoms also possess the same number of qualities as they, then while an atom of air has one quality, an atom of earth will have four qualities. Possessing four qualities it will be bigger in size, for our experience says that an increase of qualities cannot take place without an increase of size, and consequently it would cease to be atomic. If, on the other hand, we take them all to possess the same number of qualities, then there cannot be any difference in the qualities of the products, the elements, according to the principle that the qualities of the cause are reproduced in its effects. In either case, the Vaiśeṣika doctrine is defective and therefore inadmissible.

अपरिग्रहाच्चात्यन्तमनपेक्षा ॥ १७ ॥

अपरिग्रहात् Because it is not accepted **च** and **अत्यन्तम्** completely **अनपेक्षा** to be rejected.

17. And because (the atomic theory) is not accepted (by any authoritative persons like Manu and others) it is to be completely rejected.

Topic 4: Refutation of the Bauddha Realists.

समुदाय उभयहेतुकेऽपि तदप्राप्तिः ॥ १८ ॥

समुदाये The aggregate उभय-हेतुके having for its cause he two अपि even तत्-अप्राप्तिः it will not take place.

18. Even if the (two kinds of) aggregates proceed from their two causes, there would result he non-formation (of the two aggregates).

This Sûtra begins the refutation of the Bauddha chool. There are three principal schools of Buddhism, iz the Realists, who accept the reality of both the outide and the inside world, consisting respectively of xternal things and thought; the Idealists who mainin that thought alone is real; and the Nihilists, who aintain that everything is void and unreal. But all of em agree that everything is momentary—nothing sts beyond a moment.

The Realists among the Bauddhas recognize two ggregates, the external material world and the internal ental world—both together making up the universe. he external world is made up of the aggregation of oms. These atoms are of four kinds—atoms of earth, hich are hard; atoms of water, which are viscid; oms of fire, which are hot; and atoms of air, which e mobile. Of the internal world, the five Skandhas roups) are the cause. They are—Rûpa Skandha, mprising the senses and their objects; the Vijñâna

Skandha, comprising the series of self-cognitions which give rise to the notion of 'I'; the Vedana Skandha, comprising pleasure, pain, etc.; the Saṁjñâ Skandha, comprising the cognition of things by names, as, he is a man; and the Saṁskâra Skandha, comprising attachment and aversion, Dharma (merit), Adharma (demerit), etc. By the aggregation of these Skandhas the internal aggregate or the mental world is produced These are the two internal and external aggregate referred to in the Sûtras. Sûtras 18-27 refute the Realists' view.

The question now arises, how are these aggregate formed? Is there an intelligent principle behind as the cause, the guide, of the aggregation, or does it take place spontaneously? If there is an intelligent principle, is i stationary or momentary? If it is stationary, the Buddhistic doctrine of momentariness is contradicted. I it is momentary, then we cannot say that it comes into existence first and then unites the atoms, for that would mean that the cause lasts for more than one moment Again, if there is no intelligent principle as guide, how can the non-intelligent atoms and the Skandhas aggregate in a systematic way? Moreover, the activity would be eternal, and there would be no destruction or Pralaya For all these reasons the formation of aggregates canno be accounted for, and in their absence there canno exist the stream of mundane existence. Consequentl the doctrine of this school of Bauddhas is untenable.

इतरेतरप्रत्ययत्वादिति चेत्, न, उत्पत्तिमात्र-
निमित्तत्वात् ॥ १९ ॥

इतरेतर-प्रत्ययत्वात् Because of successive causali

इति चेत् if it be said न no उत्पत्ति-मात्र-निमित्तत्वात् because they are merely the efficient cause of the origin.

19. If it be said (that the formation of aggregates is possible) because of the successive causality (of Nescience etc. in the Bauddha series), we say), no, because they are merely the efficient cause of the origin (of the immediately subsequent thing in the series, and not of the aggregation).

The series is as follows: Nescience, Saṁskâra (attachment, aversion, etc.), Vijñâna (self-consciousness), name (earth, water, etc.), colour (the rudimentary ingredients of the body), abode of the six (*i.e.* the body and the senses), contact, experience of pleasures etc., desire, movement, merit and demerit, etc. In this series the immediately preceding item is the cause of the next and so we can explain the mundane existence without any combining principle, as demanded in the previous Sûtra. These constitute an uninterrupted chain of cause and effect, revolving unceasingly, and this cannot take place without aggregates. So aggregates are a reality.

The Sûtra refutes it by saying that though in the series the preceding one is the cause of the subsequent one, there is nothing which can be the cause of the whole aggregate. That the atoms cannot combine of themselves even when they are assumed to be permanent and eternal, has been shown in refuting the Vaiśeṣikas. Much more is their combination by themselves impossible when they are momentary as the Buddhists hold. Again, the individual soul, for whose enjoyment etc. this aggregate of body etc. exists, is also momentar and cannot therefore be an enjoyer; and whose agai is Liberation, since the individual soul is momentary So the series, though it stands in a relation of successiv causality cannot be the cause of the aggregates, an there being no permanent enjoyer, there is neither an need of these aggregates. So the Bauddha doctrine o momentariness is untenable.

The Sûtra can also be explained as follows: Th Bauddhas say, if we hold that the atoms stand in relation of causality, then no combining principle of th atoms would be necessary; in that case they would joi of themselves. The latter part of the Sûtra refutes th saying that the causality will explain only the produ tion of the atoms of the pot of a subsequent moment b the atoms of the pot of a previous moment, but will nc explain the combination of the atoms into an aggregat which can take place only if there is an intelligent ager beh nd, for otherwise the combination of inert an momentary atoms cannot be explained.

उत्तरोत्पादे च पूर्वनिरोधात् ॥ २० ॥

उत्तरोत्पादे At the time of the production of tl subsequent thing च and पूर्व-निरोधात् because the ant cedent one has ceased to exist.

20. And because at the time of the produ tion of the subsequent thing (even in the seri of successive causality) the antecedent thing h already ceased to exist (it cannot be the cau of the subsequent thing).

The Sûtra now refutes that even the successive causality spoken of in the series Nescience, Saṁskâras, etc. is untenable. Since everything is momentary, the antecedent thing would already have ceased to exist at the next moment, when the subsequent thing is created; so it cannot be the cause of the other. The clay that exists at the time the pot is created, is alone the cause of the pot, and not that which existed before and has ceased to exist then. If it be still maintained to be the cause, then we have to accept that existence comes out of non-existence, which is impossible. Again the acceptance of the doctrine of momentariness would go against the principle that the effect is the cause in a new form. This principle shows that the cause exists in the effect, which means that it is not momentary. Again on account of the momentariness of things 'origination' and 'destruction' will be synonymous, for if we say there is difference between the two, then we shall be forced to say that the thing lasts at least for more than one moment, and consequently we shall have to abandon the doctrine of momentariness.

असति प्रतिज्ञोपरोधो यौगपद्यमन्यथा ॥ २१ ॥

असति If non-existence (of cause) be assumed प्रतिज्ञा-उपरोध. contradiction of the proposition अन्यथा otherwise यौगपद्यम् simultaneity.

21. If non-existence (of cause) be assumed, (the effects being produced in spite of it) (there will result) contradiction of their (Bauddhas') proposition. Otherwise (there would result) simultaneity (of cause and effect).

If, to avoid the difficulty shown in the previous Sûtra, the Bauddhas say that effects are produced without a cause, then they would contradict their own proposition that every effect has a cause. If on the other hand a cause be assumed, then we have to accept that the cause and effect exist simultaneously at the next moment, *i.e.* the cause lasts for more than one moment, as already shown in the last Sûtra, which would falsify the doctrine of momentariness.

प्रतिसंख्याप्रतिसंख्यानिरोधाप्राप्तिः, अविच्छेदात् ॥ २२ ॥

प्रतिसंख्या (निरोध)-अप्रतिसंख्यानिरोध-अप्राप्तिः Conscious destruction and unconscious destruction would be impossible अविच्छेदात् owing to non-interruption.

22. Conscious and unconscious destruction would be impossible owing to non-interruption.

The Bauddhas maintain that universal destruction is ever going on, and that this destruction is of two kinds, conscious and unconscious, The former depends upon an act of thought, as when a jar is broken by a man with a stick, while the latter is the natural decay of things. The Sûtra says that either kind of destruction would be impossible, for it must refer either to the series of momentary existences or to the single members of that series. The series is continuous and can never be stopped. Why? Because the last momentary existence before such destruction must be assumed either to produce its effect or not to produce it. If it does then the series would continue and will not be destroyed. If it does not produce the effect, the last momentary existence ceases to be a fact at all, for according to the Bauddhas existence (Sattâ) means causal efficiency. Again the non-existence of the last momentary existence would lead backward to the non-existence of the previous momentary existence and so on of the whole series.

Again these two kinds of destruction cannot be found in the individual members of the series also. For owing to the momentary existence of each member no conscious destruction of it is possible. Neither can it be unconscious destruction, since the individual member is not altogether destroyed; for when a pot is destroyed we find the existence of the clay in the shreds. Even in those cases where it seems to vanish, as when a drop of water disappears on account of heat, we can infer that it continues to exist in some other form *viz* as steam.

उभयथा च दोषात् ॥ २३ ॥

उभयथा In either case च and दोषात् because of objections

23. And in either case (*i.e.* whether Nescience with its offshoots meets with conscious or unconscious destruction resulting in final release) because of the objections (that arise, the Bauddha position is untenable).

Nescience, according to the Bauddhas, is the false idea of permanency in things momentary. They say that on the destruction of it Mokṣa or Freedom is attained. Now this destruction of Nescience must be one of the two kinds referred to in the last Sûtra. If it is a conscious destruction, depending on the effort of the individual—his penance and knowledge, then this would go counter to the Buddhistic doctrine of momentariness, according to which Nescience will also be momentary and cease to exist after a moment of its own accord. And if we say that the destruction of ignorance is spontaneous, then the Buddhist instruction as to the 'path' is useless. So in either case the Bauddha position is untenable.

आकाशे चाविशेषात् ॥ २४ ॥

आकाशे In the case of Ākâśa (space) च also अविशेषात् there being no difference.

24. The case of Ākâśa also not being different (from the two-fold destruction, it also cannot be a non-entity).

According to the Bauddhas, besides the two-fold destruction Ākâśa or space is a third non-entity. It means the absence in general of any covering or occupying body. It has been shown in Sûtras 22-23 that the two kinds of destruction are not absolutely devoid of positive characteristics and so cannot be non-entities. The case of Ākâśa is also similar. Just as earth, air, etc. are recognized to be entities in consequence of their being the substratum of properties like smell etc. similarly Ākâśa also on account of its being the substratum of sound ought to be recognized as an entity. Earth etc. are experienced through their attributes, and the existence of Ākâśa also is experienced through it attribute, sound. Consequently it also must be an entity.

अनुस्मृतेश्च ॥ २५ ॥

अनुस्मृते: On account of memory च and.

25. And on account of memory (the permanency of the experience has to be recognized).

A further refutation of the momentariness of things is given here. If everything is momentary, the experiencer or enjoyer of something must also be momentary. But that the enjoyer is not momentary and abides longer is realized from the fact that people have the memory of past experiences. Memory is possible only in a person who has previously experienced it, for what is experienced by one man is not remembered by another. So the agent of the experience and the remembrance being the same, he is connected with at least two moments—which refutes the doctrine of momentariness.

नासतः, अदृष्टत्वात् ॥ २६ ॥

न Not असत: from non-existence अदृष्टत्वात् because this is not seen.

26. (Existence does) not (result) from non-existence, because this is not seen.

The Bauddhas say that from anything that is eternal and non-changing no effects can be produced; for that which does not change cannot give rise to effects. So they say that the cause undergoes destruction before the effect is produced. The seed undergoes destruction, and then the sprout comes out. In other words, existence springs from non-existence. The Sûtra refutes this by saying that if it were so, then the assumption of special causes would be meaningless. Anything might spring from anything; for non-entity is the same in all cases. There is no difference between the non-entity of a mango stone and that of an apple seed. Consequently we could expect an apple tree to come out of a mango stone. If there are distinctions between non-existences, with the result that the non-existence of a mango stone differs from that of an apple seed, and therefore they produce certain definite results, then they will no longer be non-entities, but something positive.

उदासीनानामपि चैवं सिद्धिः ॥ २७ ॥

उदासीनानाम् Of the effortless अपि even च and एवं thus सिद्धिः attainment of the goal.

27. And thus (if existence should spring from non-existence, there would result) the attainment of the goal even by the effortless.

Mere inactivity would result in the fulfilment of all ends, for there would no longer be the necessity of the cause, activity. Even final Freedom would result without any effort.

Topic 5: Refutation of the Bauddha Idealists.

नाभावः उपलब्धेः ॥ २८ ॥

न Is not अभावः non existence उपलब्धेः on account of their being experienced.

28. Non-existence (of things external) is not (true), on account of their being experienced.

From this Sûtra begins the refutation of the Idealists among the Bauddhas, according to whom only ideas exist and nothing else.

According to them the external world is non-existent. Does it mean that the objective world is absolutely non-existent like the horns of a hare, or does it mean that it is unreal even as the world seen in a dream is unreal? The Sûtra refutes the former view. In that case we could not have experienced it. The external world is an object of experience through the senses, and cannot therefore be altogether non-existent like the horns of a hare. The Buddhist may say that he does not affirm that he is conscious of no object, but only that what is seen in his consciousness alone shines as something external. But then the very nature of consciousness itself proves the existence of external things different from consciousness, for men are conscious of things or objects of perception, and nobody is conscious of his perception merely. The very fact that the Bauddhas say that the internal cognition appears 'as something external' shows that the external world is real. If it were not real, the comparison 'like something external' would be meaningless. No one says that Devadatta is like the son of a barren woman.

वैधर्म्याच्च न स्वप्नादिवत् ॥ २९ ॥

वैधर्म्यात् Owing to the difference of nature च and न is not स्वप्नादिवत् like dreams etc.

29. And owing to the difference of nature (in

consciousness between the waking and the dream states, the experience of the waking state) is not like dreams etc.

This Sûtra refutes the alternative view given in the previous Sûtra. The Bauddhas may say that perception of the external world is to be considered similar to dreams and the like. In a dream there are no external objects; yet the ideas appear in a two-fold form as subject and object. The appearance of an external world is similarly independent of any objective reality. This Sûtra refutes that view. There is a difference between the dream state and the waking state. What is seen in a dream is contradicted by waking experience, it is unreal. The dream state is a kind of memory, but the waking state is a real perception; so it cannot be rejected as untrue. Moreover, what is the proof of the existence of consciousness except experience? If that is so, why should not an object which is experienced be taken also as existing? It may be said that even the Vedântins acknowledge the unreality of the external world, since it is contradicted by the knowledge of Brahman, and that this view is based on the Śrutis. But if the Bauddhas accept the authority of the Vedas, then they would be included within the Vedântic school and no longer remain outside it, but as a matter of fact they do not accept the Vedas.

न भावः अनुपलब्धेः ॥ ३० ॥

न Is not भाव existence अनुपलब्धेः because (external things) are not experienced.

30. The existence (of Saṁskâras) is not (possible according to the Bauddhas), because (external things) are not experienced.

The Bauddhas say that though external things do not exist, yet the actual variety of notions like pot, cloth, etc. can be accounted for by the preceding Saṁskâras or mental impressions left by previous experience, even as the impressions of the waking state give rise to the variety of experience in the dream state. This view is not tenable, says the Sûtra, for mental impressions are impossible without the perception of external objects, and this the Bauddhas deny. The assumption of a beginningless series of mental impressions as cause and effect would only lead to a *regressus in infinitum* and not solve the difficulty.

क्षणिकत्वाच्च ॥ ३१ ॥

क्षणिकत्वात् On account of the momentariness च and.

31. And on account of the momentariness (of the ego-consciousness it cannot be the abode of the Saṁskâras).

The mental impressions must have an abode. Without that they cannot exist. But the doctrine of momentariness denies permanency to everything. Even the Ālayavijñâna or ego-consciousness, is momentary and cannot be that abode. Unless there is a permanent principle connecting the past, present, and future, there cannot be remembrance or recognition of an experience originating at a particular time and place.

If the Ālayavijñâna is said to be something permanent, then that would go counter to the doctrine of momentariness.

सर्वथानुपपत्तेश्च ॥ ३२ ॥

सर्वथा In every way अनुपपत्तेः being illogical च and.

32. And (as the Bauddha system is) illogical in every way (it cannot be accepted).

This Sûtra can also be interpreted as refuting the Nihilists: The translation would then be: And (as Nihilism) is illogical etc.

Nihilism of the Bauddhas goes counter to everything. It goes against the Śruti, the Smṛti, perception, inference, and every other means of right knowledge and so has to be entirely disregarded by those who are mindful of their welfare.

Topic 6: Refutation of the Jainas.

नैकस्मिन्, असम्भवात् ॥ ३३ ॥

न Not एकस्मिन् in one असम्भवात् on account of the impossibility.

33. On account of the impossibility (of contrary atributes) in one and the same thing (the Jaina doctrine is) not (true).

After the refutation of the Bauddhas the Jaina doctrine is taken up for discussion and refutation. The Jainas acknowledge seven categories, which can be mainly divided into two groups, the soul and the non soul. Again they predicate seven different views as regards the reality of everything. Everything according to them may be real, unreal, both real and unreal, different from real and unreal, indescribable, and so on. Now this view about things cannot be accepted, as it is absurd to think of the same thing as endowed with these contradictory attributes of reality, unreality, etc. According to the Jaina doctrine we cannot arrive at any certain knowledge, and this world, heaven, and even Freedom will become doubtful. According to Vedântic view, however, the world is Anirvacanîya, unspeakable, and so fit for all relative purposes.

एवं चात्माकात्स्न्र्यम् ॥ ३४ ॥

एवं In the same way च and आत्म-अकात्स्न्र्यम् non-universality of the soul.

34. And in the same way (there would arise) the non-universality of the soul.

The Jainas say that the soul is of the size of the body. If so, it would be limited and with parts; therefore it cannot be eternal. Another difficulty would be that the soul of an ant taking an elephant body as a result of its past work will not be able to fill up that body; and conversely, the soul of an elephant will not have sufficient space in an ant body. The same difficulty arises with respect to the different stages like childhood, youth, old age, etc. in a single individual.

न च पर्यायादप्यविरोधः विकारादिभ्यः ॥ ३५ ॥

न च Nor पर्यायात् in turn अपि even अविरोधः consistency विकारादिभ्यः on account of change etc.

35. Nor (can) consistency (be gained) even (if the soul is assumed to take on and discard parts) in turn (to suit different bodies), on account of the change etc. (of the soul in that case).

To get over the difficulty shown in the previous Sûtra about the soul being of the size of the body it assumes, if it be regarded as having parts and alternatively adding to and taking away from them, then another defect, *viz* the soul undergoing modification and consequently being non-eternal, would arise. If it is non-eternal and ever-changing, bondage and liberation cannot be predicated of it.

अन्त्यावस्थितेश्चोभयनित्यत्वादविशेषः ॥ ३६ ॥

अन्त्य-अवस्थितेः Because of the permanency (of the size) at the end **च** and **उभय-नित्यत्वात्** there follows the permanency of the two **अविशेषः** there is no difference.

36. And because of the permanency (of the size of the soul) at the end (*i.e.* on release) there follows the permanency of the two (preceding sizes, *viz* those at the beginning and middle), (hence) there is no difference (as to the size of the soul at any time).

The size of the soul at the time of release, the Jainas hold, is permanent. Now if this size is permanent, it cannot have been created, for nothing created is eternal and permanent. If it is not created, it must have existed in the beginning and middle as well. In other words the size of the soul was always the same, be it minute or great. Hence the Jaina theory that it varies according to the size of the body is untenable.

Topic 7: Refutation of the doctrine that God is only the efficient, not material, cause of the world.

पत्युः, असामञ्जस्यात् ॥ ३७ ॥

पत्युः The Lord's असामञ्जस्यात् on account of inconsistency.

37. The Lord's (being merely the efficient cause of the world cannot hold good) on account of the inconsistency (of that doctrine).

The Vedânta says that the Lord is both the efficient and the material cause of the world. The Naiyâyikas, Vaiśeṣikas, Yogins, and Mâheśvaras say that the Lord is the efficient cause only, and the material cause is either the atoms according to the Naiyâyikas and Vaiśeṣikas, or the Pradhâna according to the Yogins and others. He is the ruler of the Pradhâna and the souls, which are different from Him. Such a view leads to inconsistency. How? Because it makes the Lord partial to some and prejudiced against others, for some people are well off in this world, while others are miserable. The opponents here may say: How does the Vedântin get out of the difficulty? He replies: The Lord is impartial, but He directs the individuals according to their merit and demerit earned in previous existences (See Sûtras 2. 1. 34-35). For the scriptures say so, and if you accept scriptural authority in this, you will have to accept its statement, "I will be many" etc. (Tai. 2. 6), which shows that the Lord is both the efficient and material cause.

संबन्धानुपपत्तेश्च ॥ ३८ ॥

संबन्ध-अनुपपत्तेः Because relation is not possible च and.

38. And because relation (between the Lord and the Pradhâna or the souls) is not possible.

As the Lord is devoid of parts, and so also the Pradhâna and the souls, there can be no conjunction between the Lord and them, and consequently they cannot be ruled by Him. Neither can the relation be one of inherence, which subsists between entities inseparably connected as whole and part, substance and attributes, etc. This difficulty does not arise in the case of the Vedântins, firstly because the relation is inexpressible identity (Tâdâtmya) and secondly because they depend on the Śrutis for their authority and so are not expected to base their reasoning entirely on observed facts, as the opponents have to.

अधिष्ठानानुपपत्तेश्च ॥ ३९ ॥

अधिष्ठान-अनुपपत्तेः Rulership being impossible च and.

39. And on account of the rulership (of the Lord) being impossible.

These schools infer the existence of the Lord, and say that He directs the Pradhâna etc. as the potter does his clay. But the Pradhâna etc. are not objects of perception like the clay. Hence the Lord cannot direct them, for the inference must be strictly in accordance with observed facts.

करणवच्चेत्, न, भोगादिभ्यः ॥ ४० ॥

करणवत् As the senses चेत् if it be said न no भोगादिभ्यः because of enjoyment etc.

40. If it be said (that the Lord rules the Pradhâna etc.) even as (the Jîva rules) the senses (which are also not perceived), (we say) no, because of the enjoyment etc.

Even as the individual soul directs the sense organs which are not perceived, so also we can take it that the Lord rules the Pradhâna etc.—says the opponent. The analogy is not proper, for in the former case the Jîva is seen to enjoy pleasure, suffer pain, etc., from which we infer that it rules the organs. If the analogy be true, the Lord also would suffer pain and pleasure caused by the Pradhâna etc.

अन्तवत्त्वमसर्वज्ञता वा ॥ ४१ ॥

अन्तवत्त्वम् Subject to destruction असर्वज्ञता non-omniscience वा or.

41. (There would result from their doctrine the Lord's) being subject to destruction or (His) non-omniscience.

According to these schools the Lord is omniscient and eternal, i.e. not subject to destruction.

The Lord, the Pradhâna, and the souls according to the Mâheśvaras are infinite and separate. Now the question is, does the omniscient Lord know the measure of the Pradhâna, soul, and Himself or not? In either case the doctrine of the Lord's being the mere efficient cause of the universe is untenable. If the Lord knows their measure, they are all limited, and therefore a time will come when they will all cease to exist. Again, if he does not know them, then He would cease to be omniscient.

Topic 8: Refutation of the Bhâgavata or the Pâñcarâtra school.

उत्पत्त्यसम्भवात् ॥ ४२ ॥

उत्पत्ति-असम्भवात् Owing to the impossibility of origination.

42. The origination (of the individual soul from the Lord) being impossible (the Pâñcarâtra doctrine is untenable).

The Pâñcarâtra or the Bhâgavata school is now taken up for examination. It recognizes the material and efficient causality of the Lord, but propounds certain other views which are objectionable. According to it Vâsudeva is the Supreme Lord, the material and efficient cause of the world. By worshipping Him, meditating on Him, and knowing Him one attains liberation. From Vâsudeva is born Saṁkarṣaṇa, the Jîva; from Jîva Pradyumna, the Mind; from mind Aniruddha, the Ego. These are the four-fold form (Vyûha) of the Lord Vâsudeva,

Of these, the view that Vâsudeva is the Supreme Lord, to be worshipped and so on, the Vedântin accepts, as it is not against the Śruti. But the creation of the Jîva etc. he rejects, as such creation is impossible. Why? Because if the soul be created, it would be subject to destruction, and so no Liberation can be predicated of it. That the soul is not created will be shown in Sûtra 2.3.17.

न च कर्तुः करणम् ॥ ४३ ॥

न च Nor कर्तुः from the agent करणम् the instrument.

43. Nor (is it seen that) the instrument (is produced) from the agent.

As an instrument, like an axe, is not seen to be produced from the agent, the woodcutter, the Bhâgavata doctrine—that from the individual soul is produced the internal instrument or mind, and from the mind the ego—cannot be accepted. Neither is there any scriptural authority for it. The scripture plainly says that everything originates from Brahman.

विज्ञानादिभावे वा तदप्रतिषेधः ॥ ४४ ॥

विज्ञानादि-भावे If intelligence etc. exist वा or तत्-अप्रतिषेधः no warding off of that.

44. Or if the (four Vyûhas are said to) possess intelligence etc., yet there is no warding off of that (*viz* the objection raised in Sûtra 42).

The Bhâgavatas may say that all the forms are Vâsudeva the Lord, and that all of them equally possess knowledge and lordship, strength, valour, etc. and are free from faults and imperfections. In this case there will be more than one Īśvara, which is redundant and also goes against their own assumption. Even granting all this, the origination of the one from the other is unthinkable. Being equal in all respects, none of them can be the cause of another, for the effect must have some feature that is lacking in the cause. Again the forms of Vâsudeva cannot be limited to four only, as the whole world from Brahmâ down to a clump of grass is a form of the Supreme Being.

विप्रतिषेधाच्च ॥ ४५ ॥

विप्रतिषेधात् Because of contradictions च and.

45. And because of contradictions (the Bhâgavata view is untenable).

Moreover the theory involves many contradictions. Sometimes it speaks of the four forms as qualities of the Ātman and sometimes as the Ātman itself.

CHAPTER II

SECTION III

In the previous section the inconsistency of the doctrines of the various non-Vedântic schools has been shown and consequently their unreliability has been established. A doubt may arise that on account of contradiction among the Śruti texts, the doctrine that upholds Brahman as the first Cause may also be of the same class. To clear such a doubt by harmonizing the apparent contradictions in scriptural texts, the next two sections are begun. The arguments of the opponent, who tries to prove the self-contradiction of the Śruti texts, are always given first, and then follows the refutation.

Topic 1: Ether is not eternal but created.

न वियत्, अश्रुतेः ॥ १ ॥

न Not वियत् Ākaśa अश्रुतेः (as it is) not so stated by the Śruti.

1. Ākāśa (is) not (created), (as it is) not so stated by the Śruti.

To start with, the texts dealing with creation are taken up, and Ākâśa (ether) is first dealt with. In the Chândogya Upaniṣad, where the order of creation is given, the text says, "It thought, 'May I be many, may I grow forth.' It sent forth fire" (6.2.3). Here there is no mention of Ākâśa being produced by the Sat or Brahman. Hence Ākâśa has no origin, it is eternal.

अस्ति तु ॥ २ ॥

अस्ति There is तु but.

2. But there is (a Śruti text which states that Ākâśa is created).

The opponent in this Sûtra anticipates a possible objection against his arguments advanced in Sûtra 1, and explains it away in Sûtra 3. The text referred to here is, "From that Self (Brahman) sprang Ākâśa (ether)" etc. (Tai. 2. 1).

गौणी, असम्भवात् ॥ ३ ॥

गौणी Used in a secondary sense असम्भवात् on account of the impossibility.

3. (The Śruti text dealing with the origin of Ākâśa) is to be taken in a secondary sense, on account of the impossibility (of Ākâśa being created).

The Taittirîya text referred to in the previous Sûtra the opponent holds, should be taken in a secondary sense, as Ākâśa cannot be created. It has no parts and hence cannot be created. Moreover, Ākâśa is all-pervading, and therefore it can be inferred that it is eternal—without origin.

शब्दाच्च ॥ ४ ॥

शब्दात् From the Śruti texts च also.

4. Also from the Śruti texts (we find that Ākâśa is eternal).

In the last Sûtra Ākâśa was inferred to be eternal. Here the opponent cites a Śruti text to show that it is eternal. The text referred to is, "And the formless are) Vâyu and Ākâśa—these are immortal" (Bṛ. 2. 3. 3). Being immortal or eternal, it cannot have a beginning.

स्याच्चैकस्य ब्रह्मशब्दवत् ॥ ५ ॥

स्यात् Is possible च and एकस्य of the same (word 'sprang') ब्रह्मशब्दवत् like the word 'Brahman'.

5. It is possible that the same word ('sprang' be used in a primary) and (secondary sense) like the word 'Brahman'.

The opponent in the Sûtra answers a weak point in his argument, *viz* how can the same word 'sprang' in the Taittirîya text, "From that Self (Brahman) sprang Ākâśa; from Ākâśa sprang Vâyu (air), from air sprang fire" etc. (2. 1), be used in a secondary sense with respect to Ākâśa and in the primary sense with respect to air, fire etc.? He does this by referring to other Śruti texts, where the word 'Brahman' is so used. "Try to know Brahman by penance, for penance is Brahman," where Brahman is used both in a primary and in a secondary sense in the same text; also "Food is Brahman" (Tai. 3. 2), and "Bliss is Brahman" (*Ibid.* 3. 6), where Brahman is used in a secondary and primary sense respectively in two complementary texts.

प्रतिज्ञाऽहानिरव्यतिरेकाच्छब्देभ्यः ॥ ६ ॥

प्रतिज्ञा-अहानिः Non-abandonment of proposition अव्यतिरेकात् from non-distinction शब्देभ्यः from the Śrutis

6. The non-abandonment of the proposition (*viz* by the knowledge of one everything else becomes known, can result only) from the non-distinction (of the entire world from Brahman). From the Śruti texts (which declare the non-difference of the cause and its effects, this proposition is established).

This Sûtra refutes the opponent's view set forth so far and gives the conclusion. The proposition that from the knowledge of one (Brahman) everything else is known can be true only if everything in the world is an effect of Brahman. For the Śruti says that the effects are not different from their cause, and consequently the cause being known, the effects will also be known. If Ākâśa is not created from Brahman, then the proposition in question falls through; for after knowing Brahman Ākâśa still remains to be known, on account of its not being an effect of Brahman. But if it is created, then no such difficulty arises. Hence Ākâśa is created; otherwise the authoritativeness of the Vedas would b gone. The Chândogya text in which Ākâśa is not mentioned is accordingly to be interpreted in the light of the Taittirîya text; that is, Ākâśa and Vâyu have to be inserted, and the text would mean that after creating Ākâśa and Vâyu, "It created fire"

यावद्विकारं तु विभागो लोकवत् ॥ ७ ॥

यावत्-विकारं Extending to all effects whatsoever तु but विभागः separateness लोकवत् as in the world.

7. But in all effects whatsoever (there is) separateness, as (is seen) in the world.

The word 'but' refutes the idea that Ākâśa is not created. We see in the world that all created things are different from each other. A pot is different from a piece of cloth and so on. In other words, everything which has a separateness about it is created. We cannot conceive of a thing as separate from others and yet eternal. Now Ākâśa is distinct from earth etc., and hence it cannot be eternal, but must be a created thing. It may be objected that the Ātman also is divided from ether and so on and therefore It too is an effect. But that is not possible, for all things are created from the Ātman, which is their Self, and so not separate from them; therefore It is not an effect. The all-pervasiveness and eternity of Ākâśa are only relatively true; it is created and is an effect of Brahman.

Topic 2: Air springs from ether.

एतेन मातरिश्वा व्याख्यातः ॥ ८ ॥

एतेन By this मातरिश्वा air व्याख्यातः is explained.

8. By this (i.e. the foregoing explanation about Âkâśa (the fact of) air (also being an effect) is explained.

Topic 3: Brahman is not created.

असम्भवस्तु सतः, अनुपपत्तेः ॥ ९ ॥

असम्भवः: There can be no origin तु but सतः of the Sat (That which is) अनुपपत्तेः as it does not stand to reason.

9. But there can be no origin of the Sat (That which is *i.e.* Brahman), as it does not stand to reason.

The question arises whether Brahman also is an effect like Âkâśa etc. In the Śvetâśvatara Upaniṣad there occurs the text: "Thou art born with Thy face turned to all directions" (Śv. 4. 3), which clearly states that Brahman is born. This view is refuted by the Sûtra, which says that Brahman, which is existence itself, cannot be an effect, as It can have no cause "And He has neither parent nor Lord" (*Ibid.* 6. 9). Neither can non-existence be such a cause, for the Śruti says, "How can existence come out of non-existence?" (Ch. 6.2.2). Nor is it proper to say that existence is its own cause, for the effect must have some speciality not possessed by the cause. Brahman is mere existence without any distinction. We observe that only particulars are produced from the general, as different pots are from clay, and not *vice versa*. Therefore Brahman which is existence in general, cannot be the effect of any particular thing. The fact that every cause is itself an effect of some antecedent thing is repudiated by the Śruti: "That great, birthless Self is undecaying" (Bṛ. 4. 4. 25), for it leads to a *regressus in infinitum.* So Brahman is not an effect, but is eternal.

Topic 4: Fire created from air.

तेजोऽतः तथा ह्याह ॥ १० ॥

तेजः Fire अतः from this तथा so हि verily आह says.

10. Fire (is produced) from this (*i.e.* air), so verily says (the Śruti).

"From air (is produced) fire" (Tai. 2. 1.) shows that fire springs from air. Again we have, "That (Brahman) created fire" (Ch. 6. 2. 3). These two texts can be reconciled by interpreting the Taittirîya text to mean the order of sequence: Brahman, after creating air, created fire. This Sûtra refutes such an ingenious explanation and says that fire is produced from Vâyu or air. This does not contradict the Chândogya text, for it means that as air is a product of Brahman, it is from Brahman, which has assumed the form of air, that fire is produced. The general proposition that everything is created from Brahman requires that all things should ultimately be traced to that cause, and not that they should be the immediate effects. Hence there is no contradiction.

Topic 5: Water created from fire.

आपः ॥ ११ ॥

11. Water (is produced from fire).

"From fire is produced water" (Tai. 2. 1); "That created water" (Ch. 6. 2. 3). These two texts leave no doubt that water is created from fire. Here also we must understand that from Brahman, conditioned as fire, water is produced.

Topic 6: Earth created from water

पृथिवी, अधिकाररूपशब्दान्तरेभ्यः ॥ १२ ॥

पृथिवी Earth अधिकार-रूप-शब्दान्तरेभ्यः because of the subject-matter, and other Śruti texts.

12. Earth (is meant by the word 'Anna') because of the subject-matter, colour, and other Śruti texts.

"From water earth" (Tai. 2. 1); "It (water) produced Anna (lit. Food)" (Ch. 6. 2. 4). The two texts are apparently contradictory; for in one water is said to produce earth and in another food. The Sûtra says that 'Anna' in the Chândogya text means not food, but earth. Why? First on account of the subject-matter treated in the section. In "It created fire," and such other texts the Śruti describes the creation of the five elements, and so 'Anna' should refer to an element and not food. Again in a complementary passage we have "The black colour in fire is the colour of Anna" (Ch. 6. 4. 1), where the reference to colour clearly indicates that the earth is meant by 'Anna'. Hence 'Anna' in the passage under discussion means earth, and there is no contradiction between the Chândogya and Taittirîya texts. Other Śruti texts like, "That which was there as the froth on water was solidified and became this earth" (Bṛ. 1. 2. 2), clearly show that from water earth is produced.

*Topic 7 : **Brahman** as the creative principle residing in the preceding element is the cause of the subsequent element in the order of creation.*

तदभिध्यानादेव तु तल्लिङ्गात् सः ॥ १३ ॥

तत्-अभिध्यानात् Because of His reflecting एव only तु but तल्लिङ्गात् from His indicatory marks सः He.

13. But because of His reflecting only (are the subsequent elements created from the previous element in the order of creation; so) He (the Supreme Lord is the creator of air etc.). (We know this) from His indicatory marks.

Brahman is described in the Śrutis as the creator of everything. Again we find in them texts like "From Ākâśa is produced air" (Tai. 2. 1), which declare that certain elements produce certain effects independently. So the opponent holds that there is a contradiction in the Śruti texts. This Sûtra refutes that objection saying that the Lord residing within these elements produces after reflection certain effects. Why? On account of the indicatory marks. "He who inhabits the earth...and who controls the earth from within" etc. (Bṛ. 3. 7. 3) shows that the Supreme Lord is the sole ruler, and denies all independence to the elements. Again, "That fire thought, ...that water thought" (Ch. 6. 2. 3-4) shows that after reflection these elements produced the effects. This reflection is impossible for inert elements, and so we are to understand that the Lord residing within these elements thought and produced the effects. Therefore the elements become causes only through the agency of the Lord, who abides within them. Hence there is no contradiction between the two texts cited at the beginning.

Topic 8 : Reabsorption takes place in the inverse order to that of creation.

विपर्ययेण तु क्रमोऽतः उपपद्यते च ॥ १४ ॥

विपर्ययेण In the reverse order तु indeed क्रमः order अतः from that (the order of creation) च and उपपद्यते is reasonable.

14. (At Pralaya the elements are) indeed (withdrawn into Brahman) in the reverse order from that (of creation); and this is reasonable.

The question is whether at the time of cosmic dissolution the elements get withdrawn into Brahman in the order of creation, or in the reverse order. The Sûtra says that it is in the reverse order, for the effect goes back to the causal state, as ice, for instance, melts into water. Hence each thing is withdrawn into its immediate cause and so on in the reverse order, till Ākâśa is reached, which in turn gets merged in Brahman.

Topic 9: The mention of the mind, intellect, and organs does not interfere with the order of creation and reabsorption, as they are the products of the elements.

अन्तरा विज्ञानमनसी क्रमेण तल्लिङ्गादिति चेत्,
न, अविशेषात् ॥ १५ ॥

अन्तरा In between विज्ञानमनसी intellect and mind क्रमेण in the order तल्लिङ्गात् owing to indication of that इति चेत् if it be said न not so अविशेषात् on account of non-difference.

15. If it be said that in between (Brahman and the elements) the intellect and the mind (are mentioned, and therefore that ought to be the order in creation and the inverse order in re-absorption), owing to the indication (in the Śruti texts) to that effect (which upsets the order of creation of the elements), (we say) not so, on account of the non-difference (of the intellect and the mind from the elements).

In the Muṇḍaka Upaniṣad occurs the following text, "From this Self are produced Prâṇa, mind, the senses. ether. air, fire, water, and earth, the support of all" (2. 1. 3). An objection is raised that the order of creation is as described in this text, which contradicts the order of creation of elements described in the Chândogya 6. 2. 3 and other Śrutis. This objection is here refuted on the ground that the Muṇḍaka text only states that all these are produced from the Self, but gives no order of creation like the other texts. Again the intellect, mind, and organs are effects of the elements, and so they can come into existence only after the elements are created. On account of this non-difference of the organs from the elements, their origination and reabsorption are the same as those of the elements. That the organs are modifications of the elements is proved by Śruti texts like, "For the mind, my child, consists of earth, the vital force of water, the vocal organ of fire" (Ch. 6. 6. 5). Therefore the Muṇḍaka text does not upset the order of creation mentioned elsewhere.

Topic 10: Birth and death are primarily spoken of the body, and metaphorically of the soul.

चराचरव्यपाश्रयस्तु स्यात् तद्व्यपदेशो भाक्तः,
तद्भावभावित्वात् ॥ १६ ॥

चराचरव्यपाश्रय: Depending on (the bodies) of moving and stationary beings तु but स्यात् may be तद्व्यपदेश: mention of that भाक्त: secondary तद्भाव-भावित्वात् on account of (those terms) depending on the existence of that.

16. But the mention of that (*viz* birth and death of the individual soul) is apt only with reference to (the bodies) of moving and stationary beings. (With reference to the soul, however,) it is secondary, on account of (those terms) depending on the existence of that (*i.e.* body).

A doubt may arise that the individual soul, too, has birth and death, because people use such expressions as "Devadatta is born" or "Devadatta is dead", and because certain ceremonies are prescribed by the scriptures at the birth and death of people. This Sûtra refutes such a doubt and says that the individual soul has neither birth nor death. These belong not to the soul, but to the body with which the soul is connected. This connection and disconnection with the body is popularly called the birth and death of the soul. Moreover, the Śruti says, "It is the body, which bereft of the soul, dies; the soul does not die" (Ch. 6. 11. 3). So birth and death are spoken primarily of the bodies of moving and stationary beings, and only metaphorically of the soul. That birth and death mean, respectively the connection and disconnection of the soul with the body is proved by such texts as "That man, when he is born, or attains a body" etc. (Bṛ 4. 3. 8).

Topic 11: The individual soul is permanent, eternal, etc.

नात्मा, अश्रुतेर्नित्यत्वाच्च ताभ्यः ॥ १७ ॥

न Is not (produced) आत्मा the individual self अश्रुते: not being (so) mentioned by the scriptures नित्यत्वात् being eternal च also ताभ्य: from them (Śrutis).

17. The individual self is not (produced), (for it is) not (so) mentioned by the scriptures; also (on account of its) being eternal, (for so it is known) from them (the Śruti texts).

At the beginning of creation there was only "One Brahman without a second" (Ai. 1. 1), and so it is not reasonable to say that the individual soul is not born, for then there was nothing but Brahman. Again the Śruti says: "Just as from a fire tiny sparks fly in all directions, even so from this Ātman emanate all Prâṇas (organs), all worlds, all gods, and the selves" (Bṛ. 2. 1. 20, Mâdhyandina recension). So the opponent argues that the individual soul is born at the beginning of the cycle, just as Ākâśa and other elements are born. This Sûtra refutes it and says that the individual soul is not born, for there is no statement to that effect in the Śruti in the section dealing with creation. On the other hand Śruti texts clearly deny such birth to the individual soul. "Unborn, eternal" (Ka. 1. 2. 18); "This great birthless Self" (Bṛ. 4. 4. 25). It is the one Brahman without a second that enters the intellect and appears as the individual soul (Jîva). "Having created it, It entered into it" (Tai. 2. 6). Hence as there is in reality no difference between the individual soul and Brahman, the fact of the Jîva's being non-created does not contradict the text, "At the beginning there was only the Ātman without a second" (Ai. 1. 1). The creation of souls spoken of in the other texts cited is only in a secondary sense. It does not therefore contradict the text, "Having created it, It entered into it."

Topic 12 : The nature of the individual soul is intelligence.

ज्ञोऽत एव ॥ १८ ॥

ज्ञः Intelligence अतः एव for this very reason.

18. For this very reason (*viz* that it is not created), (the individual soul is) intelligence (itself).

The Vaiśeṣikas say that the individual soul is not intelligent by nature, for it is not found to be so in the state of deep-sleep (Suṣupti) or of swoon. It is only when the soul comes to the conscious plane and unites with the mind that it becomes intelligent. This Sûtra refutes such a possibility, for it is the intelligent Brahman Itself that, being limited by the Upâdhis (limiting adjuncts), the body etc. manifests as the individual soul. Therefore intelligence is its very nature, and is never altogether destroyed, not even in the state of deep-sleep or swoon. "That it does not see in that state is because although seeing then, it does not see; for the vision of the witness can never be lost, because it is immortal. But there is not that second thing separate from it which it can see" (Bṛ. 4. 3. 23). Therefore it is not true that its intelligence is lost, for it is impossible. It does not in reality lose its power of seeing; it does not see only because there is no object to see. Were intelligence actually non-existent then, who would be there to say that it did not exist? How could it be known? Moreover, he who says that he did not know anything in deep-sleep, must have been existent at that time. Otherwise how could he remember the condition of that state? Hence the intelligence of the Self is never lost under any condition.

Topic 13: The size of the individual soul.

उत्क्रान्तिगत्यागतीनाम् ॥ १९ ॥

उत्क्रान्ति-गति-आगतीनाम् Passing out, going, and returning.

19. (As the Śruti texts declare the soul's) passing out, going (to other spheres) and returning (thence), (the soul is not infinite in size).

From this up to Sûtra 32 the question of the size of the soul—whether it is atomic, medium-sized or infinite—is discussed. We have in the Śvetâśvatara Upaniṣad: "He is the one God . . . all-pervading" (6. 11); and again, "This Ātman is atomic" (Mu. 3. 1. 9). The two texts contradict each other and we have to arrive at a decision on the point. Sûtras 20-28 set forth the *prima facie* view. The opponent says we find in the scriptures texts mentioning the soul's passing out of the body, going to heaven etc., and returning from there. This is possible only if the soul is atomic, and not infinite or all-pervading; for to an infinite soul there can be no going and coming. Therefore the soul is atomic.

स्वात्मना चोत्तरयोः ॥ २० ॥

स्वात्मना (Being connected) directly with their agent च and उत्तरयोः the latter two.

20. And the latter two (the going and coming) (being connected) directly with their agent (the soul), (it is of atomic size).

Even if the soul is infinite, still it can be spoken of as passing out of the body, if by that term is meant ceasing to be the ruler of the body. But the two latter activities, *viz* the going and coming, are not possible for an entity that is all-pervading. So the soul is atomic in size.

नाणुरतच्छ्रुतेरिति चेत्, न, इतराधिकारात् ॥ २१ ॥

न अणुः Not atomic अतत्-श्रुतेः as the scriptures state

it to be otherwise इति चेत् if it be said न not so इतराधिकारात् owing to a principle other than the individual soul being the subject-matter (in those texts).

21. If it be said (that the soul is) not atomic, as the scriptures state it to be otherwise (*i.e.* all-pervading), (we say) not so, for (the one) other than the individual soul (*i.e.* Supreme Brahman) is the subject-matter (in those texts).

Śruti texts like, "He is the one God...all-pervading" (Śv. 6. 11), refer not to the individual soul, but to the Supreme Lord, who is other than the individual soul and forms the chief subject-matter of all the Vedânta texts; for that is the one thing that is to be known, and is therefore propounded by all the Vedânta texts.

स्वशब्दोन्मानाभ्यां च ॥ २२ ॥

स्वशब्द-उन्मानाभ्यां From direct statements (of the Śruti texts) and infinitesimal measure च and.

22. And on account of direct statements (of the Śruti texts as to the atomic size) and infinitesimal measure (the soul is atomic).

"This Ātman is atomic" (Mu. 3. 1. 9). Again we have, "That individual soul is to be known as part of the hundredth part of the tip of a hair divided a hundred times" (Śv. 5. 9), which shows that the soul is smaller than even the smallest. Hence the soul is atomic in size

अविरोधश्चन्दनवत् ॥ २३ ॥

अविरोधः No contradiction चन्दनवत् like sandal-paste.

23. There is no contradiction, like sandal-paste.

Even as sandal-paste applied to any particular part of the body gives an aggreeable sensation all over the body, even so the soul, though of atomic size and therefore occupying only one part of the body, may experience happiness and misery extending over the entire body.

अवस्थितिवैशेष्यादिति चेत्, न, अभ्युपगमाद्धृदि हि ॥ २४ ॥

अवस्थिति-वैशेष्यात् On account of the particular position इति चेत् if it be said न not so अभ्युपगमात् on account of the admission हृदि in the heart हि indeed.

24. If it be said that on account of the particular position (of the sandal-paste in the body the analogy is not just), (we say) not so, on account of the admission (by the scriptures of a special seat of the soul, *viz*) in the heart alone.

A possible objection is raised by the opponent against his own view. In the case of the sandal-paste we see that it occupies a particular part of the body and yet gladdens the whole body. But in the case of the soul we do not know that it occupies a particular place, and in the absence of that we cannot infer that like the sandal paste it must occupy a particular portion of the body and therefore be atomic. For even an all-pervading soul or a soul pervading the whole body like the skin can give rise to the same result. So in the absence of any proof it is difficult to settle the size of the soul. This objection the opponent refutes by saying that such Śruti texts as, "The self-effulgent one within the heart" (Bṛ. 4. 3. 7) declare that the soul has a particular abode in the body, *viz* the heart, and hence it is atomic.

गुणाद्वा लोकवत् ॥ २५ ॥

गुणात् Owing to (its) quality वा or लोकवत् as in the world.

25. Or owing to (its) quality (*viz* intelligence) as in the world.

This Sûtra gives another argument to show how an atomic soul can have experience throughout the body. In the world we find that a light placed in one corner of a room illumines the whole room. So also the soul, though atomic and therefore occupying a particular portion of the body, may, because of its quality of intelligence, which pervades the whole body, experience pleasure and pain throughout the body.

व्यतिरेको गन्धवत् ॥ २६ ॥

व्यतिरेकः The extension beyond (the object *i.e.* the soul) गन्धवत् like odour.

26. The extension (of the quality of intelligence) beyond (the soul, in which it inheres) is like odour (which extends beyond the fragrant object).

We find that the sweet odour of flowers extends beyond them to the surrounding region. Even so the intelligence of the soul, which is atomic, extends beyond the soul and pervades the whole body.

तथा च दर्शयति ॥ २७ ॥

तथा Thus च also दर्शयति (the Śruti) shows o declares.

27. Thus also (the Śruti) declares.

The Śruti also declares that it is by the quality c intelligence that the atomic soul pervades the whol body. For instance, it says: "Just so has the intelliger self penetrated this body up to the very hairs and th finger nails" (Kau. 4. 20).

पृथगुपदेशात् ॥ २८ ॥

पृथक् Separate उपदेशात on account of the teaching.

28. On account of the separate teaching (the Śruti) (that the soul so pervades the bo owing to its quality of intelligence).

A further argument is given to establish the p position of the last Sûtra. The text, "Having by Praj (intelligence) taken possession of the body" (Kau. 3. 6), shows that intelligence is different from the soul, being related as instrument and agent, and that with this ouality the soul pervades the whole body.

तद्गुणसारत्वात् तु तद्व्यपदेशः, प्राज्ञवत् ॥ २९ ॥

तद्गुणसारत्वात् On account of its having for its ssence the qualities of that (*viz* the Buddhi) तु out तद्व्यपदेशः that declaration (as to its atomic size) प्राज्ञवत् even as the Intelligent Lord (is declared to e atomic).

29. But that declaration (as to the atomic ize of the soul) is on account of its having for ts essence the qualities of that (*viz* the Buddhi), ven as the Intelligent Lord (Brahman, which s all-pervading, is declared to be atomic).

The word 'but' refutes all that has been said in Sûtras 9-28, and decides that the soul is all-pervading, beause the all-pervading Brahman Itself is said to have ntered the universe as the individual soul, which again stated to be identical with It. How then is the soul eclared to be atomic? Such declarations are on acount of its preponderating in the qualities of the uddhi (intellect) so long as it is imagined to be conected with the latter and in bondage. Passing out, oing, and coming are qualities of the Buddhi and are nly imputed to the individual soul. For the same reason lso, *i.e.* limitation of the intellect, is the Ātman rearded as atomic. It is like imagining the all-pervading

Lord as limited for the sake of Upâsanâ, devout meditation.

यावदात्मभावित्वाच्च न दोषः, तद्दर्शनात् ॥ ३० ॥

यावत्-आत्मभावित्वात् So long as the soul (in its relative aspect) exists च and न दोषः there is no defect तद्दर्शनात् because it is so seen (in the scriptures).

30. And there is no defect (in what has been said in the previous Sûtra), (as the conjunction of the soul with the intellect exists) so long as the soul (in its relative aspect) exists: because it is so seen (in the scriptures).

An objection might be raised against what has been said in the previous Sûtra that since the conjunction of the soul and the intellect, which are different entities must necessarily come to an end some time, the soul when so disjoined from the Buddhi, will either cease to exist altogether or at least cease to be a Saṁsârin (individualized). This Sûtra replies: There can be no such defect in the argument of the previous Sûtra, for this connection with the intellect lasts so long as the soul's state of Saṁsâra is not destroyed by the realization of supreme Knowledge. How is this known? It is known from the declaration of the scriptures that even at death this connection is not severed. "This infinite entity that is identified with the intellect. ...Assuming the likeness of the intellect it moves between the two worlds, it thinks, as it were, it moves, as it were" (Bṛ. 4. 3. 7). The terms "thinks, as it were", "moves, as it were" also mean that the self does not think and move on its own account, but only through its association with the intellect.

पुंस्त्वादिवत् त्वस्य सतोऽभिव्यक्तियोगात् ॥ ३१ ॥

पुंस्त्वादिवत् Like virility etc. तु verily अस्य its (*i.e.* of the connection with the intellect) सत: existing अभिव्यक्तियोगात् on account of the manifestation being possible.

31. On account of the manifestation (of the connection with the intellect in the awakened state) being possible only on its existing (potentially in Suṣupti), like virility etc.

An objection is raised that in Suṣupti or deep-sleep there can be no connection with the intellect, for it is said, "Then he becomes united with the True, he is gone to his own" (Ch. 6. 8. 1); how then can it be said that this connection lasts so long as the individualized state exists?

This Sûtra refutes it and says that even in Suṣupti this connection exists in a fine or potential form. But for this it could not have become manifest in the awakened state. Virile power becomes manifest in youth only if it exists in a potential condition in the child. So this connection with the intellect lasts so long as the individualized state exists.

नित्यापलब्ध्यनुपलब्धिप्रसङ्गोऽन्यतर-
नियमो वाऽन्यथा ॥ ३२ ॥

नित्योपलब्धि-अनुपलब्धि-प्रसङ्ग: There would result perpetual perception or non-perception अन्यतरनियमः limitation of the power of either of the two वा or else अन्यथा otherwise.

32. Otherwise (*i.e.* if the intellect or mind be not accepted) there would result either perpetual perception or perpetual non-perception, or else the limitation of the power of either of the two (*viz* the soul or the senses).

What is the necessity of accepting an internal organ (Antaḥkaraṇa), of which the intellect is only a mode? The Sûtra says that if it be not accepted, the senses being always in contact with their objects, there would always result perception of everything, for all the requisites, *viz* the soul, the senses, and the objects, are present. If, however, this be denied, then it would mean that knowledge can never result, and nothing would ever be cognized. So the opponent will have to accept the limitation of the power either of the soul or of the senses. Such a thing is not possible in the Ātman, which is changeless. Nor can it be said that the power of the senses, which is not impeded either in the previous moment or in the subsequent moment, is so limited in the middle. Hence we have to accept an internal organ (Antaḥkaraṇa), through whose connection and disconnection perception and non-perception take place. The Śruti also refers to a common experience of ours, "I was absent-minded, I did not hear it" Br. 1. 5. 3). Hence there exists an internal organ, of which the intellect is a mode, and it is the connection with this that causes the Ātman to appear as the individualized soul, as explained in Sûtra 29.

Topic 14: The individual soul as agent.

कर्ता, शास्त्रार्थवत्त्वात् ॥ ३३ ॥

कर्ता Agent शास्त्रार्थवत्त्वात् in order that the scriptures may have a meaning.

33. (The soul is) an agent, on account of scriptural (injunctions) having a meaning on that ground only.

The question as regards the size of the soul has been settled. Now another characteristic of the soul is taken up for discussion. The individual soul is an agent for only on that basis do scriptural injunctions like "He is to sacrifice" etc. have a sense. In these the Śruti enjoins certain acts to be done by the agent and if the soul be not an agent these injunctions would become meaningless.

विहारोपदेशात् ॥ ३४ ॥

विहार-उपदेशात् On account of the Śruti teaching wandering about.

34. And on account of (the Śruti) teaching (its) wandering about.

"It, taking the organs, moves about as it pleases in its own body" (Bṛ. 2. 1. 18). This text which describes the wandering of the soul in the dream state clearly shows that it is an agent.

उपादानात् ॥ ३५ ॥

35. On account of its taking (the organs).

The text quoted in the last Sûtra also shows that the soul in dream state takes the organs with it thereby declaring that it is an agent.

व्यपदेशाच्च क्रियायाम्, न चेन्निर्देशविपर्ययः ॥ ३६ ॥

व्यपदेशात् On account of mention च also क्रियायाम् in respect of action न चेत् if it were not so निर्देश-विपर्ययः the reference (would have been) of a different kind.

36. Also on account of (the scriptures) mentioning (the soul as an agent) with respect to action. If it were not so, the reference (would have been) of a different kind.

"Intelligence performs sacrifices, and it also performs all acts" (Tai. 2. 5). Here by 'intelligence' the soul is meant and not the Buddhi, thereby showing that the soul is an agent. If the intention of the Śruti were to refer to the Buddhi then it would have used the word not in the nominative case, but in the instrumental case, as 'by intelligence', meaning, through its instrumentality, as it has done elsewhere in similar circumstances. *Vide* Kau. 3. 6.

उपलब्धिवदनियमः ॥ ३७ ॥

उपलब्धिवत् As in the case of perception अनियमः (there is) no rule.

37. As in the case of perception, (there is) no rule (here also).

An objection is raised that if the soul were a free agent, then it would have performed only what is beneficial to it, and not both good and bad deeds. This objection is being refuted. Just as the soul, although it is free, perceives both agreeable and disagreeable things, so also it does both good and bad deeds. There is no rule that it should do only what is good and avoid what is bad.

शक्तिविपर्ययात् ॥ ३८ ॥

38. On account of the reversal of power (of the Buddhi, which is inadmissible).

If the Buddhi, which is an instrument, becomes the agent and ceases to function as an instrument, we shall have to imagine some other thing as the instrument. Hence the dispute is only as regards terms, for in either case an agent different from the instrument has to be admitted.

समाध्यभावाच्च ॥ ३९ ॥

समाधि-अभावात् On account of the impossibility of Samâdhi च and.

39. And on account of the impossibility of Samâdhi.

If the soul is not an agent, then the realization

prescribed by texts like, "The Ātman is to be realized" (Bṛ. 2. 4. 5), through Samâdhi would be impossible. It will not be capable of activities like "hearing reasoning, and meditation" that lead to Samâdhi, in which state perfect Knowledge dawns. Therefore there will be no Liberation for the soul. So it is established that the soul alone is the agent, and not the Buddhi.

Topic 15: The soul is an agent only so long as it is connected with the Upâdhis.

यथा च तक्षोभयथा ॥ ४० ॥

यथा Even as च and तक्षा carpenter उभयथा is both

40. And even as a carpenter is both.

In the last Sûtra the topic about the soul's being an agent is established. Now the question is raised whether this agency is its real nature or only a superimposition. The Nyâya school holds that it is its very nature. This Sûtra refutes it and says that it is superimposed on the soul and not real. For the Śruti declares, "This Ātman is non-attached" (Bṛ. 4. 3. 15). Just as a carpenter suffers when he is busy working with his tools and is happy when he leaves off work, so does the Ātman suffer when, through its connection with the Buddhi etc., it is active, as in the waking and dream states, and is blissful when it ceases to be an agent, as in deep sleep. All scriptural injunctions are with reference to the conditioned state of the Self. By nature it is inactive, and it becomes active only through a connection with its Upâdhis (adjuncts), the mind etc. The objection that if the soul is not an agent by nature, the Śruti injunctions will be meaningless, does not stand, for these scriptures do not aim at establishing it, but merely refer to an agency already existing as a result of ignorance.

Topic 16: The soul in its activity is dependent on the Lord.

परात्तु तच्छ्रुतेः ॥ ४१ ॥

परात् From the Supreme Lord तु but तत् that (agency) श्रुतेः so declares the Śruti.

41. But (even) that (agency of the soul) is from the Supreme Lord; so declares the Śruti.

The agency of the soul is also due to the Supreme Lord. The soul does good and bad deeds, being so directed by the Lord. "He makes those whom He will raise do good deeds" (Kau. 3. 8). It is through His grace that the soul attains to Knowledge and becomes free.

कृतप्रयत्नापेक्षस्तु विहितप्रतिषिद्धावैयर्थ्यादिभ्यः ॥ ४२ ॥

कृतप्रयत्न-अपेक्षः Depends on works done तु but विहित-प्रतिषिद्ध-अवैयर्थ्यादिभ्यः on account of the relevancy of injunctions and prohibitions etc.

42. But (the Lord's making the soul act) depends on works done (by it); (thus only

would) injunctions and prohibitions etc. be relevant.

This Sûtra refutes a possible doubt that since the Lord makes some persons do good and others evil, He must be cruel and whimsical. It says, that the Lord always directs the soul according to its good or bad deeds in previous births. And Saṁsâra being without beginning, there will always be previous births, with actions done in them, for the guidance of the Lord. So He cannot be accused of being cruel and whimsical. It is thus alone that the scriptural injunctions and prohibitions can have any meaning; for otherwise the Jîva will gain nothing by observing these injunctions.

This does not however mar the independence of the Lord, though it may be said that since He depends on the acts of the soul, He is not free to do what He likes; for a king who presents or punishes His subjects according to their acts does not cease to be a sovereign thereby.

Topic 17: Relation of the individual soul to Brahman

अंशो नानाव्यपदेशात्, अन्यथा चापि
दाशकितवादित्वमधीयत एके ॥ ४३ ॥

अंशः Part नानाव्यपदेशात् on account of difference being declared अन्यथा otherwise च and अपि also दाश-कितवादित्वम् being fishermen, knaves, etc. अधीयते read एके some (Śâkhâs of the Vedas).

43. (The soul is) part (of the Lord) on account

of difference (between the two) being declared and otherwise also (*i.e.* as non-different from Brahman); for in some (Sâkhâs or recensions of the Vedic texts) (Brahman) is spoken of as being fishermen, knaves, etc.

In the last topic it has been shown that the Lord rules the soul. This brings us to the question of the relation between the two. Is it that of master and servant, or as between fire and its sparks? The Sûtra says that the relation is as between fire and its spark, that is, of whole and part. But then, the soul is not actually a part, but a part, as it were—an imagined part, for Brahman cannot have any parts. Why then should it be taken as a part and not identical with the Lord? Because the scriptures declare a difference between them in texts like, "Knowing It alone one becomes a sage" (Bṛ. 4. 4. 22), "The Ātman is to be seen" (Bṛ. 2. 4. 5). This difference, however, is spoken of from the empirical standpoint; from the absolute standpoint they are identical. The text, "Brahman is the fishermen, Brahman the slaves, Brahman the knaves," etc. shows that even such humble persons as these are in reality Brahman.

मन्त्रवर्णाच्च ॥ ४४ ॥

मन्त्रवर्णात् From the words of the Mantra च also

44. Also from the words of the Mantra (it is known that the soul is a part of the Lord).

A further reason is given to show that the soul is a

part of the Lord. "One foot of it are all these beings" (Ch. 3. 12. 6)—where beings, including souls, are said to be a foot or part of the Lord.

अपि च स्मर्यते ॥ ४५ ॥

अपि Also **च** and **स्मर्यते** it is (so) stated in the Smrti.

45. And it is also (so) stated in the Smṛti.

"An eternal portion of myself having become a living soul" (Gîtâ 15. 7).

प्रकाशादिवन्नैवं परः ॥ ४६ ॥

प्रकाशादिवत् Like light etc. **न** is not **एवं** like this **परः** the Supreme Lord.

46. The Supreme Lord is not (affected by pleasure and pain) like this (individual soul), even as light etc. (are not affected by the shape of the things they touch).

If the soul is a part of the Lord, the question may arise that the Lord also experiences pleasure and pain like the soul, even as a cloth is soiled if its threads are soiled. This Sûtra refutes it and says that the Lord does not experience pleasure and pain like the soul, which on account of ignorance identifies itself with the body and mind, and thereby partakes of their pleasure and pain. Just as the light of the sun, which is all-pervading, becomes straight or bent by coming in contact with particular objects, or as the ether enclosed in a ja seems to move when the jar is moved, or as the sun appears to tremble when the water in which it is reflected trembles, but in reality none of them undergoes those changes, so also is the Lord not affected by pleasure and pain, which are experienced by that imagined part of it, the individual soul, which is a product of ignorance and is limited by the Buddhi etc.

स्मरन्ति च ॥ ४७ ॥

स्मरन्ति The Smṛtis state च and.

47. The Smṛtis also state (that).

"Of the two, the Supreme Self is said to be eternal and devoid of qualities. It is not touched by the fruits of actions any more than a lotus leaf is by water. . . ." Smṛti texts like this declare that the Supreme Lord does not experience pleasure and pain. The Śrutis too do the same.

अनुज्ञापरिहारौ देहसम्बन्धाज्ज्योतिरादिवत् ॥ ४८ ॥

अनुज्ञापरिहारौ Injunctions and prohibitions देहसम्बन्धात् on account of the connection with the body ज्योतिरादिवत् like light etc.

48. Injunctions and prohibitions (are possible) on account of the connection (of the Self) with the body; as in the case of light etc.

Even though the Self is one and indescribable, and with reference to it there can be no injunctions and prohibitions, yet as connected with a body, such injunctions and prohibitions are possible. Fire is one; but the fire of the funeral pyre is rejected, and that of a sacrifice is accepted. Similar is the case with the Ātman.

असन्ततेश्चाव्यतिकरः ॥ ४९ ॥

असन्ततेः Non-extension (beyond its own body) च and अव्यतिकरः there is no confusion (of results of actions).

49. And on account of the non-extension (of the soul beyond its own body) there is no confusion (of results of actions).

An objection is raised that on account of the unity of the Self there would result a confusion of the results of actions; that is, everyone would get the results of the actions of everyone else. This Sûtra refutes such a possibility; for an individualized soul means the connection of the Ātman with a particular body, mind, etc., and since these are not overlapping, the individual souls are different from each other. Hence there is no such possibility of confusion.

आभास एव च ॥ ५० ॥

आभासः A reflection एव only च and.

50. And (the individual soul is) only a reflection (of the Supreme Lord).

According to Vedânta the individual soul is but a reflection, an image, of the Supreme Lord in Its

Upâdhi (adjunct), the Antaḥkaraṇa (inner organ). So the reflections of the Lord in different Antahkaraṇas are different, even as the reflections of the sun in different sheets of water are different. Therefore just as the trembling of a particular reflection of the sun does not cause the other reflections to tremble so also the experiencing of happiness and misery by a particular Jîva or individualized soul is not shared by other souls. Hence there can be no confusion of the results of action.

अदृष्टानियमात् ॥ ५१ ॥

अदृष्ट-अनियमात् There being no fixity about the unseen principle.

51. There being no fixity about the unseen principle (there would result that confusion for those who believe in many souls, each all-pervading).

The Sâṁkhyas, the Vaiśeṣikas and the Naiyâyikas accept a plurality of souls, each of which is all-prevading. Under such circumstances there cannot but result a confusion of the fruits of action, for each soul is present everywhere, in close proximity to whatever causes those results in the shape of happiness or misery. Nor can this confusion be avoided by introducing the Adṛṣṭa or unseen principle, which is religious merit and demerit acquired by the souls. According to the Sâṁkhyas it inheres not in the soul, but in the Pradhâna, which is common to the souls, and as such there is nothing to fix that a particular Adṛṣṭa operates in a particular soul. According to tó the other two schools the unseen principle is created by the conjunction of the soul with the mind; and since every soul is all-pervading and therefore equally connected with all minds, here also there is nothing to fix that a particular Adṛṣṭa belongs to a particular soul. Hence that confusion of results is inevitable.

अभिसंध्यादिष्वपि चैवम् ॥ ५२ ॥

अभिसंध्यादिषु In resolve etc. **अपि** even **च** and **एवम** like this.

52. And even as regards resolve etc. (it would be) like this.

If it be maintained that the resolve etc. one makes to achieve something or to avoid something will allocate the Adṛṣṭa to particular souls, even then there will be this confusion. For resolve etc. are also formed by the conjunction of the soul and the mind. Hence the same argument applies here also.

Sûtras 51-53 refute the doctrine of the Sâṁkhyas and other schools about the plurality of souls each of which is all-pervading. It leads to absurdities.

प्रदेशादिति चेत्, न, अन्तर्भावात् ॥ ५३ ॥

प्रदेशात् From (difference of) place **इति चेत्** if it be said **न** not so **अन्तर्भावात्** on account of the self being in all bodies.

53. If it be said (that the distinction of pleasure

and pain etc. results) from (the difference of) place, (we say) not so, on account of the self being in all bodies.

The Naiyâyikas and others try to get over the difficulty shown in the previous Sûtra thus: Though each soul is all-prevading, yet if we take its connection with the mind to take place in that part of it which is limited by its body, then such a confusion is not likely. Even this cannot stand; since every soul is all-pervading and therefore permeates all bodies, and there is nothing to fix that a particular body belongs to a particular soul. Again there cannot be more than one all-pervading entity; if there were, they would limit each other and consequently cease to be all-pervading or infinite. Hence there is only one Self and not many. The plurality of selves in Vedânta is only a product of ignorance and not a reality.

CHAPTER II

Section IV

In the third section it has been shown that ether and the other elements are produced from Brahman, by reconciling the apparently contradictory texts of the Śrutis with respect to their origination. In this section the Sûtras take up for discussion texts that deal with the origination of the senses etc.

Topic 1: The organs are produced from Brahman.

तथा प्राणाः ॥ १ ॥

तथा Likewise प्राणाः the organs.

1. Likewise the organs (are produced from Brahman).

In the scriptures, in those sections which treat of the origin of things, we do not find the origination of the organs etc. mentioned. On the other hand, there are texts like, "This was indeed non-existence in the beginning. They say: What was non-existence in the beginning? Those Ṛṣis. . . .Who are those Ṛṣis? The Prâṇas (organs) are indeed the Ṛṣis" (Śat. Br. 6. 1. 1. 1), which show that the organs are eternal and not created.

This Sûtra refutes that view and says that the organs

etc. are produced just like ether etc. from Brahman. The word 'likewise' refers not to the immediately preceding topic of the last section, which is the plurality of souls, but to the creation of ether etc. spoken of in the last section. Śruti texts directly declare their origination. "From that (Self) are produced the vital force, mind, and all the organs" (Mu. 2. 1. 3). Therefore the senses are created.

गौण्यसम्भवात् ॥ २ ॥

गौणी Secondary sense असम्भवात् being impossible.

2. On account of the impossibility (of explaining the origination in a) secondary sense.

Since there are texts like the one quoted from the Śat. Br. which speak of the existence of the organs before creation, why not explain the texts which describe their creation in a secondary sense? This Sûtra refutes it, for a secondary sense would lead to the abandonment of the general assertion, "By the knowledge of one, everything else is known". Therefore they are produced from Brahman. The reference to the existence of the Prâṇas (organs) before creation in Śat. Br. is concerning Hiraṇyagarbha, which is not resolved in the partial dissolution of the world, though all other effects are resolved. Even Hiraṇyagarbha is resolved, however, in complete dissolution (Mahâpralaya).

तत्प्राक्श्रुतेश्च ॥ ३ ॥

तत् That प्राक् first श्रुतेः being mentioned च and.

3. And because that (the verb denoting origin) is mentioned first (in connection with the Prâṇas).

The texts referred to is: "From that (Self) are produced the vital force, mind and all the organs, ether, air, water, fire, and earth" (Mu. 2. 1. 3). Here the word 'produced' occurs at the very beginning of the things enumerated and if it is interpreted in its primary sense with respect to ether etc., it is all the more to be so interpreted with respect to the vital force, mind, and organs mentioned earlier. Thus a further reason is given in this Sûtra to show that the organs etc. have originated from Brahman.

तत्पूर्वकत्वाद्वाचः ॥ ४ ॥

वाचः Of the organ of speech (etc.) तत्पूर्वकत्वात् being preceded by them (the elements).

4. On account of the pre-existence of that (*viz* the elements) (before) the organ of speech (etc.).

"For truly, my boy, mind consists of earth, the vital force of water, the vocal organ of fire" (Ch. 6. 5. 4). This text clearly shows that the organs etc. are products of the elements, which in their turn spring from Brahman. Hence they too are products of Brahman. Being products of the elements, they are not separately mentioned in texts dealing with the origin of things.

Topic 2: The number of the organs.

सप्त, गतेर्विशेषितत्वाच्च ॥ ५ ॥

सप्त Seven गते: being so known (from the scriptures) विशेषितत्वात् on account of the specification च and.

5. (The organs are) seven (in number), because it is so known (from the scriptures) and on account of the specification (of those seven).

The number of the organs is ascertained in this and the next Sûtra. This Sûtra, which gives the view of the opponent, declares that there are seven organs. "The seven Prâṇas (organs) spring from It" (Mu. 2. 1. 8). These are again specified in another text, "Seven indeed are the Prâṇas (organs) in the head" (Taittirīya Saṁhitâ 5. 1. 7. 1). No doubt in some texts eight or even more organs are enumerated, but these are to be explained as modifications of the inner organ, and so there is no contradiction in the Śruti texts if we take the number as seven.

हस्तादयस्तु, स्थितेऽतो नैवम् ॥ ६ ॥

हस्तादय: Hands etc. तु but स्थिते being a fact अत: therefore न not एवम् like this.

6. But hands etc. (are also referred to as sense-organs in scriptural texts). Since this is a fact, therefore (it is) not like this (*i.e.* they are not merely seven in number).

'But' refutes the view of the previous Sûtra. "The hands are the Graha (organs)" etc. (Bṛ. 3. 2. 8). Such texts show that the hands etc. are additional sense-organs. Therefore to the seven already enumerated *viz* eyes, nose, ears, tongue, touch, speech, and inner organ, four others, *viz* hands, feet, anus, and the organ of generation, have to be added. In all, therefore, there are eleven organs. The different modifications of the inner organ, *viz* mind, intellect, ego, and Citta (memory), are not separate organs, and therefore cannot raise the number beyond eleven, which is therefore the number fixed. These are: the five organs of knowledge, the five organs of action, and the inner organ.

Topic 3: The organs are minute in size.

अणवश्च ॥ ७ ॥

अणवः Minute च and.

7. And (they are) minute.

The organs are minute. 'Minute' does not mean atomic, but fine and limited in size. It is because they are subtle that they are not seen. If they were all-pervading, then texts which speak of their passing out of the body and going and coming along with the soul at death and birth would be contradicted. Moreover, we do not perceive through the senses what is happening throughout the universe, which would be the case if they were all-pervading. Hence they are all subtle and limited in size.

Topic 4: The chief Prâṇa (vital force) also is created from Brahman.

श्रेष्ठश्च ॥ ८ ॥

श्रेष्ठः The chief Prâṇa (vital force) च and.

8. And the chief Prâṇa (vital force) (is also produced).

"From this (Self) is produced the vital force" (Mu. 2. 1. 3); again we have, "By Its own law It alone was moving without wind (the vital force)" (Ṛg-Veda 10. 129. 2). Here the words "was moving" seem to refer to the function of the vital force, and so it must have existed before creation and was therefore not created. Hence there appears to be a contradiction with respect to its origination. This Sûtra says that even the vital force is produced from Brahman. The words "was moving" are qualified by "without wind" and so does not intimate that the vital force existed before creation. It only intimates the Brahman, the Cause, existed before creation, as is known from texts like "Existence alone was there before this" (Ch. 6. 2. 1). It is called the 'chief' because it functions before all other Prâṇas and senses, *i.e.* from the very moment the child is conceived, and also on account of its superior qualities; "We shall not be able to live without you" (Bṛ. 6. 1. 13).

Topic 5: The chief vital force is different from air and sense functions.

न वायुक्रिये, पृथगुपदेशात् ॥ ९ ॥

न वायुक्रिये Not air nor function पृथक् separately उपदेशात् on account of its being mentioned.

9. (The chief Prâṇa) is neither air nor any

function (of the organs) on account of its being mentioned separately.

In this Sûtra the nature of the chief Prâṇa is discussed. The opponent holds that there is no separate principle called Prâṇa, but that it is only air and nothing else, which exists in the mouth as well as outside. The Śruti also says, "That vital force is air." Or it may be the combined effect of the functions of all the eleven organs. Just as a number of birds in a cage, when they move, also move the cage, so also the eleven organs functioning together constitute life in the body. So the resultant of these functions is Prâṇa. This is the view of the Sâṁkhyas. Hence there is no separate principle called Prâṇa (vital force).

The Sûtra refutes these views and says that Prâṇa is a separate principle, for it is mentioned separately from air and the sense functions. "The Prâṇa (vital force) indeed is the fourth foot of Brahman. That foot shines and warms as the light called air" (Ch. 3. 18. 4), where it is distinguished from air. Again, "From that (Self) are produced the vital force, mind, and all the organs" (Mu. 2. 1. 3), which shows that is not a function of any organ, for in that case it would not have been separated from the organs. The Text, "The vital force is air," is also correct, inasmuch as the effect is but the cause in another form and the vital force is air functioning within the body (Adhyâtma). The analogy of the birds in a cage is not to the point, for they all have the same kind of activity, *viz* movement, which is favourable to the motion of the cage. But the functions of the organs are not of one kind, but different from one another and they are also of a distinct nature from that of the vital force. Hence they cannot constitute life. Therefore Prâṇa (vital force) is a separate entity.

चक्षुरादिवत्तु, तत्सहशिष्टयादिभ्यः ॥ १० ॥

चक्षुरादिवत् Like eyes etc. तु but तत्-सह-शिष्टयादिभ्यः on account of (its) being taught with them and other reasons.

10. But (Prâṇa is subordinate to the soul) like eyes etc. on account of (its) being taught with them and for other reasons.

If the vital force is a separate entity from the organs, which are subordinate to it, then it, like the soul, must also be independent in the body. The Sûtra refutes this and says that the vital force is subordinate to the soul. Why? Because in the conversation of the Prâṇas which we find in the Upaniṣads it is mentioned along with the sense-organs. Now in such grouping only those of a class are grouped together. So the vital force, like the organs, is subordinate to the soul. The other reasons referred to in the Sûtra are its being composed of parts, its being insentient, and so on.

अकरणत्वाच्च न दोषः, तथा हि दर्शयति ॥ ११ ॥

अकरणत्वात् On account of (its) not being an instrument च and न not दोषः objection तथा हि because thus दर्शयति (Śruti) teaches.

11. And on account of (its) not being an instrument (there is) no objection, because thus (the scripture) teaches.

If the vital force, like the organs is also subordinate to the soul, then it must stand in the relation of an instrument to the soul like the organs. But as there are only eleven functions and as many organs already, there is no room for a twelfth organ in the absence of a twelfth sense-object. This Sûtra refutes the above objection and says that the vital force is not an instrument or organ like the eyes etc., for the acceptance of which a twelfth sense-object would be necessary; yet it has a function in the body which no sense-organ is capable of, and that is the upkeep of the body. In the text, "Preserves the unclean nest (of a body) with the help of the vital force" (Bṛ. 4. 3. 12), the vital force is said to guard the body. Again, "From whatever limb the Prâṇa goes, right there it withers" (Bṛ. 1. 3. 19); "What ever food one eats through the Prâṇa satisfies these (the organs)" (Bṛ. 1. 3. 18). All these texts show tha the function of the vital force (Prâṇa is the upkeep o the body, unlike those of the organs.

Nor is this the only function of the vital force. Ther are others, too, as the next Sûtra declares.

पञ्चवृत्तिर्मनोवद्व्यपदिश्यते ॥ १२ ॥

पञ्चवृत्तिः Having fivefold function मनोवत् like th mind व्यपदिश्यते it is taught.

12. It is taught as having a fivefold functio like the mind.

"I alone dividing myself fivefold support this bod and keep it" (Pr. 2. 3). Fivefold, *i.e.* as Prâṇa, Apân Vyâna, Udâna, and Samâna each of which has a speci function, *viz* breathing in, exhaling, functioning throughout the body and aiding feats of strength, helping the soul to pass out of the body, and digesting the food eaten and carrying it to all parts of the body. In this respect it resembles the inner organ, which though one has a fourfold aspect as mind, intellect, ego, and Citta (memory).

Topic 6: The minuteness of the vital force.

अणुश्च ॥ १३ ॥

अणुः Minute च and.

13. And it is minute.

The vital force (Prâna) is also minute, subtle, and limited like the senses. It may be objected that it is all-pervading according to the text: "Because he is equal to a gnat, equal to a mosquito, equal to an elephant, *equal to these three worlds, equal to this universe*" (Bṛ. 1. 3. 22). But the all-pervadingness spoken of here is with respect to Hiraṇyagarbha, the cosmic Prâṇa. In its universal aspect it is all-pervading; but in relation to beings in the world, in its individual aspect with which we are concerned here, it is limited. Hence the vital force is also limited.

Topic 7: The presiding deities of the organs.

ज्योतिराद्यधिष्ठानं तु तदामननात् ॥ १४ ॥

ज्योतिरादि-अधिष्ठानं Presiding over by Fire and others

तु but तत्-आमननात् on account of the scriptures teaching that.

14. But there is the presiding over by Fire and others (over the organs), on account of the scriptural teaching about that.

The dependence or independence of the Prâṇa and the organs is taken up for discussion: The scriptures say that these are presided over by the gods like Fire etc., which direct them. For example, "(Fire) having become speech entered the mouth" (Ai. 2. 4). The organs etc., being inert, cannot move of themselves. Hence they are dependent on the presiding deities.

प्राणवता, शब्दात् ॥ १५ ॥

प्राणवता With the one possessing the Prâṇas (organs

शब्दात् from the scriptures.

15. (The gods are not the enjoyers, but th soul, because the organs are connected) with th one (*i.e.* the soul) possessing them, (as is known from the scriptures.

This Sûtra makes it clear why the soul, and not th gods, is the enjoyer in the body. The relation betwee the soul and the organs is that of master and servant, s the scriptures declare; hence the enjoyment through th organs is of the soul, and not of the gods. "He wh knows, 'Let me smell this,' is the self, the nose is th instrument of smelling" (Ch. 8. 12. 4). Moreover, the are many gods in the body, each presiding over particular organ, but there is only one enjoyer. Otherwise remembrance would be impossible. Hence the senses are for the enjoyment of the soul and not the gods though they are directed by them.

तस्य च नितयत्वात् ॥ १६ ॥

तस्य Its च and नित्यत्वात् on account of permanence.

16. And on account of its (soul's) permanence (in the body it is the enjoyer, and not the gods).

The soul abides permanently in the body as the experiencer since it can be affected by good and evil and can experience pleasure and pain. It is not reasonable to think that in a body which is the result of the soul's past actions, others, *e.g.* the gods, enjoy. The gods have glorious positions and would disdain such lowly enjoyments as can be had through the human body. It is the soul that is the enjoyer. Moreover, the connection between the organs and the soul is permanent. *Vide* Śruti text, "When it departs, the vital force follows; when the vital force departs, all other organs follow" (Bṛ. 4. 4. 2). The soul is the master, and is therefore the enjoyer, in spite of the fact that there are presiding deities over the senses.

Topic 8: The organs are independent principles and not modes of the chief Prâṇa.

त इन्द्रियाणि, तद्व्यपदेशादन्यत्र श्रेष्ठात् ॥ १७ ॥

ते They इन्द्रियाणि organs तद्व्यपदेशात् being so designated श्रेष्ठात् अन्यत्र except the chief.

17. They (the other Prâṇas) except the chief (Prâṇa) are organs (and so different from the chief Prâṇa), on account of (their) being so designated (by the scriptures).

The question is raised whether the eyes etc. are but modes of the vital force or independent entities. The opponent holds the former view since the scripture says, "This is the greatest amongst us (the organs). . . . Well, let us all be of his form' They all assumed its form. Therefore they are called by this name of 'Prâṇa' " (Br. 1. 5. 21). This Sûtra refutes this and says that the eleven organs belong to a separate category, and are not modes of the vital force, because they are shown to be different in texts like: "From Him are born, the vital force, mind, and all organs" (Mu. 2. 1. 3), where the vital force and the organs are separately mentioned. The text of the Bṛhadâraṇyaka is to be taken in a secondary sense.

भेदश्रुतेः ॥ १८ ॥

18. On account of differentiating scriptural texts.

In Br. 1. 3. the organs are treated first in one section, and after concluding it the vital force is treated in a fresh section, which shows that they do not belong to the same category. Hence also the organs are independent principles, and not modes of the vital force.

वैलक्षण्याच्च ॥ १९ ॥

वैलक्षण्यात् On account of characteristic differences च and.

19. And on account of characteristic differences.

Various differences in their nature are described in the scripture. For example, the organs do not function in deep-sleep, whereas the vital force does. The organs get tired, but not the vital force. The loss of individual organs does not affect life, but the passing out of the vital force ends in the death of the body. The Śruti which speaks of the organs being called Prâṇa for their having assumed its form is to be taken in a secondary even as the servants do their master. The vital force is the leader of the organs. Therefore the organs are independent principles.

Topic 9: The evolution of names and forms is the work of the Lord and not of the individual soul.

संज्ञामूर्तिक्लृप्तिस्तु त्रिवृत्कुर्वतः, उपदेशात् ॥ २० ॥

संज्ञा-मूर्ति-क्लृप्ति: The creation of name and form तु but त्रिवृत्कुर्वत: by Him who does the tripartite (creation) उपदेशात् on account of scriptural teaching.

20. But the creation of names and forms is by Him who does the tripartite (creation), for so the scriptures teach.

A question is raised whether the individual soul or the Supreme Lord fashions gross objects of name and form after the three elements have been created by the Lord. In the Chândogya 6. 2. we have the creation of the elements by the Lord. The next section says: "That Deity thought, 'Well, let me now enter those three deities (fire, earth, and water) as (lit. through) this living self (Jîva) and reveal names and forms' " (Ch. 6. 3. 2). On the basis of this text the opponent holds that the fashioning of names and forms, that is, the creation of the gross world after the elements have been created, belongs to the individual soul and not to the Lord. This Sûtra refutes it and says that the word 'Jîva' in the text is syntactically related with 'entrance' and not with the revealing of names and forms. The individual soul has not the power to create the gross world. Moreover, the next sentence of that passage, "Then that Deity having said, 'Let me make each of these three (elements) tripartite" etc. (Ch. 6. 3. 3), clearly shows that the Supreme Lord alone reveals names and forms, and creates the gross elements and this world. How then is the production of pots etc. by a potter to be explained? There also the Lord is the inner director. It is the Lord who resides in everything and directs the whole creation.

मांसादि भौमं यथाशब्दमितरयोश्च ॥ २१ ॥

मांसादि Flesh etc. भौमं are effects of earth यथाशब्दम् according to the scriptures इतरयोः of the other two च also.

21. Flesh etc. result from earth, according to the scriptures. So also as regards the other two (*viz* fire and water).

Tripartite earth, when assimilated by man, forms

flesh etc. "The earth (food) when eaten becomes threefold, . . .its middle portion becomes flesh, and its finest portion mind" (Ch. 6. 5. 1). So also we have to understand the effects of the other two elements according to the scriptures. Water produces blood, Prâna, etc., and fire produces bone, marrow and the organ of speech.

वैशेष्यात्तु तद्वादस्तद्वादः ॥ २२ ॥

वैशेष्यात् On account of the preponderance तु but तद्वादः that special name.

22. But on account of the preponderance (of a particular element in them the gross elements) are so named (after it).

An objection is raised that if all gross elements contain the three fine elements, then why such distinctions as "This is water," "This is earth," "This is fire"? The Sûtra refutes this objection saying that as the fine elements are not found in equal proportion in each of the gross elements, they are named after that fine element which preponderates in their constitution. The repetition of "that special name" is to show that the chapter ends here.

CHAPTER III

Section I

In the second chapter all objections based on the Śruti and reasoning against the Vedântic view have been refuted. It has been shown that all other views are incorrect, and that the so-called scriptural contradictions do not exist with respect to the Vedântic view. Further, it has been shown that all entities different from the soul (like Prâṇa etc.) spring from Brahman and for the enjoyment of the soul. In this chapter the soul's travels to the different regions accompanied by those adjuncts are discussed to produce a spirit of dispassion.

Topic 1: The soul, when passing out of the body at death, is enveloped with fine particles of the gross elements.

तदन्तरप्रतिपत्तौ रंहति सम्परिष्वक्तः, प्रश्ननिरू-
पणाभ्याम् ॥ १ ॥

तदन्तरप्रतिपत्तौ With a view to obtaining a fresh body रंहति goes सम्परिष्वक्त: enveloped (with subtle parts of the elements) प्रश्ननिरूपणाभ्याम् (so it is known) from the question and answer.

1. (The soul) goes (out of the body) enveloped (with subtle parts of the elements) with a view to

obtaining a fresh body; (so it is known) from the question and answer (in the scripture).

The Sûtra discusses whether in transmigration the soul takes with it subtle parts of the gross elements as the seed, as it were, for the future body. The opponent holds that it does not take them, for it is useless, be cause the elements are easily available everywhere. Moreover, in the absence of a definite opinion to the contrary in the scriptures, we have to understand that the soul does not take subtle parts of the elements with it. This Sûtra refutes that view and says that the soul does take with it subtle parts of the elements; that this is a fact is known from the question and answer that occurs in the scriptures. "Do you know why in the fifth oblation water is called man?" (Ch. 5. 3. 3). This is the question, and the answer is given in the whole passage which after explaining how the five oblations in the form of Śraddhâ (liquid oblations in subtle form), Soma, rain, food, and seed are offered in the five 'fires' (*i.e.* objects imagined to be fires for the sake of Upâsanâ)—the heavens, Parjanya (rain-god), earth, man, and woman—ends, "For this reason is water in the fifth oblation called man." From this we understand that the soul goes enveloped with water (same as Śraddhâ). Moreover, though the elements are available everywhere, yet the seeds for a future body are not so easily available. Again the adjuncts of the individual soul, *viz* the organs etc. which go with it (*Vide* Bṛ. 4, 4. 2) cannot accompany it unless there is a material basis

त्र्यात्मकत्वात्तु भूयस्त्वात् ॥ २ ॥

त्र्यात्मकत्वात् On account of (water) consisting of three elements तु but भूयस्त्वात on account of the preponderance (of water).

2. On account of (water) consisting of three elements (the soul goes enveloped by all these elements and not merely water); but (water alone is mentioned in the text) on account of its preponderance (in the human body).

An objection is raised that the text mentions only water, and not the other elements as accompanying the soul. The Sûtra says that in water are found the other two elements also according to the tripartite creation of the gross elements. Hence all the three elements accompany the soul. The mention of water is indicatory and includes all the elements. With mere water no body can be formed. But as the watery portion in the body is preponderant, water only is mentioned in the text.

प्राणगतेश्च ॥ ३ ॥

प्राणगते: Because of the going of the sense-organs च and.

3. And because of the going of the organs (with the soul, the elements also accompany the soul).

"When it departs, the vital force follows. When the vital force departs, all the organs follow" (Bṛ. 4. 4. 2). Since the organs go with the soul, they must have a material base; hence also it is inferred that water and other elements follow the soul, thus forming a basis for the organs.

अग्न्यादिगतिश्रुतेरिति चेत्, न, भाक्तत्वात् ॥ ४ ॥

अग्न्यादिगति Entering into fire etc. श्रुतेः from the scriptures इति चेत् if it be said न not so भाक्तत्वात् on account of its being so said in a secondary sense.

4. If it be said (that the organs do not follow the soul), for the scriptures declare their entering into fire etc., (we say) not so, on account of its being so said in a secondary sense.

"When the vocal organ of a man who dies is merged in the fire, the nose in the air," etc. (Bṛ. 3. 2. 13). This text shows that at the time of death the organs are resolved into their presiding deities, and hence it cannot be said that they accompany the soul. This Sûtra refutes that view and says that such interpretations would go against many texts which declare that they do accompany the soul, as for example: "When it departs, the vital force follows; when the vital force departs, all the organs follow" (Bṛ. 4. 4. 2). Hence the text cited must be interpreted in a secondary sense like the words, "The hair on the body in the herbs" (Bṛ. 3. 2. 13).

प्रथमेऽश्रवणादिति चेत्, न, ता एव हि, उपपत्तेः ॥ ५ ॥

प्रथमे In the first of the oblations अश्रवणात् not being mentioned इति चेत् if it be said न not so ताः एव that only (*i.e.* water) हि because उपपत्तेः on account of the appropriateness.

5. If it be objected on account of (water) not being mentioned in the first of the oblations, (we say) not so, because that (*viz* water) only (is meant by the word 'Śraddhâ') on account of the appropriateness (of such an interpretation).

An objection is raised that as there is no mention of water in the first oblation: "On that altar the gods offer Śraddhâ as oblation" (Ch. 5. 4. 2), but only Śraddhâ (faith) is mentioned, to substitute water for Śraddhâ will be arbitrary. So how can it be ascertained "that in the fifth oblation water is called man?" The Sûtra says that by 'Śraddhâ' water is meant, for in that case alone syntactical unity of the whole passage remains undisturbed. Otherwise the question and answer would not agree. Moreover, faith (Śraddhâ), which is a mental attribute, cannot be offered as an oblation. Water is also called Śraddhâ in the Śruti texts: "Śraddhâ indeed is water (Taittirīya Saṁhitā 1. 6. 8. 1).

अश्रुतत्वादिति चेत्, न, इष्टादिकारिणां प्रतीतेः ॥ ६ ॥

अश्रुतत्वात् On account of not being mentioned in the Śruti इति चेत् if it be said not so इष्टादिकारिणां the performers of sacrifices etc. प्रतीतेः being understood.

6. If it be said that on account of (the soul) not being mentioned in the text (the soul does not depart enveloped with water etc.), (we say) not so, for it is understood (from the scripture

that the Jîvas who perform sacrifices etc. (alone go to heaven).

An objection is raised that in the Châandogya text cited (5. 3. 3), there is mention of water only but no reference to the soul; and it is explained how this water becomes man. So how can it be taken that the soul departs enveloped with water and then is born again as man? This Sûtra refutes it and says that if we examine all the scriptural texts like, "But they who being in the village practise sacrifices and works of public utility and give alms, go to the (deity of) smoke...to the moon" (Ch. 5. 10. 3-4), which describe the journey to the moon, we find that only the Jîvas who perform such good acts go to heaven, and that in so doing they go enveloped with water, which is supplied by the materials like curds, etc. that are offered as oblations in sacrifices; these assume a subtle form called Apûrva and attach themselves to the sacrificer.

भाक्तं वानात्मवित्त्वात्, तथा हि दर्शयति ॥ ७ ॥

भाक्त In a secondary sense वा but अनात्मवित्त्वात् on account of their (souls) not knowing the Self तथा so हि because दर्शयति (Śruti) declares

7. But (the souls' being the food of the gods in heaven is used) in a secondary sense, on account of their not knowing the Self; because (the Śruti) declares like that.

In the scriptures it is stated that those who go to heaven become the food of the gods; so how could they be enjoying the fruits of their good actions in heaven? "That is Soma, the king. He is the food of the gods. They eat him" (Ch. 5. 10. 4). This Sûtra says that the word 'food' is used not in a primary sense, but metaphorically, meaning an object of enjoyment. Otherwise, if this is the fate of souls who go to heaven, texts like, "Those who want to go to heaven shall perform sacrifices" are meaningless. Therefore what the text means is that they are objects of enjoyment to the gods even as wives, children, and cattle are to men. Thus the Jîvas, while giving enjoyment to the gods, are happy, and rejoice with them in their turn. That they are objects of enjoyment to the gods is known from texts like: "While he who worships another deity...He is like a beast to the gods. And as many beasts serve a man, so does every man serve the gods" (Bṛ. 1. 4. 10).

Therefore it is decided that the soul goes enveloped with subtle parts of the elements when it goes to other spheres for enjoying the fruits of its good Karma.

Topic 2: The souls descending from heaven have a residual Karma, which determines their birth.

कृतात्ययेऽनुशयवान्, दृष्टस्मृतिभ्याम्, यथेतमनेवं च ॥ ८ ॥

कृतात्यये On the exhaustion of (good) work अनुशयवान् possessed of residual Karma दृष्टस्मृतिभ्याम् as is known from the Śruti and Smṛti यथा इतम् as (it) went अनेवं differently च and.

8. On the exhaustion of (good) work (the soul) with the residual Karma (descends to thi

earth), as is known from the Śruti and Smṛti, along the path (it) went by (from here) and differently too.

A fresh topic is taken up for discussion—the descent of the soul from heaven. The question is raised whether it descends with any residual Karma or not. The opponent holds that there is no residual Karma, for Śruti says: "Having dwelt there till their work is consumed, they return again the way they went by" etc. Ch. 5. 10. 5), which means that all their Karma is exhausted and there is nothing left. Moreover, it is reasonable to think that Karma done in one life (as man) is worked out in the next as god.

The Sûtra, refuting this view, says that what is exhausted in heaven is only that Karma which gave the soul a birth as god in heaven, but on the exhaustion of this Karma the remaining Karma, good and bad, brings it backs to earth. Otherwise it is difficult to explain the happiness or misery of a newborn child. Neither is it possible that in one life the entire Karma of the previous life is worked out. For a man might have done both good work like sacrifices, as a result of which he is born as a god, and bad work, which can be worked out in an animal body; and the working out of both kinds of Karma simultaneously in one birth is impossible. So though by the enjoyment of heaven the result of good work like sacrifices etc. is exhausted, there are other Karmas in store according to which a man is born again in good or bad environments. The Śruti says, "Those whose conduct has been good will quickly attain some good birth" etc. (*Ibid*. 5. 10. 7). The

Smṛti also says, "With the remainder of their Karma they are born in a noteworthy place, caste, and family, with becoming appearance, longevity, knowledge, wealth, happiness, and intellect." So the soul is born with residual Karma. By what way does it descend? Following the same way that it went by, but with some difference. That they follow the same way as they went by, is understood from the mention of smoke and ether in the path (*Vide* Ch. 5. 10. 5), and that there is some difference too is known from the fact that the text omits night etc. (*Vide* Ch. 5. 10. 3), but mist etc. are mentioned (*Vide* Ch. 5. 10. 6).

चरणादिति चेत्, न, उपलक्षणार्थेति कार्ष्णाजिनिः ॥ ९ ॥

चरणात् On account of conduct **इति चेत्** if it be said **न** not so **उपलक्षणार्था** to denote indirectly **इति** thus **कार्ष्णाजिनिः** (the sage) Kârṣṇâjini (thinks).

9. If it be said that on account of conduct (the assumption of residual Karma is not neces sary for a rebirth on earth), (we say) not so, (fo the word 'conduct' is used) to denote indirectly (the remaining Karma). So (thinks) Kârṣṇâjini.

In the text cited (Ch. 5. 10. 7) the Śruti says thos of 'good conduct' get a good birth. Now conduct is on thing, and residual Karma quite another thing, eve according to the Śruti (*Vide* Bṛ 4. 4. 5). Since th Śruti does not mention residual Karma, the soul i not born with any Karma, conduct alone being th cause of good birth. This is the main objection. This the Sûtra refutes and says that 'conduct' here is used to denote good Karma. It is a case of Ajahat Lakṣaṇâ, conduct standing for Karma which is dependent on good conduct. This is the view of the sage Kârṣṇâjini.

आनर्थक्यमिति चेत्, न, तदपेक्षत्वात् ॥ १० ॥

आनर्थक्यम् Irrelevancy इति चेत् if it be said न not so तदपेक्षत्वात् on account of dependence on that.

10. If it be said (by such interpretation of the word 'conduct' good conduct would become) purposeless, (we say) not so, on account of (Karma) being dependent on that (good conduct).

An objection is raised that if the word 'conduct' be interpreted indirectly to mean 'residual Karma', leaving its direct meaning, then good conduct would be purposeless in man's life, as it has no result of its own, not being a cause of the quality of the new birth. The Sûtra denies this on the ground that only those who are of good conduct are expected to perform Vedic sacrifices. "Him who is devoid of good conduct the Vedas do not purify." Thus good conduct is an aid to Karma and therefore has a purpose. So it is the view of Kârṣṇâjini that it is Karma and not conduct that is the cause of the new birth.

सुकृतदुष्कृते एवेति तु बादरिः ॥ ११ ॥

सुकृतदुष्कृते Good and evil work एव merely इति thus but बादरिः Bâdari.

11. But (conduct) is merely good and evil work; thus (the sage) Bâdari (thinks).

This Sûtra says that as a matter of fact there is no difference between conduct and Karma in common parlance, for people say of a person who performs sacrifices etc. "That man practises righteousness," showing thereby that 'conduct' is used in the general sense of action. Thus 'men of good conduct' means those whose actions (Karma) ars priseworthy.

Therefore it is settled that those who go to heaven performing sacrifices have residual Karma as the cause of a new birth on earth.

Topic 3: The fate after death of those souls whose actions do not entitle them to go to the lunar world

अनिष्टादिकारिणामपि च श्रुतम् ॥ १२ ॥

अनिष्टादिकारिणाम् Of those who do not perform sacrifices etc. अपि even च also श्रुतम् is declared by the Śruti

12. The Śruti declares (the going to the lunar world etc.) also of even those who do not perform sacrifices etc.

Now the question of those who do not perform sacrifices etc. is taken up for discussion. The opponent holds that even they go to heaven, though they may not enjoy there like the performers of sacrifices etc., because they too require the fifth oblation for a new birth, and also because the scriptures directly say that *all* to heaven: "All who depart from this world go to the moon" (Kau. 1. 2).

संयमने त्वनुभूयेतरेषामारोहावरोहौ, तद्गति-
दर्शनात् ॥ १३ ॥

संयमने In the abode of Yama तु but अनुभूय having experienced इतरेषाम् of others (than the performers of sacrifices etc.) आरोहावरोहौ the ascent and descent तद्गति-दर्शनात् such a passage being declared by the Śruti.

13. But of others (*i.e.* those who have not performed sacrifices etc.) the ascent is to the abode of Yama, and after having experienced (the result of their evil works) the descent (to the earth again takes place). On account of such a passage (for the evil-doer) being declared by the Śruti.

This Sûtra refutes the view of the last Sûtra and says that evil-doers go not to heaven, but to the world of Yama, where they suffer and then descend again to earth. "The hereafter never rises before an ignorant person . . . thus he falls again and again under my sway" (Ka. 1. 2. 6). The ascent to the moon is only for the enjoyment of the fruits of good works and not for any other purpose; so the evil-doers do not go there.

स्मरन्ति च ॥ १४ ॥

स्मरन्ति The Smṛtis declare च also.

14. The Smṛtis also declare (thus).

Manu and others say that the evil-doers go to hell and suffer there.

अपि च सप्त ॥ १५ ॥

अपि च Moreover सप्त seven.

15. Moreover there are seven (hells).

There are seven hells mentioned in the Purâṇas, to which the evil-doers are cast to expiate their sins through suffering.

तत्रापि च तद्व्यापारादविरोधः ॥ १६ ॥

तत्र There अपि even च and तत्-व्यापारात् on accoun of his control अविरोधः there is no contradiction.

16. And on account of his (Yama's) contro even there (in those hells), there is no contra diction.

An objection is raised that since according to th Śruti the evil-doers suffer at the hands of Yama how this possible in the hell called Raurava, where Citr gupta is the presiding deity. The Sûtra says that the is no contradiction, as Citragupta is directed by Yam

विद्याकर्मणोरिति तु प्रकृतत्वात् ॥ १७ ॥

विद्याकर्मणोः Of knowledge and work इति thus तु b

प्रकृतत्वात् on account of their being the subject under discussion.

17. But (the reference is to the two roads) of knowledge and work; thus (we have to understand) on account of their being the subject under discussion.

"Now those who go along neither of these ways become those tiny, continually rotating creatures of which it may be said, 'Be born and die'. This is the third place. That is why that world (heaven) never becomes full" (Ch. 5. 10. 8). The two ways mentioned in this text we have to take as referring to those of knowledge and work, on account of these being the subject under discussion. Knowledge and work are the means to go along the Devayâna and Pitṛyâna routes. For those who are not entitled to go through knowledge along the Devayâna, the route leading to the gods, or through sacrifices etc. to the Pitṛyâna, the route leading to the fathers, the Śruti declares a third place, distinct from the Brahmaloka and the Candraloka. That the evil-doers, who form a separate group, go to this third place, and not to heaven, is made all the more explicit by the words, "That is why that world (heaven) never becomes full" (Ch. 5. 10. 8). The word 'but' refutes a possible doubt arising from a text belonging to another Śâkhâ *vide* Kau. 1. 2. So the Kauṣîtakī text which says that all go to the spheres of the moon, means all those who have performed good Karma of whatever kind, and does not include evil-doers.

न तृतीये, तथोपलब्धेः ॥ १८ ॥

न Not तृतीये in the third तथा so उपलब्धेः it being seen.

18. (The specification about five oblations does) not (apply) to the third (place), for so it is seen (from the scriptures).

It has been said in Ch. 5. 3. 3, which is quoted in the first Sûtra of this section, that the Jîva attains a new birth after five oblations. So at least for getting a new body the evil-doer will have to go to the moon, to complete the five oblations that cause the new birth. This Sûtra says that the rule about the five oblations does not apply in the case of evil-doers, for they are born irrespective of the oblations, because the Śruti says, "'Be born and die.' This is the third place." That rule applies only to the performers of sacrifices etc.

स्मर्यतेऽपि च लोके ॥ १९ ॥

स्मर्यते Are recorded अपि also च and लोके in the world.

19. And moreover (cases of birth without the completion of the five oblations) are recorded in the world.

A further argument is given to show that the fiv[e] oblations are not absolutely necessary for a futur[e] birth, and hence the evil-doers need not go to heave[n] just for conforming to this rule. For in cases like tha[t] of Droṇa, who had no mother, and of Dhṛṣṭadyumn[a] who had neither father nor mother, the last two obla[-] tions respectively were absent. Hence the rule about the five oblations is not universal, but applies only to those who perform sacrifices.

दर्शनाच्च ॥ २० ॥

दर्शनात् On account of observation च also.

20. Also on account of observation.

That this rule about the five oblations is not universal is also seen from the fact that of the four kinds of life, viviparous, oviparous, life springing from moisture, and plant life, the last two are born without any mating and consequently there is not the fifth oblation in their case.

तृतीयशब्दावरोधः संशोकजस्य ॥ २१ ॥

तृतीय-शब्द-अवरोध: Inclusion in the third term संशोकजस्य of that which springs from moisture.

21. The third term (*i.e.* plant life) includes that which springs from moisture.

There are four kinds of organic beings as described in the last Sûtra. But the Chândogya Upaniṣad 6. 3. 1 mentions only three kinds. This Sûtra says that it makes no difference for that which springs from moisture is included in plant life (Udbhid), since they both germinate, one from the earth and the other from water etc.

Hence it is a settled fact that the evil-doers do not go to heaven but only those who perform sacrifices.

Topic 4: The soul in its descent from the moon does not become identified with ether etc. but attains similarity of nature.

तत्साभाव्यापत्तिः, उपपत्तेः ॥ २२ ॥

तत्-साभाव्य-आपत्तिः Attainment of a similarity of nature with them उपपत्तेः being reasonable.

22. (The soul when descending from Candra loka) attains similarity of nature with them (*i.e* with ether, air, etc.), (that alone) being reason able.

It has been said that the righteous who descend fron the moon descend by the same path as they ascende by, but with some differences. "They return again tha way as they came by, to the ether, from the ether to th air; the sacrificer having become air, becomes smoke, etc. (Ch. 5. 10. 5). Now the question is whether th souls of such persons actually attain identity with ethe smoke, etc., or only attain a similar nature. The Sûtr says that the souls do not attain identity with them, fc it is impossible. A thing cannot become another of different nature. What the text means, therefore, that it attains similarity of nature—becomes like ethe air, etc. The soul assumes a subtle form like ethe comes under the influence of air and is connected wi smoke, etc. Therefore similarity of nature and n identity is meant.

Topic 5: The entire descent of the soul takes onl a short time.

नातिचिरेण, विशेषात् ॥ २३ ॥

न Not अतिचिरेण in very long time विशेषात् on account of the special declaration.

23. (The soul's descent from the moon through the various stages up to the earth takes) not very long time, on account of a special declaration (of the Śrutis with respect to the stages after that as taking time).

The question is raised whether the descending soul, when it attains similarity of nature with ether, air, etc., remains in those stages pretty long, or attains the next stages quickly one after another. This Sûtra says that it passes through them quickly. "Then he is born as rice and corn, herbs and trees, sesamum and beans. From thence the escape is beset with many more difficulties" (Ch. 5. 10. 6). Thus the stages after coming down on earth through rain the Śruti particularly characterizes as hard to escape from, thereby hinting that the escape from the earlier stages is easy and attained quickly.

Topic 6: When the souls enter into plants etc. they only get connected with them and do not participate in their life.

अन्याधिष्ठिते पूर्ववत्, अभिलापात् ॥ २४ ॥

अन्य-अधिष्ठते Into what is ruled by another पूर्ववत् as in the previous cases अभिलापात् for so the Śruti states.

24. (The descending soul enters) into what is ruled by another (Jîva or soul) as in the previous

cases (*viz* becoming ether etc.); for so the Śruti states.

A view is put forward that the soul's passage through the stages of corn etc. is not a mere connection with them, as the earlier stages with ether etc., but that it is actually born in the form of corn etc. For the Śruti says, "Then he is *born* as rice" etc. (Ch. 5. 10. 6). It also seems reasonable that those who fall from heaven after having exhausted their good deeds should be born as herbs, plants, etc., owing to their bad Karma such as the killing of animals that remains.

So the word 'born' is to be taken literally. The Sûtra refutes this view and says that the word 'born' implies mere connection with corn, herbs, etc., which are animated by other souls actually born as such. For in these stages there is no reference to their Karma, even as in the earlier stages of ether etc. They enter these plants etc. independently of their Karma, and while there, they do not experiencc the fruits at all. Where birth in the primary sense takes place and experience of the fruits of action begins, it is made clear by a reference to Karma, as in, "Those whose conduct has been good will quickly attain a good birth" (Ch. 5. 10. 7). Therefore the descending souls only dwell, as it were, in plants etc. animated by other souls till they get the opportunity for a new birth.

अशुद्धमिति चेत्, न, शब्दात् ॥ २५ ॥

अशुद्धम् Unholy इति चेत् if it be said न not so शब्दात् on account of scriptural authority.

25. If it be said (that sacrifices, which entail the killing of animals etc.) are unholy, (we say) not so, on account of scriptural authority.

This Sûtra refutes the point raised by the opponent in the previous Sûtra that the descending soul is enveloped by its bad Karma such as the killing of animals in sacrifices and so is born as herbs etc. The killing of animals etc. in sacrifices does not entail any bad Karma for the person, for it is sanctioned by the scriptures.

रेतःसिग्योगोऽथ ॥ २६ ॥

रेतः-सिक्-योगः Connection with one who performs the act of generation अथ then.

26. Then (the soul gets) connected with him who performs the act of generation.

"For whoever eats food and performs the act of generation, (the soul) becomes one with him" (Ch. 5. 10. 6). Here the soul's becoming literally identical with the person is impossible, and we have to understand that it gets connected with him. This further proves that the soul's becoming plants etc. in the immediately preceding stages is also mere connection with them and not actual birth as such.

योनेः शरीरम् ॥ २७ ॥

योनेः From the womb शरीरम् body.

27. From the womb a (new) body (results).

Finally the actual birth of the soul is referred to in this Sûtra. Till now it was only a connection with the successive stages, but now through its connection with a person performing the act of generation the soul enters the woman and there gets a new body fit for experiencing the results of its past residual Karma.

CHAPTER III

Section II

In the last section the passage of the soul to different spheres and its return have been explained. There are people who get disgusted with Karma or sacrifices leading to such a fate of the soul and become dispassionate. In order to make them grasp the true import of the Mahâvâkyas or the great Vedic dicta, this section sets itself to elucidate the true nature of 'That' and 'thou' contained in the Mahâvâkya, "Ṭhat thou art". In the last section the waking state of the soul (the 'thou') has been fully described. Now its dream state is taken up for discussion, to show that the soul is self-luminous. In this way the three states of the soul, *viz* waking, dream, and deep sleep, will be shown to be merely illusory, and thus the consequent identity of the Jîva and Brahman will be established.

Topic 1: The soul in the dream state.

संध्ये सृष्टिराह हि ॥ १ ॥

संध्ये In the intermediate stage (between waking and deep-sleep, *i.e.* in the dream state) सृष्टिः (there is real) creation आह (Śruti) says so हि because.

1. In the intermediate stage (between waking and deep-sleep, there is a real) creation, because (the Śruti) says so.

The question is raised whether the creation which one experiences in the dream state is as real as this world of ours, or merely Mâyâ, false, as compared with this waking world. This Sûtra, which gives the view of the opponent, holds that it is just as real, for the Śruti declares, "There are no chariots, nor horses to be yoked to them, nor roads there, but he himself creates the chariots, horses, and roads. For he is the agent" (Bṛ. 4. 3. 10). Moreover, we do not find any difference between the experience of the waking state and that of the dream state. A meal taken in dream has the effect of giving satisfaction even as in the waking state. Therefore the creation of the dream state is real and springs from the Lord Himself, even as He creates ether etc.

निर्मातारं चैके, पुत्रादयश्च ॥ २ ॥

निर्मातारं Creator च and एके some (the followers of particular Śâkhâs of the Vedas) पुत्रादय: sons etc. च and.

2. And some (Śâkhâs or recensions) (state the Self or the Supreme Lord to be) the creator (of objects of desires while we are asleep) and (objects of desires there stand for) sons etc.

A further argument is given by the opponent that the creation even in dreams is by the Lord Himself. "He who is awake in us shaping objects of desire while we are asleep . . . that is Brahman" (Ka. 2. 5. 8). Sons etc. are the objects of desire that He creates. So, as in the case of the waking state, even in dreams the Lord

Himself creates, and hence the world of dreams is also real. Therefore the dream world is not false but real like this Vyâvahârika (phenomenal) world of ours.

मायामात्रं तु, कार्त्स्न्येनानभिव्यक्तस्वरूपत्वात् ॥ ३ ॥

मायामात्रं Mere illusion तु but कार्त्स्न्येन *in toto* अनभिव्यक्तस्वरूपत्वात् on account of its nature not being manifest.

3. **But** (the dream world is) mere illusion, on account of its nature not being manifest with the totality (of attributes of the waking state).

'But' discards the view expressed by the two previous Sûtras. The nature of the dream world does not agree *in toto* with that of the waking world with respect to time, place, cause, and non-contradiction, and as such that world is not real like the waking world. There can be no appropriate time, place or cause in the dream state. Inside the body, there is not enough space for objects like chariots, horses, etc., and in a dream the soul does not leave the body; for if it did, then one who dreams of having gone to America would find himself there on waking while he went to sleep in India. Nor is the midnight proper time for an eclipse of the sun seen in a dream, nor can we conceive a child's getting children in a dream to be real. Moreover, even in dreams we see objects seen being transformed, as for example, when we see a tree turn into a mountain. "He himself creates the chariots etc." (Bṛ. 4. 3. 10), only means that objects which have no reality appear to exist in dreams just as silver does in a mother-of-pearl.

The argument that the dream world is real because it is also a creation of the Supreme Lord, like this waking world, is not true, for the dream world is not the creation of the Lord but of the individual soul. "When he dreams... himself puts the body aside and himself creates (a dream body in its place)" (Bṛ. 4. 3. 9). This text clearly proves that it is the Jîva that creates in dreams and not the Lord.

सूचकश्च हि श्रुतेः, आचक्षते च तद्विदः ॥ ४ ॥

सूचकः Omen **च** but **हि** for **श्रुतेः** from the Śruti **आचक्षते** say **च** also **तद्विदः** experts in dream-reading.

4. But (though the dream-world is an illusion) yet it serves as an omen, for (so we find) in the Śruti, (and) expert dream-readers also say (thus).

Lest it be thought that because the dream-world is an illusion, even the results indicated by dreams are to be so regarded, this Sûtra says that these dreams are yet capable of forecasting events or good and bad fortune. The thing indicated by these dreams is real, though the dreams themselves are unreal, even as the appearance of silver in a mother-of-pearl, though false, produces joy in us, which is real. The Śruti also says so: "If in this dream he sees a woman, let him know this to be a sign that his sacrifice has succeeded" (Ch. 5. 2. 8).

पराभिध्यानात्तु तिरोहितम्, ततो ह्यस्य
बन्धविपर्ययौ ॥ ५ ॥

पराभिध्यानात् By meditation on the Supreme Lord तु but तिरोहितम् that which is covered (by ignorance) ततः from Him (the Lord) हि for अस्य of the soul बन्धविपर्ययौ bondage and its opposite, *i.e.* freedom.

5. But by meditation on the Supreme Lord, that which is covered (by ignorance, *viz* the similarity of the Lord and soul, becomes manifest); for from Him (the Lord) are its (the soul's) bondage and freedom.

It has been shown that the dream-world is false. But an objection is raised against it. The individual soul is but a part of the Supreme Soul and therefore shares Its power of knowledge and rulership even as a spark and fire have alike the power of burning. As such it must also be able to create at will like the Lord. This Sûtra refutes it and says that that rulership is covered by ignorance in the Jîva state and gets manifested only when in the state of meditation on the Lord this ignorance is destroyed by the knowledge 'I am Brahman'. "When that god is known all fetters fall off. . . . From meditating on him there arises, on the dissolution of the body, the third state, that of universal Lordship" (Śv. 1. 11). Till then the Jîva cannot create at will anything real. Moreover, this does not come to man spontaneously, since the bondage and freedom of the individual soul come from the Lord. That is to say, ignorance of His true nature causes bondage, and the knowledge of it results in freedom.

देहयोगाद्वा सोऽपि ॥ ६ ॥

देहयोगात् From its connection with the body वा and स: that (the covering of its rulership) अपि also.

6. And that (the covering of the soul's rulership) also (results) from its connection with the body.

A cause for this covering up of the soul's rulership is given; and that is its connection with the body etc. Because of these limiting adjuncts, the results of nescience, its knowledge and rulership remain hidden, and this lasts so long as it erroneously thinks itself as the body etc. Hence though the soul is not different from the Lord, its powers remain hidden.

Topic 2: The soul in dreamless sleep.

Now the state of deep sleep or Suṣupti is taken up for discussion.

तदभावो नाडीषु, तच्छ्रुतेः, आत्मनि च ॥ ७ ॥

तत्-अभाव: Absence of that (dreaming), in other words Suṣupti नाडीषु in the nerves आत्मनि च and in the Self तत्-श्रुते: as it is known from the Śruti.

7. The absence of that (dreaming, *i.e.* dreamless sleep takes place) in the nerves and in the Self, as it is known from the Śruti.

In different texts Suṣupti (deep-sleep) is said to take place under different conditions. "And when a man is asleep . . . so that he sees no dreams, then he has entered into those nerves (Nâḍis)" (Ch. 8. 6. 3); "Through them he moves forth and rests in the pericardium, *i.e.* in the region of the heart" (Bṛ. 2. 1. 19); "When this being full of consciousness is asleep...lies in the ether *i.e.* the real Self which is in the heart" (Bṛ. 2. 1. 17). Now the question arises whether Suṣupti takes place in any one of these places, *i.e.* whether these are to be taken as alternatives or whether they are to be taken as standing in mutual relation so as to refer to one place only. The opponent holds that as all the words standing for the places enumerated are in the same case, *viz* the locative case, in the texts, they are co-ordinate and therefore alternatives. If mutual relation was meant, then different case-endings would be used by the Śruti. This Sûtra says that they are to be taken as standing in mutual relation denoting the same place.

There is no alternative here, for by allowing option between two Vedic statements we lessen the authority of the Veda, since the adoption of either alternative sublates for the time being the authority of the other alternative. Moreover, the same case is used where things serve different purposes and have to be combined, as, for example, when we say, "He sleeps in the palace, he sleeps on a couch," where we have to combine the two locatives into one as "He sleeps on a couch in the palace." Similarly here the different texts have to be combined, meaning that the soul goes through the nerves to the region of the heart and there rests in Brahman.

It may be questioned why, then, in deep-sleep we do not experience the relation of supporter and that which is supported with respect to Brahman and the Jîva. It is because the individual soul covered with ignorance is lost in Brahman even as a pot of water in a lake and so has no separate existence. "He becomes united with the True, he is gone to his own (Self)" (Ch. 6. 8. 1). Moreover, in the following text the three places are mentioned together, "In these the person is when sleeping he sees no dreams. Then he becomes one with the Prâṇa (Brahman) alone" (Kau. 4. 19). Hence Brahman is the soul's place of rest in deep-sleep.

अतः प्रबोधोऽस्मात् ॥ ८ ॥

अतः Hence प्रबोधः awakening अस्मात् from this.

8. Hence the awakening from this (*i.e.* Brahman).

"In the same manner, my son, all these creatures when they have come back from the True, know no that they have come back from the True" (Ch. 6. 10. 2) In this text the Śruti states that when the Jîva return after deep-sleep to the waking state, it returns from th True or Brahman, thereby showing that in Suṣupt Jîva is merged in Brahman and not in the nerve Hitâ etc. But as it is covered by ignorance it does no realize its identity with Brahman in Suṣupti.

Topic 3: The selfsame soul returns from Suṣupti.

स एव तु, कर्मानुस्मृति-शब्दविधिभ्यः ॥ ९ ॥

स एव The selfsame soul तु but कर्म-अनुस्मृति-शब्द-विधिभ्य on account of Karma, memory, scriptural authorit and precept.

9. But the selfsame soul (returns from Brahman fter Suṣupti on account of work, memory, scripural authority, and precept.

A question is raised here that just as when a drop f water has merged in the ocean it is difficult to pick it ut again, so also when the Jîva has merged in Brahian it is difficult to say that the selfsame Jîva arises om It after Suṣupti. So we have to take that some ul arises after Suṣupti from Brahman. There can be o rule that the same soul arises from It. The Sûtra futes this and says that the selfsame soul comes back ter Suṣupti for the following reasons: (1) What has en partly done by a person before going to sleep, we d him finishing after he wakes up. If it were not the me soul, then the latter would have no interest in iishing what has been partly done by another. (2) om our experience of identity of personality before d after sleep. (3) From our memory of past events. (4) om scriptural authority as in texts like, "Whatever ese creatures are here, whether a tiger, or a lion, a wolf, or a boar . . . that they become again" (Ch. 9. 3), we find that the selfsame soul returns from ahman after Suṣupti. (5) If the person who goes to ep and he who rises after it be different, then scripral precepts either as regards work or knowledge uld be meaningless. For if a person can attain entity for ever with Brahman by merely going to ep, then scriptural instruction would be useless to ain liberation.

Therefore it is the selfsame soul that rises from ahman after Suṣupti. The case of the drop of water is not quite analogous, for a drop of water merges in th ocean without any adjuncts and so is lost for ever; bu the Jîva merges in Brahman with its adjuncts. So th identical Jîva rises again from Brahman owing to i Karma and ignorance, which do not allow it to be lo in Brahman irrevocably.

Topic 4: The nature of a swoon.

मुग्धेऽर्धसंपत्तिः, परिशेषात् ॥ १० ॥

मुग्धे In a swoon अर्धसंपत्तिः partial attainment of t state of deep-sleep परिशेषात् as the only alternative le

10. In a swoon (there is the) partial attainme of the state of deep-sleep, as that is the on alternative left.

The question of swoon is taken up for discussic There are only three states of a soul while living in t body—waking, dream, and deep-sleep. Its fourth st is death. The condition of swoon cannot come in as fifth state, as no such state is known. So what is Is it a separate state of the soul, or is it but one of th states? It cannot be waking or dream, for there is consciousness or experience of anything. It is not de sleep, for that gives happiness, which swoon does n Nor is it death, for the soul returns to life. So the o alternative left is that in a swoon the soul parti attains the state of deep-sleep, inasmuch as there is consciousness in that state and it returns to life, a partially that of death, as is seen from the soul's exp ence of misery and pain in that state resulting in torted face and limbs. It is a separate state, though happens occasionally, and the reason why it is not c dered a fifth state is because it is a mixture of the ther two states.

Topic 5: The nature of the Supreme Brahman.

The preceding four topics deal with the nature of hou' or the apparent self. By proving that the creaon in dreams is false, it has been shown that though e Jîva appears apparently to enjoy happiness and isery, yet in reality it is unattached. By its mergence Brahman in deep-sleep that detachment has been mly established. By saying that the selfsame Jîva rerns from sleep the doubt as to its non-permanency s been refuted. By a reference to swoon it has been plained that though all expressions of life are tinct in that state still the Jîva is there, and hence e can be sure that even after death the soul continues exist. Thus it has been shown that the soul is selfninous, of the nature of consciousness, having easure in itself only, and beyond the various states. wing described the nature of 'thou', the nature of hat' is taken up for discussion in the succeeding tras.

न स्थानतोऽपि परस्योभयलिङ्गम्, सर्वत्र हि ॥ ११ ॥

न Not स्थानत: from (difference of) place अपि even य of Brahman उभयलिङ्गम् twofold characteristic हि ause सर्वत्र throughout (the scriptures teach otherwise).

1. Even from (difference of) place a twofold racteristic cannot (be predicated) of Brahman, ause throughout (the scriptures teach It to be erwise *i.e.* without any qualities).

In the scriptures we find two kinds of descriptio about Brahman. Some texts describe It as qualified an some as unqualified. "From whom all activities, al desires, all odours, and all tastes proceed" (Ch. 3. 14 2) speak of attributes; again "It is neither gross no minute, neither short nor long, neither redness no moisture" etc. (Bṛ. 3. 8. 8). Are we to take that bot are true of Brahman according as It is or is not con nected with adjuncts, or have we to take only one c them as true and the other as false, and if so, whicl and on what grounds? The Sûtra says that both cann be predicated of one and the same Brahman, for it against experience. One and the same thing cann have two contradictory natures at the same time. N does the mere connection of a thing with anoth change its nature, even as the redness of a flower r flected in a crystal does not change the nature of th crystal, which is colourless. The imputation of redne is due to ignorance and not real. Neither can a thir change its real nature: it means destruction. Even so the case of Brahman. Its connection with adjuncts li earth etc. is a product of nescience. Hence between t two aspects of Brahman we have to accept that which attributeless as Its true nature, for throughout t scriptures we find Brahman so described to the e clusion of Its qualified aspects. "It is without soun without touch, form, and decay" etc. (Ka. 1. 3. 1. The other description of Brahman is only for the sa of Upâsanâ and is not Its real nature.

न भेदादिति चेत्, न, प्रत्येकमतद्वचनात् ॥ १२ ॥

न Not so भेदात् on account of difference (bei

taught in the scriptures) इति चेत् if it be said न not so प्रत्येकम् with respect to each अतद्वचनात because of the declaration of the opposite of that.

12. If it be said (that it is) not so on account of difference (being taught in the scriptures), (we reply) not so, because with respect to each (such form) the Śruti declares the opposite of that.

We find that the scripture declares Brahman as having different forms in different Vidyâs or meditations. In some It is described as having four feet, in some as of sixteen digits (Kalâs) or again as having for Its body the three worlds and being called Vaiśvânara, and so on. So we have to understand on scriptural authority that Brahman is also qualified. This Sûtra refutes it and says that every such form due to Upâdhi is denied of Brahman in texts like, "The shining, immortal being who is in this earth, and the shining, immortal, corporeal being in the body are but the Self" (Bṛ. 2. 5. 1). Such texts show that in all Upâdhis like earth etc. the same Self is present, and hence there is only non-difference, oneness. It is not true that the Vedas inculcate the connection of Brahman with various forms. With regard to what we take as different, the Śruti explains at every instance that the form is not true, and that in reality there is only one formless principle.

अपि चैवमेके ॥ १३ ॥

अपि च Moreover एवम् thus एके some.

13. Moreover some (teach) thus.

Some Śâkhas (recensions) of the Vedas directly teach that the manifoldness is not true, by passing strictures on those who see difference. "He goes from death to death, who sees difference, as it were, in It" (Ka. 1. 4. 11) also Bṛ. 4. 4. 19.

अरूपवदेव हि, तत्प्रधानत्वात् ॥ १४ ॥

अरूपवत Formless एव only हि verily तत्-प्रधानत्वात् on account of that being the main purport.

14. Verily Brahman is only formless on account of that being the main purport (of all texts about Brahman).

Brahman is only formless for all the texts that aim at teaching Brahman describe It as formless. If Brahman be understood to have a form, then texts which describe It as formless would become purportless, and such a contingency with respect to the scriptures is unimaginable, for the scriptures throughout have a purport. On the other hand, texts dealing with qualified Brahman seek not to establish It, but rather to enjoin meditations on Brahman. Therefore Brahman is formless.

प्रकाशवच्चावैयर्थ्यात् ॥ १५ ॥

प्रकाशवत् Like light च and अवैयर्थ्यात् not being purportless.

15. And like light (taking form in connection

with bodies having form, Brahman takes form in connection with Upâdhis), because (texts ascribing form to Brahman) are not purportless.

If Brahman is formless, what about the texts which describe It as having form? Are they superfluous? If Brahman is without form then all Upâsanâs of the Brahman with form would be futile, for how can the worship of such a false Brahman lead to Brahmaloka and other spheres? This Sûtra explains that they are not without a purpose. Just as light, which has no form, appears to be great or small according to the aperture through which it enters a room and yet has the virtue of removing the darkness in the room, even so the formless Brahman appears to have a form, as being limited by adjuncts like earth etc.; and the worship of such an illusory Brahman can help one to attain Brahmaloka etc., which are also illusory from the absolute standpoint. Hence these texts are not altogether purportless. This, however, does not contradict the position already established, *viz* that Brahman, though connected with limiting adjuncts, is not dual in character, because the effects of these cannot constitute attributes of a substance, and moreover these limiting adjuncts are all due to Nescience.

आह च तन्मात्रम् ॥ १६ ॥

आह Declares च and तत्-मात्रम that (*i.e.* intelligence) only.

16. And (the scripture) declares (that Brahman is) that (*i.e.* intelligence) only.

Now what is the nature of that formless Brahman? "As a lump of salt is without interior or exterior, entire, and purely salt in taste, even so is the Self without interior or exterior, entire, and Pure Intelligence alone" (Bṛ. 4. 5. 13). It is mere intelligence, self-effulgent, homogenous, and without attributes.

दर्शयति च, अथो अपि स्मर्यते ॥ १७ ॥

दर्शयति (Scripture) shows च also अथो thus अपि also स्मर्यते (it is) stated by the Smṛtis.

17. (The scripture) also shows (this, and) thus also (is it) stated by the Smṛtis.

That Brahman is without any attributes is also proved by the fact that the Śruti teaches about It by denying all characteristics to It. "Now therefore the description (of Brahman): 'Not this, not this.' Because there is no other and more appropriate description than this 'Not this'" (Bṛ. 2. 3. 6). If Brahman had form, then it would be established by such texts, and there would be no necessity to deny everything and say 'Not this, not this'. So also the Smṛtis teach about Brahman: "The Highest Brahman without either beginning or end, which cannot be said either to be or not to be" (Gîtâ 13. 12); "It is unmanifest, unthinkable, and without modification, thus is It spoken of" (Gîtâ 2. 25).

अतएव चोपमा सूर्यकादिवत् ॥ १८ ॥

अतएव Therefore च also उपमा comparison सूर्यकादिवत् like the images of the sun etc.

18. Therefore also (with respect to Brahman we have) comparisons like the images of the sun etc.

That Brahman is formless is further established from the similes used with respect to it. Since this Brahman is mere intelligence, homogeneous, and formless, and everything else is denied in It, therefore we find that the scriptures explain the fact of Its having forms by saying that they are like reflections in water of the one sun, meaning thereby that these forms are unreal, being due only to limiting adjuncts.

अम्बुवदग्रहणात् तु न तथात्वम् ॥ १९ ॥

अम्बुवत् Like water अग्रहणात् not being experienced तु but न no तथात्वम् similarity.

19. But (there is) no similarity (in the case of Brahman, any second thing) not being experienced like water.

An objection is raised that the comparison of the last Sûtra is not correct. In the case of the sun, which has a form, water, which is different and at a distance from it, catches its image but Brahman is formless and all-pervading, and there can be nothing else different and at a distance from It, to serve as an Upâdhi, that can catch Its reflection. So the comparison is defective.

वृद्धिह्रासभाक्त्वमन्तर्भावात्, उभयसामञ्जस्यादेवम् ॥ २० ॥

वृद्धि-ह्रास-भाक्त्वम् Participating in the increase and

decrease अन्तर्भावात् on account of its being inside उभय-सामञ्जस्यात् on account of the similarity in the two cases एवम् thus.

20. On account of Brahman being inside (Its adjuncts) (It appears) to participate in their increase and decrease. On account of this similarity in the two cases (mentioned in Sûtra 18) it is thus (*i.e.* the comparison is not defective).

The comparison with the reflection of the sun is to be taken not on all fours but only with respect to a particular feature. Just as the reflected sun is distorted, trembles, or varies in size as the water shakes, expands, or contracts, while the real sun remains unchanged; so also Brahman participates, as it were, in the attributes of the Upâdhis; it grows with them, decreases with them, suffers with them, and so on, but not in reality. Hence on account of this similarity in the two cases the comparison is not defective.

दर्शनाच्च ॥ २१ ॥

दर्शनात् On account of scriptural instruction च and.

21. And on account of scriptural instruction.

The scripture also teaches that Brahman enters into the body and other limiting adjuncts. "He made bodies with two feet and bodies with four feet. That Supreme Being first entered the bodies as a bird. He on account of his dwelling in all bodies is called the Puruṣa" (Bṛ. 2. 5. 18). Thus also the comparison in Sûtra 18 is not defective.

Therefore it is established that Brahman is formless, of the nature of intelligence, and homogenous—without any difference.

Topic 6: 'Not this, not this' in Bṛ. 2.3.6 denies the gross and subtle forms of Brahman given in Bṛ. 2.3.1 and not Brahman Itself.

प्रकृतैतावत्त्वं हि प्रतिषेधति, ततो ब्रवीति च भूयः ॥ २२ ॥

प्रकृत-एतावत्त्वं What has been mentioned up to this प्रतिषेधति denies ततः than that भूयः something more ब्रवीति says च and.

22. What has been mentioned up to this is denied (by the words 'Not this, not this'), and (the Śruti) says something more than that (afterwards).

"Brahman has but two forms—gross and subtle, mortal and immortal, limited and unlimited, Sat (defined) and Tyat (undefined)" (Br. 2. 3. 1). Thus describing the two forms of Brahman, the gross, consisting of earth, water, and fire, and the subtle, consisting of air and ether, the Śruti says finally, "Now therefore the description (of Brahman): 'Not this, not this' etc. (Br. 2. 3. 6). Now the question is whether the double denial in 'Not this, not this' negates both the world and Brahman, or only one of them. The opponent holds that both are denied, and consequently Brahman, which is false, cannot be the substratum for a world, which is also false. In other words, it leads us to Śûnyavâda, the theory of Void. If one only is denied it is proper that Brahman is denied, for It is not seen and therefore Its existence is doubtful, and not the world, since we experience it. The Sûtra refutes this view and says that what has been described till now, *viz* the two forms of Brahman, gross and subtle, is denied by the words 'Not this, not this', the double mention of these words of denial applying to the two forms of Brahman. The word 'Iti' refers to what has been mentioned immediately before, *i.e.* the *two forms* of Brahman, the subject-matter of the discussion, and therefore cannot refer to Brahman Itself, which is not the main topic of the preceding texts. Moreover, after denying the world the Śruti says something more than that about Brahman, *viz* 'The Truth of truth' meaning thereby that Brahman alone is the one reality that exists and is the substratum of the world, which is illusory. Nor is it reasonable to suppose that the Śruti, professing to teach about Brahman, will deny it. It is the Truth of truth, *i.e.* the reality behind 'Sat', or earth, water, and fire, and 'Tyat' or air and ether, the definite and indefinite forms in nature. There is no contradiction to perception in this denial of the world, for it denies only the transcendental reality of the world and not its Vyâvahârika or phenomental reality, which remains intact. The objection, *viz* that Brahman is not experienced, and therefore it is Brahman that is denied, is baseless; for the object of the Śruti is to teach about something which is not ordinarily experienced by us; otherwise its teaching would be redundant.

तदव्यक्तम्, आह हि ॥ २३ ॥

तत् That (Brahman) अव्यक्तम् is not manifest आह (so the scripture) says हि for.

23. That (Brahman) is not manifest, for (so the scripture) says.

If Brahman exists, then why is It not perceived? The Śruti says that Brahman is unmanifest on account of our being covered with ignorance. Therefore It is not perceived by us: "He is not apprehended by the eye, nor by the other senses, nor by penance" etc. (Mu. 3. 1. 8).

अपि च संराधने, प्रत्यक्षानुमानाभ्याम् ॥ २४ ॥

अपि च And moreover संराधने in perfect meditation (It is experienced) प्रत्यक्ष-अनुमानाभ्याम् from the Śruti and Smrti.

24. And moreover (Brahman is experienced) in perfect meditation, (as we know) from the Śruti and Smṛti.

If Brahman is not manifest to us, then we can never know It, and therefore there will be no Freedom. This Sûtra says that Brahman is not known only to those whose heart is not purified, but those who are purified realize It in the state of Samâdhi when ignorance is destroyed. That this is so is known from the Śruti: "Some wise man, however, with his eyes turned inside and wishing for immortality saw the Self within" (Ka. 2. 4. 1); also Mu. 3. 1. 8. The Smṛti also says the same thing: "He who is seen as Light by the Yogins meditating on Him sleeplessly, with suspended breath, contented minds, and subdued senses" etc.

प्रकाशादिवच्चावैशेष्यं प्रकाशश्च कर्मणि, अभ्यासात् ॥ २५ ॥

प्रकाशादिवत् Like light etc. च and अवैशेष्यं (there is) no difference प्रकाशः Brahman च also कर्मणि in work अभ्यासात् on account of repeated mention (in the Śruti).

25. And as in the case of light etc. there is no difference, (so) also between Brahman (and its manifestation) in activity; on account of the repeated instruction (of the Śruti to that effect).

The nature of the Jîva and Brahman has been described. Now their identity is being explained.

If according to the last Sûtra Brahman is the object of meditation and the Jîva is the meditator, it means that there is duality, and not the unity of Brahman. This Sûtra explains it. Even as between the sun and its reflection in water etc. there is in reality no difference, the image being unreal, so also the one Brahman manifests as many in the limiting adjuncts of activity like meditation etc. Through ignorance the meditating self thinks it is different from Brahman; but in reality it is identical with Brahman. That it is so is known from repeated instruction of the Śruti in texts like, "That thou art", "I am Brahman", which deny difference.

अतो अनन्तेन, तथा हि लिङ्गम् ॥ २६ ॥

अतः Therefore अनन्तेन with the Infinite तथा thus हि for लिङ्गम् (the scripture) indicates.

26. Therefore (the individual soul become

one) with the Infinite; for thus (the scripture) indicates.

The Jîva attains identity with Brahman on the dawning of Knowledge, when ignorance with all its limiting adjuncts disappears. "He who knows that Supreme Brahman becomes Brahman Itself" (Mu. 3. 2. 9). If ᵗʰe difference were real, then one could not become Brahman Itself. Knowledge may destroy ignorance, but not what is real. Now, since the Jîva becomes Brahman, its individuality was not real, and hence it was destroyed by Knowledge, leaving only Brahman. So the difference is unreal, the identity real.

उभयव्यपदेशात्त्वहिकुण्डलवत् ॥ २७ ॥

उभयव्यपदेशात् On account of both being taught तु but हिकुण्डलवत् like that between a serpent and its coils.

27. But on account of both (*i.e.* difference and non-difference) being taught (by the Śruti) (the elation of the Jîva and Brahman is to be taken) ke that between a serpent and its coils.

Having established the identity of the Jîva and rahman, the author proceeds to elucidate it further by camining the theory of difference and non-difference. the scriptures we find also texts like, "Two birds of eautiful plumage" etc. (Mu. 3. 1. 1), which speak of fference between the Jîva and Brahman. So we have understand that the difference between them prior to beration is real, though when it is destroyed by nowledge they attain identity. Hence we have to take that their relation is one of difference and non-difference, as between a serpent and its coils. As a snake it is one but if we look at the coils, hood, etc. there is difference. Similarly between the Jîva and Brahman there is difference as well as non-difference.

प्रकाशाश्रयवद्वा, तेजस्त्वात् ॥ २८ ॥

प्रकाश-आश्रयवत् Like light and its substratum वा or तेजस्त्वात् on account of both being luminous.

28. Or like (the relation of) light and its substratum, on account of both being luminous.

Another example is given to establish the theory of difference and non-difference. The relation between the Jîva and Brahman may be taken to be like that between light and its orb. Both being luminous are non-different; yet on account of their varying extensity they are spoken of as different. So is the relation between the Jîva and Brahman one of difference and non-difference, the one being limited and the other all-pervading.

पूर्ववद्वा ॥ २९ ॥

पूर्ववत् As before वा or.

29. Or (the relation between the two, *i.e.* Jîva and Brahman) is as given before.

Having given in the two previous Sûtras the view of Bhedâbhedavâdins, the upholders of difference and non-difference, this Sûtra refutes it and establishes as the final truth what has been stated in Sûtra 25, *viz* that the difference is merely illusory and non-difference is the reality. For if the difference is also real, it can never cease to be, and all the instruction of the Śruti with respect to Liberation will be useless, for bondage is nothing but this idea of separateness, and if this is real, there can be no Liberation at all. But if the difference is due to ignorance, then Knowledge can destroy it and the reality, the non-difference may be realized. So the views given in Sûtra 27 and 28, which later on were developed by Kumârila and Bhâskara, are not correct, and the view given in Sûtra 25 alone is correct.

प्रतिषेधाच्च ॥ ३० ॥

प्रतिषेधात् On account of the denial च and.

30. And on account of the denial.

Form the Śruti texts like, "There is no other witness but He" (Bṛ. 3. 7. 23), which deny that there exists any other intelligent being apart from Brahman, and from the denial of the world by, "Not this, not this", it follows that there is no other entity but Brahman. Therefore there is only one Brahman without any difference whatsoever.

Topic 7: Brahman is one without a second, and expressions which apparently imply something else as existing are only metaphorical.

परमतः सेतून्मानसंबन्धभेदव्यपदेशेभ्यः ॥ ३१ ॥

परम् Greater अत: than this (Brahman) सेतु-उन्मान-संबन्ध-भेद-व्यपदेशेभ्य: on account of terms denoting a bank, measure, connection, and difference.

31. (There is something) superior to this (Brahman), on account of terms denoting a bank, measure, connection, and difference (used with respect to It).

To say that there is nothing except Brahman is objectionable, for we find that there is something besides Brahman on account of its being designated as a bank separating things other than Itself in texts like, "That self is a bank, a boundary" etc. (Ch. 8. 4. 1); as having size and therefore limited in texts like, "That Brahman has four feet" (Ch. 3. 18. 2)—it is well known that whatever is limited is limited by some other object; as being connected with other objects: "The embodied self when embraced by the Supreme Self" (Bṛ. 4. 3. 21), which shows that there is something else than Brahman; and as being different: "The Ātman is to be seen", thereby hinting a seer and seen. All these show that Brahman is not one without a second.

सामान्यात्तु ॥ ३२ ॥

तु But सामान्यात् on account of similarity.

32. But (Brahman is called a bank) on account of similarity.

'But' refutes the position taken in the previous Sûtra. There can exist nothing different from Brahman. It is called a bank, not because there exists something beyond It, as in the case of a bank, but on account of a similarity. The similarity is this: Just as a bank keeps back water and marks the boundary of adjacent fields, even so Brahman maintains the world and its boundaries. "Having passed the bank" (Ch. 8. 4. 2) means, having attained Brahman fully and not having crossed it, even as we say he has passed in Grammar, meaning thereby that he has mastered it.

बुद्धयर्थः पादवत् ॥ ३३ ॥

बुद्धयर्थः For the sake of easy comprehension पादवत् just like (four) feet.

33. (Brahman is depicted as having size) for the sake of easy comprehension (*i.e.* Upâsanâ); just like four feet.

The statements as to the size of Brahman, 'Brahman has four feet,' 'It has sixteen digits,' etc. are meant for the sake of Upâsanâ; for it is difficult to comprehend the Infinite, all-pervading Brahman. Just as mind conceived as the personal manifestation of Brahman is imagined to have the organ of speech, nose, eyes, and ears as its four feet, so also Brahman is imagined as having size etc. for the sake of Upâsanâ, but not in reality.

स्थानविशेषात्, प्रकाशादिवत् ॥ ३४ ॥

स्थानविशेषात् On account of special places प्रकाशादिवत् like light etc.

34. (The statements about connection and difference with respect to Brahman) are on account of special places; as in the case of light etc.

The statements regarding difference are made with reference to limiting adjuncts only and not to any difference in Brahman's nature. We speak of light inside a chamber and light outside it, though in reality light is one, the distinction being due to limiting adjuncts. So also all statements about connection are made with reference to the removal of the adjuncts, when connection with the Supreme Self is said to take place metaphorically, even as on the destruction of the chamber the light inside it may be said to be united with light in general.

उपपत्तेश्च ॥ ३५ ॥

उपपत्तेः From reasoning च and.

35. And it is reasonable.

This Sûtra explains further that connection and difference are not to be taken as real, but only metaphorically. The connection of the Jîva with Brahman in deep-sleep cannot be real. "It merges in its Self" (Ch. 6. 8. 1), shows that the connection of the soul with Brahman is a natural, inherent identity, and not as between two things. Similarly the difference referred to is not real, but due to ignorance, as can be gathered from hundreds of texts.

तथान्यप्रतिषेधात् ॥ ३६ ॥

तथा Similarly अन्य-प्रतिषेधात् on account of the express denial of all other things.

36. Similarly on account of the express denial of all other things (there is nothing but Brahman).

A further reason is given to show that there is nothing but Brahman. "The Self is all this" (Ch. 7. 25. 2); "All this is Brahman alone" (Mu. 2. 2. 11) etc. deny the existence of anything else besides Brahman. Therefore Brahman is one without a second.

अनेन सर्वगतत्वमायामशब्दादिभ्यः ॥ ३७ ॥

अनेन By this सर्वगतत्वम् all-pervadingness आयामशब्दादिभ्यः as is known from scriptural statements etc. regarding (Brahman's) extent.

37. By this (is established) the all-pervadingness (of Brahman), as is known from scriptural statements etc. regarding (Brahman's) extent.

This Sûtra explains the all-pervadingness of Brahman which follows from the fact that It is one without a second. By saying that texts describing Brahman as a bank etc. are not to be taken literally, and by denying all other things, it is proved that Brahman is all-pervading. If they were taken literally, then Brahman would be limited and not all-pervading and consequently not eternal. That Brahman is all-pervading is known from such Śruti texts as, "He is omnipresent like ether, and eternal" (Śat. Br. 19. 6. 3.2). See also Gîtâ 2. 24.

Topic 8: Īśvara the giver of the fruits of actions.

फलमतः, उपपत्तेः ॥ ३८ ॥

फलम् Fruits of actions अत: from Him उपपत्ते: for that is reasonable.

38. From Him (the Lord) are the fruits of actions; for that is reasonable.

Having described the nature of Brahman, the author proceeds now to discuss the view of the Mîmâṁsakas who say that Karma (work) and not Īśvara, gives the fruits of one's actions. According to them it is useless to set up an Īśvara for this purpose, since Karma itself can give that result at a future time.

This Sûtra refutes it and says that from Īśvara alone come the fruits of one's work. Karma is insentient and short-lived, and cannot therefore be expected to bestow the fruits of actions at a future time according to one' deserts. We do not see any insentient thing bestow fruits on those who worship it. Therefore it is only from the Lord, who is worshipped through actions, that thei results proceed.

श्रुतत्वाच्च ॥ ३९ ॥

श्रुतत्वात् Because the scripture so teaches च and.

39. And because the scripture so teaches.

The scripture declares that the fruits of actions come from the Lord. "That great, birthless Self is the eater of food and the giver of wealth (the fruit of one's work)" (Bṛ. 4. 4. 24).

धर्मं जैमिनिः, अतएव ॥ ४० ॥

धर्मं Religious merits जैमिनिः (sage) Jaimini अतएव for the same reasons.

40. Jaimini (thinks) for the same reasons (*viz* scriptural authority and reasoning) that religious merit (is what brings about the fruits of actions).

The view of the previous Sûtra is being criticized. The scripture enjoins, "He who is desirous of the heavenly world is to sacrifice" (Tâṇḍya). Since every scriptural injunction has an object, it is reasonable to think that the sacrifice itself produces the fruit. But it may be objected that since the deed is destroyed, it cannot produce a result at a future time. This is met by the positing of an Apûrva or extraordinary principle, which is produced by the Karma before it is destroyed, and through the intervention of which the result is produced in the distant future. Again, if the deed itself did not produce the result, it would be useless to perform it; and moreover it is not reasonable to imagine one cause (the Lord) for a great variety of effects.

पूर्वं तु बादरायणः, हेतुव्यपदेशात् ॥ ४१ ॥

पूर्वं The former (*i.e.* the Lord) तु but बादरायणः Bâdarâyaṇa हेतु-व्यपदेशात् on account of His being declared to be the cause (of the actions even).

41. But Bâdarâyaṇa (thinks) the former (the Lord, as the bestower of the fruits of actions) on account of His being declared to be the cause (of the actions even).

'But' refutes the view of Sûtra 40. Both Karma and Apûrva are insentient, and as such incapable of producing results without the intervention of an intelligent principle. For such a phenomenon is not experienced in the world. No one gets anything by worshipping stocks and stones. So the fruits of actions come only from the Lord, and this is all the more established, as the Lord Himself causes people to act one way or the other; and since the Jîva acts as directed by Him, He Himself is the bestower of the fruits of his actions according to his deserts. "He makes him whom He wishes to lead up from these worlds do a good deed" etc. (Kau. 3. 8); "Whichever divine form a devotee wishes to worship. . .and obtains from it the results he desires, as ordained by Me" (Gîtâ 7.21-22). Since the Lord has regard for the merit and demerit of the souls, the objection that a uniform cause is incapable of producing various effects does not stand.

In the last four topics the entity 'That' has been explained. Firstly, Brahman has been shown to be formless, self-effulgent, and without difference; secondly, by the denial of manifoldness in It it has been established that it is one without a second; and lastly, It has been proved to be the giver of the fruits of people's action in the relative world. Thus the two entities 'thou' and 'That' have been explained in these two sections.

CHAPTER III

Section III

In the last section the two entities 'thou' and 'That' f the Vedic dictum (Mahâvâkya) 'That thou art' have een explained and shown to be identical. Now the criptures prescribe various meditations that help to ttain this knowledge of identity. It is not possible for he ordinary man to grasp the Infinite. Therefore the criptures present various symbols of Brahman such as râṇa, Âkâśa, and mind, for the beginner to meditate pon. Sometimes they prescribe the cosmic form of rahman (Vaiśvânara) for meditation. These different ethods of approaching the infinite Brahman are nown as Vidyâs or Upâsanâs.

This section discusses these various Vidyâs, by eans of which the individual soul attains Brahman. n this connection the question naturally arises, hether similar Vidyâs described differently in different recensions of the Vedas are one or different, and onsequently to be combined into a single meditation r separately gone through. Here it is decided which idyâs are the same and have to be combined into one, nd which Vidyâs are different in spite of certain milarities. The principle that is followed throughout the interpretation of these Vidyâs is this: Since rahman, which is the only reality, is the resulting gnition of all Vidyâs, it may be helpful to combine the particulars of the same Vidyâ mentioned in different Śâkhâs, since they have been found efficacious by the followers of those Śâkhâs.

Topic 1: The Vidyâs with identical or similar form met with in the scriptures or in different recensions of the scriptures are one Vidyâ.

सर्ववेदान्तप्रत्ययम्, चोदनाद्यविशेषात् ॥ १ ॥

सर्व-वेदान्त-प्रत्ययम् Described in the various Vedânta texts चोदनादि-अविशेषात् on account of non-difference as regards injunction etc. (i.e. connection, form, and name.

1. (The Upâsanâs) described in the various Vedânta texts (are not different), on account of the non-difference as regards injunction etc. (*i.e* connection, form, and name).

There are Upâsanâs described variously in differen Vedânta texts. For example, the Upâsanâ of Prâṇa i described in one way in the Bṛhadâraṇyaka Upaniṣa and in a different way in the Chândogya. Are suc Upâsanâs, described differently in different Śâkhâs o the Vedas, different or same? The opponent holds tha they are different, on account of the difference in form This Sûtra refutes it and says that such meditations ar one and the same, on account of the non-difference a regards injunction, connection, name, and form c these in different Śâkhâs. Just as on account of th injunction in all Śâkhâs, "One should perform th Agnihotra" etc. (Mai. 6. 36) the daily Agnihotra sacr fice is one only, and as Jyotiṣṭoma and Vâjapeya sacrifices described in different Śâkhâs are one only, so also on account of non-difference as regards injunction such as, "He who knows the oldest and greatest" (Bṛ. 6. 1. 1) in both the Bṛhadâraṇyaka and the Chândogya Upaniṣads, the Prâṇa Vidyâ in all the Śâkhâs is one and the same. Similarly as regards the fruit or result of the Upâsanâ there is non-difference. "He who knows it to be such becomes the oldest and greatest" (*Ibid* 6. 1. 1). Prâṇa, which is the object of he meditation, is described in both as the oldest and greatest, and both the meditations are named Prâṇa Vidyâ. Therefore there being non-difference in all espects, the two Vidyâs are not different, but one. The ame is true of Dahara Vidyâ, Vaiśvânara Upâsanâ, âṇḍilya Vidyâ, etc. described in various Śâkhâs.

भेदान्नेति चेत्, न एकस्यामपि ॥ २ ॥

भेदात् On account of difference न not इति चेत् if it e said न not so एकस्यामपि even in the same (Vidyâ).

2. If it be said (that the Vidyâs are) not (one) n account of difference (in minor points), (we eply) not so, since even in the same Vidyâ here might be such minor differences).

A further objection is raised that since certain differences are seen to exist with respect to the Vidyâs escribed in different Śâkhâs, they cannot be one. For xample, in the Bṛhadâraṇyaka in the Pañcâgni Vidyâ sixth fire is mentioned as an object of worship: "The e becomes his fire" (Bṛ. 6. 2. 14); whereas in the

Chândogya we have, "But he who knows these five fires" (Ch. 5. 10. 10). Therefore on account of difference in form the two Vidyâs cannot be one. This Śûtra refutes it and says that they are one, since even in the same Vidyâ there may be differences of form. The five fires like heaven etc. mentioned in the Chândogya are identified in the Bṛhadâraṇyaka. Therefore there can be no difference in Vidyâ. Nor can the presence or absence of a sixth fire create a difference as regards form, for in the same Atirâtra sacrifice the Ṣoḍaśi vessel may or may not be taken. On the other hand, on account of the majority of fires being recognized in both, it is reasonable that we should add the sixth fire to the Vidyâ in the Chândogya. The name 'five fires' is also no objection against this increase of number, for the number five is not an essential part of the injunction. Moreover, even in the same Śâkhâ and in the same Vidyâ differences like this are seen in different chapters, yet the Vidyâ described in these different chapters is taken on all hands as one. Therefore in spite of these differences in different Śâkhâs it is reasonable that Vidyâs of the same class are one and not different.

स्वाध्यायस्य तथात्वेन हि समाचारेऽधिकाराच्च
सववच्च तन्नियमः ॥ ३ ॥

स्वाध्यायस्य Of the study of the Vedas तथात्वेन as being such हि because समाचारे in the Samâcâra (a book of that name) अधिकारात् on account of the qualification च and सववत् like that of the (seven) oblations (v. Saurya etc.) च and तन्नियमः that rule.

3. (The rite of carrying fire on the head is connected) with the study of the Vedas, because in the Samâcâra (it is described) as being such. And (this also follows) from its being a qualification (for the students of the Atharva Veda), as is the case with the (seven) oblations (*viz* Saurya etc.).

A further objection is raised. In the Muṇḍaka Upaniṣad, which deals with the knowledge of Brahman, the carrying of fire on the head by the student is mentioned. The opponent holds that on account of this particular ceremony, which obtains among the followers of the Atharva Veda, the Vidyâ of the Ātharvaṇikas is different from all other Vidyâs. The Sûtra refutes this saying that the rite of carrying fire on the head is not an attribute of the Vidyâ, but of the study of the Vedas of the Ātharvaṇikas. So it is described in the book Samâcâra, which deals with Vedic observances. From the following text, "A man who has performed the rite (*viz* carrying fire) does not read this" (Mu. 3. 2. 11) also we find it is connected with the reading or study of the Upaniṣad and not with the Vidyâ. The rite of carrying the fire is connected only with the study of that particular Veda and not others, like the seven oblations, which are not connected with the fires taught in the other Vedas, but only with those of the Atharva Veda. So the unity of Vidyâs stands in all cases.

दर्शयति च ॥ ४ ॥

दर्शयति Instructs च also.

4. (The scripture) also instructs thus.

"That which all the Vedas declare" (Ka. 1. 2. 15) shows that the Nirguṇa Brahman is the one purport of all the Vedânta texts. Therefore all Vidyâs relating to It must also be one. Thus the meditation of the Saguṇa Brahman as Vaiśvânara, who is represented as extending from heaven to the earth in the Bṛhadâraṇyaka, is referred to in the Chândogya as something well known: "But he who worships that Vaiśvânara self as extending from heaven to the earth" (Ch. 5. 18. 1), thereby showing that all Vaiśvânara Vidyâs are one. Thus since the Nirguṇa or the Saguṇa Brahman is one and not many, therefore particular Vidyâs which relate to either of them are also one and not many. This also follows from the same hymns and the like enjoined in one place being employed in other places for the sake of Upâsanâ. The same rule applies to other Vidyâs also besides the Vaiśvânara, and in consequence they are not many, though differently described in different Śâkhâs.

The unity of Vidyâs, having been established, their results are taken up for discussion.

Topic 2: Particulars of identical Vidyâs mentioned in different places or Śâkhâs are to be combined into one meditation.

उपसंहारोऽर्थाभेदाद्विधिशेषवत्समाने च ॥ ५ ॥

उपसंहार: Combination अर्थाभेदात् since there is no difference in the object of meditation विधिशेषवत् like the subsidiary rites of a main sacrifice समाने च and in the Upâsanâs of the same class.

5. And in the Upâsanâs of the same class (mentioned in different Śâkhâs) a combination (of all the particulars mentioned in all Śâkhâs is to be made), since there is no difference in the object of meditation just as (a combination of) all subsidiary rites of a main sacrifice (mentioned in different Śâkhâs is made).

From what has been discussed in the previous Sûtras it is clear that the Vidyâs described in different Śâkhâs will have to be combined in the Upâsanâ, since their object after all is one. The particulars mentioned in other Śâkhâs than one's own are also efficacious, and as such one has to combine all these, even as one does with respect to subsidiary rites like Agnihotra, connected with a main sacrifice, mentioned in several Śâkhâs.

Topic 3: Vidyâs having really different subject-matter are separate, though in other respects there are similarities.

अन्यथात्वं शब्दादिति चेत्, न, अविशेषात् ॥ ६ ॥

अन्यथात्व There is difference शब्दात् on account of (difference in) texts इति चेत् if it be said न not so अविशेषात् on account of non-difference (as regards essentials).

6. If it be said (that the Udgîtha Vidyâ of the Bṛhadâraṇyaka and that of the Chândogya) are different on account of (difference in) texts; (we say) not so, on account of the non-difference (as regards essentials).

This Sûtra represents the view of the opponent, who tries to establish that the two Vidyâs are one. "Then they said to this vital force in the mouth, 'Chant the Udgîtha for us.' 'All right", said the vital force and chanted for them" (Bṛ. 1. 3. 7); "Then this vital force that is in the mouth—they meditated on the Udgîtha 'Om' as that vital force" (Ch. 1. 2. 7). It may be objected that they cannot be one, because of the difference in texts. But this is unacceptable, because there is unity as regards a great many points. (For the similarity see texts in both). So on the grounds given in Sûtra 3. 3. 1, there is unity of Vidyâs.

न वा, प्रकरणभेदात् परोवरीयस्त्वादिवत् ॥ ७ ॥

न वा Rather not प्रकरण-भेदात् on account of difference in subject-matter परोवरीयस्त्वादिवत् even as (the meditation on the Udgîtha) as the highest and greatest (Brahman) (is different).

7. Rather (there is) no (unity of Vidyâs), on account of the difference in subject-matter, even as (the meditation on the Udgîtha) as the highest and greatest (*i.e.* Brahman) (is different from the meditation on the Udgîtha as abiding in the eye etc.).

This Sûtra refutes the former view and establishes that the two Vidyâs, in spite of similarity in many points, are different on account of difference in subject-matter. In the Chândogya only a part of the Udgîtha (hymn), the syllable 'Om' is meditated upon as Prâṇa:

"Let one meditate on the syllable 'Om' (of) the Udgitha" (Ch. 1. 1. 1). But in the Bṛhadâranyaka the whole Udgîtha hymn is meditated upon as Prâṇa. *Vide* Bṛ. 1. 3. 2. On account of this difference in the object of meditation the two Vidyâs cannot be one. The case is similar to the Upâsanâ on Udgîtha enjoined in, "This is indeed the highest and greatest Udgîtha" (Ch. 1. 9. 2), which is different from the one enjoined in the Chândogya 1.6, where the Udgîtha is meditated upon as abiding in the eye and the sun.

संज्ञातश्चेत्, तदुक्तम्, अस्ति तु तदपि ॥ ८ ॥

संज्ञात: On account of the name (being same) चेत् if तत् it उक्तम् has already been answered अस्ति exists तु but तत् that अपि even.

8. If on account of the name (of both Vidyâs being the same, it be said that they are one), it has already been answered. But even that (identity of name in Vidyâs admitted to be different) exists.

Identity of name is no reason for claiming unity of Vidyâs, since the subject-matter differs. This has already been established in the last Sûtra. Moreover, it is borne out by the scriptures. For example, the different sacrifices like Agnihotra, Darśapûrṇamâsa, etc., which all occur in Kâṭhaka, are known as Kâthakas; or even the Udgîtha Upâsanâs of Ch. 1. 6 and Ch. 1. 9. 2 are different Vidyâs.

Topic 4: Specializing the 'Om' of the Udgîtha Vidyâ is apt, as 'Om' is common to all the Vedas.

व्याप्तेश्च समञ्जसम् ॥ ९ ॥

व्याप्तेः Because (Om) extends (over the whole of the Vedas) च and समञ्जसम् is appropriate.

9. And because (Om) extends (over the whole of the Vedas), (to specialize it by the term 'Udgîtha') is appropriate.

Since 'Om' is common to all the Vedas we have to understand which particular 'Om' is to be meditated upon. By specifying that the 'Om' which is a part of the Udgîtha is to be meditated upon, we learn that it is the 'Om' of the Sâma-Veda. "Let one meditate on the syllable 'Om' (of) the Udgîtha" (Ch. 1. 1. 1).

Topic 5: Unity of the Prâṇa Vidyâ.

सर्वाभेदादन्यत्रेमे ॥ १० ॥

सर्वाभेदात् On account of non-difference everywhere अन्यत्र in the other places इमे these qualities (are to be inserted).

10. On account of the non-difference (of the Vidyâ) everywhere (*i.e.* in all the texts of the different Śâkhâs where the Prâṇa Vidyâ occurs) these qualities (mentioned in two of them are to be inserted) in the other places (*e.g.* the Kauṣîtakî Upaniṣad).

In the Chândogya and Bṛhadâraṇyaka Upaniṣads

in the Prâṇa Vidyâ we find the qualities of speech etc. as being richest and so on, are ultimately attributed to Prâṇa but not so in the Kauṣîtakî Upaniṣad, for instance. The question is whether they are to be inserted in the Kauṣîtakî also, where they are not mentioned. The Sûtra says that they have to be inserted, since the Vidyâ is the same in all the three Upaniṣads. Attributes of one and the same Vidyâ have to be combined wherever that Vidyâ occurs, although they may not be expressly mentioned.

Topic 6: In all the meditations on Brahman qualities like 'Bliss' etc., which describe Its nature, are to be combined into one meditation, and not others.

आनन्दादयः प्रधानस्य ॥ ११ ॥

अानन्दादय: Bliss and other attributes प्रधानस्य of the subject (*i.e.* Brahman).

11. Bliss and other attributes (which depict the true nature) of the subject (*i.e.* Brahman) (have to be combined from all places in the meditation on Brahman).

Brahman is described as Bliss, Knowledge, all-pervading, the self of all, true, etc. in different texts of different Śâkhâs. All the attributes are not mentioned in all places. Now the question is whether they have to be combined in the meditation on Brahman or not. This Sûtra says that they have to be combined, since the object of meditation (Brahman) is one and the same in all Śâkhâs, and therefore the Vidyâ is one.

प्रियशिरस्त्वाद्यप्राप्तिः, उपचयापचयौ हि भेदे ॥ १२ ॥

प्रियशिरस्त्वादि (Qualities like) joy being Its head etc. अप्राप्तिः are not to be taken everywhere उपचयापचयौ increase and decrease हि because भेदे (are possible) in difference.

12. (Qualities like) joy being Its head etc. are not to be taken everywhere, (being subject to increase and decrease and) increase and decrease (are possible only) if there is difference (and not in Brahman in which there is non-difference).

Attributes like joy being Its head etc. mentioned in the Taittirîya Upaniṣad are not to be taken and combined in other places where the Upâsanâ of Brahman is enjoined, because the terms 'joy', 'satisfaction', 'great satisfactions', 'bliss', etc. indicate qualities which have increase and decrease relatively to each other and to other experiencers (Jîvas), and therefore can exist only where there is difference. But Brahman being absolutely without any difference, these attributes cannot constitute Its nature, and as such they are to be confined to the texts prescribing them and not taken in other places.

इतरे त्वर्थसामान्यात् ॥ १३ ॥

इतरे Other attributes तु but अर्थसामान्यात् on account of identity of purport.

13. But other attributes (like Bliss etc. are to be combined) on account of identity of purport.

Attributes like Bliss, Knowledge, all-pervading, etc. which describe the nature of Brahman are to be combined, for their purport is the one and indivisible, unconditioned Brahman. These attributes are mentioned with a view to the knowledge of Brahman and not for Upâsanâ.

Topic 7: *Ka. 1. 3. 10-11 simply aims at teaching that the Self is higher than everything else.*

आध्यानाय प्रयोजनाभावात् ॥ १४ ॥

आध्यानाय For the sake of meditation प्रयोजन-अभावात् as there is no use.

14. (Kâṭhaka 1. 3. 10-11 tells about the Self only as the highest) for the sake of meditation, (and not about the relative position of the objects etc.) as there is no use of it.

"Higher than the senses are the objects, higher than the objects there is the mind. . .higher than the Self there is nothing, this is the limit, the Supreme Goal" (Ka. 1. 3. 10-11). The opponent holds that these sentences are separate and not one, as referring to the Ātman alone; therefore it is the aim of the Śruti to teach that the objects are superior to the senses, and so on. This Sûtra refutes it and says that it is one sentence and means that the Ātman is superior to all these. This information is given for the sake of meditation on the Ātman, which results in the knowledge of It. The Ātman alone is to be known, for the knowledge of It gives Freedom. But the knowledge of the fact that objects are superior to the senses and so on, serves no useful purpose, and as such it is not the aim of the Śruti to teach this.

आत्मशब्दाच्च ॥ १५ ॥

आत्मशब्दात् On account of the word 'Self' च and.

15. And on account of the word 'Self'.

The view established in the last Sûtra is confirmed by the fact that the subject of the discussion is called the Self. "That Self is hidden in all beings and does not shine forth" (Ka. 1. 3. 12), thereby hinting that the other things are non-Self. But the enumeration of the series is not altogether useless, inasmuch as it helps to turn the mind, which is outgoing, gradually towards the Ātman, which is hard to realize without deep meditation.

Topic 8: The self referred to in Ai. 1. 1 is the Supreme Self and consequently the attributes of the Self given in other places are to be included in this Aitareyaka meditation.

आत्मगृहीतिरितरवत्, उत्तरात् ॥ १६ ॥

आत्म-गृहीतिः The Supreme Self is meant इतरवत् as in other texts (dealing with creation) उत्तरात् on account of the subsequent qualification.

16. (In the Aitareya Upaniṣad 1. 1) the Supreme

Self is meant, as in other texts (dealing with creation), on account of the subsequent qualification.

"Verily in the beginning all this was the Self, one only; there was nothing else whatsoever" etc. (Ai. 1. 1). Does the word 'Self' here refer to the Supreme Self or to Hiraṇyagarbha? It refers to the Supreme Self. Even as the word 'Self' in other texts dealing with creation refers to It and not to Hiraṇyagarbha: "From the Self sprang forth ether" (Tai. 2. 1). Why? Because in the subsequent text of the Aitareya we have, "It thought, 'Shall I send forth worlds?' It sent forth these worlds" (Ai. 1. 1-2). This qualification, *viz* that 'It thought' before creation, is applied to Brahman in the primary sense in other Śruti texts. So from this we learn that the Self refers to the Supreme Self and not to Hiraṇyagarbha.

अन्वयादिति चेत्, स्यात्अवधारणात् ॥ १७ ॥

अन्वयात् Because of the context इति चेत् if it be said स्यात् it might be so अवधारणात् on account of the definite statement.

17. If it be said that because of the context (the Supreme Self is not meant, but Hiraṇyagarbha), (we reply that) it is so (*i.e.* the Supreme Self is meant) on account of the definite statement (that the Ātman alone existed at the beginning).

In the Aitareya Upanisad 1. 1 the Self is said to

have created the four worlds. But in the Taittirîya and other texts the Self creates ether, water, etc.—the five elements. Now it is well known that creation of the worlds is by Hiraṇyagarbha with the help of the elements created by the Supreme Self. So the Self in the Aitareya cannot mean the Supreme Self but Hiraṇyagarbha. The Sûtra refutes it and says that on account of the statement, "Verily in the beginning all this was the Self, one only" (Ai. 1. 1), which declares that there was one only without a second, it can only refer to the Supreme Self and not to Hiraṇyagarbha. Therefore we have to take that the Supreme Self after creating elements as described in other Śâkhâs created the four worlds.

The object of Sûtras 16 and 17 in establishing that the Supreme Self is meant is that the attributes of the Supreme Self given in other places are to be combined in the Aitareyaka meditation.

Topic 9: Rinsing the mouth is not enjoined in the Prâṇa Vidyâ, but only thinking the water as the dress of Prâṇa.

कार्याख्यानादपूर्वम् ॥ १८ ॥

कार्याख्यानात् On account of being a restatement of an act (already enjoined by the Smṛti) अपूर्वम् what has not been so enjoined elsewhere.

18. On account of (the rinsing of the mouth with water referred to in the Prâṇa Vidyâ) being a restatement of an act (already enjoined by th

Śmṛti), what has not been so enjoined elsewhere (is here enjoined by the Śruti).

In the Châṇdogya 5. 2. 2. and the Bṛhadâraṇyaka 6. 1. 14 we find a reference to the rinsing of the mouth with water before and after a meal, thinking that thereby Prâṇa is dressed. The question is whether the Śruti enjoins both or only the latter. The Sûtra states that since the former, the act of rinsing, is already enjoined on every one by the Smṛti, the latter act of thinking the water as the dress of Prâṇa is alone enjoined by the Śruti.

Topic 10: Vidyâs in the same Śâkhâ which are identical or similar have to be combined, for they are one.

समान एवञ्च, अभेदात् ॥ १९ ॥

समाने In the same Śâkhâ एवम् (it is) like this च also अभेदात् on account of non-difference.

19. In the same Śâkhâ also (it is) like this (*i.e.* here is unity of Vidyâ), on account of the non-difference (of the object of meditation).

In the Agnirahasya in the Vâjasaneyi Śâkhâ there is a Vidyâ called Śâṇḍilya Vidyâ, in which occurs the passage, "Let him meditate on the Self which consists of mind" etc. (Śat. Br. Mādhy. 10. 6. 3. 2). Again in the Bṛhadâraṇyaka, which belongs to the same Śâkhâ we have, "This Being identified with the mind" etc. (Br. 5. 6. 1). Do these two passages form one Vidyâ, in which the particulars mentioned in either text are to be combined, or are they different Vidyâs? The Sûtra says that they are one Vidyâ, since the object of meditation in both cases is the Self consisting of mind. The rule as regards the combining of particulars of a similar Vidyâ in the same Śâkhâ is the same as in the case of such Vidyâs occurring in different Śâkhâs. Therefore the Śâṇḍilya Vidyâ is one.

Topic 11: The names 'Ahar' and 'Aham' of the Supreme Brahman as abiding in the sun and in the right eye respectively, given in Bṛ. 5. 1-2, cannot be combined, as these are two separate Vidyâs.

संबन्धादेवमन्यत्रापि ॥ २० ॥

संबन्धात् On account of the connection एवम् like thi[s] अन्यत्र in other cases अपि also.

20. In other cases also (*e.g.* in the Vidyâ of th[e] Satya Brahman) on account of the connectio[n] (*i.e.* the object of the meditation being the Saty[a] Brahman) (we have to combine particulars lik[e] this (*i.e.* as in the Śâṇḍilya Vidyâ).

This Sûtra sets forth the view of the opponent. "Saty[a] is Brahman....That which is Satya is that sun—th[e] being who is in that orb and the being who is in th[e] right eye" (Bṛ. 5. 5. 1-2). This gives the abode of th[e] Satya Brahman with respect to the gods and the bod[y] and two secret names of the Satya Brahman are als[o] taught in connection with these abodes; the former [i]

'Ahar' and the latter 'Aham'. Now on the analogy of the Śâṇḍilya Vidyâ, since the object of meditation is one, *viz* the Satya Brahman, we must combine the particulars. Therefore both the names 'Ahar' and 'Aham' have to be combined with respect to Satya Brahman.

न वा, विशेषात् ॥ २१ ॥

न वा Rather not विशेषात् on account of difference.

21. Rather not (so) on account of the difference (of abode).

This Sûtra refutes the view of the previous Sûtra. Though the Vidyâ is one, still owing to difference in abodes the object of meditation becomes different; hence the different names. Therefore these cannot be exchanged or combined.

दर्शयति च ॥ २२ ॥

दर्शयति (The scripture) declares च also.

22. (The scripture) also declares (that).

The scripture distinctly states that the attributes are not to be combined, but kept apart; for it compares the two persons, the person in the sun and in the right eye. If it wanted the particulars to be combined, it would not institute such a comparison.

Topic 12: Attributes of Brahman mentioned in Râṇâyaṇîya-khila are not to be taken into consideration in other Brahma Vidyās e.g. the Śâṇḍilya Vidyâ, as the former is an independent Vidyâ on account of the difference of Brahman's abode.

सम्भृतिद्युव्याप्त्यपि चातः ॥ २३ ॥

सम्भृतिः Supporting (the universe) द्युव्याप्तिः pervading the sky अपि also च and अतः for the same reason (as in the previous Sûtra).

23. For the same reason (as in the previous Sûtra) the supporting (of the universe) and pervading of the sky (attributed to Brahman in the Râṇâyaṇîya-khila) also (are not to be included in other Upâsanâs of Brahman).

In a supplementary text of the Râṇâyaṇîyas there occurs the passage, "The powers, which were collected together, were preceded by Brahman; the pre-existent Brahman in the beginning pervaded the whole sky.' Now these two qualities of Brahman are not to be included in other places treating of Brahma Vidyâ for the same reason as is given in the last Sûtra, *viz* difference of abode. Moreover, these qualities and those mentioned in other Vidyâs like the Śâṇḍilya Vidyâ are of such a nature as to exclude each other, and are not suggestive of each other. The mere fact of certain Vidyâs being connected with Brahman does not constitute their unity. Brahman, though one, is, on account of its plurality of powers, meditated upon in manifold ways. The conclusion therefore is that the Upâsanâ referred to in this Sûtra is an independent Vidyâ standing by itself.

Topic 13: The Puruṣa Vidyâ in the Chândogya and the Taittirîya are not one.

पुरुषविद्यायामिव चेतरेषामनाम्नानात् ॥ २४ ॥

पुरुषविद्यायाम्-इव As in the Puruṣa Vidyâ (of the Chândogya) च and इतरेषाम् of the others अनाम्नानात् not being mentioned (in the Taittirîya).

24. And (since the qualities) as (mentioned) in the Puruṣa Vidyâ (of the Chândogya) are not mentioned (in that) of the others (*i.e.* in the Taittirîya) (the two Puruṣa Vidyâs are not one).

In the last Sûtra the Vidyâs were held to be different as there was no recognition of the fundamental attribute of the one Vidyâ in the other. This Sûtra cites an example where such a fundamental attribute occurs in both. On this ground the opponent argues that the two Vidyâs are one. In the Chândogya there is a Vidyâ about man in which he is identified with the sacrifice: "Man is the sacrifice." In the Taittirîya Araṇyaka (10.64) also occurs a similar Vidyâ where man is so identified: "For him who knows thus, the self of the sacrifice is the sacrificer" etc. The fundamental attribute referred to is that man is identified with sacrifice in both. This Sûtra says that in spite of this, the two Vidyâs are not one, for the details differ. Moreover, the result of the Vidyâ in the Taittirîya is the attainment of the greatness of Brahman, while that of the Chândogya is long life. Therefore the two Vidyâs are separate, and there can be no combination of particulars in the two places.

Topic 14: Detached Mantras like "Pierce the whole (body of the enemy)" etc. and sacrifices mentioned at the beginning of certain Upaniṣads do not form part of the Brahma Vidyâ included in the Upaniṣads.

वेधाद्यर्थभेदात् ॥ २५ ॥

वेधादि Piercing etc. अर्थभेदात् because they have a different meaning.

25. (Certain Mantras relating to) piercing etc. (are not part of the Vidyâs though mentioned near by) because they have a different meaning.

At the beginning of the Upaniṣad of the Ātharvaṇikas we have, "Pierce the whole (body of the enemy), pierce his heart" etc. Similarly at the beginning of other Upaniṣads of other Śâkhâs we have Mantras. The question is, whether these Mantras and the sacrifices referred to in the Brâhmaṇas in close proximity to the Upaniṣads are to be combined with the Vidyâs prescribed by these Upaniṣads. The Sûtra says that they are not to be combined, for their meaning is different inasmuch as they indicate acts of a sacrifice and therefore have no connection with the Vidyâs. The piercing, for example, is connected with some ceremony to destroy one's enemy.

Topic 15: The statement made in one of the texts that the good and evil deeds of a person who has attained Knowledge go to his friends and enemies respectively, is valid for all texts where discarding of good and evil Karma by such a person is mentioned.

हानौ तु, उपायनशब्दशेषत्वात्, कुशाच्छन्दः-
स्तुत्युपगानवत्, तदुक्तम् ॥ २६ ॥

हानौ Where (only) the discarding (of good and evil) s mentioned तु but उपायन-शब्दशेषत्वात् on account of he word 'receiving' being supplementary (to the ord 'discarding') कुशा-छन्दः-स्तुति-उपगानवत् as in the case f Kuśas (sticks for keeping count of hymns), metres, raise, and recitation तत् that उक्तम् has been stated y Jaimini).

26. But where (only) the discarding (of good nd evil) is mentioned, (the receiving of this good nd evil by others has to be included), on account f this word 'receiving' being supplementary (to e word 'discarding'), as in the case of Kuśas, etres, praise, and recitation. That (*viz* that it ould be so done) has been stated (by Jaimini in ûrva Mîmâṁsâ).

Having dealt with the combination of particulars ith respect to similar Vidyâs, the author now proceeds deal with the combination of the effects with respect the Upâsaka.

Jaimini has said that statements with respect to

Kuśas, metres, praise, and hymns have to be complete from other texts. In some places Kuśas are simply mentioned, but another text specifies that they are to be made of fig wood. The first Śruti will have to be completed in the light of the other. Similarly with respect to metres, praise, and recitation. This principle is here applied to the effects of the Upâsaka's actions in connection with the Vidyâs mentioned in the Upaniṣad We find certain texts mentioned the discarding of good and evil by a person attaining Knowledge. *Vide* Ch. 8. 13. Another text not only mentions this, but also adds that the good and evil are obtained by his friends and enemies, respectively. *Vide* Kau. 1. 4. This Sûtra says that the obtaining of the good and evil by his friends and enemies has to be inserted in the Chândogya text according to Jaimini's principle explained above.

This Sûtra may also be explained in another way the discussion on 'discarding' is different. It may be argued that the verb 'Dhu' in the text of the Chândogya and Kauṣîtakî may be interpreted as trembling and not as getting rid of, in which case it would mean that good and evil still cling to a person who attains Knowledge, though their effects are retarded owing the Knowledge. This Sûtra says that such a meaning not correct, for the subsequent portion of the text in the Kauṣîtakî shows that others get this good and evil and this is not possible unless the person who attains Knowledge discards them.

Topic 16: The discarding of good and evil by the knower of Brahman takes place at the time of death and not his way to Brahmaloka.

साम्पराये, तर्तव्याभावात्, तथा ह्यन्ये ॥ २७ ॥

साम्पराये At the time of death तर्तव्य-अभावात there being nothing to be attained तथा so also हि for अन्ये others.

27. (He who attains Knowledge gets rid of his good and evil works) at the time of death, there being nothing to be obtained (by him on the way to Brahmaloka through works); for other texts also say so.

The question is raised as to when the individual soul gets rid of the effects of its good and evil works. "He comes to the river Virajâ and crosses it by the mind alone, and there he shakes off good and evil" (Kau. 1. 4). On the basis of this text the opponent holds that the effects are got rid of on the way to Brahmaloka and not at the time of death. This Sûtra refutes it and says that the man of realization gets rid of them at the time of death. The Saṁcita and Āgâmi Karma (work) is destroyed with Knowledge and the Prârabdha is destroyed at death. So at the time of death he is rid of all effects of his good and evil deeds. The reasons for this conclusion are: On the way to Brahmaloka, the destination of the knower of Brahman, it is not possible to discard good and evil effects for then the soul has no gross body, and so cannot practise any Sâdhanâ that will destroy them. Nor does the soul experience anything on the way, for which one would have to admit the persistence of good and evil till then. Rather they are destroyed by the Vidyâ practised by the aspirant before he leaves the body. The scripture also says, "Having shaken off his evil as a horse shakes off his hairs" etc. (Ch. 8. 13. 1). Moreover, it is not, possible to cross the river Virajâ unless one is free from all good and evil. Therefore we have to take it that all the good and evil are discarded at the time of death and the Kauṣîtakî text has to be explained accordingly.

छन्दतः, उभयाविरोधात् ॥ २८ ॥

According to his liking उभय-अविरोधात् on account of there being harmony between the two

28. (The interpretation that the individual soul practising Sâdhanâ) according to his liking (gets rid of good and evil while living, is reasonable) on account of there being harmony (in that case) between the two (*viz* cause and effect as well as between the Chândogya and another Śruti).

Since the individual soul attains Brahman after death as a result of the Vidyâ, why not understand that the getting rid of good and evil, the result of the Vidyâ, is also attained after death? Not so, for it is possible to practise Sâdhanâ to one's liking only during one's lifetime, and from Sâdhanâ alone results the destruction of good and evil. And it is not reasonable to say that the cause being there, the effect is delayed till some time after death. Therefore there is harmony between the texts quoted above The attainment of Brahmaloka is not possible so long as there is a body, but there is no such difficulty about the shaking off of good and evil.

Topic 17: The knower of the Saguṇa Brahman alone goes by the path of the gods after death and not the knower of the Nirguṇa Brahman.

गतेरर्थवत्त्वमुभयथा, अन्यथा हि विरोधः ॥ २९ ॥

गतेः Of the soul's journey (after death) along the path of the gods अर्थवत्त्वम् utility उभयथा in two ways अन्यथा otherwise हि for विरोधः a contradiction.

29. (The soul's) journey along the path of the gods is applicable in two ways (*i.e.* differently) for otherwise (there would result) a contradiction.

A question is raised that just as the getting rid of good and evil is understood as being followed by their acceptance by others, so also the journey after death along the Devayâna, the path of the gods, which is sometimes mentioned as following the discarding of good and evil, is common to all Upâsakas, those of the Nirguṇa as well as the Saguṇa Brahman This Sûtra says that it is true only of the worshipper of the Saguna Brahman, for Brahmaloka being located elsewhere in space, the journey has a meaning in his case only But the knowledge which results from absorption in the Nirguṇa Brahman is merely the destruction of ignorance. So what meaning has journey for such a person? If the journey applies to him also, then it would contradict Śruti texts like, "Shaking off good and evil, free from passions, he reaches the Highest Unity" (Mu. 3. 1. 3). How can one who has become Brahman, the pure, the one without movement, go to another place by Devayâna? Since he has already attained his goal, *viz* unity, the journey along the Devayâna is meaningless for him. Therefore the worshipper of the Saguṇa Brahman alone goes by the Devayâna.

उपपन्नः, तल्लक्षणार्थोपलब्धेः, लोकवत् ॥ ३० ॥

उपपन्नः Is reasonable तत्-लक्षणार्थ-उपलब्धेः for the characteristics which render such journey possible are seen लोकवत् as in the world.

30. (The differentiation mentioned above) is reasonable, for the characteristics which render such a journey possible are seen (in the case of Saguṇa Upâsanâ but not in that of Nirguṇa Upâsanâ); as (is seen) in the world.

The differentiation between the paths of the worshippers of the Saguṇa and Nirguṇa Brahman is reasonable, because the characteristics or reasons for such a journey of the worshipper of the Saguṇa Brahman, are seen in the Vidyâ described in the Kauṣîtakî Upanisad. For the texts mention certain results which can be attained by the worshipper only by going to different places, such as mounting the couch and holding conversation with Brahman. But with perfect Knowledge or destruction of ignorance, which results from Nirguṇa Upâsana, no purpose is served by such a journey. The distinction is analogous to what is seen in the world. To reach a village we have to go by the path which leads to it. But no such journey is required to get rid of our illness.

Topic 18: All the worshippers of the Saguṇa Brahman go after death by the path of the gods to Brahmaloka, and not merely those who know the Pañcâgni Vidyâ etc., wherein such a path is specifically mentioned.

अनियमः सर्वासाम्, अविरोधः शब्दानुमानाभ्याम् ॥ ३१ ॥

अनियमः (There is) no restriction सर्वासाम् (Devayâna applies equally) to all (Vidyâs of the Saguṇa Brahman) अविरोधः there is non-contradiction शब्द-अनुमानाभ्याम् as is seen from the Śruti and Smṛti.

31. (The passage of the soul by the path of the gods) is not restricted (only to certain Vidyâs of the Saguṇa Brahman); (it applies equally) to all (Vidyâs of the Saguṇa Brahman). There is no contradiction, as is seen from the Śruti and Smṛti.

In the Pañcâgni Vidyâ of the Chândogya the result of such a meditation is said to be the passage after death to Brahmaloka by the path of the gods (Devayâna). But such a result is not explicitly stated in the case of the Vaiśvânara Vidyâ. The question is whether through this Vidyâ also one goes after death along the Devayâna or not. This Sûtra says that all worshippers of the Saguṇa Brahman, whatever their Vidyâs, go after death by this path. For so it is seen from the Śruti and Smṛti. "Those who meditate thus (through Pañcâgni Vidyâ) and also those who meditate in the forest endowed with Śraddhâ and Tapas go by the path of the gods" (Ch. 5. 10. 1). This text clearly shows that those who meditate upon these five fires, and those dwellers in the forest who, endowed with faith and austerity, worship the Saguṇa Brahman through any other Vidyâ, both go by the path of the gods. For the support of this view by the Smṛti see Gîtâ 8. 26.

Topic 19: Perfected souls may be reborn for the fulfilment of some divine mission.

यावदधिकारमवस्थितिराधिकारिकाणाम् ॥ ३२ ॥

यावत्-अधिकारम् So long as the mission is not fulfilled अवस्थितिः (there is corporeal) existence आधिकारिकाणाम् of those who have a mission to fulfil.

32. Of those who have a mission to fulfil (there is corporeal) existence, so long as the mission is not fulfilled.

Ṛṣi Apântaratama was born again as Vyâsa. Sanatkumâra was born as Skanda. So also other Ṛṣis like Vasiṣṭha and Nârada were born again. Now these Ṛṣis had attained the knowledge of Brahman, and yet they had to be reborn. If that is so, what is the utility of such knowledge of Brahman?—says the opponent. The Sûtra refutes it and says that ordinarily a person after attaining Knowledge is not reborn. But the case of those who have a divine mission to fulfil is different. Those perfected sages have one or more births until their mission is fulfilled, after which they are not born again. But then they never come under the sway of ignorance although they may be reborn. Their case is analogous to that of a Jîvanmukta, who even after attaining

Knowledge continues his corporeal existence as long as the Prârabdha Karma lasts. The divine mission of these people is comparable to the Prârabdha Karma.

Topic 20: The negative attributes of Brahman mentioned in various texts are to be combined in all meditations on Brahman.

अक्षरधियां त्ववरोधः, सामान्यतद्भावाभ्यामौपसदवत्,
तदुक्तम् ॥ ३३ ॥

अक्षरधियां Of the conceptions of the (negative) attributes of the Immutable (Brahman) तु but अवरोध combination सामान्यतद्भावाभ्याम् on account of the similarity (of defining Brahman through denials) and the object (*viz* Immutable Brahman) being the same पउसदवत् as in the case of the Upasada (offerings) तत् it उक्तम् has been said (by Jaimini).

33. But the conceptions of the (negative) attributes of the Immutable (Brahman) are to be combined (from different texts where the Immutable Brahman is treated, in all meditations on the Immutable Brahman, as they form one Vidyâ), on account of the similarity (of defining the Immutable Brahman through denials) and the object (the Immutable Brahman) being the same, as in the case of the Upasad (offerings). It has been said (by Jaimini in Pûrva Mîmāṁsâ).

"O Gârgî, the knowers of Brahman say this Immutable (Brahman) is that. It is neither gross nor minute, neither short nor long" etc. (Bṛ. 3. 3. -8). Again we have, "The supreme knowledge is that by which the Immutable (Brahman) is attained. That which is imperceivable, ungraspable" etc. (Mu. 1. 1. 5-6) The question is whether the negative attributes in these two texts are to be combined so as to form one Vidyâ, or they are to be treated as two separate Vidyâs. The opponent holds that these attributes do not directly specify the nature of Brahman like the positive attributes, bliss, truth, etc., and so the principle established in Sûtra 3. 3. 11 does not apply here, for no purpose is served by such a combination. So each denial is valid only for the text in which it occurs and not for other places. This the Sûtra refutes and says that such denials are to be combined, for the method of teaching Brahman through denial is the same, and the object of instruction is also the same, *viz* the Immutable Brahman. The rule of Sûtra 3. 3. 11 applies here also, though there we were concerned with positive attributes and here with negative attributes which teach Brahman by an indirect method. The case is analogous to the Upasada offerings. The Mantras for giving these offerings are found only in the Sâma-Veda. But the priests of the Yajur-Veda use this Mantra given in the other Veda. This principle is decided by Jaimini in Pûrva Mîmâṁsâ. Similarly here also in the meditation on the Immutable (Brahman) the negative attributes have to be combined.

Topic 21: Muṇḍaka 3. 1. 1 and Kaṭha 1. 3. 1. form one Vidyâ.

इयदामननात् ॥ ३४ ॥

इयत्-आमननात् On account of describing as this much.

34. Because (the same thing) is described as such and such.

"Two birds of beautiful plumage. . .one of them eats the sweet and bitter fruits thereof, the other witnesses without eating" (Mu. 3. 1. 1). Again we have, "There are the two ... enjoying the results of their good deeds" etc. (Ka. 1. 3. 1). In these two texts do we have two different Vidyâs, or one only? The opponent holds that these are two Vidyâs for unlike the meditation on the Immutable, where the object of meditation was one, as shown in the previous Sûtra, here there are different objects of meditation. That it is so is clear, for of the texts cited above, the Muṇḍaka text says only one eats the fruit, while the other does not; in Kaṭha, however, both of them enjoy the results of their good actions. So the object of meditation is not dentical. The Sûtra refutes it and says that they form one Vidyâ, for both describe the same Lord as existing hus and thus, *i.e.* in the form of the Jîva. In other words, the object of the two texts is to teach about the upreme Brahman and show the identity of the Jîva nd Brahman. It has been explained in 1. 2. 11 that he Supreme Lord does not actually enjoy the fruits of ctions, but is said to do so because of His being menoned along with the Jîva, which does, as when we y, 'The men with the umbrella,' where only one of hem has the umbrella. Therefore the object of the editation being one, the Vidyâs are also one.

Topic 22: Bṛhadâraṇyaka 3. 4. 1 and 3. 5. 1 constitute one Vidyâ.

अन्तरा भूतग्रामवत् स्वात्मनः ॥ ३५ ॥

अन्तरा As being the innermost of all भूतग्रामवत् as in the case of the elements स्वात्मनः (teaching) of the same Self.

35. The same Self (is taught) as being the innermost of all, as in the case of the elements.

In the Bṛhadâraṇyaka we find Uṣasta questioning Yâjñavalkya thus: "Explain to me the Brahman that is immediate and direct—the self that is within all" and Yâgñavalkya replies: "That which breathes through Prâṇa is your self, that is within all," (Bṛ. 3. 4. 1). In the same Upaniṣad 3. 5. 1, to the same question put by Kahola, Yâjñavalkya replies: "That which transcends hunger and thirst, grief and delusion, decay and death. Knowing this very Self" etc. The opponent holds that these two are separate Vidyâs, because the answers given being different, the objects referred to must be different. The Sûtra refutes this and says that the object is one, the Supreme Self, for it is impossible to conceive two Selves being simultaneously the innermost of all in the same body, even as none of the five elements constituting the body can be the innermost of all in the true sense of the term, though relatively one element can be inside another. Similarly one Self alone can be the innermost of all. Therefore the same Self is taught in both the answers.

अन्यथा भेदानुपपत्तिरिति चेत्, न, उप-
देशान्तरवत् ॥ ३६ ॥

अन्यथा Otherwise भेद-अनुपपत्तिः the repetition cannot be accounted for इति चेत् if it be said न not so उपदेशान्तरवत् like another instruction (in the Chândogya).

36. If it be said (that the two Vidyas are separate, for) otherwise the repetition cannot be accounted for, (we say) not so; (it is) like (the repetition) in another instruction (in the Chândogya).

An objection is raised that unless the two texts refer to two different Selves, the repetition of the same subject would be meaningless. This Sûtra says that it is not like that. The repetition has a significance. It is intended to make the student understand the subject more convincingly from different angles, and so the repetition does not justify us to take that two different Selves are taught here, even as the repetition of the teaching 'Thou art That' nine times does not entitle us to take the whole teaching in the Chândogya as more than one Vidyâ. The difference in answer is due to the fact that the second answer tells something special about the Self. In the first it is taught that the Self is different from the body; in the second, that It is beyond relative attributes.

Topic 23: The Śruti enjoins reciprocal meditation in Ai. Ā. 2. 2. 4. 6 and not merely one way.

व्यतिहारः, विंशिषन्ति हीतरवत् ॥ ३७ ॥

व्यतिहारः Reciprocity (of meditations) विशिषन्ति (the scriptures) prescribe (this) हि for इतरवत as in other cases.

37. (There is) reciprocity (of meditation), for the scriptures prescribe this, as in other cases.

In the Aitareya Āraṇyaka we have, "What I am, that He is; what He is, that am I" (2. 2. 4. 6). The question here is whether the meditation is to be of a reciprocal nature, *i.e.* identifying the worshipper with the being in the sun, and then, inversely, identifying the being in the sun with the worshipper; or only in the first named way. The opponent holds that the meditation is to be one way only and not in the reverse way also. For the first meditation has a meaning, inasmuch as it raises the Jîva to the level of Brahman, but lowering Brahman to the Jîva state is meaningless. The present Sûtra refutes this view and says that the meditation is to be both ways, for otherwise such a statement would be useless. Śruti expressly prescribes the reverse meditation, even as it prescribes elsewhere that the Lord is to be meditated upon as having true determination (Satya Saṅkalpa) and so on. This is not lowering Brahman, since He who has no body can be worshipped even as possessing a form.

Topic 24: *Bṛhadâraṇyaka 5.4.1 and 5.5.2 treat of one Vidyâ about Satya Brahman.*

सैव हि सत्यादयः ॥ ३८ ॥

सा एव The same (Satya-Vidyâ) हि because सत्यादय (attributes like) Satya etc.

38. The same (Satya-Vidyâ is taught in both

places), because (attributes like) Satya etc. (are seen in both places).

In the Bṛhadâraṇyaka 5. 4. 1 we have, "He who knows this great, adorable, first born (being) as the Satya Brahman, conquers these worlds." Again in 5. 5. 2 we have, "That which is Satya is that sun—the being who is in that orb and the being who is in the right eye...he destroys evils." Are these two Satya-Vidyâs one or different? The Sûtra says that they are one, inasmuch as the second text refers to the Satya of the earlier text by saying, "That which is Satya" etc. But it may be said that the result of these two meditations is different, as is seen from the texts: In the first it is said that such a person conquers those worlds, and in the second, that he destroys evils. In reality, however, there is only one result in both cases, and the mention of result in the latter case is merely by way of praise of the further instruction given about Satya.

Topic 25: Attributes mentioned in Ch. 8. 1. 1 and Bṛ. 4. 4. 22 are to be combined on account of a number of common features in both the texts.

कामादीतरत्र तत्र च, आयतनादिभ्यः ॥ ३९ ॥

कामादि (True) desire etc. इतरत्र in the other तत्र (those mentioned) in the other च and आयतनादिभ्यः on account of the abode etc.

39. (Qualities like true) desire etc. (mentioned in the Chândogya are to be inserted) in the other

(*i.e.* in the Bṛhadâraṇyaka) and (those mentioned) in the other (*i.e.* in the Bṛhadâraṇyaka are also to be inserted in the Chândogya), on account of the abode etc. (being the same in both).

In the Chândogya 8. 1. 1 we have "There is the city of Brahman and in it the palace-like lotus and in that the small ether. . . .That is the Self" etc. Again in the Bṛhadâraṇyaka 4. 4. 22 we have, "That great birthless Self which is identified with the intellect...lies in the ether that is within the heart." The question is whether the two constitute one Vidyâ and hence the particulars are to be combined, or not. The Sûtra says that they form one Vidyâ, and the qualities mentioned in each are to be combined in the other, for many points are common to both. There is the same abode, the same Lord is the object of meditation, and so on. There is, however, one difference between the two texts. The Chândogya treats of the Saguṇa Brahman while the Bṛhadâraṇyaka treats of the Nirguṇa Brahman. But then as the Saguṇa Brahman is in reality one with the Nirguṇa, this Sûtra prescribes combination of qualities for glorifying Brahman, and not for the purpose of Upâsanâ.

Topic 26: Prâṇâgnihotra need not be observed on days of fast.

आदरादलोपः ॥ ४० ॥

आदरात् On account of the respect shown अलोपः there can be no omission.

40. On account of the respect shown (to the Prâṇâgnihotra by the Sruti) there can be no omission (of this act).

This Sûtra gives the view of the opponent.

In the Vaiśvânara Vidyâ of the Chândogya the Upâsaka, before he takes his meals is asked first to offer food to each of the Prâṇas, saying, "To Prâṇa I offer this." The Śruti attaches such importance to this Prâṇâgnihotra that it enjoins food to be offered to the Prâṇas even before entertaining guests, whom all Hindus are supposed to attend before they take any food. The question is whether this Prâṇâgnihotra is to be observed even on days of fasting. This Sûtra says that there should be no omission of it, and so it must be observed even on fasting days by sipping at least a few drops of water, since the Śruti attaches such importance to it.

उपस्थितेऽतः, तद्वचनात् ॥ ४१ ॥

उपस्थिते When food is served अत: from that तत्-वचनात् for so (the Śruti) declares.

41. When food is served, from that (the Prâṇâgnihotra is to be performed), for so (the Sruti) declares.

This refutes the view expressed in the last Sûtra and says that the Prâṇâgnihotra need not be performed on fasting days, for the Śruti says, "Therefore the first food which comes is meant for Homa. And he who offers that first oblation should offer it to Prâna, saying

Svâhâ" (Ch. 5. 19. 1). The importance given by the Śruti is only to the effect that the first portion of the food, on those days when it is taken, should be offered to the Prâṇas, and not that it should be observed even on fasting days.

Topic 27: Upâsanâs mentioned in connection with certain sacrifices are not parts of them and hence are not inseparably connected with them.

तन्निर्धारणानियमः, तद्दृष्टेः, पृथग्घ्यप्रतिबन्धः फलम् ॥ ४२ ॥

तत्-निर्धारण-अनियमः No rule about the inviolability of that तत्-दृष्टेः that being seen (from the Śruti) पृथक् separate हि for अप्रतिबन्धः non-obstruction फलम् result.

42. There is no rule about the inviolability of that (*i.e.* Upâsanâs connected with certain sacrifices); that is seen (from the Śruti itself); for a separate effect (belongs to the Upâsanâs), *viz* non-obstruction (for the results of the sacrifice).

The question whether certain Upâsanâs mentioned with some sacrifices are part of those sacrifices and therefore inseparably connected with them, is taken up for discussion. This Sûtra says that such Upâsanâs do not form a part of the sacrifice, for there is no rule as to their inseparability. On the other hand the scripture clearly says that the sacrifice can be performed with or without them. "Therefore both he who knows this and he who does not, perform the sacrifice" (Ch. 1. 1. 10

See also Ch. 1. 10. 9. The Śruti, moreover, mentions a separate effect of the Upâsanâs apart from that of the sacrifice, *viz* the non-obstruction (*i.e.* enhancement) of the results of the sacrifice. "The sacrifice which a man performs with knowledge etc. is more powerful" (Ch. 1. 1. 10). It means that the original sacrifice would have got its own results, but the Upâsanâ enhances those results. So the results of the sacrifice with or without the Upâsanâ are different. Therefore the Upâsanâ does not form part of the sacrifice, and hence may or may not be performed according to the pleasure of the sacrificer. Non-obstruction may be explained thus: The sacrifice without the Upâsanâ would have had the prescribed results, but the Upâsanâ prevents any obstruction to those results. This, however, does not make it a part of the sacrifice. Sometimes the results of the sacrifice are delayed owing to the intervention of any bad Karma of the sacrificer, but the Upâsanâ destroys the effect of that, and the results are attained earlier. Here, however, the sacrifice does not depend upon the Upâsanâ for its results, though they might have been delayed. Hence the Upâsana is not a part of the sacrifice, and is therefore optional.

Topic 28: Meditations on Vâyu and Prâṇa are to be kept separate in spite of the essential oneness of these two.

प्रदानवदेव, तदुक्तम् ॥ ४३ ॥

प्रदानवत् As in the case of the offerings एव exactly तत् that उक्तम् has been stated.

43. (The meditations on Vâyu and Prâna are

different owing to their different functions, though the two are essentially one); (it is) exactly as in the case of the offerings (of cakes to Indra the ruler, the monarch, and the sovereign separately). This has been stated (by Jaimini in Pûrva Mîmâṁsâ-Sûtras).

In the Saṁvarga Vidyâ of the Chândogya, meditation on Prâṇa with reference to the body and on Vâyu with reference to the gods is prescribed. Now many texts declare that Prâṇa and Vâyu are one in essence. So the opponent holds that the two meditations can be combined. The Sûtra refutes the view and says that they are to be kept apart, in spite of the non-difference in nature of Vâyu and Prâṇa; for their functions due to their different abodes are different. Just as oblations are separately given to Indra the ruler, the monarch, and the sovereign according to his different capacities, though he is one god; so the meditations on Vâyu and Prâṇa have to be kept apart. This principle is established by Jaimini in Pûrva Mîmâṁsâ.

Topic 29: The fires in Agnirahasya of the Bṛhadâraṇyaka are not part of the sacrificial act, but constitute a separate Vidyâ.

लिङ्गभूयस्त्वात्, तद्धि बलीयः, तदपि ॥ ४४ ॥

लिङ्ग-भूयस्त्वात् On account of the abundance of indicatory marks तत् it (an indicatory mark) हि for बलीयः stronger तत् that अपि also.

44. On account of the abundance of indic

tory marks (the fires of the mind, speech, etc. in the Agnirahasya of the Vâjasaneyins do not form part of the sacrifice), for it (an indicatory mark) is stronger (than the context). That also (has been stated by Jaimini).

In Agnirahasya of the Śatapatha Brâhmaṇa certain fires, named after mind, speech, eyes, etc. are mentioned. The question is whether these form part of the sacrifice mentioned therein, or form an independent Vidyâ. The Sûtra says that in spite of the *prima facie* view which arises from the context, these constitute an independent Vidyâ. For there are many indicatory marks to show that these fires form a Vidyâ; and indicatory marks are more forceful than the context, according to Pûrva Mîmâṁsâ.

पूर्वविकल्पः प्रकरणात्स्यात्क्रिया, मानसवत् ॥ ४५ ॥

पूर्व-विकल्पः Alternative forms of the one mentioned first प्रकरणात् on account of the context स्यात् ought to be क्रिया part of the sacrifice मानसवत् like the imaginary drink.

45. (The fires spoken of in the previous Sûtra are) alternative forms of the one mentioned first (*i.e.* the actual sacrificial fire) on account of the context; (they) ought to be part of the sacrifice like the imaginary drink.

The opponent raises a fresh objection. In a certain sacrifice a Soma drink is offered to Prajâpati, wherein the earth is regarded as the cup and the sea as the Soma. This is a mental act only, and yet it forms a part of the sacrifice. So these fires also, though mental, *i.e.* imaginary, are yet part of the sacrifice, and not an independent Vidyâ, because of the context. They are rather an alternative form of the first-mentioned actual fire.

अतिदेशाच्च ॥ ४६ ॥

अतिदेशात् On account of the extension (of the attributes of the first to these fires) च and.

46. And on account of the extension (of the attributes of the actual fire to these imaginary fires).

The opponent gives a further reason in support of his view. The Śruti in that passage attributes all the qualities of the actual fire to these imaginary fires. Hence they are part of the sacrifice.

विद्यैव तु, निर्धारणात् ॥ ४७ ॥

विद्या Vidyâ एव indeed तु but निर्धारणात् because (the Śruti) asserts it.

47. But (the fires) rather form a Vidyâ, because (the Śruti) asserts it.

'But' refutes the opponent. The Sûtra says that the fires constitute a Vidyâ, for the text asserts that "The are made of knowledge only", and that "By knowledge and meditation they are made for him."

दर्शनाच्च ॥ ४८ ॥

दर्शनात् Because (of the indicatory marks) seen च and.

48. And because (of the indicatory marks) seen.

The indicatory marks are those referred to in Sûtra 44.

श्रुत्यादिबलीयस्त्वाच्च न बाधः ॥ ४९ ॥

श्रुत्यादि-बलीयस्त्वात् Because of the greater force of the Śruti etc. (*i.e.* indicatory mark and syntactical connection) च and न बाधः cannot be refuted.

49. And because of the greater force of the Śruti etc. (*i.e.* indicatory mark and syntactical connection), (the view that the fires constitute a Vidyâ) cannot be refuted.

The Sruti directly says, "All these fires are kindled with knowledge alone." The indicatory mark is this: "All beings kindle these fires for him, even when he is asleep." This continuity of the fires indicates that they are mental ones. An actual sacrifice is not continued during sleep. The syntactical connection is: "Through meditation alone are these fires of the worshipper kindled." These three are more forcible than more context.

अनुबन्धादिभ्यः प्रज्ञान्तरपृथक्त्ववत्, दृष्टश्च, तदुक्तम् ॥ ५० ॥

अनुबन्धादिभ्य: From the connection and so on (extension etc.) प्रज्ञान्तर-पृथक्त्ववत् even as other Vidyâs are separate दृष्ट: (it is) seen च and तत्-उक्तम् this has been said (by Jaimini).

50. From the connection and so on (extension etc.) (the fires constitute a separate Vidyâ), even as other Vidyâs (like the Śâṇḍilya Vidyâ) are separate. And (it is) seen (that in spite of the context a sacrifice is treated as independent). This has been said (by Jaimini in Pûrva Mîmâṁsâ-Sûtras).

This Sûtra gives additional reasons in support of the view set forth in Sûtra 47. The text connects for purposes of Saṁpat Upâsanâ (meditations based on) resemblance) parts of a sacrifice with mental activities, *e.g.* "These fires are started mentally, the altars are set up mentally. . .everything connected with this sacrifice are done mentally." This is possible only if there is a sharp difference between things resembling each other.

The fires form a separate Vidyâ even as the Śâṇḍilya Vidyâ, Dahara Vidyâ, etc. form separate Vidyâs although mentioned along with sacrificial acts. Moreover, it is seen in the sacrificial portion of the Vedas the sacrifice Āveśṭi, though mentioned along with the Râjasûya sacrifice, is yet regarded as an independent sacrifice by Jaimini in his Pûrva Mîmâṁsâ-Sûtras.

न सामान्यादपि, उपलब्धेः, मृत्युवत्, नहि
लोकापत्तिः ॥ ५१ ॥

न Not सामान्यात् अपि in spite of the resemblance उपलब्धे: for it is seen मृत्युवत् as in the case of death न हि लोकापत्ति: for the world does not become (fire because of certain resemblances).

51. In spite of the resemblance (of the fires to the imaginary drink, they do) not (form part of the sacrificial act), for it is seen (from the reasons adduced that they constitute an independent Vidyâ); (the mental affair here is) as in the case of death, for the world does not become (fire because of certain resemblances).

This Sûtra refutes the argument of the opponent given in Sûtra 45. The resemblance cited by the opponent there cannot stand, for on account of the reasons already adduced, *viz* the Śruti, indicatory mark, etc., the fires in question subserve the purpose of man only, and not any sacrifice. Mere resemblance cannot justify the opposite view. Anything can resemble anything in certain respects; still the things are different. The resemblance cited is like the common epithet 'death' applied to fire and the being in the sun. "The being in that orb is death indeed" (Śat. Br. 10. 5. 2. 3). "Fire is death" (Bṛ. 3. 2. 10). This resemblance cannot make fire and the being in the sun one. Again we have: "This world is a fire indeed, O Gautama, the sun its fuel" etc. (Ch. 5. 4. 1). Here from the similarity of fuel and so on the earth does not actually become fire.

परेण च शब्दस्य ताद्विध्यम्, भूयस्त्वात्त्वनुबन्धः ॥ ५२ ॥

परेण From the subsequent (Brâhmaṇa) च and शब्दस्य of the text ताद्विध्यम् the fact of being such भूयस्त्वात् on account of the abundance तु but अनुबन्धः connection.

52. And from the subsequent (Brâhmaṇa) the fact of the text (under discussion) being such (*i.e.* enjoining a separate Vidyâ) (is known). But the connection (of the imaginary fires with the actual fire is) on account of the abundance (of the attributes of the latter that are imagined in these fires).

In a subsequent Brâhmaṇa we have, "By knowledge they ascend there where all wishes are attained. Those skilled in works do not go there" etc. Here Vidyâ is praised and work depreciated. From this we find that what has been shown, *viz* that the fires form a Vidyâ, is the injunction of the Śruti. The connection of the fires with the actual fire is not because they form part of the sacrifice, but because many of the attributes of the real fire are imagined in the fires of the Vidyâ.

Topic 30: The Self is a separate entity from the body.

Till now the Upâsanâs have been discussed. But

the utility of these Upâsanâs depends on the existence of an individual apart from the body who can reap the results of the Upâsanâs. In the absence of such an individual the Upâsanâs and even Vedânta teachings become useless. So in this topic the existence of an Ātman apart from the body is taken up for discussion.

एक आत्मनः शरीरे भावात् ॥ ५३ ॥

एके Some (deny) आत्मनः (the existence) of an Ātman (besides the body) शरीरे (सति) भावात् (for It) exists (only) when there is a body.

53. Some (deny) (the existence) of an Atman separate from the body), (for It) exists (only) when there is a body.

This Sûtra gives the view of the Cârvâkas or materialists, who deny the existence of an Ātman other than the body. They say that man is only a body, having consciousness for its quality, and that consciousness is like the intoxicating property that is produced when certain materials are put together, none of which singly is intoxicating. They arrive at this conclusion in this way. Consciousness is seen to exist only when there is a body. Independent of the body it is nowhere experienced. Hence it is only a quality of the body. Therefore, there is no separate Self in this body.

व्यतिरेकः, तद्भावाभावित्वात्, न तु, उपलब्धि-
वत् ॥ ५४ ॥

व्यतिरेकः Separateness तद्भाव-अभावित्वात् for (consciousness) does not exist even when there is the body न not (so) तु but उपलब्धिवत् as in the case of cognition.

54. But not (so); (a Self) separate (from the body does exist), for (consciousness) does not exist even when there is the body (after death); as in the case of cognition.

This Sûtra refutes the view expressed in the previous one. Consciousness cannot be a quality of the body, for we do not find consciousness in a body after a person dies. So this consciousness is a quality of something different from and residing in the body. Again the Cârvâkas also accept that the cognizer is different from the thing cognized. If so, since we experience our body, we who cognize it must be different from our body: and this thing which cognizes this body of ours is the Self, and consciousness is a quality of this Self, rather its nature.

Topic 31: Upâsanâs connected with sacrificial acts, e.g. the Udgîtha Upâsanâ, are valid for all Śâkhâs.

अङ्गावबद्धास्तु न शाखासु हि प्रतिवेदम् ॥ ५५ ॥

अङ्गावबद्धाः (Upâsanâs) connected with parts (of sacrificial acts) तु but न not शाखासु to (particular) Śâkhâs हि because प्रतिवेदम् in each Veda.

55. But (the Upâsanâs) connected with parts (of sacrificial acts are) not (restricted) to (particular) Śâkhâs only of each Veda (but to all its

Śâkhâs), because (the same Upâsanâ is described in all).

There are certain Upâsanâs mentioned in connection with sacrificial acts, as, for example, the meditation on 'Om' which is connected with the Udgîtha as Prâṇa, or the meditation on the Udgîtha as the earth and so on. The question is whether these meditations are enjoined with reference to the Udgîtha and so on as belonging to a certain Śâkhâ of a Veda or as belonging to all its Śâkhâs. The doubt arises because the Udgîtha and so on are chanted differently in different Śâkhâs, and as such they may be considered different. This Sûtra refutes the view that they are so restricted, because the text speaks of these Upâsanâs in general, and so they are one in all the branches.

मन्त्रादिवद्वाऽविरोधः ॥ ५६ ॥

मन्त्रादिवत् Like Mantras etc. वा or else अविरोधः there is no contradiction.

56. Or else like Mantras etc. there is no contradiction (here).

Just as Mantras etc. mentioned in only one Śâkhâ are used in another Śâkhâ with respect to that particular rite, so also the Upâsanâs connected with particular rites in one Śâkhâ of the Veda can be applied to the other Śâkhâs.

Topic 32: Vaiśvânara Upâsanâ is one entire Upâsanâ

भूम्नः क्रतुवज्ज्यायस्त्वं, तथा हि दर्शयति ॥ ५३ ॥

भूम्न: On the entire form क्रतुवत् as in the case of sacrifice ज्यायस्त्वं importance तथा so हि for दर्शयति (the Śruti) shows.

57. Importance (is given to the meditation) on the entire form (of Vaiśvânara) as in the case of sacrifice; for so (the Śruti) shows.

In the Chândogya Upaniṣad 5. 11-18 we have the Vaiśvânara Vidyâ, the meditation on the cosmic form of the Lord, where we are asked to imagine that His head is the heavens, His eye the sun, and so on. In those sections we find different results mentioned for each part of the Upâsanâ. For example, the result of meditating on His head as the heavens is: "He eats food, sees his dear ones, and has Vedic glory in his house" (Ch. 5. 12. 2). Now the question is whether the Śruti here speaks only of one Upâsanâ on the whole cosmic form, or also piecemeal Upâsanâs. This Sûtra says that it is the former. The separate results mentioned for detached. Upâsanâs are to be combined into one aggregate with the principal meditation. That the Śruti intends only the entire Upâsanâ is moreover known from the fact that it discourages part Upâsanâ in such expressions as "Your head would have fallen if you had not come to me" (Ch. 5. 12. 2). The case is similar to certain sacrifices which include several minor sacrifices, the combined result of which completes that of the main sacrifices. That only one entire Upâsanâ is intended is also inferred from the fact that the section begins thus: "Which is our Self, which is the Brahman" (Ch. 5. 11. 1)—which shows that the entire Brahman is sought as the object of meditation. It ends also thus: "Of that Vaiśvânara Self Sutejas is the head" etc. (Ch. 5. 18. 2).

Topic 33: Various Vidyâs like the Śâṇḍilya Vidyâ Dahara Vidyâ, and so on are to be kept separate and not combined into one entire Up^sanâ.

नाना, शब्दादिभेदात् ॥ ५८ ॥

नाना Different शब्दादि-भेदात् owing to difference of words etc.

58. Various Vidyâs like the Śâṇḍilya, Dahara, etc. are) different owing to difference of words etc.

In the last Sûtra it was shown that though the Śruti mentions meditations on parts of the cosmic form, yet the meditation on the entire form is what is intended by the Śruti. Following this argument the opponent says that as the object of meditation is the one Lord, we are to combine all the different Vidyâs like the Śâṇḍilya Vidyâ, Dahara Vidyâ, Satya Vidyâ, and so on into one composite meditation on the Lord. This Sûtra refutes that view and says that these different Vidyâs are separate, because the Śruti prescribes them using different words, 'He knows', 'Let him meditate', 'Let him form the idea', etc. and this difference of terms is acknowledged to be a test of the difference of acts by Pûrva Mimâmsâ. 'Etc.' refers to other reasons like the difference in qualities. Though the object of meditation is the one Lord, yet owing to the difference in qualities that are imagined in different Upâsanâs He is different. Moreover, it is an impossibility to combine all the various Vidyâs into one. So the different Vidyâs are to be kept separate, and not combined into one general meditation.

Topic 34: Among Vidyâs relating to Brahman any one alone should be selected according to one's choice.

विकल्पः, अविशिष्ट-फलत्वात् ॥ ५९ ॥

विकल्पः Option अविशिष्ट-फलत्वात् on account of (all Vidyâs) having the same result.

59. There is option (with respect to the several Vidyâs), because the result (of all the Vidyâs) is the same.

As the result of all the Vidyâs is the realization of Brahman, it is enough if one takes up any one of them according to his liking and sticks to it till he reaches the goal. And once Brahman is realized through one of these Vidyâs, resorting to another is useless. Besides, to practise more than one meditation at a time would only distract one's mind and thereby retard one's progress Therefore one must restrict oneself to one particular Vidyâ.

Topic 35: Meditations yielding special desires may or may not be combined according to liking.

काम्यास्तु यथाकामं समुच्चीयेरन्न वा, पूर्वहेत्व-
भावात् ॥ ६० ॥

काम्याः Vidyâs for particular desires तु but यथाकाम according to one's desire समुच्चीयेरन् one may combine न वा or not पूर्व-हेतु-अभावात् on account of the absence of the preceding reason.

60. But Vidyâs for particular desires may be combined or not according to one's desire on account of the absence of the reason (mentioned in the) previous (Sûtra).

In the last Sûtra it was said that any *one* of the Vidyâs about Brahman should be taken up, and that more than one at a time should not be taken up, because each Vidyâ was quite sufficient and more than one would distract the mind. Now there are various Vidyâs which are practised not for the realization of Brahman, but to yield some particular desire. As, for example, in the Chândogya 3. 15. 2; 7. 1. 5. The question is whether one is to restrict oneself to only one of these Vidyâs, or can practise more than one at a time. This Sûtra says that as the results are different, unlike that of the Brahma-Vidyâs, one can take up more than one Vidyâ or not according to one's pleasure.

Topic 36: Meditations connected with members of sacrificial acts may or may not be combined according to liking.

अङ्गेषु यथाश्रयभावः ॥ ६१ ॥

अङ्गेषु With regard (to meditations) connected with members (of sacrificial acts) यथा-आश्रय-भावः it is as with (the members) with which they are connected.

61. With regard (to meditations) connected with members (of sacrificial acts) it is as with (the members) with which they are connected.

Sûtras 61-64 give the view of the opponent. Differen instructions connected with a sacrifice are mentioned ir the different Vedas. Now the scriptures themselves say that all these members mentioned in the differen Vedas are to be combined for the due performance o the main one. The question now is, what is the rule to be followed with respect to the Upâsanâs connectec with these members? This Sûtra says that the same rule which applies to the members applies also to the Upâsanâs connected with them. In other words, al these Upâsanâs are also to be combined.

शिष्टेश्च ॥ ६२ ॥

शिष्टेः From the injunction of the Śruti च and.

62. And from the injunction of the Śruti.

Even as the members are scattered in the differer Vedas, so are also the meditations connected with then There is no difference as regards the injunction of th Śruti with respect to these meditations.

समाहारात् ॥ ६३ ॥

63. On account of the rectification.

A further reason is given by the opponent.

"Now verily that which is Udgîtha is 'Om', and that which is 'Om' is Udgîtha. (If one knows this) then from the seat (*i.e.* through proper functioning) of the Hotṛ (he) rectifies all defective singing (of the Udgâtṛ)" (Ch. 1. 5. 5). Here it is said that the mistakes committed by the Udgâtṛ (chanting priest of the Sâma-Veda) are rectified by the recitation of the Hotṛ (invoking priest of the Ṛg-Veda), which shows that the meditations, though they are given in the different Vedas, are yet interlinked. So all of them have to be observed.

गुणसाधारण्यश्रुतेश्च ॥ ६४ ॥

गुण-साधारण्य-श्रुतेः From the Śruti declaring the feature 'Om' as being common to all the Vedas च and.

64. And from the Śruti declaring the syllable 'Om' which is a common feature (of the Udgîtha Vidyâ), to be common to all the Vedas.

"Through this does the Vedic Vidyâ proceed" (Ch. 1. 1. 9). This is said with reference to the syllable 'Om' which is common to all the Vedas and all the Upâsanâs in them. This shows that as the abode of all Vidyâs is common, so are the Vidyâs that abide in it, and therefore all of them are to be observed.

न वा, तत्सहभावाश्रुतेः ॥ ६५ ॥

न वा Rather not तत्सहभाव-अश्रुतेः their correlation not being mentioned by the Śruti.

65. (The meditations connected with members of sacrificial acts are) rather not to be combined), as the Śruti does not say that they are so correlated.

This and the following Sûtra give the conclusion. The rule for combining the instructions regarding sacrifices that are scattered in all the Vedas cannot be applied with respect to the Upâsanâs connected with them. In the former case, if the instructions are not combined, the sacrifice itself will fail. But not so if the Upâsanâs are not practised, for Upâsanâs only enhance the results of the sacrifice. (*Vide* 3. 3. 42). They are not inseparable from the sacrifice. So they may or may not be practised.

दर्शनाच्च ॥ ६६ ॥

दर्शनात् Because the Śruti says so च and.

66. And because the Śruti says so.

"The Brahmâ (superintending priest) who knows this protects the sacrifice, the sacrificer, and all the other priests" (Ch. 4. 17. 10). This shows that the scriptures do not intend that all the meditations should go together. If it were so, then all the priests would know all of them and there is no sense in the Śruti distinguishing the qualified superintending priest from the rest.

The meditations, therefore, may or may not be combined according to one's taste.

CHAPTER III

SECTION IV

In the last section were discussed the Vidyâs, the means to the knowledge of Brahman. This section discusses whether this knowledge of Brahman is connected with ritualistic work through the agent, or whether it independently serves the purpose of man (Puruṣârtha). Man tries to attain the fulfilment of his desires, discharge of duties, acquisition of wealth, and Liberation. The question is whether knowledge of Brahman serves any of these purposes, or is merely connected with sacrificial acts in so far as it imparts to the agent a certain qualification.

Topic 1: Knowledge of Brahman is not subordinate to sacrificial acts.

पुरुषार्थोऽतः, शब्दादिति बादरायणः ॥ १ ॥

पुरुषार्थः Purpose of man **अतः** from this **शब्दात्** from the scriptures **इति** thus (says) **बादरायणः** Bâdarâyaṇa.

1. From this (results) the purpose of man, because of the scriptures; thus (says) Bâdarâyaṇa.

Bâdarâyaṇa basing his arguments on the Śruti texts says that the knowledge of Brahman effects man's highest purpose and is not a part of sacrificial acts. It leads to Liberation. The scriptural authority referred to is texts like: "The knower of the Self goes beyond grief" (Ch. 7. 1. 3); "He who knows that Supreme Brahman becomes indeed Brahman" (Mu. 3. 2. 9); "The knower of Brahman attains the Highest" (Tai. 2. 1).

शेषत्वात्पुरुषार्थवादो यथाऽन्येष्विति जैमिनिः ॥ २ ॥

शेषत्वात् On account of being supplementary (to sacrificial acts) पुरुष-अर्थवादः are mere praise of the agent यथा even as अन्येषु in other cases इति thus (says) जैमिनिः Jaimini.

2. Because (the Self) is supplementary (to sacrificial acts), (the fruits of the knowledge of the Self) are mere praise of the agent, even as in other cases; thus says Jaimini.

According to Jaimini the Vedas merely prescribe acts to attain certain purposes including Liberation, and nothing more. He argues that the knowledge of the Self does not yield any independent results, as Vedânta holds, but is connected with the acts through the agent. No one undertakes a sacrificial act unless he is conscious of the fact that he is different from the body and that after death he will go to heaven, where he will enjoy the results of his sacrifices. Texts dealing with Self-knowledge serve merely to enlighten the agent and so are subordinate to sacrificial acts. The fruits, however, which the Vedânta texts declare with regard to Self-knowledge are merely praise, even as texts declare such results by way of praise with respect to other matters. In short, Jaimini holds that by the knowledge that his Self will outlive the body, the agent becomes qualified for sacrificial actions, even as other things become fit in sacrifices through purificatory ceremonies.

आचारदर्शनात् ॥ ३ ॥

आचार-दर्शनात् Because of the conduct found (from the scriptures).

3. Because we find (from the scriptures such) conduct (of men of realization).

"Janaka, emperor of Videha, performed a sacrifice in which gifts were freely distributed" (Bṛ. 3. 1. 1); "I am going to perform a sacrifice, sirs" (Ch. 5. 11. 5). Now both Janaka and Aśvapati were knowers of the Self. If by this knowledge of the Self they had attained Liberation, there was no need for them to perform sacrifices. But the two texts quoted show that they did perform sacrifices. This proves that it is through sacrificial acts alone that one attains Liberation, and not through the knowledge of the Self, as the Vedântins hold.

तच्छ्रुतेः ॥ ४ ॥

तत्-श्रुतेः Because the scriptures directly declare that.

4. That (*viz* that knowledge of the Self stands

in a subordinate relation to sacrificial acts) the scriptures directly declare.

"That alone which is performed with knowledge, faith, and meditation becomes more powerful" (Ch 1. 1. 10); This text clearly shows that knowledge is a part of the sacrificial act.

समन्वारम्भणात् ॥ ५ ॥

5. Because the two (knowledge and work) go together (with the departing soul to produce the results).

"It is followed by knowledge, work, and past experience" (Bṛ. 4. 4. 2). This text shows that knowledge and work go together with the soul and produce the effect which it is destined to enjoy Knowledge independently is not able to produce any such effect.

तद्वतो विधानात् ॥ ६ ॥

तद्वत: For such (as know the purport of the Veda

विधानात् because (the scriptures) enjoin (work).

6. Because (the scriptures) enjoin (work) for such (as know the purport of the Vedas).

The scriptures enjoin work only for those who have a knowledge of the Vedas, which includes the knowledge of the Self. Hence Knowledge does not independently produce any result.

नियमाच्च ॥ ७ ॥

नियमात् On account of prescribed rules च and

7. And on account of prescribed rules.

"Performing works here let a man wish to live a hundred years" (Īś. 2); "Agnihotra is a sacrifice lasting up to old age and death; for through old age one is freed from it or through death" (Śat. Br. 12. 4. 1. 1). From such prescribed rules also we find that Knowledge stands in a subordinate relation to work.

अधिकोपदेशात्तु बादरायणस्यैवम्, तद्दर्शनात् ॥ ८ ॥

अधिक-उपदेशात् Because (the scriptures) teach (the Supreme Self to be) something over and above तु but बादरायणस्य Bâdarâyaṇa's (view) एवम् such *i.e* correct तत्-दर्शनात् for that is seen (from the scriptures).

8. But because (the scriptures) teach (the Supreme Self to be) other (than the agent), Bâdarâyaṇa's (view is) correct; for that is seen (from the scriptures).

Sûtras 2-7 give the view of the Mîmâṁsakas, which is refuted in Sûtras 8-17

The Vedânta texts do not teach the limited self, which is the agent, but the Supreme Self, which is different from the agent. Thus the knowledge of the Self which the Vedânta texts declare is different from that knowledge of the self which an agent possesses.

The knowledge of such a Self, which is free from all limiting adjuncts, not only does not help, but puts an end to all actions. That the Vedânta texts teach the Supreme Self is clear from such texts as the following: "He who perceives all and knows all' (Mu. 1. 1. 9); "Under the mighty rule of this Immutable, O Gârgî" etc. (Br. 3. 8. 9).

तुल्यं तु दर्शनम् ॥ ९ ॥

तुल्यं Equal तु but दर्शनम् declarations of the Śruti.

9. But the declarations of the Śruti equally support both views.

This Sûtra refutes the view expressed in Sûtra 3. There it was shown that Janaka and others even after attaining Knowledge were engaged in work. This Sûtra says that scriptural authority equally supports the view that for one who has attained Knowledge there is no work. "Knowing this very Self the Brâhmanas renounce the desire for sons, for wealth, and for the worlds, and lead a mendicant life" (Bṛ. 3. 5. 1). We also see from the scriptures that knowers of the Self like Yâjñavalkya gave up work. " 'This much indeed is (the means of) immortality, my dear.' Saying this Yâjñavalkya left home" (*Ibid.* 4. 5. 15). The work of Janaka and others was characterized by non-attachment, and as such it was practically no work; so the Mîmâṁsâ argument is weak.

असार्वत्रिकी ॥ १० ॥

10. (The declaration of the scripture referred to in Sûtra 4) is not universally true.

The declaration of the Śruti that knowledge enhances the fruit of the sacrifice does not refer to all knowledge, as it is connected only with the Udgîtha, which is the topic of the section.

विभागः शतवत् ॥ ११ ॥

विभागः (There is) division of knowledge and work **शतवत्** as in the case of a hundred (divided between two persons).

11. (There is) division of knowledge and work, as in the case of a hundred (divided between two persons).

This Sûtra refutes Sûtra 5. "It is followed by knowledge, work, and past experiences" (Bṛ. 4. 4. 2). Here we have to take knowledge and work in a distributive sense, meaning that knowledge follows one and work another. Just as when we say a hundred be given to these two persons, we divide it into two halves and give each man fifty. There is no combination of the two. Even without this explanation Sûtra 5 can be refuted. For the text quoted refers only to knowledge and work, which concern the transmigrating soul, and not an emancipated soul. For the passage, "Thus does the man who desires (trasmigrate)" (*Ibid*. 4. 4. 6) shows that the previous tẹxt refers to the transmigrating self. And of the emancipated soul Śruti says, "But the man who never desires (never transmigrates)" etc. (*Ibid*. 4. 4. 6).

अध्ययनमात्रवतः ॥ १२ ॥

12. (The scriptures enjoin work) only on those who have read the Vedas.

This Sûtra refutes Sûtra 6

Those who have read the Vedas and known about the sacrifices are entitled to perform work. No work is prescribed for those who have knowledge of the Self from the Upaniṣads. Such a knowledge is incompatible with work.

न, अविशेषात् ॥ १३ ॥

न Not अविशेषात् owing to the absence of any specification.

13. Because there is no special mention (of the Jñâni, it does) not (apply to him).

This Sûtra refutes Sûtra 7. The text quoted there from the Īśâ Upaniṣad is a general statement, and there is no special mention in it that it is applicable to a Jñâni also. In the absence of such a specification it is not binding on him.

स्तुतयेऽनुमतिर्वा ॥ १४ ॥

स्तुतये For the praising (of Knowledge) अनुमति permission वा or rather

14. Or rather the permission (to do work) is for praising (Knowledge).

The injunction to do work for the knowers of the Self is for the glorification of this Knowledge. The praise involved in it is this: A knower of the Self may work all his life, but on account of this Knowledge he will not be bound by its effects.

कामकारेण चैके ॥ १५ ॥

कामकारेण According to their choice च and एके some.

15. And some according to their choice (have refrained from all work).

In Sûtra 3 it was said that Janaka and others were engaged in work even after Knowledge. This Sûtra says that some have of their own accord given up all work. The point is that after Knowledge some may choose to work to set an example to others, while others may give up all work. There is no binding on the knowers of the Self as regards work.

उपमर्दं च ॥ १६ ॥

उपमर्दं Destructions च and.

16. And (the scriptures say that the) destruction (of all qualifications for work results from Knowledge).

Knowledge destroys all ignorance and its products like agent, act, and result. "But when to the knower of Brahman everything has become the Self, then what should one see and through what" etc. (Bṛ. 4. 5. 15).

The knowledge of the Self is antagonistic to all work and so cannot possibly be subsidiary to work.

ऊर्ध्वरेतःसु च, शब्दे हि ॥ १७ ॥

ऊर्ध्वरेतःसु To those who observe continence च and शब्दे (this Āśrama is mentioned) in the scriptures हि because.

17. And (Knowledge belongs) to those who observe continence (*i.e.* to Sannyâsins); because (this fourth Āśrama is mentioned) in the scriptures.

The scriptures declare that Knowledge is gained in that stage of life in which continence is prescribed, *i.e.* the fourth stage or Sannyâsa Āśrama. To a Sannyâsin there is no work prescribed except discrimination. So how can knowledge be subservient to work? That there is a stage of life called Sannyâsa we find from the scriptures themselves in texts like: "There are three branches of duty; sacrifice, study and charity are the first. . . . All these attain to the worlds of the virtuous; but only one who is firmly established in Brahman attains immortality" (Ch. 2. 23. 1-2): "Desiring this world (the Self) alone monks renounce their homes" (Bṛ. 4. 4. 22). See also Mu. 1. 2. 11 and Ch. 5. 10. 1. Everyone can take to this life without being a householder etc., which shows the independence of Knowledge.

Topic 2: Sannyâsa is prescribed by the scriptures.

परामर्शं जैमिनिरचोदना च, अपवदति हि ॥ १८ ॥

परामर्शं Mere reference जैमिनिः Jaimini अचोदना there is no injunction च and अपवदति हि because (the scripture) condemns (it).

18. Jaimini (thinks that in the texts referred to in the last Sûtra there is) a mere reference (to Sannyâsa), and not injunction, because (other texts) condemn (Sannyâsa).

In the text quoted in the last Sûtra (Ch. 2. 23. 1) Jaimini says that as there is no word showing that Sannyâsa is enjoined on man, it is a mere reference and not an injunction. The Bṛhadâraṇyaka text quoted in the last Sûtra says that some persons do like that. Śruti here makes a mere statement of fact. It does not enjoin Sannyâsa. Moreover, the text here praises steadfastness in Brahman. "But only one who is firmly established in Brahman attains immortality." Sacrifice, study, charity, austerity, studentship, and lifelong celibacy result in the attainment of the virtuous world. But immortality is gained only by him who is firmly established in Brahman. That is what the text says. Further, there are other texts which condemn Sannyâsa. "Having brought to your teacher the wealth that he likes, do not cut off the line of progeny" (Tai. 1. 11); "To him who is without a son (this) world does not belong" (Tai. Br. 7. 13. 12) and so on.

अनुष्ठेयं बादरायणः, साम्यश्रुतेः ॥ १९ ॥

अनुष्ठेयं Ought to be gone through बादरायणः Bâdarâyaṇa साम्यश्रुतेः for the scriptural text refers equally to all the four Āśramas.

19. Bâdarâyaṇa (thinks that Sannyâsa or monastic life) also must be gone through, for the scriptural text (cited refers equally to all the four Āśramas (stages of life).

In the text cited, sacrifice etc. refer to the householder's life, penance to Vânaprastha, studentship to Brahmacarya and 'one who is firmly established in Brahman' to Sannyâsa. So the text equally refers to all the four stages of life. The text relating to the first three stages refers to what is enjoined elsewhere. So also does the text relating to Sannyâsa. Hence Sannyâsa also is enjoined and must be gone through by all.

विधिर्वा धारणवत् ॥ २० ॥

विधिः Injunction वा or rather धारणवत् as in the case of the carrying (of the sacrificial fuel).

20. Or rather (there is an) injunction (in this text), as in the case of the carrying (of the sacrificial fuel).

This Sûtra now tries to establish that there is an injunction about Sannyâsa in the Chândogya passage cited. There is a Śruti text referring to Agnihotra performed for the manes, which runs as follows: "Let him approach, carrying the sacrificial fuel below; for above he carries it for the gods." The last clause Jaimini interprets as an injunction, though there is no word in it to that effect, because such an injunction is nowhere else to be found in the scriptures. On account of its newness (Apûrvatâ) it is an injunction. Following this argument this Sûtra says that in Ch. 2. 23. 1 there is an injunction with respect to Sannyâsa, and not a mere reference, as it is not enjoined anywhere else. Moreover, there are Śruti texts which directly enjoin Sannyâsa: "Or else he may wander forth from the students' life or from the house, or from the forest" (Jâb. 4).

Again Jaimini himself says that even glorification, to be relevant, must be in a complementary relation to an injunction. In the text cited steadfast devotion to Brahman is being praised, and so it has an injunctive value. Now is it possible for one engaged in sacrificial rites etc. to be wholly devoted to Brahman? Devotion to Brahman means constant meditation on It without any disturbing thought. Such a thing is impossible for a householder engaged in ritualistic work. It is possible only for a Sannyâsin who has renounced all work, and not for others.

Neither is it true that Sannyâsa is prescribed only for those who are lame, blind, etc., and therefore unfit for ritualistic work. The text cited above (Jâb. 4) makes no such difference. Moreover, Sannyâsa is meant as a means to the realization of Brahman, and it is to be acquired in a regular prescribed way. "The wandering mendicant with coloured dress, shaven-headed, accepting no gifts, qualifies himself for the realization of Brahman." Therefore Sannyâsa is prescribed by the scriptures and Knowledge, because it is enjoined on Sannyâsins, is independent of work.

Topic 3: Scriptural statements as in Ch. 1. 1. 3 which refer to Vidyâs are not merely glorificatory but enjoin the meditations.

स्तुतिमात्रमुपादानादिति चेत्, न, अपूर्वत्वात् ॥ २१ ॥

स्तुतिमात्रम् Mere praise उपादानात् because of their reference (to parts of sacrificial acts) इति चेत् if it be said न not so अपूर्वत्वात् on account of its newness.

21. If it be said (that reference as in Ch 1. 1. 3) are mere praise because of their reference (to parts of sacrificial act), (we say) not so, because here it is mentioned for the first time.

"That Udgîtha (Om) is the best essence of the essences, the supreme, deserving the highest place, the eighth" (Ch. 1. 1. 3), "This earth is Ṛk, and fire Sâman" (*Ibid.* 1. 6. 1). The opponent holds that these are mere praise, and no injunction to meditate on 'Om' and so on. These passages are akin to. "The ladle is the earth", "The tortoise is the sun", which simply glorify the ladle and so on. This view of the opponent is refuted in the latter half of the Sûtra. The analogy is not correct. Glorification to have a purpose must be in complementary relation to an injunction. The passages quoted for analogy stand in proximity to injunctive passages, and so they can be taken as praise. But the passage of the Chândogya where Udgîtha 'Om' is described as the essence of essences, is mentioned in the Upaniṣad, and so cannot be taken along with the injunctions about Udgîtha in the Karmakâṇḍa. As such on account of the newness it is an injunction and not mere glorification.

भावशब्दाच्च ॥ २२ ॥

भाव-शब्दात् There being words expressive of injunction च and.

22. And there being words expressive of injunction.

"Let one meditate on 'Om' (of) the Udgîtha" (Ch. 1. 1. 1). In this passage we have a clear injunction to meditate on 'Om'. On the face of this we cannot interpret the text cited in the last Sûtra as merely glorificatory of 'Om'.

Topic 4: The stories recorded in the Upaniṣads do not serve the purpose of Pâriplavas and so do not form part of the ritualistic acts. They are meant to glorify the Vidyâ taught in them.

पारिप्लवार्था इति चेत्, न, विशेषितत्वात् ॥ २३ ॥

पारिप्लवार्थाः For the purpose of Pâriplavas इति चेत् if it be said न not so विशेषितत्वात् on account of (certain stories alone) being specified.

23. If it be said (that the stories that occur in the Upaniṣads are) for the purpose of Pâriplavas, (we say) not so, because (certain stories alone) are specified (by the Śruti for this purpose).

In the Aśvamedha sacrifice, which lasts for one year, the sacrificer and his family are expected to hear at intervals the recital of certain stories. These are known as Pâriplavas, and form part of the ritualistic acts. The question is whether Upaniṣadic stories also serve this purpose, in which case they become part of the rites, and this means that the whole of Jñânakâṇḍa becomes subservient to Karmakâṇḍa. The stories referred to are those relating to Yâjñavalkya and Maitreyi, Pratardana and so on, which we find in the Bṛhadâraṇyaka Kauṣîtakī and other Upaniṣads.

This Sûtra denies that they serve the purpose o Pâriplavas, for the scripture specifies the stories tha are meant for this purpose. Any and every story canno serve this purpose. Upaniṣadic stories are not mer tioned in this category.

तथा चैकवाक्यतोपबन्धात् ॥ २४ ॥

तथा So च and एकवाक्यता-उपबन्धात् being connected a one whole.

24. And so (they are meant to illustrate th nearest Vidyâs), being connected as one whole.

The stories while not serving the purpose of Pâr plavas are intended to introduce the Vidyâs. The sto form is meant to catch the imagination of the studen who will thereby be more attentive to the Vid described.

Topic 5: Sannyâsins need not observe ritualistic acts, Knowledge serves their purpose.

अतएव चाग्नीन्धनाद्यनपेक्षा ॥ २५ ॥

अतएव Therefore च and अग्नि-इन्धनादि-अनपेक्षा no necessity of lighting fires etc.

25. And, therefore, there is no necessity of lighting fires, and so on.

In Sûtra 3. 4. 1 it was said that the knowledge of the Self results in the attainment of the highest Puruṣârtha or goal of life. Therefore the lighting of fires for sacrifices and other similar acts enjoined on the householders etc. need not be observed by Sannyâsins, as Knowledge alone fulfils their object.

Topic 6: Nevertheless works prescribed by the scriptures are useful as they are an indirect means to Knowledge.

सर्वापेक्षा च यज्ञादिश्रुतेः अश्ववत् ॥ २६ ॥

सर्वापेक्षा There is the necessity of all works च and यज्ञादि-श्रुतेः for the scriptures prescribe sacrifices etc. (as means to Knowledge) अश्ववत् even as the horse.

26. And there is the necessity of all works, for the scriptures prescribe sacrifices etc. (as means to the attainment of Knowledge, though they are unnecessary for the attainment of its results, *viz.* Liberation), even as the horse (is used to draw a chariot and not for ploughing).

From the previous Sûtra we may conclude that works are altogether useless. This Sûtra says that all these works are useful, and that even the scriptures prescribe them, since they serve as a means to Knowledge. But they have no part in producing the result of this Knowledge, *viz* Liberation. It comes only from Knowledge and not from work. Work purifies the mind, and the knowledge of the Self is manifested in such a pure mind. So works have a place as a means to Knowledge, though an indirect one.

शमदमाद्युपेतः स्यात्तथाऽपि तु, तद्विधेस्तदङ्गतया
तेषामवश्यानुष्ठेयत्वात् ॥ २७ ॥

शम-दमादि-उपेतः स्यात् One must possess calmness, self control, and the like **तथा अपि** even if it be so **तु** but **तद्विधेः** since they are enjoined **तदङ्गतया** as helps to knowledge **तेषाम्-अवश्य-अनुष्ठेयत्वात्** and therefore they have necessarily to be observed.

27. But even if it be so (*i.e.* even though there is no injunction to do work to attain Knowledge in the text [Br. 4. 4. 22]) one must possess calmness, self-control, and the like, since these are enjoined as helps to Knowledge, and therefore have necessarily to be observed.

"The Brâhmaṇas seek to know It through the study of the Vedas, sacrifices, charity" etc. (Bṛ. 4. 4. 22). In this text there is no word to show that sacrifice is enjoined on one who wants to know Brahman. So th opponent says that there is no need at all of work for an aspirant of Knowledge. This Sûtra says that even if it be so, yet control of the senses etc. are enjoined by the Śruti: "Therefore he who knows it as such becomes self-controlled, calm . . . sees Self in his self" etc. (Bṛ. 4. 4. 23). This passage is injunctive in character, for 'therefore' expresses praise of the subject-matter and hence is connected with an injunction, because in the absence of an injunction the praise would be purposeless. Since these qualities are enjoined, they have necessarily to be practised. Self-control etc. directly help the attainment of Knowledge, while work helps it indirectly.

Topic 7: Restrictions as regards food may be waived only when life is at stake.

सर्वान्नानुमतिश्च प्राणात्यये, तद्दर्शनात् ॥ २८ ॥

सर्व-अन्न-अनुमतिः Permission to take all sorts of food प्राणात्यये when life is jeopardized तत्दर्शनात् because the Śruti declares that.

28. (Only) when life is jeopardized (there is) permission to take food indiscriminately, because the Śruti declares that.

"For one who knows this, there is nothing that is not food" (Ch. 5. 2. 1). The opponent holds that on account of the newness of the statement it is enjoined on one who meditates on Prâṇa. Such a statement being found nowhere else, it has an injunctive value.

This Sûtra refutes it and says that it is not an injunction, but only a statement of fact, and where the idea of an injunction does not arise, we are not justified in assuming one. Prohibited food may be eaten only when life is in danger, as was done by the sage Câkrâyaṇa when he was dying for want of food. This fact we get from the Śruti.

अबाधाच्च ॥ २९ ॥

अबाधात् Because of a non-contradiction (thus) च and.

29. And because (thus) (the scriptural statements with respect to food) are not contradicted.

"When the food is pure the mind becomes pure" (Ch. 7. 26. 2). This statement will not be contradicted only if the explanation given is taken, and not otherwise.

अपि च स्मर्यते ॥ ३० ॥

अपि च Moreover स्मर्यते the Smṛtis say so.

30. Moreover the Smṛtis (also) say so.

The Smṛtis also say that both those who have Knowledge and those who have not can take any food when life is in danger; then it is not sinful. But they prohibit various kinds of food as objectionable.

शब्दश्चातोऽकामकारे ॥ ३१॥

शब्दः The scriptural text च and अतः hence अकामकारे prohibiting licence.

31. And hence the scriptural text prohibiting licence.

There are scriptural passages prohibiting one from doing everything just as one pleases. Licence, freedom from all discipline, cannot help us to attain Knowledge. "Therefore a Brâhmaṇa must not drink liquor" (Kâṭhaka Saṁ.). Such Śruti texts are meant for this discipline. Therefore it is established that the Śruti does not enjoin on one who meditates on Prâṇa to take all kinds of food indiscriminately.

Topic 8: The duties of the Āśrama are to be performed by even one who is not desirous of Knowledge

विहितत्वाच्चाश्रमकर्मापि ॥ ३२ ॥

विहितत्वात् Because they are enjoined च and आश्रम कर्म duties of the Āśrama (order of life) अपि also.

32. And the duties of the Āśrama (are to be performed) also (by him who does not desire Liberation), because they are enjoined (on him by the scriptures).

In Sûtra 25 it was said that works are a means to Knowledge. The question is raised, since it is so why should one who does not desire Knowledge do these works? This Sûtra says that since these duties are enjoined on all who are in these Āśramas or stages of life, *viz* student life, householder's life, and hermit life, one should observe them.

सहकारित्वेन च ॥ ३३ ॥

सहकारित्वेन As a means to Knowledge च and.

33. And (the duties are to be performed also) as a means to Knowledge.

Here we have to understand that the duties are helpful in producing Knowledge, but not its fruit, *viz* Liberation, which is not attainable except through Knowledge.

सर्वथापि त एव, उभयलिङ्गात् ॥ ३४ ॥

सर्वथा अपि In all cases ते एव the same duties (have to be performed) उभय-लिङ्गात् because of the two-fold indicatory mark.

34. In all cases the same duties (have to be performed), because of the two-fold indicatory mark).

The question is raised whether the work done as enjoined on the Āśramas and those done as aids to Knowledge are of two different kinds. This Sûtra says that in either case, whether as duties of the Āśramas or as aids to Knowledge, the same duties are to be done, as is seen from the Śruti and the Smṛti texts.

"The Brâhmaṇas seek to know It through the study of the Vedas, sacrifices" etc. (Bṛ. 4, 4, 22). This text shows that sacrifices etc. enjoined in Karmakâṇḍa for different purposes are to be performed as means to Knowledge also. The Smṛti also says the same thing. "He who performs obligatory work without desire for fruits" etc. (Gîtâ 6. 1). Those very obligatory duties subserve Knowledge also.

अनभिभवं च दर्शयति ॥ ३५ ॥

अनभिभवं Not being overpowered च and दर्शयति the scripture shows.

35. And the scripture shows (that one endowed with Brahmacarya) is not overpowered (by anger etc.).

"For that self does not perish which one attains by Brahmacarya" (Ch. 8. 5. 3). This text also shows that like work, Brahmacarya etc. are also means to Knowledge. One endowed with it is not overcome by anger, jealousy, etc., and his mind not being disturbed he is able to practise Knowledge.

Therefore works are obligatory on the Āśramas and are also means to Knowledge.

Topic 9: Those who stand midway between two Āśramas are also entitled to Knowledge.

अन्तरा चापि तु, तद्दृष्टेः ॥ ३६ ॥

अन्तरा (Persons standing) in between (two Āśramas) च and अपि तु also तद्दृष्टेः such cases being seen.

36. And (persons standing) in between (two Āśramas) are also (entitled to Knowledge), because such cases are seen.

The question is raised whether persons of dubious position—who have not the means etc. to do the duties of an Āśrama, or who stand midway between two Āśramas, as for example a widower—are entitled to Knowledge or not. The opponent holds that they are not, since they cannot do the works of any Āśrama which are means to Knowledge. This Sûtra says that they are entitled, for such cases are seen from the scriptures, as for example Raikva and Gârgî, who had the knowledge of Brahman. *Vide* Ch. 4. 1 and Bṛ. 3. 6 and 8.

अपि च स्मर्यते ॥ ३७ ॥

अपि च Further स्मर्यते the Smṛti records such cases.

37. The Smrti also records such cases.

Samvarta and other Ṛṣis, without doing the works enjoined on the Āśramas, became great Yogîs.

विशेषानुग्रहश्च ॥ ३८ ॥

विशेष-अनुग्रहः Favour due to special works च and.

38. And special works favour (Knowledge).

A widower, who cannot be said to be a householder in the proper sense of the word or a poor man who has not the means to perform the duties of the Āśrama, can attain Knowledge through special works like prayer fasting, Japa etc., which are not opposed to the condition of those who do not belong to any Āśrama.

अतरित्वतरज्ज्यायो लिङ्गाच्च ॥ ३६ ॥

अत: Than this तु but इतरत् the other ज्याय: better लिङ्गात् because of the indicatory marks च and.

39. But better than this is the other (state of being in some Āśrama or other), (being maintained by the Śruti and the Smṛti) and because of the indicatory marks (in the Śruti and the (Smṛti).

Though it is possible for one who stands between two Āśramas to attain Knowledge, yet both the Śruti and Smṛti say directly and indirectly that it is a better means to Knowledge to belong to some Āśrama. "The Brâhmaṇas seek to know It through. . .sacrifices" etc. (Bṛ. 4. 4. 22)—this is a direct statement of the Śruti; "Any other knower of Brahman who has done good deeds" etc. (Bṛ. 4. 4. 9), and "Let not a-Brâhmaṇa stay even for a day outside the Āśrama"—these are indirect statements of the Śruti and Smṛti respectively.

Topic 10: One who has taken the vow of lifelong celibacy (Sannyâsa) cannot revert back to his former stages of life.

तद्भूतस्य तु नातद्भावः, जैमिनेरपि, नियमातद्रूपा-
भावेभ्यः ॥ ४० ॥

तद्भूतस्य For one who has attained that (the highest Āśrama) तु but न no अतद्भाव: ceasing from that जैमिने: of Jaimini (is this opinion) अपि also नियम-अतद्रूप-अभावेभ्य: on account of restrictions prohibiting such reversion.

40. But for one who has risen to the highest Āśrama (*i.e.* Sannyâsa) there is no reverting (to the preceding ones), on account of restrictions prohibiting such reversion. Jaimini also (is of this opinion).

The question whether one who has embraced Sannyâsa can go back to the previous Āśrama is taken up for discussion. This Sûtra says that he cannot, because the Śruti expressly forbids it. "He is to go to the forest, he is not to return from there." But there are no rules allowing a reversion, like those which sanction the ascent to higher Āśramas. It is also against approved custom. So one cannot revert from Sannyâsa.

Topic 11: Expiation for one who transgresses the vow of lifelong celibacy.

न च आधिकारिकमपि, पतनानुमानात्
तदयोगात् ॥ ४१ ॥

न Not च and अधिकारिकम् (expiation) mentioned in the chapter dealing with the qualification अपि even पतन-अनुमानात् because a fall (in his case) is inferred from the Smṛti तदयोगात् and because of its inefficacy (in his case).

41. And (the expiation), although mentioned in the chapter dealing with qualifications (in Pûrva Mîmâṁsâ), is not (with reference to one who has taken the vow of lifelong celibacy), because a fall (in his case) is inferred from the Smṛti, and because of its (of the expiatory ceremony) inefficacy (in his case).

The case of those who have taken the vow of lifelong celibacy and yet have transgressed this vow through a mistake in judgement, it is taken up for discussion. The opponent's whose view is given in this Sûtra, holds that for such transgressions there is no expiation. For no such ceremony is mentioned with respect to them, the one mentioned in Pûrva Mîmâṁsâ 6. 8. 22 referring to ordinary Brahmacârins, who are students, and not to Naiṣṭhika Brahmacârins. It can also be inferred that the Smṛti declares such lapses as not expiable. A beheaded man cannot be cured. "For him who lapses after having embraced the vow of a Naiṣṭhika Brahmacârin I see no expiatory ceremony by which such a suicide can be purified." The Smṛti here does not refer to the ordinary Brahmacârin, and so the expiatory ceremony applies only to them and not to the Naiṣṭhika. Moreover, the ceremony referred to in Pûrva Mîmâṁsâ is not efficacious in his case, for, to perform the ceremony he will have to light the sacrificial fire and therefore have to marry, which means that he will cease to be a Naiṣṭhika thereafter.

उपपूर्वमपि तु एके भावम्, अशनवत् तदुक्तम् ॥ ४२ ॥

उपपूर्वम् Prefixed with 'Upa', *i.e.* an Upapâtaka or

a minor sin अपि तु but एके some भावम् the existence अशनवत as in the case of eating तत् this उक्तम् is explained in Pûrva Mîmâṁsâ.

32. But some (consider this transgression on the part of the Naiṣṭhika) a minor sin (and therefore claim) the existence (of expiation for it), as in the case of eating (prohibited food by ordinary Brahmacârins). This is explained in Pûrva Mîmâmsâ.

Some, however, think that such lapses on the part of a Naiṣṭhika, other than disloyalty to teacher's wife etc., are minor sins and not major ones, and so can be expiated by proper ceremonies, even as ordinary Brahmacârins who take prohibited food are again purified by expiatory ceremonies. The reference to the text denying any such ceremony in his case is meant only to bring home to the Naiṣṭhika Brahmacârin the grave responsibility on his part so that he may struggle with all his soul. Similarly in the case of the recluse and the Sannyâsin. As a matter of fact, the Smṛti does prescribe the purificatory ceremony for both the recluse and the Sannyâsin. "The recluse when he has broken his vows undergoes the Kṛcchra penance for twelve nights and then develops a place which is full of trees and grass." The Sannyâsin also undergoes the purificatory ceremony, with certain modifications.

Topic 12: The lifelong celibate who lapses in his vows to be shunned by society.

बहिस्तूभयथापि स्मृतेराचाराच्च ॥ ४३ ॥

बहिः Outside तु but उभयथा-अपि in either case स्मृतेः from the Smṛti आचारात् from custom च and.

43. But in either case (they are to be kept) outside the society, on account of the Smṛti and custom.

Whether the lapses be regarded as major sins or minor sins, in either case good people are to avoid such transgressors; because the Smṛti and approved custom both condemn them.

Topic 13: The meditations connected with the subordinate members of sacrificial acts are to be gone through by the priest and not by the sacrificer.

स्वामिनः, फलश्रुतेरित्यात्रेयः ॥ ४४ ॥

स्वामिनः To the sacrificer फल-श्रुतेः from the declaration of results in the Śruti इति this आत्रेयः Ātreya.

44. To the sacrificer (belongs the agentship in meditations), because the Śruti declares a fruit (for it); thus Ātreya (thinks).

The question is raised as to who is to observe the meditations connected with subordinate members of sacrificial acts, whether it is the sacrificer or the priest. The opponent, represented by the sage Ātreya, holds that it is to be observed by the sacrificer, as the Śruti declares a special fruit for these meditations.

आर्त्विज्यमित्यौडुलोमिः, तस्मै हि परिक्रीयते ॥ ४५ ॥

आर्त्विज्यम् The duty of the Ṛtvik (priest) इति thus औडुलोमिः Audulomi तस्मै for that हि because परिक्रीयते he is paid.

45. (They are) the duty of the Rtvik (priest), thus thinks Audulomi, because he is paid for that (*i.e.* the performance of the whole sacrifice).

Since the priest is paid for all his acts, and thereby the fruit of all his acts is, as it were, purchased by the sacrificer, the meditations also come under this category and have to be observed by the priest and not the sacrificer. This is the view of the sage Audulomi.

श्रुतेश्च ॥ ४६ ॥

श्रुतेः From the Sruti च and.

46. And because the Śruti so declares.

"Whatever blessing the priests pray for at the sacrifice, they pray for the good of the sacrificer" (Śat. Br 1. 3. 1. 26). Such texts declare that the fruit of meditations in which the priest is the agent, goes to the sacrificer. Therefore Audulomi's view is correct, being supported by the Śruti texts.

Topic 14: In Bṛ. 3. 5. 1. meditativeness is enjoined besides scholarship and the childlike state

सहकार्यन्तरविधिः पक्षेण तृतीयं तद्वतः विध्या-
दिवत् ॥ ४७ ॥

सहकार्यन्तरविधिः Injunction of another auxiliary (to Knowledge) पक्षेण as an alternative तद्वत: for one who possesses it (*i.e.* Knowledge) तृतीयम् a third one विध्यादिवत् as in the case of injunctions and the like.

47. (The meditative state is) the injunction of another auxiliary (to Knowledge), which is a third one (besides the two expressly enjoined), as an alternative (where the knowledge of diversity is persistent) for one who possesses Knowledge; as in the case of injunctions and the like.

"Therefore a knower of Brahman, having done with scholarship should remain like a child (free from anger, passions, etc.); and after having finished with this state and with learning he becomes meditative (Muni)" (Bṛ. 3. 5. 1). The question is whether the meditative state is enjoined or not. The opponent holds that it is not enjoined, as there is no word indicating an injunction. The text merely says that he becomes a Muni or meditative, whereas with respect to scholarship and the state of a child free from all passions, it expressly enjoins, 'one should remain' etc. Moreover, scholarship refers to Knowledge and therefore includes Munihood which also more or less refers to Knowledge. Therefore there is no newness with respect to Munihood in the text, it being included in scholarship already, and not being an Apûrva it has no injunctive value.

This Sûtra refutes this view and says that Munihood or meditativeness is enjoined in the text as a third requisite besides scholarship and the state of a child. For Munihood is not merely Knowledge but meditativeness, continuous devotion to Knowledge and as such it is different from scholarship. Hence, not having been referred to before, it is a new thing (Apûrva), and therefore the text has injunctive value. Such meditativeness has a value for a Sannyâsin who is not yet established in the knowledge of unity, and persistently experiences diversity owing to past impressions.

कृत्स्नभावात्तु गृहिणोपसंहारः ॥ ४८ ॥

कृत्स्नभावात् On account of the householder's life including all तु verily उपसंहारः (the chapter) ends गृहिणा with the householder.

48. Verily, on account of the householder's life including (duties from) all (the other stages of life), the chapter ends with the (enumeration of the duties of the) householder.

In the Chândogya Upaniṣad we find that after enumerating the duties of the Brahmacârin it enumerates those of the householder, and there it ends without any mention of Sannyâsa. If this also is one of the Āśramas, why is nothing said about it in that place? The Sûtra says that in order to lay stress on the householder's life, to show its importance, the Śruti ends there without referring to Sannyâsa, and not because it is not one of the prescribed Āśramas

The householder's life is important because for him are prescribed, besides his own duties, those of other Āśramas like study, control of the senses, etc. It includes more or less duties of all Āśramas.

मौनवदितरेषामप्युपदेशात् ॥ ४९ ॥

मौनवत् Even as the state of a Muni (Sannyâsa) इतरेषाम् of the others अपि even उपदेशात् on account of scriptural instruction.

49. Because the scripture enjoins the other (stages of life, *viz* Brahmacarya and Vânaprastha) even as it enjoins the state of a Muni (Sannyâsa).

Just as the Śruti enjoins Sannyâsa and householder's life, so also it enjoins the life of a recluse and that of a student. Hence the scriptures enjoin all the four Āśramas or stages of life to be gone through, in sequence or alternatively. The plural number 'others' instead of the dual is to denote the different classes of these two stages of life.

Topic 15: Childlike state means the state of innocence, being free from anger, passion, etc.

अनाविष्कुर्वन्, अन्वयात् ॥ ५० ॥

अनाविष्कुर्वन् Without manifesting himself अन्वयात् on account of the context.

50 (The childlike state means) without manifesting himself, on account of the context.

In the passage of the Bṛhadâraṇyaka quoted in Sûtra 47, the childlike state is enjoined on an aspirant after Knowledge. The question is what is exactly meant by this? Does it mean to be like a child without any idea of purity and impurity and doing whatever one likes, or does it mean to be guileless and without the sense of egoism as a child? The Sûtra says it is the latter and not the former, because that is detrimental to Knowledge. It means one has not to manifest or give vent to any of the passions and has to be guileless and without the sense of egoism. It refers to the innate innocence of a child. Such a meaning alone is appropriate to the context, purity and innocence being helpful to Knowledge.

Topic 16: The time of the origination of Knowledge when the Vidyâ is practised.

ऐहिकमप्यप्रस्तुतप्रतिबन्धे, तद्दर्शनात् ॥ ५१ ॥

ऐहिकम् In this life अपि even अप्रस्तुत-प्रतिबन्धे if there is no obstruction to it (the means adopted) तत्-दर्शनात् because it is so seen from the scriptures.

51. (The fruition of Knowledge may take place) even in this life if there be no obstruction to it (the means adopted), because it is so seen from the scriptures.

From Sûtra 26 the various means to Knowledge have

been discussed. The question now is whether Knowledge resulting from these means comes in this life or in the life to come. This Sûtra says that it may come in this life only if there is no obstruction to its manifestation from extraneous causes. For it often happens that when the fruition of Knowledge is about to take place it is retarded by the fruit of some other stronger work, which is also about to fructify. In such cases Knowledge comes in the next life. That is why the scriptures declare that it is difficult to realize the Self. "Even to hear of It is not available to many; many even having heard of It cannot comprehend" etc. (Ka. 1.2.7). The Gîtâ also says: "There he is united with the intelligence acquired in his former body" etc. (Gîtâ. 6. 43); "The Yogî, striving assiduously, purified of taint, gradually gaining perfection through many births, then reaches the highest goal" (*Ibid.* 6. 45). Moreover, that Knowledge sometimes fructifies in the next life is known from the life of Vâmadeva who possessed Knowledge even while he was in the womb. This shows that it must have been the result of his past actions, for he could not have practised any Vidyâs in the womb. Knowledge did not manifest in his previous life owing to obstruction, and this being removed when he was in the womb, Knowledge fructified as a result of his past Sâdhanâ

Topic 17: There is no difference in Liberation i.e. in the cognition of Brahman—it is of one kind in all cases.

एवं मुक्तिफलानियमः, तदवस्थावधृतेस्तदवस्थाव-
धृतेः ॥ ५२ ॥

एवं Like this मुक्तिफल-अनियमः there is no rule with

respect to Liberation, the fruit (of Knowledge) तत् अवस्था-अवधृतेः because the Śruti asserts that state (to be immutable).

52. With respect to Liberation, the fruit (of Knowledge) there is no rule like this, because the Śruti asserts that state (to be immutable).

In the last Sûtra it was seen that Knowledge may result in this life or the next according to the absence or presence of obstructions and the intensity of the means adopted. Similarly a doubt may arise that there may be some such rule with respect to Liberation also, which is the fruit of Knowledge. In other words, the question is whether Liberation can be delayed after Knowledge, and whether there are degrees of Knowledge according to the qualifications of the aspirant. This Sûtra says that no such rule exists with respect to Liberation. Because the Śruti texts assert that the nature of final release is uniform, without any variations of degree in it. The state of final release is nothing but Brahman. "The knower of Brahman becomes Brahman," and there can be no variety in it, as Brahman is without qualities. Difference is possible only where there are qualities, as in the case of the Saguna Brahman about which according to difference in Vidyâs there may be difference in the cognitions. But with respect to the cognition of Brahman, it can be only one and not many. Neither can there be any delay in the attainment of Liberation after Knowledge has dawned, for knowledge of Brahman itself is Liberation.

The repetition of the clause 'Because the Śruti asserts that state' is to show that the chapter ends here.

CHAPTER IV

Section I

In the third chapter the means to Knowledge were discussed. In this chapter the result of Knowledge and some other topics are taken up for discussion. In the beginning, however a special discussion connected with means to Knowledge is dealt with.

Topic 1: The meditation on the Ātman enjoined by the scriptures is to be repeated till Knowledge is attained.

आवृत्तिः, असकृदुपदेशात् ॥ १ ॥

आवृत्तिः Repetition (is necessary) असकृत् repeatedly उपदेशात् on account of instruction by the scriptures.

1. The repetition (of hearing, reflection, and meditation on the teaching of the Self is necessary), on account of the repeated instruction by the scriptures.

"The Self, my dear Maitreyî, should be realized—should be heard of, reflected on, and meditated upon" (Bṛ. 2. 4. 5). "The intelligent aspirant after Brahman, knowing about this alone, should attain intuitive knowledge (*Ibid.* 4. 4. 21). The question arises whether what is enjoined in this is to be done once only or repeatedly. The opponent holds that it is to be observed once only, even as sacrifices like Prayâja are to be performed once only to yield the desired result. This Sûtra refutes the view and says that the hearing etc. must be repeated till there is intuition of Brahman. Of course, if the knowledge of Brahman is attained by a single act, it is well and good; otherwise there is the necessity of repetition till the Knowledge dawns. It is the repetition of these acts that finally leads to intuition. The case of the Prayâja is not to the point. For there the result is Adṛṣṭa, which yields fruit at some particular future time. Here the result is directly perceived, and so, if the result is not there, the process must be repeated till the result is seen. Moreover, scriptural texts like the first one cited above give repeated instruction, thereby signifying the repetition of the means. Again 'meditation' and 'reflection' imply a repetition of the mental act, for when we say, 'he meditates on it', we imply the continuity of the act of remembrance of the object Similarly with respect to 'reflection'. It follows, therefore, that there must be repetition of the instruction This holds good even in those cases where the texts do not give instruction repeatedly, as for example, in the second text cited above.

लिङ्गाच्च ॥ २ ॥

लिङ्गात् On account of the indicatory mark च and.

2. And on account of the indicatory mark.

"Reflect upon the rays, and you will have many sons" (Ch. 1. 5. 2). This text prescribes repeated meditation by asking to meditate on the Udgîtha as the rays instead of as the sun. And what holds good in this case is equally applicable to other meditations also. And it is not true that repetition is not necessary. If it were so, the Śruti would not have taught the truth of the statement 'That thou art' repeatedly. There may be people who are so advanced, and so little attached to the world of sense objects, that in their case a single hearing of the statement may result in Knowledge. But generally such advanced souls are very rare. Ordinary people, who are deeply rooted in the idea of the body and the senses, do not realize the truth by a single enunciation of it. This wrong notion of theirs goes only through repeated practice of the truth, and it is only then that Knowledge dawns. So repetition has the effect of removing this wrong notion gradually, till even the last trace of it is removed. When the body consciousness is completely removed, the Self manifests Itself in all purity.

Topic 2: In the meditations on the Supreme Brahman the meditator is to comprehend It as identical with himself.

आत्मेति तूपगच्छन्ति ग्राहयन्ति च ॥ ३ ॥

आत्मेति As the self तु but उपगच्छन्ति acknowledge ग्राहयन्ति teach च also.

3. But (the Śruti texts) acknowledge (Brahman) as the self (of the meditator) and also teach others (to realize It as such).

The question whether Brahman is to be comprehended by the individual soul as identical with it or separate from it, is taken up for discussion. The opponent holds that Brahman is to be comprehended as different from the individual soul on account of their essential difference. For one is subject to misery, while the other is not. This Sûtra refutes the view and holds that Brahman is to be comprehended as identical with one's self; for in reality the two are identical, the experience of misery etc. by the individual soul—in other words, the Jîvahood—being due to the limiting adjunct, the internal organ. (*Vide* 2. 3. 29 *ante*). For instance, the Jâbâlas acknowledged it. "I am indeed Thou, O Lord, and Thou art indeed myself." Other scriptural texts also say the same thing: "I am Brahman" (Bṛ. 1. 4. 10); "This self is the Brahman" (Mâ. 2). These texts are to be taken in their primary, and not secondary sense, as in, "The mind is Brahman" (Ch. 3. 18. 1), where the text presents the mind as a symbol for contemplation.

Hence we have to meditate on Brahman as being the self.

Topic 3: Where symbols of Brahman are used for contemplation, the meditator is not to comprehend them as identical with him.

न प्रतीके, न हि सः ॥ ४ ॥

न Not प्रतीके in the symbol न is not हि because सः he.

4. (The meditator is) not (to see the self) in the symbol, because he is not (that).

"The mind is Brahman" (Ch. 3. 18. 1) In such meditations, where the mind is taken as a symbol of

Brahman, is the meditator to identify himself with the mind, as in the case of the meditation "I am Brahman"? The opponent holds that he should, for the mind is a product of Brahman according to Vedânta, and as such it is one with It. So is the individual soul, the meditator, one with Brahman. Hence it follows that the meditator also is one with the mind, and therefore he should see his self in the mind in this meditation also. This Sûtra refutes it. In the first place, if the symbol, mind, is cognized as identical with Brahman, then it ceases to be a symbol, even as when we realize an ornament as gold, we forget its individual character of being an ornament. Again, if the meditator is conscious of his identity with Brahman, then he ceases to be the individual soul, the meditator. The act of meditation can take place only where these distinctions exist, and unity has not been realized; and where there is knowledge of diversity, the meditator is quite distinct from the symbol. As such he is not to see his self in the symbol.

Topic 4: In meditations on symbols the latter are to be viewed as Brahman and not in the reverse way.

ब्रह्मदृष्टिः, उत्कर्षात् ॥ ५ ॥

ब्रह्म-दृष्टिः Viewing as Brahman उत्कर्षात् on account of the elevation.

5. (The symbol is) to be viewed as Brahman (and not in the reverse way), on account of the elevation (of the symbol thereby).

In meditations on symbols as in, "The mind is Brahman", "The sun is Brahman", the question is whether the symbol is to be regarded as Brahman, or Brahman as the symbol The Sûtra says that the symbols, the mind and the sun, are to be regarded as Brahman and not *vice versa*. Because it is only by looking upon an inferior thing as a superior thing that we can progress, and not in the reverse way. Inasmuch as our aim is to get rid of the idea of differentiation and see Brahman in everything, we have to meditate upon these symbols as That.

Topic 5: In meditations on the members of sacrificial acts the idea of the divinity is to be superimposed on the members and not vice versa.

आदित्यादिमतयश्चाङ्ग, उपपत्तेः ॥ ६ ॥

आदित्यादि-मतयः The ideas of the sun etc. च and अङ्गे in a subordinate member (of sacrificial acts) उपपत्तेः because of consistency.

6. And the ideas of the sun etc. (are to be superimposed) on the subordinate members (of sacrificial acts), because (in that way alone would the statement of the scriptures) be consistent.

"One ought to meditate upon that which shines yonder as the Udgîtha" (Ch. 1. 3. 1); "One ought to meditate upon the Sâman as five-fold" etc. (Ch. 2. 2 1.). In meditations connected with sacrificial acts as given in the texts quoted, how is the meditation to be observed? For example, in the first cited text, is the sun to be viewed as the Udgîtha, or the Udgîtha as the sun? Between the Udgîtha and the sun there is nothing to show which is superior, as in the previous Sûtra, where Brahman being pre-eminent, the symbol was viewed as Brahman. This Sûtra says that the members of sacrificial acts, as here the Udgîtha, are to be viewed as the sun and so on. Because by so doing the fruit of the sacrificial act is enhanced, as the scriptures say. If we view the Udgîtha as the sun, it undergoes a certain ceremonial purification and thereby contributes to the Apûrva, the invisible fruit of the whole sacrifice. But by the reverse way, the sun being viewed as the Udgîtha, the purification of the sun by this meditation will not contribute to the Apûrva, inasmuch as the sun is not a member of the sacrificial act. So if the statement of the scriptures that the meditations enhance the result of the sacrifice, is to come true, the members of the sacrificial acts are to be viewed as the sun etc.

Topic 6: One is to meditate sitting

आसीनः, सम्भवात् ॥ ७ ॥

आसीन: Sitting सम्भवात् because of the possibility.

7. (One has to practise Upâsanâ) sitting, because (in that way alone) it is possible.

As Upâsanâ or contemplation is a mental affair, the posture of the body is immaterial—says the opponent. This Sûtra says that one has to meditate sitting, for it is not possible to meditate while standing or lying down.

In Upâsanâ one has to concentrate one's mind on a single object, and this is impossible if one is standing or lying.

ध्यानाच्च ॥ ८ ॥

ध्यान On account of meditation (implying that) च and.

8. And on account of meditation (implying that).

The word 'Upâsanâ' also means exactly what meditation means, *viz* concentrating on a single object, with fixed look, and without any movement of the limbs. This is possible only in a sitting posture.

अचलत्वं चापेक्ष्य ॥ ९ ॥

अचलत्वं Immobility च and अपेक्ष्य referring to.

9. And referring to (its) immobility (the scriptures attribute meditativeness to the earth).

"The earth meditates as it were"—in such statements meditativeness is ascribed to the earth on account of its immobility or steadiness. So we learn that steadiness is a concomittance of meditation, and that is possible only while sitting and not while standing or walking.

स्मरन्ति च ॥ १० ॥

स्मरन्ति The Smṛti texts say च also.

10. The Smṛti texts also say (the same thing).

"Having made a firm seat for one's self on a pure spot" etc. (Gîtâ 6. 11)—in this text the sitting posture is prescribed for meditation.

Topic 7: With respect to meditation there is no restriction of place.

यत्रैकाग्रता तत्र, अविशेषात् ॥ ११ ॥

यत्र Wherever एकाग्रता concentration of mind तत्र there अविशेषात् for want of any specification.

11. Wherever concentration of mind (is attained), there (it is to be practised), there being no specification (as to place).

The object of meditation is to attain concentration, and so any place is good if concentration is attained in that place. That is why the scriptures say, "Select any place suitable and convenient"; "Where the mind is buoyant there one should concentrate", and so on. But places that are clean, free from pebbles, fire, sand, and so on, are desirable, as such places are helpful to meditation. But all the same there are no fixed rules as to place.

Topic 8: Meditations are to be observed till death.

आ प्रायणात्, तत्रापि हि दृष्टम् ॥ १२ ॥

आ प्रायणात् Till death तत्र then अपि even हि because दृष्टम is seen (from the scriptures).

12. Till death (meditations have to be observed), because (their observance) even at that moment is seen (from the scriptures).

In the first topic of this section it was said that meditations on Brahman are to be repeated till Knowledge dawns. The question is now taken up about other meditations which are practised for attaining certain results. The opponent holds that such meditations can be stopped after a certain time; they would still yield results, like sacrifices performed only once. This Sûtra says that they are to be continued till death, for the Śruti and Smṛti say so. "With whatever thought he passes away from this world" (Śat. Br. 10. 6. 3. 1). "Remembering whatever form of being he leaves this body" etc. (Gîtâ 8. 6). Such a thought at the time of death as fixes the course of life hereafter cannot be had at that moment without lifelong practice. Hence meditations must be practised till death.

Topic 9: Knowledge of Brahman frees one from the effects of all past and future evil deeds.

तदधिगम उत्तरपूर्वाघयोरश्लेषविनाशौ, तद्-
व्यपदेशात् ॥ १३ ॥

तत्-अधिगमे When that is realized उत्तर-पूर्व-अघयोः of the subsequent and previous sins अश्लेष-विनाशौ non-clinging and destruction तत्-व्यपदेशात् because it is declared (by the scriptures).

13. When that (Brahman) is realized (there

result) the non-clinging and destruction of the subsequent and previous sins respectively, because it is (so) declared (by the scriptures).

The state of Jîvanmukti is described here. The opponent holds that Liberation is attained, in spite of Knowledge, only after one has experienced the results of one's sins committed before illumination. For the Smṛtis say, "Karma is not destroyed before it has given its results". The law of Karma is inexorable. This Sûtra says that when a person attains Knowledge, all his past sins are destroyed and future sins do not cling to him. For by realizing Brahman he experiences that he never was, nor is, nor will be an agent, and such a person cannot be affected by the result of sins. The scriptures also declare that. "Just as cotton growing on reeds is burnt when thrown into fire, even so are burnt the sins of one who knowing this offers Agnihotra" (Ch. 5. 24. 3); "The fetters of the heart are broken, all doubts are solved, and all works are destroyed when He who is high and low is seen" (Mu. 2. 2. 8); "As water does not wet the lotus leaf, even so no sins cling to him who knows It" (Ch. 4. 14. 3). What the Smṛtis say about the inexorability of the law of Karma is true only of ordinary people, and does not hold good in the case of the knowers of Brahman. And in this way alone can Liberation result—by snapping the chain of work. Otherwise Liberation can never take place.

Topic 10: Good deeds likewise cease to effect the knower of Brahman.

इतरस्याप्येवमसंश्लेषः, पाते तु ॥ १४ ॥

इतरस्य Of the other अपि also एवम् thus असंश्लेषः non-clinging पाते at death तु but.

14. Thus there is non-clinging of the other (*i.e.* virtue) also; but at death (Liberation *i.e.* Videhamukti is certain).

As a knower of Brahman has no idea of agency he is not affected by good deeds also. He goes beyond vice and virtue. "He overcomes both" (Bṛ. 4. 4. 22). And as he is not touched by vice or virtue after illumination, and as his past sins are destroyed by Knowledge, his Liberation at death is certain.

Topic 11: Works which have not begun to yield results are alone destroyed by Knowledge and not those which have already begun to yield results.

अनारब्धकार्ये एव तु पूर्वे, तदवधेः ॥ १५ ॥

अनारब्ध-कार्ये Works which have not begun to yield results एव only तु but पूर्वे former works तदवधेः that (death) being the limit.

15. But (of his) former works only those which have not begun to yield results (are destroyed by Knowledge); (for) death is the limit (set by the scriptures for Liberation to take place).

In the last two topics it has been said that all the past works of a knower of Brahman are destroyed. Now past works are of two kinds: Saṁcita (accumulated) *i.e.*

those which have not yet begun to bear fruit, and Prârabdha (commenced) *i.e.* those which have begun to yield results, and have produced the body through which a person has attained Knowledge. The opponent holds that both these are destroyed, because the Muṇḍaka text cited says that all his works are destroyed. Moreover, the idea of non-agency of the knower is the same with respect to Saṁcita or Prârabdha work; therefore it is reasonable that both are destroyed when Knowledge dawns.

The Sûtra refutes this view and says that only the Saṁcita works are destroyed by Knowledge, but not the Prârabdha, which are destroyed only by being worked out. So long as the momentum of these works lasts, the knower of Brahman has to be in the body. When they are exhausted, the body falls off, and he attains perfection. His Knowledge cannot check these works, even as an archer has no control over the arrows already discharged which come to rest only when their momentum is exhausted. The Śruti declares that in texts like, "And for him the delay is only so long as he is not liberated (from this body); and then he is one (with Brahman)" (Ch. 6. 14. 2). If it were not so, then there would be no teachers of Knowledge. Therefore the Prârabdha works are not destroyed by Knowledge.

Topic 12: Obligatory works are however excepted from the rule mentioned in topic 10.

अग्निहोत्रादि तु तत्कार्यायैव, तद्दर्शनात् ॥ १६ ॥

अग्निहोत्रादि (Daily) Agnihotra etc. तु but तत्-कार्याय

contribute to the same result as that (knowledge) एव only तत्-दर्शनात् that being seen (from the scriptures).

16. But (the results of daily) Agnihotra etc. (are not destroyed by Knowledge; these) contribute to the very same result as Knowledge (*i.e.* Liberation), because that is seen from the scriptures.

Among works some are enjoined for attaining certain results such as heaven, and there are others like the daily Agnihotra which yield no such results and yet are enjoined as a sort of discipline. The opponent holds that even these regular works (Nitya Karma) performed before the dawning of Knowledge are destroyed, even as works done with desires (Kâmya Karma), for from the standpoint of the knower of Brahman his non-agency with respect to both is the same. This Sûtra refutes that view and says that the regular works performed in the past are not destroyed. Works are of two kinds: those which yield specific results, and those which help to produce Knowledge. Obligatory regular works performed before Knowledge are of this latter kind. And since Knowledge leads to Liberation, the regular works also may be said to contribute indirectly to that. Hence their results persist till death.

अतोऽन्यापि ह्येकेषामुभयोः ॥ १७ ॥

अतः From this अन्या different अपि also हि indeed एकेषाम् of some (Śâkhâs) उभयोः of both.

17. (There are) indeed (good works) also

different from this (daily Agnihotra and the like), (with reference to which is the statement) of some (Śâkhâs); (this is the view) of both (Jaimini and Bâdarâyaṇa).

Besides the Nitya Karma or regular works like the daily Agnihotra and the like there are other good works which are performed with a view to certain results. It is with reference to these that the following statement of some Śâkhâs is made: "His sons get his inheritance —friends his good works and enemies his evil actions." Both Jaimini and Bâdarâyaṇa are of opinion that works done with a desire do not help the origination of Knowledge.

Topic 13: Sacrificial works not combined with knowledge or meditations also help in the origination of Knowledge.

यदेव विद्ययेति हि ॥ १८ ॥

यत् एव Whatever विद्यया with knowledge इति thus हि because.

18. Because (the statement), "Whatever (he does) with knowledge", indicates this.

Regular works (Nitya Karma) which help the origination of Knowledge are of two kinds: Those combined with meditations, those unaccompanied by them. Since work combined with meditations is superior to work done without meditations, the opponent holds that the former alone helps the origination of Knowledge. This Sûtra refutes it and says that in the statement, "That alone which is performed with knowledge . . . becomes more powerful" (Ch. 1. 1. 10), the comparative degree shows that works done without knowledge, that is, not combined with meditations, are not altogether useless, though the other class is more powerful.

Topic 14: On the exhaustion of Prârabdha work through enjoyment the knower of Brahman attains oneness with It.

भोगेन त्वितरे क्षपयित्वा संपद्यते ॥ १९ ॥

भोगेन By enjoyment तु but इतरे of the other two works क्षपयित्वा having exhausted संपद्यते becomes one (with Brahman).

19. But having exhausted by enjoyment the other two works (*viz* good and evil works that have begun to bear fruit), (he) becomes one (with Brahman).

The opponent argues that even as a knower of Brahman sees diversity while living, so also even after death he will continue to see diversity; in other words, he denies that the knower of Brahman attains oneness with Brahman at death. This Sûtra refutes it and says that the Prârabdha works are destroyed through fruition, and though till then the knower of Brahman has to be in the relative world as a Jîvanmukta, yet when these are exhausted by being worked out, he attains oneness with Brahman at death. He no longer sees any diversity, owing to the absence of any cause like the Prârabdha, and since all works including the Prârabdha are destroyed at death, he attains oneness with Brahman.

CHAPTER IV

Section II

In the previous section it was shown that by the destruction of actions which have not as yet begun to yield results a knower of Brahman attains Jîvanmukti, and that on the exhaustion of the Prârabdha work he attains Videhamukti at death and becomes one with Brahman. Thus in a general way the result of Knowledge has been set forth. The remaining three sections deal at length with the nature of Liberation, which is attained on the exhaustion of the Prârabdha Karma. In this particular section the path of the gods, by which the knower of the Saguṇa Brahman travels after death, is described. With this end in view it begins with the exposition of the successive steps by which the soul passes out of the body at death.

Topic 1: At the time of death the functions of the organs are merged in mind.

वाङ्मनसि, दर्शनाच्छब्दाच्च ॥ १ ॥

वाक् **Speech** मनसि in mind दर्शनात् because it is so seen शब्दात् from scriptural statements च and.

1. Speech (is merged) in mind, because it is so seen, and there are scriptural statements (to that effect).

"When, my dear, the man departs from here, his speech merges in mind, mind in Prâṇa, Prâṇa in Fire, and Fire in the Highest Deity" (Ch. 6. 8. 6). This text describes what happens at the time of death. It says that speech gets merged in mind, mind in Prâṇa, and so on. Now the question is whether the organ of speech as such gets merged in mind, or only its function. The opponent holds that as there is no mention in the text about the function of speech getting merged, we have to understand that the organ itself gets merged in mind.

The Sûtra refutes this view and says that only the function of the organ of speech gets merged in mind. Mind is not the material cause of the organs, and as such they cannot get merged in it. It is only in the material cause that the effects get merged, and as mind is not the material cause of the organs, we have to understand here by speech not the organ, but its function. A function of the organ, unlike the organ itself, can get merged in mind, even though it is not the cause of that function, just as the burning property of fire, which has its start in wood, becomes extinct in water. The scriptural statement therefore refers to the function of speech, the function and the thing to which it belongs being viewed as one. We also notice that a dying man first loses his function of speech, though his mind is still functioning. So we have to understand from experience also that the function of speech, and not the organ itself, is merged in mind.

अत एव च सर्वाण्यनु ॥ २ ॥

अतः एव For the same reason च and सर्वाणि all (organs) अनु after.

2. And for the same reason all (organs) follow (mind, *i.e.* get their functions merged in it).

For the same reasons as stated in Sûtra 1 the functions of the remaining organs follow, *i.e.* get merged in mind. "The fire is verily the Udâna, for they in whom the fire has been extinguished, go for rebirth with their organs absorbed in mind" (Pr. 3. 9). This text shows that the functions of all the organs get merged in mind.

Topic 2: The function of mind gets merged in Prâṇa.

तन्मनः प्राणे, उत्तरात् ॥ ३ ॥

तत् That मनः mind प्राणे in Prâṇa उत्तरात् from the subsequent clause (of the Śruti).

3. That mind (is merged) in Prâṇa, (as is seen) from the subsequent clause (of the Śruti cited).

That mind, in which the functions of the different organs get merged, in its turn gets merged in Prâṇa, for the Śruti cited in Sûtra 1 says, "Mind in Prâṇa". The opponent holds that here, unlike the case of the organs, it is mind itself, and not its function, that gets merged in Prâṇa, inasmuch as Prâṇa can be said to be the material cause of mind. In support of his contention he cites the following texts: "Mind consists of food, Prâṇa of water" (Ch. 6. 6. 5) and "Water sent forth earth" (Ch. 6. 2. 4). When mind is merged in Prâṇa, it is the same thing as earth being merged in water, for mind is food or earth, and Prâṇa is water.

Hence the Śruti here speaks not of the function of mind, but of mind itself getting merged in Prâṇa. The Sûtra refutes this view and says that this relation of causality by an indirect process does not justify our understanding that mind itself is merged in Prâṇa. So here also it is the function alone that gets merged, and this is justified on the same grounds as given in Sûtra 1, *viz* scriptural statement and experience. We find that mind ceases to function in a dying man, even while his vital force is functioning.

Topic 3: The function of the vital force gets merged in the individual soul.

सोऽध्यक्षे, तदुपगमादिभ्यः ॥ ४ ॥

सः That (Prâṇa) अध्यक्षे in the ruler (Jîva) तत्-उपगमादिभ्यः on account of (statements expressing) approach to that etc.

4. That (Prâṇa) is merged in the ruler (Jîva) on account of (statements expressing) approach to that etc.

In the text cited in Sûtra 1 we have, "Prâṇa (is merged) in fire," How then can it be said that the function of Prâṇa is merged in the individual soul, asks the opponent. The Sûtra justifies its view on the ground that statements about Prâṇas coming to the Jîva etc. are found in scriptural texts. "All the Prâṇas approach the departing man at the time of death" (Bṛ. 4. 3. 38). Also, "When it departs, the vital force follows" (Bṛ.

4. 4. 2). The text cited in Sûtra 1 does not, however, contradict this view, as the following Sûtra shows.

भूतेषु, तच्छ्रुतेः ॥ ५ ॥

भूतेषु In the elements तत्-श्रुतेः from the Śruti texts to that effect.

5. In the elements (is merged) (the Jîva with the Prâṇas), as it is seen from the Śruti.

If we understand, "Prâṇa (is merged) in fire" as meaning that the Jîva with Prâṇa is merged in fire, there is no contradiction between this Śruti text and what is said in the last Sûtra. So Prâṇa is first merged in the individual soul and then the soul with Prâṇa takes its abode in the fine essence of the gross elements, fire etc., the seed of the future body.

नैकस्मिन्, दर्शयतो हि ॥ ६ ॥

न Not एकस्मिन् in one दर्शयतः (both) declare so हि for.

6. (The soul with Prâṇa is merged) not in one (element only), for both (the Śruti and Smṛti) declare so.

At the time of death, when the soul leaves one body and goes in for another, it together with the subtle body abides in the fine essence of all the gross elements and not in fire only, for all the elements are required for a future body. *Vide* 3. 1. 2.

Topic 4: The mode of departure from the body up to the way is common to both a knower of the Saguṇa Brahman and an ordinary man.

समाना चासृत्युपक्रमात्, अमृतत्वं चानुपोष्य ॥ ७ ॥

समाना Common च and आ सृति-उपक्रमात् up to the beginning of their ways अमृतत्वं immortality च and अनुपोष्य not having burnt (ignorance).

7. And common (is the mode of departure at the time of death for both the knower of the Saguṇa Brahman and the ignorant) up to the beginning of their ways; and the immortality (of the knower of the Saguṇa Brahman is only relative), not having burnt (ignorance).

For the knower of the Nirguṇa Brahman there is no departure at all. Leaving his case, the opponent says that the mode of departure from the body for the knower of the Saguṇa Brahman and the ignorant ought to be different, as they attain different abodes after death, the former reaching Brahmaloka and the latter being reborn in this world. This Sûtra says that the knower of the Saguṇa Brahman enters at death the nerve Suṣumnâ, and then goes out of the body, and takes to the path of the gods, while the ignorant enter some other nerve and go by another way to have rebirth. But till they enter on their respective ways, the method of departure at death is common to both, for it is something pertaining to this life, and like happiness and misery it is the same for both.

Topic 5: The merging of fire etc. at death in the Supreme Deity is not absolute merging.

तदाऽपीतेः, संसारव्यपदेशात् ॥ ८ ॥

तत That आ अपीतेः up to the attainment of Brahman (through Knowledge) संसार-व्यपदेशात् because (scriptures) declare the state of relative existence.

8. That (fine body lasts) up to the attainment of Brahman (through Knowledge), because (the scriptures) declare the state of relative existence (till then).

In the text cited in Sûtra 1 we have, "And fire (is merged) in the Supreme Deity." The opponent argues that as fire and the other elements are merged in the Supreme Deity, which is the cause of these elements, this is only the final dissolution, and so everyone at death attains Liberation. This Sûtra says that this merging is not absolute merging, but the one we experience in deep-sleep. Only the functions of these elements are merged, and not the elements themselves. The final dissolution does not take place till Knowledge is attained; for the scriptures declare that till then the individual soul is subject to relative existence: "Some souls enter the womb to have a body" etc. (Ka.. 2. 5. 7). If the merging at death were absolute, then there could be no rebirth.

सूक्ष्मं प्रमाणतश्च, तथोपलब्धेः ॥ ९ ॥

सूक्ष्मं Subtle प्रमाणतः as regards size च and तथा so उपलब्धेः because it is experienced.

9. (This fine body) is subtle (by nature) and size, because it is so experienced.

The body formed from the essence of the gross elements in which the soul abides at the time of death is subtle by nature and size. This is understood from scriptural statements which declare that it goes out along the Nâḍis (nerves). So it is necessarily subtle or small in size. Its transparency explains why it is not obstructed by gross bodies, or is not seen when it passes out at death.

नोपमर्दनातः ॥ १० ॥

न Not उपमर्दन by the destruction अत: therefore.

10. Therefore (this subtle body is not destroyed) by the destruction (of the gross body).

अस्यैव च-उपपत्तेः-एष ऊष्मा ॥ ११ ॥

अस्य एव To this (fine body) alone च and उपपत्ते: because of possibility एष: this ऊष्मा (bodily) heat.

11. And to this (fine body) alone does this (bodily) heat belong, because this (only) is possible.

The bodily heat observed in living animals belongs to this subtle body and not to the gross body, for the heat is felt so long as there is life and not after that.

Topic 6: The Prâṇas of a knower of the Nirguṇa Brahman do not depart from the body at death.

प्रतिषेधादिति चेत्, न, शारीरात् ॥ १२ ॥

प्रतिषेधात् On account of denial इति चेत् if it be said न not so शारीरात् from the individual soul.

12. If it be said (that the Prâṇas of a knower of Brahman do not depart), on account of the Śruti denying it; (we say) not so, (because the scripture denies the departure of the Prâṇas) from the individual soul (and not from the body).

This Sûtra gives the view of the opponent.

"His Prâṇas do not depart" (Bṛ. 4. 4. 6). This text refers to a knower of the Nirguṇa Brahman. It says that his Prâṇas do not depart at death. The opponent holds that the denial of the departure of the Prâṇas is from the soul and not from the body. It says that the Prâṇas do not depart from the soul—not that they do not depart from the body, for in the latter case there will be no death at all. This is made all the more clear from the Mâdhyandina recension which says, "From him" etc. Therefore the soul of one who knows Brahman passes out of the body with the Prâṇas.

स्पष्टो ह्येकेषाम् ॥ १३ ॥

स्पष्ट: Clear हि for एकेषाम् of some (schools).

13. For (the denial of the departure) is clear (in the texts) of some (schools).

This Sûtra refutes the view of the previous one by connecting the denial to the body and not to the soul.

That the Prâṇas do not depart from the body is made clear from Śruti texts like " 'Yâjñavalkya,' said he, 'When this (liberated) man dies, do his Prâṇas go up from him, or do they not?' 'No, replied Yâjñavalkya, 'they merge in him only' " etc. (Bṛ. 3. 2. 11). Therefore we have to take even the Mâdhyandina reading 'from him' to refer to the body. It is not true that if the Prâṇas do not depart there will be no death, for they do not remain in the body, but get merged, which makes life impossible, and we say in common parlance that the person is dead. Moreover, if the Prâṇas did depart with the soul from the body, then a rebirth of such a soul would be inevitable, and consequently there would be no Liberation. So the Prâṇas do not depart from the body in the case of the knower of Brahman.

स्मर्यते च ॥ १४ ॥

स्मर्यते The Smṛti says (so) च and.

14. And the Smṛti (also) says (so).

"The gods themselves are perplexed, looking for the path of him who has no path" (Mbh. 12. 270. 22) which thus denies departure for the knower of Brahman.

Topic 7: The organs of the knower of the Nirguṇa Brahman get merged in It at death.

तानि परे, तथाह्याह ॥ १५ ॥

तानि Those परे in the Supreme Brahman तथा so हि for आह (the scripture) says.

15. Those (Prâṇas) (are merged) in the Supreme Brahman, for so (the scripture) says.

This Sûtra describes what happens to the Prâṇas (organs) and the fine essence of the gross elements in which they abide, in the case of a knower of Brahman who dies. These organs and the elements get merged in the Supreme Brahman. "The sixteen digits of this witness, the Puruṣa, having their goal in Him are dissolved on reaching Him" (Pr. 6. 5). The text, "All the fifteen parts of their body enter into their causes" etc. (Mu. 3. 2. 7) gives the end from a relative standpoint, according to which the body disintegrates and goes back to its cause, the elements. The former text speaks from a transcendental standpoint, according to which the whole aggregate is merged in Brahman, even as the illusory snake is merged in the rope when knowledge dawns.

Topic 8: The digits (Kalâs) of the knower of the Nirguṇa Brahman attain absolute non-distinction with Brahman at death.

अविभागः, वचनात् ॥ १६ ॥

अविभागः Non-distinction वचनात् on account of the statement (of the scriptures).

16. (Absolute) non-distinction (with Brahman

of the parts merged takes place) according to the statement (of the scriptures).

"Their names and forms are destroyed, and people speak of the Puruṣa only. Then he becomes devoid of digits and immortal" (Pr. 6. 5). The digits get absolutely merged in the Supreme Brahman. The merging in the case of the knower of Brahman is absolute, whereas in the case of an ordinary person it is not so; they exist in a fine potential state, the cause of future rebirth. But in the case of the knower of Brahman, Knowledge having destroyed ignorance, all these digits which are but its effects, get merged absolutely, without any chance of cropping up again.

Topic 9: The soul of the knower of the Saguṇa Brahman comes to the heart at the time of death and thence goes out through the Suṣumnâ.

तदोकोऽग्रज्वलनं तत्प्रकाशितद्वारः विद्यासामर्थ्यात् तच्छेषगत्यनु-
स्मृतियोगाच्च, हार्दानुगृहीताः शताधिकया ॥ १७ ॥

तत्-ओकः-अग्रज्वलनं The illumining of the top of its (soul's) abode (the heart) तत्-प्रकाशित-द्वारः with the passage illumined by this light विद्या-सामर्थ्यात् owing to the efficacy of knowledge तत्-शेष-गति-अनुस्मृति-योगात् because of the appropriateness of constant meditation of the way which is a part of that knowledge च and हार्दानुगृहीताः being favoured by Him who resides in the heart शताधिकया by the one that is beyond the hundred.

17. (When the soul of a knower of the Saguṇa Brahman is about to depart from the body, there is) the illumining of the top of its abode (the heart); with the passage (for the exit of the soul) illumined by this light (the soul departs), being favoured by Him who resides in the heart, along that nerve which is beyond the hundred (*i.e.* the hundred and first nerve or the Suṣumnâ) owing to the efficacy of the knowledge and the appropriateness of his constant meditation on the way which is a part of that knowledge.

This Sûtra describes the exit from the body of a knower of the Saguṇa Brahman. It has already been stated in Sûtra 7 that till the soul's entering on the path, the mode of departure of a knower of the Saguṇa Brahman and an ignorant man is the same. The Bṛhadâraṇyaka text describing the death of a person says, "When this self becomes weak and senseless, as it were, the organs come to it...it comes to the heart" (Bṛ. 4. 4. 1); again, "The top of the heart brightens. Through that brightened top the self departs, either through the eye or through the head, or through any other part of the body" (*Ibid.* 4. 4. 2). These texts show that at the time of death the soul together with the organs comes to the heart. At that moment the departing soul, on account of its past works, has a peculiar consciousness picturing to it its next life, and goes to the body which is revealed by that consciousness. This is what is referred to as the illumining of the top of the heart. With this particular consciousness the soul goes out, along one of the nerves that issue from the heart, to the eyes, or ears, or the skull, or other parts of the body, which it finally leaves through that particular exit. The question now is whether this departure is the same for a knower of the Saguṇa Brahman and an ordinary man. This Sûtra says that though the illumining of the top of the heart is common to both, yet the knower of the Saguṇa Brahman, through the grace of the Lord who abides in the heart, departs through the skull only, while others depart through other parts. This is consistent with his knowledge and constant meditation on the way out through the hundred and first nerve, the Suṣumnâ. The following text elucidates it: "There are a hundred and one nerves of the heart; one of them penetrates the head; going up along that, one attains Immortality; the others serving for departure in various directions" (Ch. 8. 6. 6).

Topic 10: The soul of a knower of the Saguṇa Brahman follows the rays of the sun after death and goes to Brahmaloka.

रश्म्यनुसारी ॥ १८ ॥

रश्मि-अनुसारी Following the rays.

18. (The soul of knower of the Saguṇa Brahman when he dies) follows the rays (of the sun).

In the Chândogya Upaniṣad we have, "... so do these rays of the sun go to both the worlds, this as well as the other. They proceed from the sun and enter into these nerves" (8. 6. 2); again, "When he thus departs from this body, then along these very rays he proceeds upwards" etc. (8. 6. 5). In these texts we learn that the soul of the knower of the Saguṇa Brahman, afte departing from the body along the Suṣumnâ, follow the rays of the sun. A doubt arises whether the soul o one who passes away in the night also follows the rays The Sûtra says that the soul, whether it departs in th night or during the day, follows the rays.

निशि न इति चेत्, न, संबन्धस्य यावद्देहभावित्वात्, दर्शयति च ॥ १९ ॥

निशि In the night न not इति चेत् if it be said न no संबन्धस्य यावत्-देह-भावित्वात् because the connection con tinues as long as the body lasts दर्शयति (the Śruti) declares च also.

19. If it be said (that the soul does) not (follow the rays) in the night, (we say) not so, because the connection (of the nerves and the rays) continues as long as the body lasts; (the Śruti) also declares (this).

The text quoted in the last Sûtra, Ch. 8. 6. 2, shows that the connection between the rays and the nerves lasts as long as the body lasts. So it is immaterial whether the soul passes out by day or by night. Moreover, the sun's rays continue even during the night, though we do not feel their presence owing to the fact that at night their number is limited. The Śruti also says, "Even by night the sun sheds his rays." The result of knowledge cannot be made to depend on the accident of death by day or night.

Topic 11: The soul of the knower of the Saguṇa Brahman goes to Brahmaloka even if he should die during the southern course of the sun.

अतश्चायनेऽपि दक्षिणे ॥ २० ॥

अत: For the same reason च and अयने during the sun's course अपि even दक्षिणे southern.

20. And for the same reason (the soul follows the rays) even during the sun's southern course.

An objection is raised by the opponent that the soul of the knower of Brahman who passes away during the southern course of the sun does not follow the rays to Brahmaloka, as both the Śruti and Smṛti say that only one who dies during the northern course of the sun goes there. Moreover, it is also written that Bhîṣma waited for the northern course of the sun to leave the body. This Sûtra says that for the same reason as mentioned in the last Sûtra, *i.e.* the unreasonableness of making the result of knowledge depend on the accident of death happening at a particular time, the knower of the Saguṇa Brahman goes to Brahmaloka even if he should die during the southern course of the sun. In the text, "Those who know thus . . . go to light, from light to day, from day to the bright half of the month, and from that to the six months of the northern course of the sun" (Ch. 5. 10. 1), the points in the northern course of the sun do not refer to any division of time but to deities as will be shown under 4. 3. 4. Bhîṣma's waiting, however, was for upholding approved custom and for showing that on account of his father's boon he could die at will.

योगिनः प्रति च स्मर्यते स्मार्ते चैते ॥ २१ ॥

योगिनः प्रति With respect to the Yogis च and स्मर्यते the Smṛti declares स्मार्ते belonging to the class of Smṛtis च and एते these two.

21. And (these times) the Smṛti declares with respect to the Yogis; and these two (Yoga and Sâṁkhya according to which they practise Sâdhanâ) are classed as Smṛtis (and not Śrutis).

In the Gîtâ we have passages which declare that persons who die during the day etc. do not return any more to this mortal world. *Vide* Gîta 8. 23, 24. On the strength of these texts, the opponent says that the decision of the previous Sûtra cannot be correct. This Sûtra refutes that objection saying that these details as to time mentioned in the Gîta apply only to Yogis who practise Sâdhanâ according to Yoga and Sâṁkhya systems; and these two are Smṛtis, not Śrutis. Hence the limitations as to time mentioned in them do not apply to those who meditate on the Saguṇa Brahman according to the Śruti texts.

CHAPTER IV

SECTION III

In the last section the departure of the soul of a knower of the Saguṇa Brahman by the path of the gods has been described. This section deals with the path itself.

Topic 1: The path connected with deities beginning with that of the flame is the only path to Brahmaloka.

अर्चिरादिना, तत्प्रथितेः ॥ १ ॥

अर्चिः-आदिना (On the path connected with deities) beginning with that of the flame तत्-प्रथितेः that being well known (from the Śruti).

1. (On the path connected with deities) beginning with that of the flame (the soul of the knower of the Saguṇa Brahman travels to Brahmaloka after death), that being well known (from the Śruti.)

In the last section it was stated that the knower of the Saguṇa Brahman travels by Devayâna or the path of the gods to Brahmaloka. About this path itself different texts make different declarations. The Chândogya and the Bṛhadâraṇyaka say that the departed soul of such a person reaches first the deity identified with the flame.

Vide Ch. 5. 10. 1 and Bṛ. 6. 2. 15. The Bṛhadâraṇyaka in connection with another Vidyâ says that it reaches the air. *Vide* Bṛ. 5. 10. 1. The Kauṣîtakî Upaniṣad says that it reaches the world of fire. *Vide* Kau. 1. 3. The Muṇḍaka says that it travels by the path of the sun. *Vide* Mu. 1. 2. 11. The question is whether these texts refer to different paths or are different descriptions of the same path, the path of the gods. The opponent holds that these texts refer to different paths to Brahmaloka. The Sûtra refutes this view and says that all the texts refer to and give only different particulars of the same path, the path connected with deities beginning with that identified with the flame. Why? On account of its being well known from the Śruti texts that this is the path for all knowers of Brahman. "Those who know this (Pañcâgni Vidyâ) and those who in the forest meditate with faith and penance, reach the deity identified with flame" etc. (Ch. 5. 10. 1) shows that this path connected with deities beginning with that of the flame belongs to all knowers of Brahman whatever be the Vidyâ through which they have attained that knowledge. Moreover, the goal attained, *viz* Brahmaloka, being the same in all cases, and there being no justification for regarding the path as different on account of their being treated in different chapters, since some part of the path is recognized in all texts, we have to conclude that all the texts refer to the same path, but give different particulars, which have all to be combined for a full description of the path.

Topic 2: The departing soul reaches the deity of the year and then the deity of the air.

वायुमब्दात्, अविशेषविशेषाभ्याम् ॥ २ ॥

वायुम् The deity of the air अब्दात् from the deity of the year अविशेष-विशेषाभ्याम् on account of the absence and presence of specification.

2. (The departed soul of a knower of the Saguṇa Brahman goes) from the deity of the year to the deity of the air, on account of the absence and presence of specification.

In the last Sûtra it was stated that the different texts give different particulars or stages of the same path. This Sûtra fixes the order of the stages. The Kauṣîtakî describes the path as follows: "This Upâsaka, having reached the path of the gods, reaches the world of Agni (fire), of Vâyu (air), of Varuṇa, of Indra, of Prajâpati, and then of Brahman" (Kau. 1. 3). Again the Chândogya Upaniṣad describes the path as follows: "They reach the deity identified with the flame, from him to the deity of the day, from him to the deity of the bright half of the month, from him to the deities identified with the sixth months of the northern path of the sun, from them to the deity of the year, from him to the deity of the sun, from him to the deity of the moon, from him to the deity of lightning" (Ch. 5. 10. 1).

In these two texts the first deity they reach is said to be the deity of the flame or fire. So the starting point is clearly pointed out by both texts, for they say that having reached the path of the gods the departed souls reach this deity. Combining these two texts we have to place the deity of air in between the deity of the year and the deity of the sun. Why? Because of the absence and presence of specification. "When a man departs from this world, he reaches the (deity identified with) air, *which makes an opening for him....He goes upwards through that and reaches the (deity of the) sun*" (Bṛ. 5. 10. 1). This text fixes that air comes immediately before the sun because we perceive a regular order of succession. But as regards air coming after the deity of the flame there is no specification, but simply a statement: "He comes from the world of fire to that of air." In between these two stages we have several other stages which the Chândogya text mentions. Again in the text, "From the deities identified with the six months in which the sun travels northward he reaches the deity identified with the world of the gods" (Bṛ. 6. 2. 15). To keep the immediate sequence of the deity identified with air and that identified with the sun, we must understand that the soul passes from the deity of the world of the gods to the deity of the air. Again in the texts of the Chândogya and the Bṛhadâraṇyaka, the deity of the world of the gods is not mentioned in the former and the deity of the year in the latter. Both have to be included in the full description of the path, and since the year is connected with the months, the deity of the year precedes the deity of the world of the gods.

Topic 3: After reaching the deity identified with lightning the soul reaches the world of Varuṇa.

तडितोऽधि वरुणः, संबन्धात् ॥ ३ ॥

तडितोऽधि After the deity of lightning वरुण: (comes) Varuṇa (rain-god) संबन्धात on account of the connection.

3. After (reaching) the deity of lightning (the soul reaches) Varuṇa, on account of the connection (between the two).

The Chândogya text reads, "From the sun to the moon, from moon to lightning." The Kauṣîtakî text reads, 'From Vâyu to Varuṇa." Combining these two texts we have to place Varuṇa after lightning, on account of the connection between the two. Varuṇa is the god of rain, and lightning precedes rain. So after lightning comes Varuṇa. And after Varuṇa come Indra and Prajâpati, for there is no other place for them, and the Kauṣîtakî text also puts them there.

So the complete enumeration of the stages of the path of the gods is as follows: First the deity of the flame or fire, then the deity of the day, the deity of the bright half of the month, the deities of the six months when the sun travels to the north, the deity of the year, the deity of the world of gods, the deity of the air, the sun, the moon, the deity of lightning, the world of Varuṇa, the world of Indra, the world of Prajâpati, and finally Brahmaloka.

Topic 4: Flame etc. referred to in the text describing the path of the gods mean deities identified with the flame etc. which conduct the soul stage after stage till Brahmaloka is reached.

आतिवाहिकाः, तल्लिङ्गात् ॥ ४ ॥

आतिवाहिका: (These are) deities conducting the soul
तत्-लिङ्गात् on account of indicatory marks of that

4. (These are) deities conducting the soul (on the path of the gods), on account of indicatory marks to that effect.

In the texts cited in the previous Sûtras, flame, bright half of the month, year, etc. are the deities identified with these, which receive the departed soul and conduct it on its way to Brahmaloka. That deities are meant here, and not marks or places of enjoyment, is indicated by the text of the Chândogya, which ends thus: "From the moon to the lightning. Then a being who is not a man leads them to Brahman" (Ch. 4. 15. 5, 5. 10. 1). This text shows that unlike the previous guides who were more or less human, this particular guide is not human in nature.

उभयव्यामोहात्तत्सिद्धेः ॥ ५ ॥

उभय-व्यामोहात् From the benumbed state of both
तत्-सिद्धेः: that is established.

5. (That deities are meant in those texts) is established, because both (*i.e.* the traveller and the path) are benumbed (*i.e.* unconscious).

The departed souls, because their organs etc. are withdrawn into the mind, are incapable of guiding themselves. And the flame etc. being without intelligence cannot guide the souls. Hence it is proved that intelligent deities identified with the flame etc. guide the souls to Brahmaloka. Moreover, as the organs of the departed souls are withdrawn into the mind, they cannot enjoy, and so flame and the rest cannot be worlds where they enjoy.

वैद्युतेनैव ततः, तच्छ्रुतेः ॥ ६ ॥

वैद्युतेन By (the superhuman) guide connected with lightning एव alone ततः from thence तत्-श्रुतेः that being known from the Śruti.

6. From thence (the souls are guided) by the very same (superhuman) person who comes to lightning, that being known from the Śruti.

After they have reached the deity identified with lightning, they are led by that very superhuman person who takes charge of them from the deity of lightning to Brahmaloka through the worlds of Varuṇa, Indra, and Prajâpati. This is known from Ch. 4. 15. 5, 5. 10. 1, and Bṛ. 6. 2. 15. Varuṇa and others do not actually guide the souls like the earlier guides, since the superhuman person guides them all through after lightning up to Brahmaloka. They only favour the souls either by not obstructing or helping them in some way.

Therefore it is established that by flame etc. deities are meant.

Topic 5: The Brahman to which the departed souls go by the path of the gods is the Saguṇa Brahman.

कार्यं बादरिः, अस्य गत्युपपत्तेः ॥ ७ ॥

कार्यं The relative (Brahman) बादरिः Bâdari अस्य its गति-उपपत्तेः on account of the possibility of being the goal.

7. The relative (Brahman) (is attained by the soul going by the path of the gods), (so says) Bâdari on account of the possibility of its being the goal (of a journey).

In the previous Sûtra the way was discussed. Now from this Sûtra onwards the discussion is about the goal reached. The Chândogya text quoted in connection with the way, says, "Then a being who is not a man leads them to Brahman" (Ch. 5. 10. 1). The question is whether this Brahman is the Saguṇa Brahman or the Supreme Brahman. Bâdari says it is the Saguṇa Brahman, for such a journey is possible only with respect to the Saguṇa Brahman, which is finite and therefore occupies a particular place to which the souls may go. But it is not possible with respect to the Nirguṇa Brahman, which is all-pervading.

विशेषितत्वाच्च ॥ ८ ॥

विशेषितत्वात् On account of the qualification च and.

8. And on account of the qualification (with respect to this Brahman in another text).

"And conducts them to the *worlds* of Brahman" (Bṛ. 6. 2. 15). The plural number is not possible with respect to the Supreme Brahman, while it is possible in the case of the Saguṇa Brahman, which may abide in different conditions.

सामीप्यात् तु तद्व्यपदेशः ॥ ९ ॥

सामीप्यात् On account of the nearness तु but तत्-व्यपदेशः (its) designation as that.

9. But on account of the nearness (of the Saguṇa Brahman to the Supreme Brahman, it is) designated as that (Supreme Brahman).

'But' sets aside any doubt that may arise on account of the word 'Brahman' being used for the Saguṇa Brahman in the Chândogya text. This designation, the Sûtra says, is because of the nearness of the Saguṇa Brahman to the Supreme Brahman.

कार्यात्यये तदध्यक्षेण सहातः परम्, अभिधानात् ॥ १० ॥

कार्य-अत्यये On the dissolution of the Brahmaloka तत्-अध्यक्षेण सह along with the ruler of that world (*i.e.* Supreme Brahman) अतः परम् higher than that (*i.e.* the Saguṇa Brahman) अभिधानात् on account of the declaration of the Śruti.

10. On the dissolution of the Brahmaloka (the souls attain), along with the ruler of that world, what is higher than that (*i.e.* the Supreme Brahman), on account of the declaration of the Śruti.

If the souls going by the path of the gods reach the Saguṇa Brahman then how can a statement like "They no more return to this world" (Bṛ. 6. 2. 15) be made with respect to them, as there can be no permanency anywhere apart from the Supreme Brahman? This Sûtra explains it saying that at the dissolution of the Brahmaloka the souls, which by that time have attained Knowledge, along with the Saguṇa Brahman attain what is higher than the Saguṇa Brahman, *i.e.* the Supreme Brahman. So the Śruti texts declare.

स्मृतेश्च ॥ ११ ॥

स्मृते: On account of the Smṛti च and.

11. And on account of the Smṛti (texts supporting this view).

परं जैमिनि॰, मुख्यत्वात् ॥ १२ ॥

परं The Supreme (Brahman) जैमिनि: (so says) Jaimini मुख्यत्वात् on account of that being the primary meaning (of the word 'Brahman').

12. The Supreme (Brahman) (is attained by the souls going by the path of the gods), (so says) Jaimini, on account of that being the primary meaning (of the word 'Brahman').

Sûtras 12-14 give a *prima facie* view of the matter.

Jaimini thinks that the word 'Brahman' in the Chândogya text refers to the Supreme Brahman, as that is the primary meaning of the word.

दर्शनाच्च ॥ १३ ॥

दर्शनात् On account of the Śruti texts च and.

13. And because the Śruti declares that.

"Going upwards by that he reaches immortality" (Ch. 8. 6. 6; Ka. 2. 6. 16). This text says that the soul which passes out of the body by the nerve Suṣumnâ reaches immortality, and this can be attained only in the Supreme Brahman.

न च कार्ये प्रतिपत्त्यभिसन्धिः ॥ १४ ॥

न Not च and कार्ये in the Saguṇa Brahman प्रतिपत्ति-अभिसन्धिः the desire to attain Brahman.

14. And the desire to attain Brahman (which an Upâsaka has at the time of death can) not (be with respect to) the Saguṇa Brahman.

"I come to the assembly-house of Prajâpati" (Ch. 8. 14. 1). This desire to attain 'the house' cannot be with respect to the Saguṇa Brahman, but is appropriate only with respect to the Supreme Brahman. For the text quoted says earlier, "And that within which these (names and forms) are contained is *Brahman,*" where the Supreme Brahman is referred to.

Sûtras 12-14 give the opponent's view against what has been said in Sûtras 7-11. The arguments of Sûtras 12-14 are refuted thus: The Brahman attained by those who go by the path of the gods cannot be the Supreme

Brahman. They attain only the Saguṇa Brahman. The Supreme Brahman is all-pervading, the Inner Self of all. Such a Brahman cannot be attained, for It is the Self of everyone. Journey or attainment is possible only where there is difference, where the attainer is different from the thing attained. What is called realization of the Supreme Brahman is nothing but the removal of ignorance about It. In such a realization there is no going or attaining. When the ignorance is removed Brahman manifests Itself. But the attainment of Brahman spoken of in the texts connected with the path of the gods is not merely the removal of ignorance but actual. Such an attainment is not possible with respect to the Supreme Brahman. Again the passage, "I enter the assembly-house of Prajâpati", etc. can be separated from what precedes and be connected with the Saguna Brahman. The fact that Ch. 8. 14. 1 says, "I am the glory of the Brâhmaṇas, of the kings" cannot make it refer to the Nirguṇa Brahman, for the Saguṇa Brahman can also be said to be the Self of all, as we find in texts like "He to whom all works, all desires belong" etc. (Ch. 3. 14. 2). The reference to the journey to Brahman, which belongs to the sphere of relative knowledge, in a chapter which deals with Supreme Knowledge is only by way of glorification of the latter. Therefore the view expressed in Sûtras 7-11 by Bâdari is the correct one.

Topic 6: Only those who have worshipped the Saguṇa Brahman without a symbol attain Brahmaloka..

अप्रतीकालम्बनान्नयतीति बादरायणः, उभयथाऽदोषात्,
तत्क्रतुश्च ॥ १५ ॥

अप्रतीक-आलम्बनात् Those who do not use a symbol (of Brahman) in their meditations नयति (the superhuman being) leads इति बादरायणः so says Bâdarâyaṇa उभयथा if this distinction is made अदोषात् there being no contradiction तत्-क्रतुः as is the meditation on that (so does one become) च and.

15. Bâdarâyaṇa says that (the superhuman being) leads (to Brahmaloka only) those who do not use a symbol (of Brahman) in their meditations, there being no contradiction if this distinction is made, and (it being construed by the principle) as is the meditation on that (so does one become).

The question is raised whether all worshippers of the Saguṇa Brahman go to the Brahmaloka, being led by the superhuman being mentioned in Ch. 4. 15. 5. The opponent holds that they do, according to 3. 3. 31 *ante,* where it is expressly stated that all, whatever be their Vidyâ, go to Brahmaloka. This Sûtra says that only those worshippers of the Saguṇa Brahman who do not use any symbol of Brahman in their meditation go there. This, however, does not contradict what is said in 3. 3. 31 if we understand that by 'all' are meant all those worshippers who do not take the help of any symbol. Moreover, this view is justified by the Śruti and Smṛti declarations which say, "In whatever form they meditate on Him, that they become." In the worship of the symbols the meditations are not fixed on Brahman, the symbols being the chief thing in them, and so the worshipper does not attain Brahmaloka. But the case of one who worships the five fires is different, as there is a direct scriptural statement saying that he goes to Brahmaloka. Where there is no such direct scriptural statement, we have to hold that only those whose object of meditation is Brahman, go to Brahmaloka, not others.

विशेषं च दर्शयति ॥ १६ ॥

विशेषं Difference च and दर्शयति the scripture declares

16. And the scripture declares a difference (with respect to meditations on symbols).

"One who meditates upon name as Brahman becomes independent so far as name reaches" (Ch. 7. 1. 5); "One who meditates upon speech as Brahman becomes independent so far as speech reaches" (Ch. 7. 2. 2). In these texts the Śruti tells of different results according to difference in the symbols. This is possible because the meditations depend on symbols, while there could be no such difference in results if they depended on the one non-different Brahman. Hence it is clear that those who use symbols for their meditations cannot go to Brahmaloka like those who meditate on the Saguṇa Brahman.

CHAPTER IV

Section IV

In the last section the attainment of Brahmaloka by the worshippers of the Saguṇa Brahman has been dealt with. This section deals with the realization of the Supreme Brahman by Its worshippers.

Topic 1: The released soul does not acquire anything new but only manifests its true nature.

संपद्याविर्भावः, स्वेनशब्दात् ॥ १ ॥

संपद्य Having attained आविर्भाव: there is manifestation (of its real nature) स्वेनशब्दात from the word 'own'.

1. (When the Jîva) has attained (the highest light) there is manifestation (of its real nature), as we know from the word 'own'

"Now this serene and happy being, after having risen from this body, and having attained the highest light, reaches its own true form" (Ch. 8. 3. 4). The opponent explains this text as follows: The individual soul which has got rid of its identification with the three bodies, *viz* gross, subtle, and causal, after attaining Brahman exists in the state of Liberation. This Liberation was not a pre-existent thing, but something that is newly acquired like heaven, as the word 'reaches' in the text clearly shows. Therefore Liberation is something new that is acquired by the Jîva. The Sûtra refutes this view and says that the word 'own' shows that Liberation was a pre-existent thing. The Jîva manifests its own nature, *i.e.* its real nature, which was so long covered with ignorance. This is its attainment of Liberation. It is nothing that is newly acquired.

मुक्तः, प्रतिज्ञानात् ॥ २ ॥

मुक्तः Released प्रतिज्ञानात् from the premiss.

2. (The Self which manifests Its true nature attains) Liberation, (as is known) from the premiss (made in the scriptures).

If Liberation is nothing new that is acquired by the Jîva, then what is its difference from bondage? The Jîva in the state of bondage was subject to the three states of wakefulness, dream, and deep-sleep, and was experiencing happiness and misery, imagining itself to be finite. On being freed from all these misconceptions it realizes its true nature, which is Absolute Bliss. This removal of all misconceptions is what is known as Liberation. Between these two states there is a world of difference. How is it known that in this state the Jîva is liberated? From the premiss made in the scriptures—says the Sûtra. "I will explain It to you further" (Ch. 8. 9. 3, 8. 10. 4, 8. 11. 3)—here the Śruti proposes to expound that Self which is free from all imperfections, and it begins thus: "The being without the body is not touched by pleasure and pain" (Ch. 8. 12. 1) and concludes, "Thus does this serene being rising above its body and having reached the highest light, appear in its own true nature" (Ch. 8. 12. 3).

आत्मा, प्रकरणात् ॥ ३ ॥

आत्मा The Supreme Self प्रकरणात् on account of the context.

3. (The 'light' attained by the Jîva is) the Supreme Self; on account of the context.

The 'Light' attained by the Jîva which is referred to in the Ch. 8. 3. 4 is the Supreme Self, and not any physical light, for the Self is the subject-matter which is introduced thus: "The Self which is free from evil, undecaying," etc. (Ch. 8. 7. 1). The word 'light' is also used to denote the Self in texts like, "Upon that immortal Light of all lights the gods meditate as longevity" (Bṛ. 4. 4. 16).

Topic 2: The relation of the released soul with Brahman is one of non-separation.

अविभागेन, दृष्टत्वात् ॥ ४ ॥

अविभागेन As inseparable दृष्टत्वात् for it is so seen from the scriptures.

4. (The Jîva in the state of Liberation exists) as inseparable (from Brahman), for it is so seen from the scriptures.

The question is raised whether the Jîva in the state of Liberation exists as different from Brahman or as one with, and inseparable from, It. The Sûtra says that it exists as inseparable from Brahman, for the scriptures say so. "That thou art" (Ch. 6. 8. 7); "I am Brahman" (Bṛ. 1. 4. 10); "Being but Brahman, he is merged in Brahman" (Ch. 4. 4. 6)—all these texts declare that the released soul is identical with Brahman. Passages which speak of difference have to be explained in a secondary sense as expressing unity.

Topic 3: Characteristics of the soul that has attained the Nirguṇa Brahman.

ब्राह्मेण जैमिनिः, उपन्यासादिभ्यः ॥ ५ ॥

ब्राह्मेण As possessed of the attributes of Brahman जैमिनिः (so says) Jaimini उपन्यासादिभ्यः on account of the reference etc.

5. (The liberated soul exists) as possessed of the attributes of Brahman; (so says) Jaimini, on account of the reference etc.

It has been said that the liberated soul attains Brahman. But Brahman has two aspects; one the unconditioned aspect as Pure Intelligence and Knowledge; the other as described in the Chândogya 8. 7. 1. "The Self which is free from evil, undecaying, undying, free from sorrow, hunger and thirst, with true desires and volition" etc. The question is, which aspect does the liberated soul attain? Jaimini says that it is the conditioned aspect. Why? On account of the reference to the nature of the Self as being such in the text cited. 'Etc.' includes Vidhi and Vyapadeśa. The Vidhi or injunction referred to is, "That is to be sought after," which the same Chândogya text enjoins later on, and Vyapadeśa or assertion is the mention of the qualities of omniscience and omnipotence in the same text—"Obtains all worlds and all desires." On these grounds Jaimini thinks that the liberated soul attains the conditioned aspect of Brahman.

चितितन्मात्रेण, तदात्मकत्वादित्यौडुलोमिः ॥ ६ ॥

चिति-तन्मात्रेण Solely as Pure Intelligence तत् आत्मकत्वात् that being its true nature इति thus औडुलोमिः Auḍulomi (thinks).

6. (The liberated soul exists) solely as Pure Intelligence, that being its true nature; thus Auḍulomi (thinks).

This Sûtra gives another view about the liberated state, which is that of the sage Auḍulomi. The soul being solely of the nature of Pure Intelligence, it exists as such in the liberated state. Qualities like being free from sin and omniscience are fanciful, and mean only the absence of sin etc.

एवमप्युपन्यासात् पूर्वभावादविरोधं बादरायणः ॥ ७ ॥

एवम् Thus अपि even उपन्यासात् on account of reference पूर्वभावात् the former qualities existing अविरोधं there is no contradiction बादरायणः (so says) Bâdarâyaṇa.

7. Even if it be so (*i.e.* if the liberated soul exists as Pure Intelligence), on account of former qualities existing owing to reference (we can accept them from the relative standpoint, for) there is no contradiction (between the two); (so thinks) Bâdarâyaṇa.

Even though from the absolute standpoint the nature of the liberated soul is Pure Intelligence, yet from the relative standpoint qualities referred to by Jaimini can be accepted, as this does not contradict Auḍulomi's view. The released soul never thinks of itself as omniscient, omnipotent, etc., but exists as Pure Intelligence. But from our relative standpoint we can say of such a released soul as being omniscient etc., because Pure Intelligence is beyond our conception. The two views describe the liberated soul from two different standpoints, and so there is no contradiction between the two. So says Bâdarâyaṇa.

Topic 4: The soul which has attained the Saguṇa Brahman effects its desires by mere will.

संकल्पादेव तु, तच्छ्रुतेः ॥ ८ ॥

संकल्पात् Through will एव only तु but तत्-श्रुतेः on account of the scriptures saying that.

8. But through mere will (the released souls attain their purpose), for the scriptures say so.

The question of those who attain Brahmaloka through the worship of the Saguṇa Brahman by means of Vidyâs like the Dahara Vidyâ is taken up for discussion in this Sûtra. In this Vidyâ it is said, "If he be desirous of the world of the fathers, by his mere will they come to him" (Ch. 8. 2. 1). The question is whether will alone suffices to get the result, or a further operative cause is necessary. This Sûtra says that by mere will the result comes, for the Śruti so declares. The will of the released is different from our will, and has the power of producing results without any operative cause.

अत एव चानन्याधिपतिः ॥ ९ ॥

अतः एव For the very reason च and अनन्याधिपतिः he is without a lord.

9. And for this very reason the released soul is without a lord.

A liberated soul is master of himself. "For them there is freedom in all worlds" (Ch. 8. 1. 6).

Topic 5: A released soul which has attained Brahmaloka can exist with or without a body according to its liking.

अभावं बादरिः, आह ह्येवम् ॥ १० ॥

अभावं Absence (of body and organs) बादरिः Bâdari (considers) आह (the Śruti) says हि because एवम् thus.

10. There is absence (of body and organs, in the case of the released souls) (considers) Bâdari, because (the scripture) says thus.

In the previous Sûtra it was told that if one attains Brahmaloka, by his mere wish things come to pass. This shows that that soul possesses a mind. The question naturally arises whether it possesses a body and the organs. Bâdari says that it does not, for the scripture says so. "And it is by means of this divine eye of the mind that he sees the desires and rejoices" (Ch. 8. 12. 5), which shows that it possesses only the mind and not the organs etc.

भावं जैमिनिः, विकल्पामननात् ॥ ११ ॥

भावं Existence जैमिनि: Jaimini विकल्प-आमननात because the scripture declares (the capacity to assume) diverse forms.

11. (The released soul) possesses (a body and the organs), considers Jaimini, because the scriptures declare (the capacity on the part of such a soul to assume) diverse forms.

"He being one becomes three, five, seven, nine" (Ch. 7. 26. 2). This text says that a released soul can assume more than one form, which shows that it possesses besides the mind, a body and the organs. This is the view of Jaimini.

द्वादशाहवदुभयविधं बादरायणोऽतः ॥ १२ ॥

द्वादशाहवत् Like the twelve days' sacrifice उभयविधं (is) of both kinds बादरायण: Bâdarâyaṇa अत: from this.

12. From this Bâdarâyaṇa (surmises) (that the released soul is) of both kinds, like the twelve days' sacrifice.

From the two-fold declaration of the scriptures Bâdarâyaṇa thinks that a released soul which has attained Brahmaloka can exist both ways—with or without a body according to its liking. It is like the twelve days' sacrifice, which is called a Sattra as well as an Ahîna sacrifice.

तन्वभावे संध्यवत्, उपपत्तेः ॥ १३ ॥

तनु-अभावे In the absence of a body संध्यवत् as in dreams, (which stand midway between waking and deep-sleep) उपपत्ते: this being reasonable.

13. In the absence of a body (the fulfilment of desires is possible) as in dreams, since this is reasonable.

भावे जाग्रद्वत् ॥ १४ ॥

भावे When the body exists जाग्रत्-वत् as in the waking state.

14. When the body exists (the fulfilment of desires is) as in the waking state.

Topic 6: The released soul which has attained the Saguṇa Brahman can animate several bodies at the same time.

प्रदीपवदावेशः, तथा हि दर्शयति ॥ १५ ॥

प्रदीपवत् Like a flame आवेशः animating तथा so हि because दर्शयति the scripture shows.

15. (The released soul's) animating (different bodies) is like that of a flame, because so the scripture shows.

In Sûtra 11 it was stated that a liberated soul can assume many bodies at the same time for enjoyment. The opponent holds that this is useless, as enjoyment is possible only in that body in which the soul and mind exist, while other bodies are lifeless puppets, since the soul and mind, which cannot be divided, cannot exist in more than one body. The Sûtra refutes this view and says that the other bodies are not lifeless puppets, for a released soul can, on account of its power, animate all these bodies, just as the flame of a lamp can enter into different wicks lighted from it. The soul through its powers creates bodies with internal organs corresponding to the original internal organs, and being limited by these, divides itself as many. Hence all the created bodies have a soul, which makes enjoyment through all of these possible. This we get from the scriptures.

स्वाप्ययसंपत्त्योरन्यतरापेक्षम्, आविष्कृतं हि ॥ १६ ॥

स्वाप्यय-संपत्त्योः Of deep-sleep and absolute union (with Brahman) **अन्यतर-अपेक्षम्** having in view either of these two **आविष्कृत** this is made clear (by the Śruti) **हि** for.

16. (The declaration of absence of all cognition is made) having in view either of the two states, *viz* deep-sleep and absolute union (with Brahman), for this is made clear (by the scriptures).

"What should one know and through what" (Bṛ 2. 4. 14); "But there is not that second thing separate from it which it can know" (*Ibid.* 4. 3. 30); "It becomes like water, one, the witness, and without a second" (*Ibid.* 4. 3. 32). These texts deny cognition to a released soul; so how is it possible for a released soul to assume several bodies and enjoy—says the opponent. This Sûtra says that these texts refer either to the state of deep-sleep or to that of Liberation, in which the soul attains absolute union with the Nirguṇa Brahman, as is made clear by the scriptures from the context in each case. But what we have been discussing in the previous Sûtras is the case of one who has attained not absolute union with Brahman, but only Brahmaloka. This state is quite different from the other two states, and as such cognition is possible in it, there being diversity, as also enjoyment, even as in heaven, the difference being that from Brahmaloka one does not return to this earth, whereas from heaven one returns to this mortal world after the exhaustion of the virtue which raised him to the status of a god.

Topic 7: The released soul which has attained Brahmaloka has all the lordly powers except the power of creation etc.

जगद्व्यापारवर्जम् प्रकरणात्, असन्निहितत्वाच्च ॥ १७ ॥

जगद्व्यापारवर्जम् Except the power of creation etc. प्रकरणात् on account of (Īśvara being) the subject-matter असन्निहितत्वात् on account of (released souls) not being mentioned च and.

17. (The released soul attains all lordly powers) except the power of creation etc., on account of (Īśvara being) the subject-matter (of all texts where creation etc. are described), and (the released souls) not being mentioned (in that connection).

The question is raised whether those who by worshipping the qualified Brahman attain Brahmaloka and lordly powers, have limited or unlimited powers. The opponent holds that it should be unlimited because of the scriptural texts, "They can roam at will in all the worlds" (Ch. 7. 25. 2, 8. 1. 6); "To him all the gods offer worship" (Tai. 1. 5). This Sûtra says that the released souls attain lordly powers without the power of creating, preserving, and destroying the universe. Barring this power they get all other powers. Why? Because Īśvara is the subject-matter of all the texts dealing with creation etc., while the liberated souls are not mentioned at all in this connection. Moreover, this would lead to many Īśvaras, which may give rise to a conflict of wills with respect to creation etc. Therefore the powers of the liberated souls are not absolute but limited, and are dependent on the will of Īśvara.

प्रत्यक्षोपदेशादितिचेत्, न, आधिकारिकमण्डलस्थोक्तेः ॥ १८ ॥

प्रत्यक्ष-उपदेशात् On account of direct teaching इति-चेत् if it be said न not आधिकारिकमण्डलस्थ-उक्तेः because the scripture declares (that the soul attains Him) who entrusts the sun etc. (with their offices) and resides in those spheres.

18. If it be said (that the released soul attains absolute powers) on account of direct teaching (of the scriptures), (we say) no, for the scriptures declare (that the released soul attains Him) who entrusts the sun etc. (with their offices) and resides in those spheres.

"He becomes the lord of himself" (Tai. 1. 6). From the direct teaching of the Śruti the opponent holds that the released soul attains absolute powers. The Sûtra says that his powers depend on the Lord, for the text cited further on says, "He attains the Lord of the mind", the Lord who abides in spheres like the sun etc. and entrusts the sun etc. with offices. Therefore from this latter part of the text it is clear that the released soul gets its powers from the Lord and depends on Him. Hence its powers are not unlimited.

विकारावर्ति च तथा हि, स्थितिमाह ॥ १९ ॥

विकार-अवर्ति Which is beyond all effected things च and तथा so हि because स्थितिम् existence आह the scripture declares.

19. And (there is a form of the Supreme Lord) which is beyond all created things, because so the

scripture declares (His) existence (in a two-fold form).

"Such is the greatness of it; greater than it is the Puruṣa. One foot of His is all beings. His (other) three feet are what is immortal in heaven" (Ch. 3. 12. 6). This text declares that the Supreme Lord abides in two forms, the transcendental and the relative. Now he who worships the Lord in His relative aspect does not attain the transcendental aspect, for the Śruti says, "As one meditates upon That, so one becomes." Similarly, since the worshipper is not able to comprehend the relative aspect of the Lord in full, as possessed of infinite attributes and powers, but is able to comprehended Him only partially, he attains only limited powers, and not unlimited powers like the Lord Himself.

दर्शयतश्चैवं प्रत्यक्षानुमाने ॥ २० ॥

दर्शयत: (The two) show च and एवं thus प्रत्यक्ष-अनुमाने perception and inference.

20. And thus perception and inference show.

This Sûtra says that the transcendental aspect of the Lord is established by both the Śruti and Smṛti. That form which the previous Sûtra cited merely as an example, this Sûtra establishes on the authority of the Śruti and Smṛti. "There the sun shines not, nor the moon, nor stars" etc. (Mu. 2. 2. 10): "That the sun illumines not, nor the moon, nor the fire" etc. (Gîtâ, 15. 6).

भोगमात्रसाम्यलिङ्गाच्च ॥ २१ ॥

भोगमात-साम्य-लिङ्गात् Because of indications of equality with respect to enjoyment only च and.

21. And because of the indications (in the scriptures) of equality (of the released soul with the Lord) only with respect to enjoyment.

That the powers of the released soul are not unlimited is also known from the indications in the Śruti that the equality of these souls with the Lord is only with respect to enjoyment, and not with respect to creation etc. "As all beings take care of this Deity, so do they take care of him" (Bṛ. 1. 5. 20); "Through it he attains identity with this Deity, or lives in the same world with it" (*Ibid.* 1. 5. 23). All these texts describe equality only with respect to enjoyment, and mention nothing as regards creation etc.

अनावृत्तिः शब्दात्, अनावृत्तिः शब्दात् ॥ २२ ॥

अनावृत्तिः Non-return शब्दात् on account of scriptural declaration.

22. (There is) no return (for these released souls); on account of scriptural declaration (to that effect).

If the powers of the released souls are limited, then like all limited things they, too, will come to an end, and consequently the released souls will have to come back from Brahmaloka to this mortal world—says the opponent. This Sûtra refutes such a contingency on scriptural authority. Those who go to Brahmaloka by the path of the gods do not return from there. "Going up by that way, one reaches immortality" (Ch. 8. 6. 6); "They no more return to this world" (Bṛ. 6. 2. 15).

The repetition of the words "No return" etc. is to show that the book is finished.

INDEX TO SUTRAS

GENERAL INDEX

Advaita Vedânta, does not uphold Pantheism, 83
 See also Vedânta
Adhyâsa (Superimposition), 1-16
 objections against, answered, 3-7
 is due to ignorance, 6
 defined by Śaṅkara, 7-10
 according to others, 10-12
 the basis of our experience, 12-14
Adṛṣṭa (the Unseen Principle) of the Vaiśeṣikas, 183 ff.
 in what does it inhere, 183
 cannot be the cause of the first motion of the atoms, 183
 yields fruit of actions at some future time, 410
Agnihotra, 323, 377
Agnirahasya, the fires in, constitute a separate Vidyâ, 356-62
Air, springs from ether, 213
 the cause of fire, 215
 See also Vâyu
Ajâ, is not the Pradhâna but causal matter, 123-5
Ajahat, Lakṣaṇâ, 271
Ajâtaśatru, 130
Ākâśa (Ether), Brahman is to be understood by the word, 47-8, 89
 the small, in the heart, is Brahman, 92-8
 external and internal, 93, 95-6
Ākâśa, the small, the Jîva retires to, in deep-sleep, 93-4
 which reveals names and forms is Brahman, 113-14
 cannot be a nonentity, 194
 not eternal, 209-13
 the cause of air 213-14
Akṣara (Imperishable), is Brahman, 89-91
Ālayavijñâna, 199-200
Ānandamaya, *see* "Self consisting of bliss"
Antaḥkaraṇa (the internal organ), the necessity of accepting an, 232
Apūrva, 266-7, 313-14, 415
Āśmarathya, his views, 80, 134, 136
Āśramas, all the four, enjoined by the scriptures, 384, 404-5
 the duties of, compulsory, 393-5
 persons not belonging to any of the, are also entitled to Knowledge, 395-7
Ātharvaṇikas, their rite of carrying fire on the head, 319
Ativâdin, who is an, 88
Ātman, as limited by the Upâdhis is atomic etc., 229, 236
 is changeless, 232
 knowledge of, gives Freedom, 327-8
 See also Self, Soul
Atoms, as the First Cause, 153, 203
 refutation of the atomic theory of the Vaiśeṣikas, 140, 153-4, 181-7
Ātreya, 401
Avidyâ (Ignorance) the cause of all duality, 1-2
 defined, 12-14
 the means of right knowledge and the scriptural texts belong to the sphere of, 13
 See also Mâyâ, Nescience
Avyakta (the Undeveloped, in Kaṭha 1.3.10-11 means causal substance, and not the Pradhâna, 116 ff., 122-3
 is dependent on the Supreme Lord, 119-20

as the person in the sun and the eye, 45-6, 67-71
limitations are imagined in, for Upâsanâ, 45-6, 68-9, 308-9
as Ākâśa (Ether), 47-8
as Prâṇa, 48-9, 53-7
as Light, 49
as the metre Gâyatri, 51-2
as the Being consisting of mind, 58-64
smallness of, 62
as abiding in the heart, 63
does not experience pleasure or pain, 63, 240-1
and the individual soul, 63, 161-2, 223, 238-41
as the Eater, 64-5
as distinguished by Bliss, 70
is the Ruler within, 71-3
is Vaiśvânara, 75-81
as the resting place of heaven, earth, etc., 82-8
all is, 83
is not manifold, 83
as the Witness, 86
is Bhūman, 86-9
is Truth, 89
is Akṣara (Imperishable), 89-91
the Highest Person in Pr. 5.5 is, 91-2
as "the small Ākâśa", 92-8
body is the city of, 93
the light of all lights, 98-9, 112-13
as the person of the size of the thumb, 99-101
the Prâṇa in Ka. 2. 6. 2 is, 112
as the revealer of names and forms, 113-14
the Nature of the Supreme, 113, 293-312
as the Self consisting of knowledge, 114-15
wished to be many, 129
the Self of all, 129
Kau. 4. 19 refers to, 130-2
is the Self to be seen through hearing etc., 132-7
is both the material and efficient cause of the world, 137-40, 163-5, 173
is the cause of the world though of a different nature from it, 145-53
is existence itself, 148, 214
objections to, being the cause of the world, refuted, 145-53, 154-73, 182-3
has only apparently changed into the world, 150, 166-7, 173
the individual soul an image of, in the mind, 155
is realized in Samâdhi, 156, 303-4
world is non-different from, 157, 161
the world exists in, potentially, during Pralaya, 160
the Cause through Mâyâ, 167
the power of Mâyâ of, established, 168
creative through sportive impulse, 169-70
partiality or cruelty cannot be attributed to, 170-2
is endowed with all the attributes necessary for creation, 173
the material and efficient cause of the world, 203-6
everything orginates from, 207
is not created, 214-15
elements become creative through the agency of, 217-18
at Pralaya the elements are absorbed in, in the reverse order, 218-20
organs are produced from, 246-8
the Chief Prâṇa is created from, 250-1
the soul in dreamless sleep rests in, 289-2
nature of Supreme, 293-312
takes form in connection with Upâdhis, 297, 299-300